SEAN CONNERY

NEITHER SHAKEN
NOR STIRRED

SEAN CONNERY

NEITHER SHAKEN
NOR STIRRED

Andrew Yule

LITTLE, BROWN AND COMPANY

A *Little, Brown* Book

First published in the USA in 1992 by Donald I. Fine, Inc.
First published in Great Britain in 1993
by Little, Brown and Company

Copyright © Andrew Yule 1992

The moral right of the author has been asserted.

A CIP catalogue record for this book
is available from the British Library.

ISBN 316 90347 7

Typeset by Solidus (Bristol) Limited
Printed and bound in Great Britain by
BPCC Hazell Books Ltd
Member of BPCC Ltd

Little, Brown and Company (UK) Limited
165 Great Dover Street
London SE1 4YA

Acknowledgements

My thanks to interviewees Sidney Lumet, Terry Gilliam, Richard Lester, Fred Zinnemann, John Boorman, Thomas Schuhly, Jake Eberts, Dennis Selinger, Peter Noble, Sue Lloyd, Gareth Wardell, Maidie Murray, William McIlvanney, Robert Hardy, Maxine Daniels, Eric Boyd, William Hamilton, Jack Vinestock and Stephen Weeks. I would like to express appreciation also to the following authors for their earlier work on Sean Connery: Emma Andrews (*Sean Connery, A Biography*), Ken Passingham (*Sean Connery: A Biography*), Richard Gant (*Gilt-Edged Bond*), Michael Feeney Callan (*Sean Connery, His Life and Films*) and Andrew Rissik (*The James Bond Man*) – and to the following journalists (UK): Lindsay Mackie, Andrew Young, Cameron Docherty, William Russell and Ian Bell of *The Herald*; Andy Dougan, *Glasgow Evening Times*; Hugh Herbert, *Guardian*; Tom Hutchinson, *The Scotsman*; Allan Hunter, Tom Condon and Steve Briggs, *Scotland on Sunday*; Bob Dow, Brian Glanville, Russell Miller and George Perry, *Sunday Times*; Pauline McLeod, Trudi Pacter, Corinna Honan, Julie Hamilton talking to Peter Donnelly, and Neil Connery, *Sunday Express*; Ken Smart and

Bill Jacobs, *Edinburgh Evening News*; Diane K. Shaw, *Empire Magazine*; Geoff Andrew and Chris Peachment, *Time Out*; Margaret Hinxman, *Mail on Sunday*; (US): William Wolf, *Cue Magazine*, *Variety*; Kurt Loder, *Rolling Stone*; Laura Cunningham, *Cosmopolitan*; Jonathan Mandell, *NY Sunday News*, *Playboy*; Robert Scheer and John H. Richardson, *Premiere*, *Movies USA*; Christopher Perez, *Village View*; Susan Spillman, *USA Today*; and Carrie Rickey, *Philadelphia Enquirer*.

Special thanks also to Russell Galen of Scott Meredith (US), Michael Thomas of A.M. Heath (UK), Adam Levison of Donald I. Fine, Inc. (US), and Barbara Boote of Little, Brown (UK).

Fondly dedicated to
Cathy, Eunice, Jess and Margo,
'the Waverley girls'

Chapter 1

'Apart from Laurence Olivier and Marlon Brando, there's no other actor I'd rather watch.'

Pauline Kael

James and Elizabeth Connery's move with their family from Ireland to Glasgow, Scotland in the 1880s was undertaken in a mood of quiet desperation. Born in 1839, James had survived the terrible potato famine of the next decade to emerge, like his father Jimmy before him, a hardy survivor, a 'travelling man' forever on the move from one encampment to another, peddling linen piece-goods and colourful gee-gaws and offering knife-sharpening on the side. He could also, when the occasion demanded, give a ferocious account of himself in bareknuckle fist-fighting.

It was in 1865 that James had met Elizabeth McPhillips, a bright, long-limbed lass of just eleven summers who proved a good match for her tall, darkly handsome suitor. Their eldest son, James, was born in 1866; a daughter, Elizabeth, in 1870; youngest son Thomas in 1879. The death of grandfather Jimmy and his wife Mary was the catalyst for the family's search for a new life 'across the water', the land of plenty, full of opportunities for the whole family. Unfortunately their children's lack of formal schooling left them ill-prepared for any tasks other than surviving by their wits or by the sweat of their brows.

The city in which the family landed was booming, with Clyde shipbuilding the cornerstone of its prosperity – it accounted for a third of the world's merchant fleet before 1912 – together with the flourishing tobacco and cotton trades. Glasgow had a tradition of high death rates eclipsed by even higher birth rates, the population explosion having been fuelled by an unprecedented influx of immigrants escaping Ireland, as well as refugees from the depopulation of the Scottish Highlands; in 1850 over 50 per cent of the population of 400,000 was not city-born. The result was chronic overcrowding, with open sewers flowing freely through many slums, leading to rampant disease. The switch from the Clyde River to freshwater supplies from Loch Catrine helped bring typhus under control by the 1880s, while deaths from infant mortality fell from a peak of 200 per 1,000 in 1850 to 116 by 1910, with the population nudging one million.

The Connery brothers could hardly have been less alike. James was introverted and sickly as a child and beset by a series of stomach ulcers in his teens. In 1888, against his parents' advice, the twenty-two-year-old married Jane Costello, a local charmer four years his senior. Like her father before her, Jane was a soft-goods hawker who worked the weekend markets around the city, James supplementing his wife's trade by sharpening cutlery and taking in shoe repairs. A daughter, Elizabeth, named after his sister and mother, was born in 1892. Her death from whooping cough after just three and a half months left both parents devastated. A second child, James, arrived in 1894 and for a while looked like succumbing to the same ailment. He rallied, but was never robust.

Jane's drinking, already heavy since her daughter's death, rapidly became chronic. By 1897, aged thirty-five, she had drunk herself to death; James arrived home one night to find her slumped in a heap on the floor, their child crouched beside her, crying and bewildered. For the second time in five years his 'X' mark was affixed to a death certificate. In 1900, aged thirty-four, James died of a combination of enteric fever and perforated ulcers, leaving his son an orphan. Despite his aunt Elizabeth's tenderest administrations, young James's death from bronchial pneumonia in 1904, aged ten, brought his branch of the Connery line to a tragic end.

Thomas Connery was a wild, precocious child, at once the apple of his parents' eye and their great despair, for there seemed to be no taming the wanton wildness in him. Swarthily handsome like his father, he had his own horse and cart and was earning a living as a scrap-metal pedlar in his teens. Aged twenty-two, after years of breaking hearts, he became smitten by a young lass he encountered one night as she left the East End cloth mill where she had begun training as a calenderer.

Jeanie McNab was known throughout the district as 'bonnie Jeanie', for she was indeed a radiantly beautiful chestnut-haired girl, and just thirteen years old. A year after they met she bore Thomas a son, Joseph. Although there was no legal impediment at the time to their being wed, Thomas had no truck with convention and saw no necessity for marriage – he loved Jeanie and intended to stick by her, and she loved him and swore the same, so that was an end of it. That young Joseph was shown as illegitimate on his birth certificate was neither here nor there, the stigma attached diminishing to the point of disappearance the lower down the social scale one dwelt. To Thomas it was of no greater consequence than the 'X' mark that branded him – like his late brother – illiterate.

The couple first set up home in Garscube, a mean hinterland of Glasgow, in a rented slum building in Church Place. By the time James, a second son, came along in 1905, they had moved to the scarcely more salubrious Ann Street in the city's teeming Cowcaddens district. If Jeanie had come round to the idea of being wed, marriage remained off the agenda as far as Thomas was concerned. Sister Elizabeth, meanwhile, had married a Dundee man and was working in that city's jute trade.

The death of Thomas's brother in 1900, his nephew in 1904,

and his parents – Elizabeth in 1907, James in 1914 – spelled the end of the family's Glasgow ties. On the basis that the grass had to be greener, he loaded the family belongings on his horse and cart and carried Jeanie and their brood the forty-five miles to Scotland's capital city of Edinburgh. There they settled in a crowded tenement in the Canongate, a predominantly Irish enclave at the poverty-stricken end of the Royal Mile. Although Thomas had nothing to contribute to the renowned engineering and printing industries of the 'Athens of the North', he was able to make ends meet between a spot of buying and selling off his cart, and doubling as a bookie's runner during the harsh winter months. Unschooled as he was, the redoubtable, now balding and occasionally fearsome head of the house turned out to be a dab hand at the necessary arithmetic.

The arrival of Thomas and his raggle-taggle troop in the metropolis – its own history of pestilence in the form of cholera outbreak long behind it – might have been more notable had the ostensibly sober-sided yet decidedly schizophrenic city not already been chock full of other colourful characters. Instead, the larger-than-life family found itself perfectly at home with an assortment of well-established worthies. There was 'Coconut Tam', peddler of coconut slices; 'Pie Davis' the meatpie specialist; 'Bible Beanie'; 'Funeral Wullie'; 'Ken the Kilty' (adept at ignoring the street urchins' taunt, 'Kilty, kilty cauld bum, never had a warm bum'); and a whole host of others answering to less obvious, but equally intriguing nicknames: 'Farthing Bob' of the Watergate; 'Tarry Jean'; 'Mutton Hole Tam'; and their own 'Betsy Mustard' of the Canongate.

By his early twenties Thomas and Jeanie's eldest son Joseph, a bout of inherited family ulcers notwithstanding, was more than ready for any challenge that came his way, his five-foot eight-inch frame a solid, well-muscled 180 pounds. Following his courtship of a beguiling, statuesque local girl, twenty-year-old Euphemia MacLean, the couple were wed on 28 December 1928. At the ceremony Joe's mental arithmetic proved no match for his untutored father's; he gave his age as twenty-four, inadvertently lopping two years off.

Joe and 'Effie' settled down to domesticity in a two-roomed redbrick ground-floor flat in Fountainbridge, an industrial area discreetly tucked away in the south-west of the Old City. Partly named after the bridge running over the Dalry burn stretching from South Borough Loch via Lochrin to the Water of Leith at Coltbridge, and partly after a fountain that had graced the thoroughfare in the eighteenth century, it was a vital artery to the west from West Port, the main entrance to Edinburgh through the Flodden Wall at the Grassmarket. Brother Jimmy, meanwhile, another powerfully built lad, elected to stay close by his parents in the Canongate after marrying Catherine McKenzie.

The cold-water tenement house at 176 Fountainbridge accommodated four families on each of its three landings, Joe and Effie's flat consisting of a large living room that doubled as a kitchen, and an adjoining bedroom. Above the stone sink hung a pulley to dry clothes when inclement weather made use of the back drying green impossible. A cast-iron fireplace, complete with two side ovens, a top plate and hob, provided the warmth of the house, which was laid wall-to-wall with sturdy ship's linoleum for further insulation. A single lavatory on the stairwell was shared by the other families.

For a remuneration of £2 a week Joe found employment at the nearby North British Rubber Works; 'the rubber mill', as it was known locally, turned out Wellington boots, tyres and industrial clothing. Its acrid fumes intermingled with the sickly stench of Mackay's sweetie factory and the yeast-laden smoke from McEwan's brewery across the road from the Connery 'stair', allowing the district to contribute fully to Edinburgh's less flattering alternative nickname of 'Auld Reekie'.

On 25 August 1930, a few minutes after six o'clock in the evening, Effie Connery gave birth to a $10\frac{1}{2}$ lb baby son. The tenement was abuzz with excitement as she returned from Edinburgh's Royal Maternity Hospital with her precious bundle, to be greeted by her proud and smiling husband, fresh from a celebration with his mates at the Fountain pub (Foy's) across the way. The couple christened the child Thomas after his grandfather; at home his first cot was the bottom drawer of the wardrobe at the foot of his parents' bed.

Young Tommy learned about life on the pavements, roads, and in the back closes of Fountainbridge many years before adopting his professional name of 'Sean Connery'. First he was known as 'Tich' during his early days at school, then as 'Big Tam' when he began sprouting at age twelve. He and his pals eagerly waited their turn at 'bools' – assorted glass and steel marbles – or took part in games of Dodgy ('Tig! You're it!'), Allevo (basically, hide and seek: 'Allevo, allevo, the game's up the pole!'), rounders, kick the can, conkers (chestnuts) and heid-the-ba', at all of which he quickly proved adept.

The young lad with the shock of gypsy-like dark brown hair, rapidly thickening eyebrows and dancing brown eyes laughed and teased with his mates as the girls played their own games of skipping and peevers (pavement hopping) and chanted the sinister street rhyme derived from Edinburgh's infamous nineteenth-century body snatchers:

> Doon the close and up the stair.
> Butt an' ben wi' Burke and Hare,
> Burke's the butcher, Hare's the thief,
> Knox the man that buys the beef.

Another popular limerick was derived from the silver screen:

> One, two, three a-leerie,
> I spy Wallace Beery,
> Sitting on his bumbaleerie,
> Kissing Shirley Temple.

An occasional treat was a bath undertaken in a tin tub in front of the fire. This was fine when Effie was in charge, in between the occasional charring she undertook; Joe, like as not, unwilling to bother heating the water, would lift Tommy bodily into the sink and turn on the cold tap. Later the lad was provided with 'saxpence' for a weekly visit to the Dalry public baths for a hot tub. Since the soap provided free was coarse, pungent carbolic, and not at all to his liking, Tommy invariably packed his own inside his towel.

On a visit to Portobello baths when he was five, Tommy had no time for the shallow end, which was considered for kids and 'jessies'. 'Let's go up the deep end, Dad,' he pleaded. 'I'm not scared.' Joe took him there on his back, then allowed him to swim halfway across under his watchful eye. He need not have worried; his son took to water like a fish. A special treat on the way home was either a toffee 'doddle', stretched toffee lengths twisted and snipped into bite-sized chunks, or a slider or cone 'poke' from Sammy the 'Hokey-pokey' man whose ice-cream parlour adjoined the family tenement. ('Hokey Pokey, penny a lump, That's the stuff to mak' you jump.')

Another worthy a few doors away was Asa Wassy, the local rag and bone scrap merchant, open seven days a week for the sale or purchase of everything from an elephant's toe-nail to a kirby-grip. Asa, of Jewish descent, had misplaced his real name in the mists of time. The story in Fountainbridge was that he had come into a little money after selling his original scrapyard. 'You'll be getting fancy ideas now you're well off,' he was teased. 'Och,' he replied, 'that's no' for me. I just want to be known *as ah was*.' From that day forth the Fountainbridgers took him at his word and dubbed him Asa Wassy, the name he proudly displayed above the entrance to his Aladdin's cave.

Although Tommy for a while liked nothing better than to perch on the cart his Uncle Jimmy had taken over from his father, and ride with him, guiding the big, old workhorse from the Canongate to the Grassmarket, street football, and games with his pals at 'the biggie', the green patch behind his tenement, soon emerged as the great delight of his life. Playing centre-forward for Bruntsfield Primary was a decided compensation for having to attend school.

A fellow classmate at Bruntsfield was Eric Boyd, a raggedy lad who sat beside 'Tich' from their first day together in the class of forty pupils. The 'bright boys' were allowed to sit at the back of the class, while Tommy and fellow 'thickies' Eric, Angus Grant, Peter McVittie, Donald Black and George Jack were invariably grouped at the front, two to a desk. Like Tommy, Eric was a loner, with no particularly close chums he can remember. 'Maybe that's why we got on so well,' he suggests. 'Tommy was a popular boy, though, well liked.'

Eric also recalls his friend as 'fairly posh', at least in Fountainbridge terms. In a school photograph Tommy can be seen resplendent in tweed jacket, neatly buttoned shirt and carefully knotted tie, hair neatly parted, standing out in a collection of ragamuffins sporting rough woollen 'jaggy jerseys' and looking as if they'd been dragged through a hedge backwards. 'His father was never out of work and his mother worked,' says Eric, 'so in local terms Tommy had a better deal than many of us.'

Tommy was designated a 'droner' in music class and excluded from singing lessons as tone deaf, unable to sing a note; while others were practising their vocal calisthenics, he was confined to his desk with a book. Out of school he was as wild as any, clambering up the hill alongside Bruntsfield after school hours with his four-wheel 'guider', a wooden board with perilous rope-pulled steering, then racing across the main road, dodging tramcars with reckless, madcap abandon.

Close as they were, a series of imagined slights led to an argument between Eric and Tommy that ended in a playground brawl. By the time the commotion reached the ears of the teachers, who immediately rushed out to separate the two, bloody noses were in evidence. The boys found themselves dragged in front of the 'beak' in short order. 'Who started it?' he demanded to know, flourishing his dreaded leather-thonged tawse. '*He* did, sur,' the lads replied in unison, pointing at each other. Then they burst out giggling – until six belts of 'the strap' went some way to curbing their amusement.

With their differences melted in the shared heat of their punishment, the incident had the effect of bonding them even closer. They were back again, fighting side by side, on the annual 'Scotch and Irish day' in Fountainbridge, where rival gangs, armed with balls made of stones wrapped in newspapers, twirled their primitive weapons on the end of string lengths before releasing the missiles to devastating effect. Others stuffed petrol-soaked rags into Tate & Lyle syrup cans before setting them ablaze. 'Oddly enough,' says Eric – currently a Justice of the Peace, no less! – 'nobody ever seemed to get seriously hurt. And there was a fairness about Tommy. He never ran with the herd, and was never a bully. If he saw someone else being done down he would be in there like a shot.'

Effie thriftily eked out the meagre family budget as best she could, performing wonders in the kitchen with simple nourishing fare like Irish stew and Scotch broth, always accompanied by filling portions of bread and potatoes washed down with milk from St Cuthbert's dairy round the corner in Grove Street. In Effie's hands a pennyworth of carrot and turnip and a ham bone would be transformed into a soup fit for a king. Thanks to a hotpot kept constantly on the hob, there was no such thing as discarded leftovers, and bread and butter pudding was best made, the legend currently ran, with bread that had gone stale. There was no such meal as 'lunch' in Edinburgh, or indeed throughout Scotland at the time, except for extreme uppercrusters. For ordinary folk 'dinner' was eaten at lunchtime, 'tea' or 'high tea' at dinnertime (normally some time between four and seven o'clock) and if you were lucky you got a bite of 'supper' before retiring.

Effie was eight months pregnant with her second child in November 1928, when grandpa Thomas, by now bald as a coot, thoroughly cantankerous, and irreverently known as 'Old Baldy' by his grandson, called round with startling news. After living with Jeanie McNab for thirty-six years, he had decided to make an honest woman of her; they were to be married in St Patrick's Roman Catholic Church that very week.

Fond as they were of the couple, Joe and Effie had mixed feelings; with the move to Edinburgh most of the family's new friends had assumed, reasonably enough in the absence of any information to the contrary, that Thomas and Jeanie were already man and wife. Their getting wed now would draw attention to the family 'secret' – that Joe and Jimmy were both illegitimate. Did Thomas, at this late date, really want to draw attention to this skeleton in the Connery cupboard? And after all this time, *why* was he suddenly so hellbent on tying the knot? The old reprobate stubbornly refused to offer any explanation and simply informed them that his mind was made up; right, reason, or none, he was going ahead. True to his word, he married Jeanie on 24 November 1938.

A few weeks later Effie contributed to the Connerys' pre-Christmas upheaval, presenting Joe with a second son, Neil. Sleeping in a bed settee in the kitchen by this time, Tommy had a chuckle to himself when he saw the wardrobe's bottom drawer being pressed into service once more as a cot for young Neil. Two years later his brother joined him in the kitchen.

From the age of nine, with Joe working twelve-hour shifts, Tommy saw little of his father, who took scant interest in his son's scholastic achievements – or lack of them, for that matter. Joe's role model seemed to be his own father, the venerable 'Baldy', long since prone to kicking everyone in sight when he came home in a temper, then proceeding to hurl his tea in the fireplace. Although exposed to these occasional outbursts, young Tommy saw that life went on – wages were handed over, provisions stocked, differences settled, beds made, the house kept warm, children grew up. He also saw that the real influence in the home emanated from the distaff side, despite the constant implication that women, like children, should be seen and not heard. ('Speak when you're spoken to, wum-man.')

Life for Joe had consisted of getting through school, in between heroic bouts of truancy, so that work and earnings could commence; it simply never occurred to him that it might be any different for his sons. There was no father as far as Tommy was concerned, in many of the ways that boys need a father – someone to check school grades, or listen to their account of a fabulous goal scored. Without this sounding board, and with very few pats on the back – Effie following her husband's example – Tommy's self-confidence suffered. Joining the lifeboys – the junior edition of the Boys' Brigade – and later the Sea Cadets, helped a little, there being a variety of surrogate fathers on tap at the weekly meetings.

With Effie now charring regularly for an extra thirty bob a week, Tommy undertook all of the shopping and the occasional washing of the tenement stairs. Although he hated the chores, he knew there was no question of rebellion; it was something that had to be done. That his boyhood was inexorably slipping away, however, was undeniable, and caused considerable resentment.

The reason behind Tommy's grandfather 'doing the right thing' out of the blue and marrying Jeanie McNab soon emerged. He had known for some time that this was her dearest wish and had not hesitated when advised that the love of his life was dying of inoperable cancer.

Jeanie, still bonnie at fifty-two, and Mrs Connery at long last, passed away in 1940, just two years after Thomas, the reformed reprobate, finally turned up trumps.

Chapter 2

'Most actors are simple, but complicated. Sean is uncomplicated, but not simple.'

Terence Young

'I think Paramount is the only company I haven't sued. They all steal.'

Sean Connery

Aged nine, on his way home from school one day, Tommy decided he might as well be in for a pound as a penny. Dropping by Kennedy's stables, he landed a job pushing a handcart, delivering milk. This entailed a five o'clock rise and half a day's work in all weathers before school; after his lessons he worked for several more hours as a butcher's assistant at the big local meat market in Dundee Street. The two jobs combined brought in £3 a week, all of which was handed over to Effie. She never failed to bank her son's share, after a reasonable deduction for the household. ('Tak' care o' the pennies, son, and the pounds'll tak' care o' themselves.')

With the outbreak of war the little Tommy saw of his father was further reduced with Joe's transfer to Rolls Royce's

Glasgow plant. An accident there, in which his wrist and nose were broken, resulted in eighteen months' convalescence back in Edinburgh. During this period Joe took over his father's daily collection of betting 'lines'. One morning, slightly the worse for an over-indulgence in the 'craitur' the night before, he overslept and missed the collection.

When Joe turned up in Foy's that night for 'a hair of the dog', he was puzzled when several punters demanded their winnings. 'But I never collected any slips today,' he protested. 'No,' they chorused, 'but your faither did!' He was left with no alternative but to pay up. It was a week before an unrepentant 'Baldy' returned from his impromptu holiday in Glasgow, resplendent in a spanking new suit and hat. There was no point in recrimination; Joe had simply failed to collect the bets and had been left to face the music. Sentiment, as ever, had proved a commodity in short supply in the Connery household. Once his health was restored, Joe found employment as a furniture removal man.

In 1940, to avoid a major disaster in the event of a direct bomb hit, Tommy's school classes were broken up into small groups of less than a dozen and dispersed to houses in the community. In the event Edinburgh escaped wartime bombing, the closest call being a raid on the strategic Forth Road Bridge that missed its target. The move from the classroom was Tommy's first taste of feeling like an outsider; whether real or imagined, he felt out of place and unwelcome in what he saw as the grand houses where classes were held. He was only welcome, it was made clear, as a milk delivery boy. With the poverty of his own circumstances graphically underlined, questions began to form, attitudes take shape. Just where did these people *get* all their money? Had they earned it or had it all been left to them? *Jesus*, life was unfair.

His scholastic progress was unremarkable, with the exception of English, at which he excelled, and a smattering of bookies' arithmetic mainly inherited from his grandfather. He had a keen appreciation of both sides of the religious coin from his determinedly non-denominational parents and mainly

Catholic relatives, together with Fountainbridge's polyglot mixture of 'Proddies', 'Papes', 'Piscies' and 'Wee Frees'. Even the various football teams – Hearts, Hibs and St Bernard's – were strictly segregated by the fans: 'Hearts ever, Hibs, never', the rallying cry of the 'Proddie' side of the religious divide.

Sex education was nowhere to be found on the school curriculum. Nor was it required, at least not beyond the fundamentals, with everyone in the tenement flats messing around long before they reached their teens, making it impossible for even the youngest not to discover, albeit in a skewed version, the facts of life. The great puritan strain in Scotland helped no end to intrigue everyone, rampantly desperate to know what was so terrible that it could only be discussed by their elders in furtive whispers. As for the violence, it was seldom of the mindless variety. Tough, vicious and bloody though it was, the cheeks that were slashed by open razors and the bones that were broken almost invariably represented retribution for some genuine wrong. And Fountainbridgers, no matter how poverty-racked, never stole from one another. Hardly anyone bothered to lock their doors, and freely negotiable milk tokens could be safely left beside the empties.

By the time he was four, Neil was joining in Tommy's games of football, often improvising with a ball made from rolled-up newspaper tied with string or a spare length of elastic. Only a hundred yards from their home lay the Union Canal, where the two boys would head with their jeelie jars and Effie's cut-down old stockings to fish for baggies and beardies, and where Tommy would boat with his bigger pals on the lower basin. Johnstone's boatyard was a favourite haunt, where the proprietor would pay the lads to row the boats back when customers dumped them upstream to avoid paying the hire fee. When one of them fell in – a fairly regular occurrence – old man Johnstone would help dry the lad off and administer cod liver oil as he warmed up, wrapped in towels, around the pot-bellied stove in his yard. Unlike the fracas between Tommy and Eric, the fisticuffs between the men from the breweries that invariably took place on the adjoining banks of the canal were no-holds-barred affairs fought to the bitter end until only one person was left standing.

Effie's parents had moved several years earlier from Gorgie, another tenement suburb of Edinburgh, to the peace and tranquillity of the Fifeshire countryside, where they bred pigs and kept chickens on a modest scale. Tommy and Neil spent many a happy holiday in Grandpa and Granny MacLean's tiny two-roomed cottage in the rolling hills near Dunfermline. They both worshipped Neil MacLean; to them the big, retired borough engineer was a hero from another, more romantic age.

Although geographically not far removed from the bustle of Fountainbridge – from the cottage they could look south to the Forth of Firth and the purple Pentland Hills, further off to the east Edinburgh's Castle Rock – to Tommy and Neil the Dunfermline countryside was an exotic Eden. The contrast between the harshness of the tenements and the gentle pastoral beauty of the country, the grime of the city streets and the freshness of dappled woodland and sun-bedecked fields, made the two brothers aware of how much more lay beyond their limited horizons.

Their mornings began with a cold-water splash, much like back home – only from a spring outside the cottage that tasted sweeter by far than any water they had ever known. Young Neil chortled and nudged his brother delightedly as they watched Grandpa MacLean expertly bore a hole with a penknife in the top and bottom of new-laid eggs, the better to suck them dry. Every morning the lads would be given a pitcher by Granny MacLean and dispatched to the nearby farm to collect milk, still fresh and warm from the cow. Left to their own devices one morning, they stared bemusedly at the tethered animal before huddling together. How *did* it work? The bucket went below the udder, of that much they were certain. When Tommy concluded that they had to crank the cow's tail up and down to pump the milk out, young Neil heartily concurred. The farmer's look of astonishment as he surveyed their efforts undoubtedly echoed that of the disconcerted cow.

The enormous Clydesdale horse on the farm was a natural

magnet. At Neil's insistence Tommy would lift him on the animal's back, where he perched and clung for dear life to the chestnut mane, one eye apprehensively on the distant turf and rocks below. When Tommy hoisted himself up behind his brother on one occasion, Neil performed a hapless slow-motion slide, ending up under the horse's belly, all the while gamely hanging on for dear life to the mane. Luckily the Clydesdale exercised endless patience; only when the lads had finished all their perambulations, and were settled on its massive back, did it break into a gentle walk. With Tommy on his own a canter would be considered.

To relax after this high excitement a visit was made to the local pond to splash bare-legged and fish for tadpoles, newts and frogs. By the time some of the creatures had been transferred from their natural habitat to an old bath in the garden, Granny MacLean was calling them in for tea. Though no less simple and homely than they were used to, the country food she cooked was a revelation. They already knew the delights of the haggis, minced sheep's intestine wrapped in its own belly-bag, best served piping hot and accompanied by mashed, buttered and peppered turnips. Hot scones straight from the griddle, however, were an unaccustomed luxury, while the mystery of lambs' hearts and sheep's heads roasted over an open fire proved something else again.

As at home, hardly a night passed for the boys without a pillow fight to the death. Tommy invariably won, grabbing his smaller brother, wrapping him in a sheet and knotting the corners together, leaving him helpless and in stitches from laughing.

The other escape route for Tommy and Neil lay in the magic of the silver screen, for which they faithfully lined up every rainy Saturday afternoon following a jostle at the sink and the 'cat's dite' lick and a promise Effie insisted upon. For the price of a jamjar, then tuppence rising to sixpence, they were transported at one of the neighbourhood 'gaffs' not only to other countries, but to other worlds. Their nearest 'local' was the tiny Coliseum fleapit that during the week featured

CineVariety – a live singer, dancer or comedian before the feature. Further afield was the Tollcross cinema dubbed 'the Toll-X', the Operetta near the Bridges known as the 'O-P', or the exotically named Blue Halls in nearby Lauriston, where the Flash Gordon serial would be followed by a Popeye, Mickey Mouse or Donald Duck cartoon, then by the latest Roy Rogers, Hopalong Cassidy, Gene Autry or Johnny Mack Brown western. These were Tommy's favourites; passports to a world where justice always triumphed, there were clearly defined good guys and bad guys among the cowboys, and, as far as he could see, few big houses and little inherited wealth. Infuriatingly, though, there always seemed to be time for a song or two between the action sequences. Maybe that was why, a Fountainbridger's natural inclination to side with the underdog apart, Tommy tended to sympathize with the Indians rather than the cowboys when range war was the issue.

In Toll-X manner the half-million good folk of Edinburgh had also coined their own names for the various theatrical palaces of entertainment in the city: the lofty Alhambra was the Alabam, the venerable Palace the Scabby Alice, the august Empire the Hemp Wire, while the Dominion, for some obscure reason, was known to one and all as the Money Boy. East of Lothian Road lay the tiny Palladium, the 'Ally-Pally', where many a popular Scottish comedian, like Charlie Kemble, Sammy Murray or Tommy Lorne spent packed seasons in between the famous 'Pally pantos'.

Tommy passed from 'Tich' to 'Big Tam' in his final year at Bruntsfield as he suddenly shot up. Although skinny, he was broad-shouldered and strong with it, inadvertently demonstrating this one day by gripping the glass door handle of his parents' bedroom and crushing it in his hand. Neil watched, perplexed, as his brother danced up and down, clenching his palm and yelling at the top of his voice. His parents at first thought he was 'acting it', until they caught sight of the bloody glass shards embedded in his hand.

At the end of Tommy's primary school education he was faced with a choice of two secondary establishments –

Boroughmuir, specializing in languages and economics, or Darroch, which leaned more towards technical skills like metalwork and crafts. Football-daft Tommy claimed that Darroch was his obvious choice; since rugby instead of soccer was played at the grammar school, he had deliberately set out to fail the eleven-plus qualifying exam. Whether this was true or not, there was no pretence that Darroch was anything other than a long way second best to Boroughmuir and reserved strictly for the dunderheads of the neighbourhood; with its gaunt, grey edifice located in Upper Gilmore Street, just above the canal, it was mockingly dubbed 'Canal Academy'.

A Darroch contemporary, Craigie Veitch, recalled the school as being staffed by no-nonsense teachers with strong right arms, the better with which to belt the pupils. He detected nothing of the long-haired poet about the big, hard-as-nails schoolboy Tommy had become; despite his easy-going ways, anyone who messed him about soon found himself the recipient of a thick ear and a black eye.

In the winter of 1943 he painstakingly built his own sledge, a pride and joy he painted black and dubbed 'The Coffin'. After a heavy fall of snow he carted the sledge off to the Meadows, known to the locals as 'the Meedies'; the area left after the draining of the Old Borough Loch had been transformed into one of the city's finest public parks. After an hour or so of breathlessly running up the slopes, then hurtling down again on the hard-packed snow, he collided with the roots of a tree halfway down. The sledge came to a juddering stop, propelling Tommy forward to connect head-first with a particularly stout tree trunk.

'You're late for your tea,' Effie scolded when he trailed in, pale and silent, having stumbled half a mile in a state of shock. Concerned at his lack of response, she looked up from the hob at her son. 'Is something wrong?' she asked. Tommy, muttering that he was fine, turned towards the sink, affording Effie a view of the back of his head and the blood that had matted his hair and was trickling down his neck. She screamed at the sight, then frantically yelled through the thin tenement walls to her next-door neighbour to run down and phone for an ambulance. Thirty-two stitches were required to close the jagged wound.

After five days spent in hospital and a further ten days of convalescence, Tommy was not only back on his feet, but back at 'the Meedies' on his hastily repaired 'Coffin'. Scars apart, another aspect of the misadventure left a lasting impression. He had been forced to share a ward with four elderly people, one of whom had died right next to him in the middle of the night. The memory of the terrifying death rattle would linger with him for the rest of his life.

Tommy left Darroch when he was thirteen, without a single qualification, to begin his first full-time occupation at St Cuthbert's Co-operative Society Dairy stables. Initially he assisted a roundsman nine years his senior – Alexander Harper ('Alex') Kitson, later to head the Scottish Horse and Motormen's Association, then the powerful Transport and General Workers' Union. One year later Tommy was awarded his own horse and cart as an emergency wartime junior van man, and £2 a week.

Every morning Effie continued to ensure that he was up at five and breakfasted on hot porridge with lashings of milk before the sprint over to the stables. He passed on his nickname of 'Tich' to his pony, since he was the smallest of the line-up. Hitched to one of St Cuthbert's distinctive red carts, Tommy and the other delivery boys made a tremendous din as they trotted over Dean Bridge on the way to Cramond and Davidson's Mains, the horses' hooves genteelly counterpointing the almighty clatter of the milk crates.

As soon as his tour was over, around 3 p.m., he wolfed down his tea and disappeared again to do an evening paper round that brought him an extra five shillings. After deducting his pocket money and rent he would pay a regular weekly visit to the Post Office savings bank, swelling the account his mother had opened for him four years earlier. ('Mony's a mickle mak's a muckle, son.')

After supper he would beg Effie's brass polish to shine

Tich's harness, as well as the blacklead she used for the fireplace for his hooves. Only then was the day's work done, whether it be eight, nine, or ten o'clock at night. On the rare evenings he visited the Clanhouse Dancehall next door to the stable, it was back home first for a personal application of spit and polish.

From the time he started working, the attitude of his parents, like theirs before them, was the one prevalent throughout Scotland: 'You make your own bed and you lie on it.' Tommy accepted this, and neither asked for, nor received advice; his father didn't feel like giving it, and his mother felt it wasn't 'her place'. Well, that was fine; he would either make it on his own or not at all.

Tommy was not, it has to be said, the most resourceful of milk roundsmen. When a harness broke soon after he started his delivery one day, he blotted his copybook by gormlessly ditching Tich and his fully laden cart at the side of a busy main street, and hightailing it back to the stable. His foreman looked at him incredulously as he strolled in and off-handedly reported the incident.

One night when Tich had a bad attack of colic Tommy churned a mixture of turnip, bruised oats and cut hay, doling this out to the ailing pony before sleeping all night beside him. A year later, after entering the annual best horse and cart competition, hours were spent burnishing the brasswork and painstakingly plaiting his pony's mane. The reward was a rosette for Tich, proudly displayed in a victory trot through Fountainbridge, and a 'Highly Commended' card for himself. Neil remembers his brother bounding up the stairs to the family's flat – they had moved to the second floor when a slightly bigger apartment had become available – looking as if he'd won the pools. He also recalls him turning up with a brooch for Effie inscribed 'Mother' that had set him back all of his week's paper round.

The youth's decisive sexual initiation, later than most in the area if his pals were to be believed, came when he was fourteen. Walking down the street one day, he found himself being followed by a determined-looking and downright attractive uniformed ATS woman. When she caught up with him there was a whispered suggestion that they might repair to a nearby underground air-raid shelter. Although the one they chose had been flooded, with hastily assembled single planks forming a perilously makeshift walkway, the encounter was all the more urgent and exciting for its suddenness and improvised nature. Among the heady cocktail of emotions any youngster might have felt, with measures of elation, shame, relief and wonderment swilling around, Tommy's overwhelming sensation was one of immense gratitude. The ex-virgin could hold his head up with the best of his mates.

His subsequent secretiveness about his girlfriends began after two young girls with a crush on him turned up at his home one night. 'Is Tommy coming out?' they asked Joe. 'Not tonight,' he replied with a smile, 'his mother's giving him his bath.' As the girls giggled their way along Fountainbridge, Tommy, who had overheard, turned on his dad. 'Fancy telling them a thing like that,' he protested. 'Whatever will they think of me?' From then on, following this 'reddie', his discretion became obsessive, although Neil and Effie both knew when he was heading for Binn's Corner, the famous lovers' trysting-place at the West End of Princes Street. 'All dressed up tonight, aren't we?' Neil would tease as he prepared to slip out.

Whenever he saw Tommy about to venture out for the evening on his own, Neil knew to look out for the trademark farewell, an ear-to-ear grin and a bright 'Cheerio, folks', accompanied by a wiggle of the fingers that served as a wave. The morning after his brother had been to a local dance Neil would ask, 'Get a click?' Whether Tommy would reply, 'Away and bile yer heid', 'Haud yer wheesht' or simply 'Shut yer gub', the admonition was usually delivered with a shy smile.

The quest for romance apart, the one constant in Tommy's life remained football. At sixteen he played for Grove Vale Juniors, then joined a pal, fellow junior vanman Willie Hamilton, in the 'first-class juveniles' team of Oxgang Rovers. With the well-known Scottish nail put through every penny of his Christmas tips, Tommy's savings of £75 began to burn a hole in his pocket. His plea for a motorbike having been adamantly turned down by his father – Tommy was too young, he was told, and the whole idea was too dangerous – his fancy turned elsewhere. To everyone's astonishment he went out and bought a piano, parting with the princely sum of £56 10s, and another £1 to have it delivered.

Since none of the family was in any way musical, the neighbours, not to mention the family itself, were thunderstruck with the purchase. Tommy, it seemed, had taken his cue from some of the non-western movies he'd seen. Pianos lent a grand air to houses – or was it that only grand houses had pianos?

Bored with the routine in which he saw himself being permanently grounded, and without a word to anyone, Tommy hopped a tram to the South Queensferry naval recruitment base and signed on for seven years' active service, five more in the reserves. Now there would be a chance to explore the world, take that slow boat to China, cruise to Zanzibar ... Joe's reaction was deadpan, young Neil was agog with envy, Effie's response was the natural one to a first-born leaving the nest.

Instead of the faraway places with strange-sounding names Tommy had anticipated, months of training at Bultaw Camp, next to Lochinvar, as an armourer, was followed by a transfer to HMS *Formidable* at Portsmouth. There was no romantic Hawaii or Hong Kong with exotic, pliant females; he was stuck instead scrubbing decks, feet frozen solid.

Outside of football and the Navy boxing team, he found little in which he could excel – unless the 'Goulash à la Connery' he occasionally cooked up for his mates was counted. Instead of the element of security the Navy might have provided, he felt stifled and frustrated. Soon he began to assume the disgruntled elements of the regular seamen – barrack-room lawyering and swinging the lead; 'Bullshit baffles brains' became his slogan. The result was the Connery legacy of a duodenal ulcer, which brought about his discharge after less than three years, aged nineteen. There was a legacy of resentment as well, for although he had wanted to leave, he disliked being pushed.

Being invalided out proved to Connery how unsuited he was for the discipline of a service career. 'Trepidations, anxieties, fears' were self-diagnosed as the cause of his ulcer, while he freely acknowledged that he also loathed following orders. Although he tried his utmost to make light of it back home, Tommy had caught a shattering glimpse during his brief service of how the world was ordered. He was a boy seaman, and there was an able seaman above him, and if he reached his status there was a naval seaman over him. Beyond that there was a leading seaman, then a petty officer and a chief petty officer. The nagging knowledge that his lack of qualifications barred him from even setting foot on the bottom rung of this ladder did nothing to appease the gnawing pain inside.

Any suggestion that Tommy had 'worked his ticket' was countered by the ulcers that ran in the family and had helped to kill his great-uncle James. Joe had suffered from them as well, as would brother Neil. Once demobbed, however, he abandoned all pretence of following the diet sheet the Navy had provided; soon the only physical reminders of his spell in the service were the twin tattoos on his right forearm – SCOTLAND FOR EVER, and MUM & DAD below, both spelled out in red and blue.

The death of seventy-year-old Thomas Connery in 1949, nine years after the loss of his wife, spelled out the end of one era and heralded the birth of another. It was late in what had been a gloomy, overcast day when an insistent knock came on the door of the Connerys' tenement. When Effie opened the door, she beheld a tall Indian gentleman, two battered cardboard suitcases at his feet, a selection of oriental silks flourished over one arm. Even as Effie began to shake her head at his suggestion that she buy something, the hawker offered to tell her fortune if she did.

A blue and gold silk fringed article duly purchased, the Indian completed the bargain. 'Ah, I see you have a son, lady,' he intoned, gazing directly into her palm. 'No, two sons. Two big, strong handsome sons. One day, lady, one of your sons will be famous – very, very famous.'

Effie knew a con-man when she heard one. 'That'll be the day,' she said, closing the door gently but firmly.

Chapter 3

'The Scots have nothing in common with the English. The Scots are Scottish – period. Bond is English and I'm Scottish. And I don't like the English at all because I'm Scottish. Period!'

Sean Connery

'If a girl's attractive, you're seventy-five per cent there. I mean seventy-five per cent towards looking as if you're accomplishing what you're supposed to be accomplishing.'

Sean Connery

In the Edinburgh to which Tommy Connery returned, there was no lack of descendants to the worthies of yesteryear. Although 'Mutton Hole Tam', 'Tarry Jean' and the like were long since gone, in their place stood Theodore Napier, a regular sight along Princes Street in full Highland dress, claymore at the ready, white hair tumbling to his shoulders, an eagle's feather secured to his Balmoral by a silver buckle. Napier was the self-styled Last of the Jacobites, his constant toast a vow of loyalty to 'the King o'er the water'.

Then there was 'Three Hat Sanny', also known as 'Mr Penny' because of his regular habit of tossing streams of ha'pennies around Edinburgh's posher areas. To those who knew Sanny to be an eccentric toff himself, there remained the question: Why not distribute his largesse to the needy poor? The answer was his defiant need to let 'the nobs' know that despite his appearance – fedora topped by sou'wester, with a huge bowler perched above for good measure, tattered ankle-length overcoat and green-mouldy wellingtons – he had more money than all of them put together and cared nothing for it. Even some city tradesmen joined in the grand tradition. Did 'Lumsden the Sweep (Lums Done)' choose his profession because of his name? 'Small is beautiful' was certainly the philosophy of another character who proudly proclaimed on his tiny van 'Just Myself, Decorator'.

After his stint in the Navy Tommy decided there was no question of returning, tail-between-his-legs, to his old milk round: 'Big Tam the Milkman' had gone for good. Instead, he took a variety of jobs that had but two factors in common – they brought in cash, and carried no chance of advancement. Delivering coal and working in a steel strip mill kept him in beer and clothes, while the unquestionable dead-end aspect left him increasingly moody and as restless as ever.

With a year of this under his belt, and just as he had reached the stage of disconsolately packing everything in and emigrating to Canada, the British Legion offered a disablement scholarship. After a minimum of deliberation, with Joe wryly remarking that at least he would have something to show for his years in the Navy, a Glasgow training college and a course of French polishing was chosen.

Back in Edinburgh Tommy picked up odd jobs practising the skill – none too well – working on one occasion at a local bank, where a teller remembers him slowly applying sandpaper and oils to a table while slyly eyeing up the girls at the same time. Even when he eventually found steady employment at Jack Vinestock's Craighouse Gardens Cabinet Works, dissatisfaction quickly set in with the humdrum 8–5, five-days-a-week routine. Basically he was in no way interested in the job, his head still bursting with airy-fairy ideas about a vague break-through he might achieve. 'He couldn't polish your boots, that's the truth,' says Jack Vinestock, the founder's son who served his apprenticeship in his father's shop, albeit at a loftier level, at the same time as Tommy. 'He was a popular boy, though, especially with the girls.'

At the suggestion of a fellow-polisher, Johnny Hogg, who doubled in the evenings as a dresser at the King's Theatre at Tollcross, Tommy landed the job of assistant dresser over Christmas. Looking after the wardrobe gave him a tantalizing whiff of theatrical life that remained long after his brief spell had ended.

The tall – six feet two inches at eighteen – but still-skinny Tommy took up weight-lifting at the urging of a friend, Jimmy Laurie, a physical culture enthusiast. Although his rugged good looks had always attracted the girls, Tommy still lacked confidence in that direction; a physique to match his looks was bound to help. For a joining fee of fifteen shillings and 1s 6d a week subscription, he signed on at the Dunedin Amateur Weight Lifting Club, a humble tin shed situated at one end of the 'Meedies' that reeked of liniment and sweat. Here he faithfully trooped every Monday, Wednesday and Friday, investing in a tracksuit, chest expanders and dumb-bells for use at home.

Soon he landed a job for the summer as a lifeguard at Portobello, the holiday town on the Forth six miles from Edinburgh. Although boasting one of the largest saltwater pools in Britain, complete with impressive artificial waves, the council had blundered aesthetically by locating it in the shadow of a giant gas works. It still proved popular, despite the unvarying Arctic temperature of the water. At first Tommy was content to catch a tram from the Post Office at the East End of Princes Street that took him all the way to Portobello for a penny. When the Navy offered £90 as a one-off disability settlement, he blew the cash on a second-hand three-horse-power motorbike – still against his father's advice – and said goodbye to public transport.

At weekends Neil was permitted to accompany Tommy. Observing his brother standing at the edge of the pool one day, looking extremely elegant in white slacks and sweater and talking to another lifeguard, Neil judged that a spot of skylarking was in order. He swam into the middle of the huge pool as the waves began rolling and thrashed about. 'Help!' he yelled. 'Help! Save me!' Tommy had his sweater halfway off and was about to dive to the rescue when he saw it was his brother and realized he was being had. 'Drown!' he suggested, deadpan, turning back to his colleague.

No matter what other interests Tommy took up, football was never neglected. A spell in 1950 with the Fet-Lor's Amateurs – Fettes College and Loretto Public School's Boys' Club – led to playing semi-professionally for Bonnyrigg Rose, a mining town junior league team. This in turn sparked the interest of East Fife, then in the Scottish First Division. To everyone's surprise Tommy declined their offer of a £25 signing fee, taking the long view that his career in the game would be strictly limited. He vowed that whatever he eventually chose, it would be a career for life.

During a fitness class one evening Archie Brennan, a former Mr Scotland, noted Tommy's impressively developing musculature and suggested that he supplement his income by modelling at the Edinburgh School of Art in Lauriston. This he did for a spell, stripped down to a minute G-string pouch that created no end of interest, whether Tommy was tossing a discus or reclining on a lounger. He earned fifteen shillings for a one-hour sitting, which included a brief break of ten to fifteen minutes. 'It's murder staying in one pose all that time,' he complained to Neil, adding bashfully, 'The girls always want to sketch me up close. It's *embarrassing*.'

Student artist Richard De Marco created several splendid oil paintings of Tommy and was one of the few who deigned to share his meal breaks with him, ignoring the protocol that dictated a clear class divide between artists and models. De Marco recalls him as 'very straight, slightly shy', and still disturbed at the medical reason behind his naval discharge. He was also, says De Marco, 'too, too beautiful for words, a virtual Adonis', a claim amply attested to by his renderings of the Connery physique.

With his height, dark good looks and rapidly filling-out figure, Tommy was a natural clotheshorse for the latest in single-button semi-drape jackets, slim-fitting trousers, crêpe-soled 'brothel creepers', Billy Eckstine folded-collar shirts and crocheted string ties. When the doting supporters who followed his football prowess were added to the Portobello girls and his dance hall fans, his list of admirers soon verged on the legendary. Friends still recall him as someone who took his pleasures fairly seriously, and was discriminating, not to say downright choosy, about the company he kept.

Neil, who had left Darroch himself by this time and started work as a plasterer's apprentice, was uniquely placed to observe how seldom Tommy wanted for female companionship. Often he would see him roaring along Fountainbridge, a girl on the pillion, headed in the evening for the West End, or by day for the beach at Gullane, a popular east coast resort, to picnic, swim and canoodle.

He knew there was something special afoot when Tommy finally brought a girl home with him to introduce to his parents. Isa Farmer was dark-haired, petite and pretty. She lived close by in the Grassmarket, where the lovebirds would often linger at the bottom of Castle Wynd. For several months Tommy was Isa's regular 'fellie', Isa Tommy's 'knockabout'. Just when they seemed on the point of getting engaged, however, the romance fizzled.

At the end of the season at Portobello Tommy reverted to French polishing, working for brief periods at various cabinet-makers in the city, one of whom specialized in the building and buffing of coffins. Here Tommy found the boss a remarkable man who knew everyone; seconds after hearing that one of his potential customers was ill, he would nip round and mentally measure them up with a practised eye. Sometimes, he marvelled, the customers even managed to cheat the proprietor and live! In any case, he considered it a waste of his time polishing coffins only to see his best work lowered into the ground – even if it was only mahogany bleached to resemble oak, one of the proprietor's many wheezes.

On many a rush job he stayed all night, sleeping in the coffin on which he was working. He found it comfortable enough, provided he brought his own pillow. And there was a side benefit – it kept his body firm.

His hand was kept in at modelling, working for Vince, a men's mail-order catalogue firm. He would leave Edinburgh at the crack of dawn on his motorbike, pose in their Manchester studio in briefs and swimming trunks, then head back home exhausted that same evening, his fee securely tucked away. A welter of labouring jobs followed the coffin polishing: humping coal again for several weeks, digging ditches, mixing cement and bricklaying, cleaning the printing presses at the *Edinburgh Evening News*, as well as part-time bouncing at the Fountainbridge. 'For God's sake settle at something,' Effie admonished her son. 'Oh, no,' Tommy replied, 'I'm going to keep going from job to job until I find the right one, and the right money. I'm not going to be like my dad and work for sweeties all my life.'

In the way that one thing leads to another, his weight training combined with his Palais stint to produce a second encounter with the world of show business. Every Trades' Week, the period in July when Edinburgh loosens its corsets and industry ceases, the 'Dilly-Dally' (Palais) proudly presented a special attraction to lure the stay-at-homes in the shape of the famous Ray Ellington Orchestra. (They had to, for the competition was fierce. Nearer Tollcross they were up against the Cavendish ballroom – not so plush, but still hugely popular thanks to the excellent resident Tommy Sampson Orchestra.) When ex-army physical training instructor Ellington was introduced to Tommy in 1951, a mutual interest was discovered. For the rest of the engagement the two men worked out regularly backstage with the dumb-bells and weights Ellington never travelled without.

Another theatrical stint followed an advertisement placed in the *Evening News*: 'Six spear carriers wanted, must be over 6' tall. Apply Empire Theatre, Nicholson Street.' The extras were required for the touring production of *Sixty Glorious Years*, a celebratory pageant on Queen Victoria about to commence a five-week engagement. Star Anna Neagle was at the very height of her popularity, following the hugely successful screen partnership with Michael Wilding that dated back to 1946 with *Piccadilly Incident* and was followed by *Spring in Park Lane* a year later, then *Maytime in Mayfair*. 'I'm not just carrying the spear, Mum,' Tommy boasted. 'I'm a guardsman as well.'

One defiant luxury he seldom went without, come hell or high water, was a weekly visit to Ritchie's restaurant, where his steak and mushroom dinner, followed by an ice-cream sundae, set him back ten shillings. On Saturday nights he would either meet his mates at Pontin Street Market Bar, the Fair Exchange pub opposite the 'Pally' or on his home turf of Foy's, where the low snick of snooker cue on ball mingled with the clack of dominoes. Several pints would be downed in the process of a game, with his father stood a round or two while he was about it. Armed with a 'cairry-oot' of a crate of beer and borrowed glasses, he regularly invited his school pal Eric, football mate Willie Hamilton, electrician Billy Bird, brewers' dray driver Danny Fraser, together with half a dozen others, back home for a sing-song.

He was concerned about the hair loss he was beginning to suffer; although there was only early evidence of thinning, it was a major cloud on his personal horizon. Would the girls still go for him if he lost his locks? He looked back ruefully on the 'Baldy' nickname he had given his grandfather, a condition Joe himself had inherited. Was this the shape of things to come? Allowing for hair tonic, the once-a-week feast and a moderate amount of smoking and drinking, Tommy was saving regularly and biding his time. The question he increasingly asked was: What was it all for?

For a while Tommy fell foul of the Valdors, one of the most notorious gangs in Edinburgh. They patrolled their beat of Leith's dockside, armed with razors, lengths of bicycle chains and lead-weighted hose, threatening anyone foolish enough to get in their way. Their girlfriends, known as the Black Angels because of their all-black short skirts and skintight sweaters, contributed razor combs and stiletto heels to the gang's armoury. Their first encounter with Connery came in the Lothian Street billiards hall he frequented. As he lined up a shot one night he saw one of the Valdors hanging around the jacket he had slung over a chair, while a few other members of the gang circled. Although he was convinced his pockets had been rifled, the suspect proved empty-handed when challenged; Tommy had interrupted him too soon. The looks he was given as he warned the rest of the gang to keep away indicated that the Valdors regarded him as unfinished business.

The following evening the gang were out in force at the Palais, several members following Tommy to the balcony overlooking the main floor. Deciding that attack was the best method of defence, he grabbed one by the throat and one by the biceps, then applied the pressure he had worked to achieve over months at the Dunedin. He knew exactly when to let go, however, and roundly cracked their heads together as the rest of the gang backed away.

From then on, although the Valdors treated him with great respect – 'Hello there, Tam,' they would greet him prior to beating a hasty retreat – the contemptuous Fountainbridge response, 'Kiss ma erse' was never far from Tommy's lips. His reputation as a 'hard man', a true Edinburgh 'keelie', was solidly established. 'All of us lads liked to "act the hard man" to attract the girls,' Jack Vinestock recalls with a smile. 'With Tommy's build and looks he hardly needed to bother.'

Some light relief after the episode was provided by the visit to Scotland on a triumphant theatrical tour of Tommy's childhood hero Roy Rogers, complete with Dale Evans and Trigger. The high excitement all of Edinburgh felt when they appeared at the Empire was climaxed by Trigger being conveniently stabled round the corner at St Cuthbert's for the season. A story that convulsed Edinburgh in the wake of the visit had a wee boy on a tram steadily avoiding the conductor, who sniffed something decidedly malodorous every time he passed. 'Here, you wee bugger, that's a lump of shite you've got in your hand,' he accused him finally.

'I know,' said the little lad, smiling beatifically, 'but it's *Trigger*'s shite!'

Chapter 4

'If you were his friend in these early days you didn't raise the subject of Bond. He was, and is, a much better actor than just playing Bond, but he became synonymous with Bond. He'd be walking down the street and people would say, "Look, there's James Bond." That was particularly upsetting to him.'

Michael Caine

'You want to get some press attention and get yourself talked about?' Jimmy Laurie asked Tommy one day as they took a breather from the weights at the Dunedin. 'Then come down to London with me and we'll both enter the Mr Universe contest. Even if we don't win anything, we'll have a smashing time down in the smoke.'

There was no need to ask Tommy twice; off the two friends went, eager and pent up for the competition, and equally ready to savour the delights of the metropolis. For three weeks they stayed in a Chelsea bed-sit, taking the tube to the massive Scala Theatre, where the equally massive Mr Universe hopefuls lined up daily for the qualifying heats.

Laurie drew a complete blank in the competition; Tommy,

34

chest hair shaved and body suitably oiled for the occasion, won a disappointing third in the tall man's category and was awarded a bronze medallion. He fumed that muscle-bound Americans had scored so resoundingly, impressing on size alone, and was shattered to discover they would refuse even to run for a bus in case they shed vital bulk and inches. Not to be allowed to run, swim and play football would have made the whole exercise meaningless for Tommy.

While in London he heard that auditions were being held at the Drury Lane Theatre for a touring version of the smash-hit musical *South Pacific*. Was it possible, he wondered, after his backstage work at the King's and spear-carrying at the Empire, that he could land an actual role? Although he did his homework before turning up, he was nervous when questioned about his qualifications for the job. (If only he had known it, his most obvious asset was the body beautiful he had developed. Fed up with a parade of undernourished professional applicants, director Joshua Logan had instructed that gymnasia be scoured for heftier types.) 'Acting? What do I know about acting?' he echoed. 'Well, I was a soldier in *Sixty Glorious Years*. I can sing "There is Nothing Like a Dame" – and I can do handsprings.' He nervously fumbled the loose-leaf script he was given, scattering the sheets. 'Hurry up, clumsy,' he was told. 'I haven't got all day.'

'Neither have I,' he retorted, impetuously tossing the remaining pages into the air and furiously striding into the wings. Lips pursed, positively oozing resentment, he was called back. 'Are these your shoulders?' he was asked, in an attempt to break the ice. 'They are,' he dourly replied. Another copy of the script was handed over, which he was asked to read in an American accent. Calling upon his years of training in the Coliseum, Blue Halls, Toll-X and 'O-P', he did just that, following up with a full-throated version of 'I Belong to Glescae'. To his astonishment and delight he was informed that the job was his. 'What's the wage?' he promptly asked. 'It doesn't concern me,' came the haughty reply. 'But it does concern *me*,' Tommy snapped.

'I've got it! I've got it!' he told his family back in Auld Reekie. 'I've got the part in *South Pacific*. This is the start, I know it is. This is what I've been looking for.' Although it was the bottom rung of the ladder, Tommy at last had the feeling there was a chance to climb.

It was time for a name change; it was also 1954, and *Shane*, the classic George Stevens western, had just swept the country. It provided Alan Ladd with his finest hour, and, by some accounts, Tommy with his new name, as 'Shane' became the inspiration for 'Sean'. While he would forever remain Tommy or 'Big Tam' to his mates, henceforth he decided he would be known professionally as Thomas Sean Connery. 'They said it was too big,' he later recalled. 'I didn't know if I was going to stay an actor, so I used Sean – Sean Connery.'

At a party to mark the end of his first week in *South Pacific*, Connery was introduced to Maurice Mickelwhite, a struggling young actor trying to break in his new monicker of Michael Caine (also derived from a 1954 Hollywood hit, *The Caine Mutiny*. Just think: it could just as easily have been Shane Mickelwhite and Tommy Caine!) With his unabashed Cockney accent, Caine recalls feeling distinctly pleased at the sound of another working-class accent. All he and his new-found friend needed now, he reflected, was a change of attitude from the dictum that only plummy-voiced classically trained actors could hope to make it big.

Although Connery entered *South Pacific* as one of the Seabees chorus boys, he had not only landed a small part by the time the tour reached Edinburgh, as Marine Cpl Hamilton Steeves, but was understudying two of the juvenile leads, his salary increased from £12 to £14 10s a week. When the show returned to Edinburgh a year later, by public demand, he had been promoted to the featured role of Lieut. Buzz Adams that Mary Martin's son, Larry Hagman, had played in the West End production. He fairly swelled with pride when his name was added to the programme. There it was in print: Sean Connery. Now it was official.

He was still introduced as 'Tommy' to black songstress

Maxine Daniels during her run at the Empire Theatre with drummer Tony Crombie and the Rockets in a hastily assembled rock 'n' roll show for impresario Bernard Delfont. Maxine, born Gladys Lynch in Stepney, London, with an English mother, a dad hailing from Barbados and a brother in pop singer/entrepreneur Kenny Lynch, was mightily impressed with the tall, hirsute young Scot with the devilish twinkle in his eye. Flattered as she was when he asked her out for dinner, she expressed some surprise at the flaunting of convention. This was sectarian Scotland in the mid-1950s, after all, where it was not at all usual for mixed couples to date, even in the show-business milieu. 'I like good-looking women,' Tommy straightforwardly explained. 'Good-looking *black* women?' Maxine persisted. '*All* good-looking women,' Tommy empha-sized, with a look of shy, hopeful pleading on his face that Maxine found totally irresistible.

When together they swept into Edinburgh's fashionable West End Café they were immediately the centre of attention, all heads in the crowded establishment turning to take in the petite Maxine, stunning in a peacock-green three-piece outfit, and Tommy towering over her in modified black drape jacket, matching drainpipe trousers and navy blue 'slim Jim' tie. After dinner in the more intimate setting of an after-hours drinking club, Maxine threw the would-be Lothario with her news that she was a faithful, happily married housewife with a baby daughter.

'We were both kids in our mid-twenties,' Maxine, now a proud, still youthful grandmother twice over, recalled during a break in her latest tour in autumn 1991. 'Tommy was a gorgeous, wonderful hunk of man, so polite, so obviously sincere, so thoroughly nice. One of my most popular numbers back then, before and after the rock 'n' roll tour, was "Nice Work if You Can Get It". Looking back on my encounter with Tommy, it seems appropriate. In another lifetime, in different circumstances, he and I might have been wonderful together.'

From the beginning of *South Pacific*'s tour, Connery had been in his element with the new-found freedom derived from living the life of a 'travelling player', darting from town to town on his humble motorbike. The backstage camaraderie had been marred just a little by one of the actors with whom he shared a dressing room. This particular character hogged the mirror, constantly struck poses, and came over to Connery as a monumental pain-in-the-neck 'theatrical'. Glad to see the back of him when he left, he sat, nonchalantly naked, as his replacement arrived. Clad in a fur coat and clutching a teddy bear, versatile entertainer Victor Spinetti initially looked every bit as bad as his predecessor. The newcomer beheld the resplendent Connery physique, eyes travelling down the torso, appreciatively taking in every inch. 'A pigeon sitting on two eggs?' Connery suggested. 'Not a pigeon,' Spinetti admiringly replied, 'more like an eagle!'

Although at first Connery had never thought matters through to the extent of considering himself an aspiring 'serious' actor, there was a perceptible change after the tour first left Scotland and was in the middle of a nine-week run through Christmas and the New Year at the Opera House, Manchester. By then veteran American actor/director Robert Henderson had become his unofficial guru on all matters theatrical. When the name of Henrik Ibsen was dropped, Connery was nonplussed. 'Who's he?' he asked. Henderson not only explained that the Norwegian was one of the world's foremost modern dramatists, but loaned his friend copies of Ibsen's *Hedda Gabler*, *The Wild Duck* and *When We Dead Awake*. Somewhat to Henderson's astonishment, Connery swiftly digested these – and came back asking for more.

He went on to list several literary classics for his friend to study – Marcel Proust's *Remembrance of Things Past*, Tolstoy's *War and Peace*, Turgenev's *Fathers and Sons*, James Joyce's *Ulysses* and *Finnegan's Wake*, the letters written between Bernard Shaw and Ellen Terry, Thomas Wolfe's *Look Homeward, Angel*, as well as all of Shakespeare's plays and the works of Shaw. Connery wasted no time in borrowing each of these in turn from local libraries, although the discovery that Proust's work ran to twelve volumes came as a considerable shock. Still he studied them all assiduously, and always with a dictionary handy by his side. Soon he had moved on to 'method' acting maestro Stanislavski's *An Actor Prepares* and *My Life in Art*, and slowly began to recognize and appreciate the truth behind Thomas Wolfe's admonition, 'You can't go home again.' His bridges, in his own mind at least, were being well and truly burned.

He came into his own in another respect in Manchester, leading *South Pacific*'s football team against the local juniors. Manchester United's Matt Busby turned up to watch and was impressed enough by Connery's prowess to offer him a trial at Old Trafford. Henderson advised against it, arguing that his future lay in acting if he could 'talk like Dostoevsky and look like a truck driver ... Speak one thing, look another.' After a night of agonizing, Connery decided against the move, forefeiting the chance to earn big money in the short term. Having found his milieu at last, he decided to stick with learning his stagecraft and improving his literary knowledge.

He watched, entranced, as Carol Sopel, a dark-haired beauty with a ballerina's slender figure, joined the cast. Soon they were inseparable, spending all their spare time together in between Connery's recital of Ibsen and Shaw and gamely attempting to flatten out his glottal stops. Sopel's erstwhile boyfriend, a dapper, energetic young agent named Dennis Selinger, was left to ponder, in the wake of their whirlwind romance, that all was fair in love and war.

Since Sopel was just as eager as Connery to learn her trade, the twosome never missed a repertory performance in each town they visited, and within weeks none of the cast and crew had any doubt that Connery had marriage on his mind. His plans were dealt an unexpected, crushing blow when Sopel's Orthodox Jewish parents declared the union out of the question; they would never consent to their daughter marrying outside the faith. Connery told Henderson the devastating news, leaving his friend pondering on the irrationalities of life and thinking how dreadfully sad it was to see such a big, brawny Scots lad helplessly sobbing.

Still on the tour, now well into its second year in 1956 – and very much on the rebound from Sopel – Connery met an extremely attractive blonde, Julie Hamilton, in a London pub. A showbiz photographer with the *Daily Mail*, Hamilton had visited the Lyric Theatre in Hammersmith in April 1956 to see her actor friend Ronald Fraser, joining him and his wife-to-be Lizzie for a drink after the show. 'I'd like you to meet a pal of mine,' Fraser had declared in his beautifully modulated tones. Hamilton found herself confronted with a character she immediately diagnosed as 'large and rather boring'. His whole manner, topped off with the give-away tattoos, she saw as bearing all the hallmarks of a navvy; not at all the type to appeal to the protected and self-confessedly virginal twenty-one-year-old Hamilton. 'Hello, my name's Connery. Sean Connery,' said the apparition, in a Scottish brogue thick enough to slice. 'God, what an appalling person,' she thought to herself, and proceeded to put the memory of the introduction behind her.

Connery's reaction was a complete contrast; yet again the impressionable, headstrong twenty-six-year-old had fallen head over heels in love. For months afterwards he popped up at parties, in pubs, in friends' houses, and always – as far as Hamilton was concerned – with a soft, slightly dopey grin on his face. It was the sort of smile she had never seen before, with nothing lecherous or even sexy about it, just a rather soppy, sweetly appealing 'I like you'. Still Hamilton remained immune to the Connery charm. *That accent!* No wonder actors who met him for the first time thought he was Polish!

It took almost six months from their first meeting, and a whole host of silly smiles, before the turning point was reached at Ronnie Fraser's wedding in Hampstead. Hamilton was a bridesmaid, and discovered that the groom had turned up for the ceremony in a kilt and full Highland gear, accompanied by a similarly attired Connery. It was as if a switch had been thrown. To Hamilton he suddenly looked absolutely devastating – the most beautiful sight, she swears, that she had ever seen in her life.

Chapter 5

'I'm a bloody Scot and I always will be. And like all Scots I'm a bit introspective, don't like lies and prefer straight dealing. I don't actually lose my temper much, except at incompetence and when the golf goes badly.'

Sean Connery

After Fraser's wedding reception, as Connery and Hamilton walked together to her Hampstead home, the couple were continually ogled in the street. At first Hamilton thought everyone was looking at her in her bridesmaid's dress, until it dawned on her that it was the dashing Adonis by her side drawing the stares. (And being London rather than Edinburgh, there was no chorus of 'Kilty, kilty, cauld bum' to endure.) With her parents – Jill Craigie and Labour Member of Parliament Michael Foot – gone for the weekend, the couple spent the next twenty-four hours together, their affair well and truly under way. Hamilton was in love, overcome by the sheer beauty and physicality of the man.

While still with the *South Pacific* company, Connery had already made a determined first step into films, playing an extra in Anna Neagle's *Lilacs in the Spring*. The few pounds he earned for this and other 'bits' were salted away against the dry spell that inevitably followed the end of *South Pacific*'s tour. By then Robert Henderson had found him digs in London's Maida Vale, off King's Road, sharing with several other struggling young actors. For a while he had to dip into his savings, his £6 unemployment benefit more than swallowed up by rent, meals and the elocution lessons both Henderson and Hamilton urged. Gratefully he accepted an offer of regular babysitting from journalist Peter Noble and his actress wife Mary, the stints earning him a generous ten shillings a night, with another ten bob thrown in if he had to change a nappy.

Even with this largess, Connery's motorbike soon had to be sacrificed, and replaced by a £2 boneshaker of a ladies' bicycle. Hamilton helped by popping round with food to his damp basement flat, while he resourcefully tried his hand at the cheap but nourishing Irish stew that was his mother's speciality. Strangely, it never tasted the same. Effie worried about her absent son, and on occasions rightly so. Confined to bed with a fever, he kept his illness to himself: only when a friend mentioned it in passing months later did he blushingly confirm having been laid up for three weeks.

Babysitting for the Nobles brought him an introduction to visiting Hollywood actress Shelley Winters. Her first glimpse of 'one of the tallest and most charming and masculine Scotsmen' she had ever seen was of Connery sitting in a corner of the Nobles' lounge animatedly telling their four-year-old a leprechaun story. She later shared several fish and chip suppers and bottles of beer with both Connery brothers – Neil stayed with Sean for a while on leave from Army conscription – and recalls the aspiring star's tiny bedroom, lined with bookshelves, one thin mattress covering the floor, topped with an embroidered Indian throw. Although the kitchen stove was the only source of heat, she claims to have spent some of her 'warmest nights' in Connery's company. Hearing that he was about to be evicted, she coaxed Noble to slip him some money from her, with a cover story that he had received a windfall advance for a book.

As Connery later moved round a succession of digs, Hamilton occasionally stayed overnight before retreating to the home comforts her mother and stepfather afforded. TV presenter Llew Gardner became Connery's landlord for a while. As a young man he had worked for the Communist *Daily Worker* and had inherited thirteen volumes of the collected works of Stalin. When Connery brought home an old bed with only three legs, the unwanted books came in extremely useful as the fourth prop. 'It was Joe's last great humanitarian act,' Gardner maintains, 'that he should supply support for the future James Bond's athletic sex.'

Although Connery and Hamilton's parents got on extremely well, Craigie was dead set against his talk of marriage to her daughter; marrying an unsuccessful actor simply would not do. Hamilton would look on as her doughty beau picked her stepfather's brains. Watching them together was one of the things that made her love Connery. His determination to learn and improve the quality of his life was accompanied by a complete lack of vanity that she felt was his most attractive quality.

On one visit to the family's country cottage in Leatherhead, Connery expressed concern that Craigie spent so much time there on her own. When a friend's dog had pups he acquired one for her as a future guard dog. 'Vanessa', who looked like a Tibetan terrier crossbred with several other exotic strains, became famous long before Connery, caricatured in cartoons and immortalized in newspaper pictures after accompanying Foot on the first Aldermaston anti-nuclear march.

With Connery persistently talking of marriage, Hamilton promised to do her best. 'What would you say,' she tentatively asked her mother, 'if I said I was thinking, only *thinking* of marrying Sean?' Craigie's explosion of rage at the very idea required all of Foot's considerable diplomatic skill to calm her down. It became a regular pattern for Hamilton to greet Connery red-eyed from her latest tearful encounter at home. Despite her love for him, she was still young and insecure enough to be unable to go against her mother's wishes. It was a situation that proved a terrible strain all round, not least for Connery, who saw the decision facing Hamilton as utterly clear-cut. If this was heading for a rerun of the Carol Sopel episode, he felt that his ego could take only so much, especially with the difficulty he was having finding work and representation.

While he was still searching for an agent sufficiently convinced of his prospects to take him on, Robert Henderson helped out with a £6 a week walk-on in a production of Agatha Christie's *Witness for the Prosecution* being staged at the Kew Theatre. A chance meeting with fellow-scot Ian Bannen in the foyer proved the start of an enduring friendship. 'My memory of him then,' says Bannen, 'is of a towering, huge fellow with hair everywhere – all over his cheeks, huge eyebrows like a squirrel's tail, the lot. I felt I wouldn't have liked to meet him down some alley.' More small roles followed for Connery in *Point of Departure* and *A Witch in Time* at Kew, in turn leading to an appearance at Oxford in *The Bacchae*, playing Pentheus to Yvonne Mitchell's Agare, then opposite Jill Bennett in Eugene O'Neill's *Anna Christie*. During this period he was out of work for a dispiriting seven months.

Following a tiny role as a boxer on television in *The Square Ring* during the Oxford run, eager-beaver Connery found himself picked out from the crowd by Canadian-born TV director Alvin Rakoff while filming *The Condemned*. Rakoff was so impressed that he gave Connery a second role in the middle of the Dover location filming – now he was both the soldier throwing the grenade *and* the villain on the receiving end, while back in the studio a third role was added! A play entitled *Epitaph* followed, together with a role in an episode of *Dixon of Dock Green* as a young hoodlum.

The agent who finally agreed to represent Connery, in spring 1957, was Richard Hatton, an up-and-comer anxious to make his mark in the profession. He promptly landed his client bottom billing and the role of Spike, the stooge to veteran Alfie Bass's villain in a low-budget British B-movie, *No Road Back*, for which director Montgomery Tully had imported the ques-

tionable star power of American Skip Homeier to bolster Paul
Carpenter and Margaret Rawlings. Bass was struck by Connery's intelligence and dedication and found to his surprise that
they even had cabinet-making backgrounds in common. He also
observed Connery's incredible success rate with the starlets and
wardrobe assistants who fluttered around. There were occasions
when Bass diplomatically vacated the dressing room they shared
to help his young friend with his assignations. In a profession
where questions are often raised, there was never the slightest
doubt about Connery's sexual orientation.

'I was supposed to be this stupid character who stuttered,' he
recalled of his role. 'The third heavy, I think. Alfie Bass and
Paul Carpenter set me up. They told me to inform the director
that a page of unspeakable dialogue I had should be cut. Bold
as brass, on my first film, I did just that. The pay-off, naturally,
was that I discovered the director stuttered and he'd written the
script! He was very nice about it, as I recall. Can't think
why . . .'

Next came *Hell Drivers*, an 'A' film with Cy Endfield at the
helm that offered Connery eleventh billing of 'Johnny' behind
Stanley Baker and the usual British repertory company including Herbert Lom, Sid James – and Alfie Bass.

Neither RKO's release of *No Road Back* nor Rank's
distribution of *Hell Drivers* caused the slightest ripple on the
cinematic scene; nor did bottom billing as 'second welder'
Connery contributed to a 73-minute 'B' entitled *Time Lock*.
Based on an early television play by Arthur 'Airport' Hailey,
the movie was shot in fifteen days, on a budget of just £17,500,
and constituted the first flowering of the team of director
Gerald Thomas and producer Peter Rogers, prior to stumbling
on their lucrative 'Carry On' formula.

Unknown to Connery or anyone else at the time, he was
headed for a series of his own that would cut across all frontiers
and shatter international records.

When Connery's first big break finally arrived, it was courtesy
of one of his screen idols – and, ironically enough, the actor

who had played Shane's deadly adversary. Jack Palance was
scheduled to fly to London to play the lead in Rod Serling's
play, *Requiem for a Heavyweight*, for BBC-TV. When a film
commitment forced him to cancel, director Alvin Rakoff had
just ten days before rehearsals commenced to find another actor
to portray Mountain McClintock, the tragic ex-champion boxer
whose downfall and humiliation is orchestrated by his unscru-
pulous manager. Several actors auditioned, with ex-profes-
sional boxer Freddie Mills under consideration for a while. It
was Rakoff's girlfriend, Jacqueline Hill, who had worked with
Connery at Oxford, who recommended that he be auditioned.
When asked why, her reasoning was peculiarly feminine and
totally practical: 'Every woman would like to watch Connery.'
The question was, could he sustain the lead in a ninety-minute
drama to be transmitted live?

With George Margo, Warren Mitchell, Fred Johnson and
Hill herself on hand to support his McLintock, Connery landed
the coveted lead. The enormous sympathy that he felt for his
character's predicament was evident from the first rehearsals.
Playing the tiny role of the boxer who succeeds McLintock –
glimpsed at the end of the play being shepherded past his
predecessor – was his friend Michael Caine, still an impov-
erished young hopeful on the verge of big things.

Joe, Effie and Neil watched, enthralled, as BBC-TV's
Sunday Night Play of 31 March 1957 unfolded. 'By heavens,
that was smashing,' Joe declared as the credits rolled, a
sentiment shared by his eighteen-year-old son and – in her own
quiet way, for demonstrativeness was not in her nature – his
misty-eyed wife.

The morning after the transmission Richard Hatton's phone
began buzzing. Although Connery was being pursued by a
variety of independent producers, the Rank Organisation and
20th Century-Fox, he kept them all hanging on and invited
Julie Hamilton to accompany him to Edinburgh to meet his
parents while he weighed up the offers. Since he had yet to pass
his driving test Hamilton did the honours in her sports two-
seater on the road north. Although the minute Connery

household was hardly what she was used to, she found it immaculately kept by Effie and possessing a wonderful, warm atmosphere.

Their romance having already been weakened by her mother's adamant rejection of Connery as a suitor, as well as by Hamilton's increasing possessiveness, she was now subjected to an old Scotch custom she found singularly unendearing. As the couple sat and talked one night, Connery consulted his watch, then looked restlessly over at his brother and mimed the lifting of a pint glass. Neil understood the signal, automatically donned his jacket and accompanied Sean over to Foy's, leaving Hamilton fuming on her own. No sooner had the first round of drinks been set up in their masculine preserve than she crashed through the door and confronted the two men. 'I think you might have asked me along for a drink,' she said, determinedly sitting herself down opposite them. In the uneasy silence that followed Neil sensed the beginning of the end of the relationship.

Back in London, with the decision taken to sign with 20th Century-Fox, Hamilton persuaded Connery to use his £25 BBC fee to make a deposit on a place of his own, rather than continue to pay rent for digs. A first-floor studio flat above a pair of garages in Wavell Mews, St Johns Wood, was located, and furnished with a considerable contribution from Hamilton's mother. Craigie wished Connery well – just so long as further talk of marriage was off the agenda.

Hamilton's insecurity increasingly turned to jealousy when Connery chose to go out with his friends. 'Although I'd no cause to be jealous – Sean was always a one-woman man – I behaved stupidly,' she later admitted. 'He'd go out drinking with the boys and I'd automatically assume women were present. There were quarrels and rows. I was to blame, I was the stupid one.'

Connery felt confident he could look forward to a whole series of roles in Fox's output. And if ever an actor was made for Cinemascope – the system Fox had pioneered in 1953 with *The Robe* – surely he was that actor. Astonishingly, the only steady feature of the contract turned out to be Fox's then-lavish £120 a week; another five years would elapse, with the deal on the verge of expiry, before he would appear in his first film for the studio, the all-star World War II epic personally produced by Fox chief Darryl Zanuck, *The Longest Day*.

First he was loaned out to MGM for a tepid thriller, *Action of the Tiger*, joining their fading ex-contract star Van Johnson and Martine Carol, then being touted as 'France's Lana Turner', on location in southern Spain. While director Terence Young knew at an early stage that he had a stinker on his hands, the untutored Connery entertained notions that the movie, his first in colour, might be the one to kickstart his film career. Young did his best to disabuse him of the notion – he later described *Action of the Tiger* as 'a dreadful film, very badly directed' – and promised to make it up to him at some unspecified time in the future. Already he had detected a quality inherent even in Connery's portrayal of a drunken ship's mate: 'He had this strange thing already back then, a sexual quality. To say it was star quality was going too far, he didn't have enough to do in the film to extend him, but he definitely was a fine-looking hunk of a man and a darned good actor.' Martine Carol, it turned out, felt the same way. 'This boy should be playing the lead instead of Van Johnson,' she informed Young. 'He has a big star quality.'

In August 1957 Connery detoured back to the small screen to appear in the ATV Playhouse presentation of *Anna Christie*, the Eugene O'Neill play familiar to him from Oxford. Playing opposite him this time, in the role of the angst-ridden woman of the night, was a petite, devastatingly attractive green-eyed ash blonde of Italian–Scottish ancestry, twenty-four-year-old Diane Cilento.

Born in Rabaul, New Guinea, her childhood had been spent in Queensland, Australia, where her father, Sir Raphael, was knighted for his services to tropical medicine. Her gynaecologist mother, Lady Caroline, travelled thousands of miles a year, treating patients in outlying areas. Cilento was the first member of her family to have broken away from the field of medicine.

Her education had taken place in several countries. She attended boarding school in Towoomba, Queensland until she was fifteen, when her family moved to New York with her father's posting to the United Nations. There she became a Washington Irving High School girl, attending New York's PS 83. Her theatrical interests found an outlet in ballet classes in Carnegie Hall before her enrolment at the American Academy of Dramatic Art. Her first stage job was with the Barter Theater Company of Virginia, playing minor roles and working backstage while touring the Mid-West and southern states of America. In 1950 she headed for England, a student once more, working her way through the Royal Academy of Dramatic Art in jobs that ranged from wine shop assistant to selling programmes in a circus.

On leaving, she secured bit parts at the Mercury Theatre in London's Notting Hill before a move to the Library Theatre in Manchester, where she achieved her first big success as Shakespeare's Juliet. Back in London she appeared in *Arms and the Man* at the Arts Theatre, *One's Fair Daughter* at the Kew and *The Big Knife*, opposite American actor Sam Wanamaker, at the Duke of York's. When film offers began to arrive she chose *The Angel Who Pawned Her Harp* – with the ubiquitous Alfie Bass in the cast – for her first starring role. Painfully twee as this was, it apparently – together with her performance in *The Big Knife* – led to a contract from Alexander Korda.

Cilento continued as a stage actress while her film career developed, playing Helen of Troy opposite Michael Redgrave in Giraudoux's comedy, *Tiger at the Gates*. The production was a great success, the Variety Club voting her Most Promising Actress of the Year. A transfer to Broadway in 1954 ran for seven months and brought her a nomination for a coveted Tony statuette as well as the New York Drama Critics' Award for the Best Actress of the Year. Although there were rumours of several offers from Hollywood, notably from director Elia Kazan to appear in Tennessee Williams's *Baby Doll*, she claimed to have turned them all down, priding herself on being someone who could not be bought and sold. Transport around town for the cigar-smoking Cilento was a Vespa motor scooter. Conventions, she declared, were for the birds. She was, and would always remain, a free spirit.

In February 1955, the twenty-two-year-old took time off to marry Italian Andrea Volpe, a some-time writer, poet and jack-of-all-trades one year her senior. 'I must have been mad,' she later confessed, looking back on the episode, 'but in those days, it was the thing to do, to get married.' The couple lived separately for long periods, their marriage determinedly 'open'. When Cilento was busy filming the latest movie version of J.M. Barrie's *The Admirable Crichton* with Kenneth More for director Lewis Gilbert, Volpe occupied his time by working as a publicist and translator for Korda.

By the time Cilento began touring in a musical version of Sir Max Beerbohm's *Zuleika Dobson* early in 1957, prospects for the marriage looked shaky. Volpe had been forbidden to visit his wife in Manchester and Wolverhampton in the troubled musical and finally caught up with her at a hotel in Oxford at one o'clock in the morning.

He found his wife screaming hysterically, blood pouring from her slashed wrists, shattered glass strewn on the floor. After emergency medical attention she was whisked off to a nursing home; following a few days' rest the couple flew to Italy. 'The trouble was with the show,' she told reporters in Palermo, Sicily, during her recuperation. 'There were so many changes I couldn't stand it any longer. I was told of some of the changes in the script only five minutes before I was due to go on stage for curtain-up and I thought it would ruin my career. I got to the point where I could stick knives in people without a qualm. Back in my hotel I threw a tantrum. I broke a glass and went to the bathroom. I stood there with the glass in my hand – but I don't remember any more.'

In Rome Cilento moved in with Volpe's family for two months before returning to England to film *The Truth about*

Women. She was pregnant, she announced, and intended to have the child in Australia, surrounded by her family. With Volpe back in Rome readying himself for Italian National Service, the stage was set for the fateful first encounter with Connery.

Chapter 6

'You don't bullshit Connery. He wants people to be able
to live with themselves. He also likes to know the score.'

Guy Hamilton

'In my eye Sean had it from the word go. He had
charisma. He looked great, had a great line in chat and,
well, look at the way he was built!'

Michael Caine

Soon after rehearsals began for *Anna Christie*, Connery ended
his relationship with Julie Hamilton. 'We were at the mews,'
Hamilton recalled. 'Sean was looking at me with his mind far
away. Suddenly he said, "She's got the most incredible eyes."
I said, "Who?" He said, "Diane." I knew immediately he was
in love with her. Then he said gently, but quite bluntly, "I don't
think I love you the same way anymore."' He went on to
explain how he had fallen for Cilento at first sight, just as he
had with Hamilton and Sopel before her. 'I'd better go, then,'
was Hamilton's response as she stumbled for the door.

Next day, back to pick up her things, she took the opportunity, through tears of anger, to scrawl a couple of rude words

on the bedroom mirror with her lipstick. Although they were eventually able to meet as friends, Hamilton still felt a terrible sadness that it was all over. Several years elapsed before she could bear to watch Connery on television, or in the cinema.

She bumped into him after her marriage on an outing with her baby son. When Connery asked his name, she replied that it was 'Jason'. 'A fine name,' he replied, smiling. 'If I have a son I'll call him Jason, too.' To Hamilton it was a source of great delight when Connery married Cilento; that hers had been the name on his lips when she was ditched somehow made everything all right. 'I suppose we all think our first love is the right one,' she rationalized. 'Of course life isn't as easy as all that. Sean was a very special person at a point in my life, but I have no regrets.'

Connery wasted no time in suggesting after-hours rehearsals to Cilento to perfect their teamwork on *Anna Christie*. When she agreed and invited him over to her flat, the first impression she gained was that he had a tremendous chip on his shoulder. He would stretch out on the floor and just lie there, dormant, almost as if he were trying to annoy her. Cilento wisely neglected to react and eventually realized that he had no ulterior motives and was just being himself. Although his purchase of her Vespa scooter may have helped to clinch the romance, she claimed that it took a year before they fell in love since 'he was not nearly as attractive in those early days'.

'Diane swept me off my feet,' was the gospel Connery expounded to anyone who would listen. He went on to describe her as 'the girl who has the most inner sex appeal for me'.

Following her return to Australia soon after the completion of *Anna Christie*, Cilento's daughter, Giovanna Margaret, was born in December 1957. A couple of months later she was back in England with 'Gigi', installed in a Bayswater flat, ready to face the world and resume her career and relationship with Connery. A divorce from Volpe was now only a matter of time.

Noting that Connery's movements had been 'very stodgy' in *Anna Christie*, she encouraged him to enrol in movement classes run by Yat Malmgeren, an ex-dancer with the Kurt

Jooss Ballet Company. The Swede taught the study of action, attitudes and drives based on the concepts of time and motion evolved by the Hungarian dancer Rudolf von Laban. Soon the couple were attending his classes three times a week, learning a cohesive terminology that eliminated any problem in communications, where so often expressions can mean one thing to one person and another to someone else. It was a remarkable eye-opening period for Connery. Unlike external weight-lifting exercises to which he was accustomed, Malmgeren's technique involved tackling oneself from within, from the head through to the base of the spine. He found himself physically awakened, and a much better-tuned instrument.

Connery's next movie loan-out from Fox produced his second contact with a fading MGM nova, this time Lana Turner herself. The studio had 'released' their tempestuous star early from her long-term contract, only a few years after she had arguably delivered her finest-ever screen performance in Vincente Minnelli's *The Bad and the Beautiful*. Her fate had been sealed when the desperate studio, reeling from the effects of TV on the box-office, had pushed her into a slew of highly coloured, risible fare that few actresses could have survived. A less than effervescent remake of *The Merry Widow* proved untimely. *Latin Lovers*, which had Turner searching for romance in South America, was turgid, paper-thin and pointless. *The Flame and the Flesh* transferred much the same 'plot' to Europe and was distinguished only by the presence of a number one hit song, 'No One But You', warbled by Billy Eckstine, the singer whose style in shirts Connery, and half the youth of Scotland, had admired so much in the early fifties. *Diane* was a medieval mish-mash with a young and rightly embarrassed Roger Moore in attendance. The nadir for both Turner and MGM was reached with 1955's Biblical howler, *The Prodigal*.

Having already completed filming 20th Century-Fox's screen adaptation of Grace Metalious' controversial *Peyton Place*, she had set up *Another Time, Another Place* with

Lanturn Productions, her own independent company, with a release negotiated through Paramount. Exercising complete cast approval, Turner took one look at Connery's dashing face and figure and wholeheartedly approved. With Barry Sullivan and Glynis Johns also set, filming was due to begin at MGM's Borehamwood studios north of London in November 1957. Fourth-billed below the title was Connery's war correspondent Mark Trevor, with whom Turner's Sara Scott falls in love in 1944. When he is killed in a plane crash – unfortunately for Connery, thirty minutes into the movie – Sara spurns old flame Carter Reynolds (Sullivan) and makes a sentimental journey to Mark's Cornish village, only to discover he had a wife (Johns) and son.

To add to her career problems MGM's deposed Queen was in deep trouble in her personal life. Earlier in the year she had broken up with her latest husband, screen Tarzan Lex Barker, following her discovery that he had been systematically sexually abusing her teenage daughter Cheryl. Consolation had been sought in the arms of Johnny Stompanato – alias John Holliday, Jay Hubbard, John Truppa, John Valentine and John Steele – a small-time Mafia hood, some-time bodyguard to godfather Mickey Cohen, part-time gift shop owner and full-time gigolo, nicknamed 'Oscar' after the Award-worthy size of his endowment. The swarthy, olive-skinned Stompanato had ambitions to extend his holding on Turner from the bedroom suite to the executive suite, producing future films for her company. Turner's denial of a public role for him had already produced a series of monumental rows between them.

Soon after she arrived alone to begin filming, the cast and crew detected a changed magnetic field between Connery and the star. 'Lana was Sean's "type",' Peter Noble confirms. 'How far did it go? With all that red-hot chemistry, one would imagine all the way. Sean certainly entertained Lana at his flat, as well as several others, and accompanied her on a number of outings.' Rumours of an affair unerringly winged their way across the Atlantic, neatly coinciding with the arrival of Turner's latest protestations of love to her gangster boyfriend.

Confused and infuriated by the mixed signals, and determined to maintain his grip on Turner, Stompanato borrowed the airfare from an obliging Mickey Cohen and flew to London.

At first Turner successfully isolated him in rented premises in Hampstead, protesting that it would be impossible to work with him around. Smelling a rat, he bribed her chauffeur to drive him out to the studio and arrived in time to see Turner and Connery settling down, on camera, to a passionate embrace. Screaming with rage, Stompanato produced a revolver and ran up to the couple, pushing aside the rolling camera, director Lewis Allen and startled crew. 'You keep away from her,' he yelled, waving the gun in Connery's face. Without a moment's hesitation, as if it were a well-rehearsed scene from the movie itself, Connery wrapped one huge fist round Stompanato's gun hand and twisted until he dropped the weapon. With the other he delivered a right hook to Stompanato's nose that smashed him to the floor. A mortified Turner looked on as her boyfriend was led away struggling by the hastily summoned security guards, a spattering of blood on his lime-green suit – and vowing bloody vengeance. The tension on the set was comically broken by the young assistant director nervously enquiring, 'Is that a wrap?'

Although Stompanato never reappeared at the studio he still made his presence felt. Turner was obviously under a constant strain, which she took out on at least one member of the cast, dubbing Glynis Johns 'the bitch of the world'. The limit was reached a few days before Christmas when Turner appeared on set hardly able to speak; it turned out that Stompanato had beaten her up the night before and almost smothered her with a pillow; her bruised larynx and facial swelling might have been worse had a maid not heard her screams and intervened. Turner was in no mood to demur when the movie's associate producer suggested that Scotland Yard be informed. That very day Stompanato was forcibly deported.

Their argument, it turned out, had started with Turner joyfully breaking the news of the smash Stateside opening of *Peyton Place*; after years of unrelenting flops she had actually managed to claw her way back. Why, Fox were predicting it would be the biggest box-office hit of the year! There was even talk of her being nominated for an Academy Award for her performance! Amid the euphoria Stompanato had mistakenly judged the moment right to push his own movie plans, again underestimating Turner's determination to keep her business and private life entirely separate.

Fox's expectations for *Peyton Place* turned out to be accurate; the film was not only a smash but collected a clutch of Oscar nominations, including Best Actress for Turner. During her daughter Cheryl's visit to Britain over Christmas and New Year, the star kept up a steady stream of correspondence with Stompanato. A two-month vacation in Mexico was planned with a strategic return to Hollywood on the eve of the Oscar presentations. Within hours of finishing work on *Another Time, Another Place* and her fond farewell to Connery, Turner departed for the reunion with Stompanato.

While the couple fought their way through their Mexican hayride, Louella Parsons, self-styled Hollywood 'house mother' to whom Turner's 'bitch of the world' sobriquet might have been more accurately directed, took it upon herself to tut-tut in print: 'I sincerely hope it isn't true that Lana Turner, who is now in Acapulco, is marrying Johnny Stompanato.' Between Parsons' touching concern and the type of press attention that accompanied her arrival back in California – 'Lana Turner Returns with Mob Figure' – the ever-practical star knew that whatever future she had with Stompanato would have to be conducted strictly behind closed doors.

He was notable by his absence from Turner's side both at the award ceremony, where she lost out to Joanne Woodward for *Three Faces of Eve*, and later at the party Fox threw at the Hilton. Instead, it was Connery who filled his place as one of the guests at her table, boosting their appearance together in their soon-to-be-released movie, and revelling in his first trip to the States. To fifteen-year-old Cheryl he was an adorably gentle giant. As they danced together and she remarked on the rippling back muscles she could feel through his tuxedo, he told her, in his appealing soft-spoken Scottish burr, of his assault on the Mr Universe title in 1952. She saw that he was completely spellbound, not only by Hollywood, but by her glamorous mother. At one point he nudged her and whispered, 'Look over there at your mom. That's what I call a *star*.'

Livid at his exclusion from the glitz and glamour of the evening, and well aware of Connery's renewed presence, Stompanato lay in wait for Turner that night in her bedroom. 'He beat me up,' she sobbed to her daughter next morning. 'He slapped me so hard that the earrings scratched my cheeks. He punched me and threw me around. He held a razor to my face. I tried not to scream because I was afraid you might wake up—'. Cheryl, it turned out in later court testimony, had listened, shaking with terror, to the entire proceedings.

She witnessed another, even more terrible scene a few days later on Good Friday. 'You'll fuckin' well do as I say!' Stompanato screamed at her mother. 'You think you can order people around? From now on I'll be doing the ordering! When I say "Hop" you'll hop! When I say "Jump" you'll jump! Baby, you'll do what I tell you!'

Back in her room, Cheryl listened as the violent threats escalated. Stompanato was going to destroy Turner's face, then go after her mother and daughter. 'I'll cut you up,' he yelled. 'I'll get you if it takes a day, a week, a year! I'll cut your face up. I'll mutilate you so you'll be so repulsive you'll have to hide forever. And if I can't do it myself, I'll find somebody who will!'

Panic-stricken, Cheryl raced downstairs to the kitchen and grabbed a nine-inch butcher's knife, hoping to scare Stompanato. Back upstairs, terrified to enter her mother's bedroom, she waited outside the door, the knife beside her. The last words she heard from Stompanato were, 'Cunt, you're dead.' As she picked up the knife and the door flew open, she saw her mother framed there, hand on the knob, with Stompanato behind her, fists raised. Cheryl rushed forward in a panic, past her mother, plunging the blade deep into Stompanato's stomach. Gurgling horribly, he staggered a couple of paces forward before twisting himself off the weapon and collapsing backwards on the bed. By the time a doctor had been summoned he was dead. 'Johnny was going to hurt Mother,' Cheryl explained, sobbing, to the Chief of Police.

In the weeks of investigation that followed, Turner's love letters to Stompanato, describing in considerable detail what she called 'our love, our hopes, our dreams, our sex and longings', were splashed across the tabloids, courtesy of Mickey Cohen. 'I thought it was fair,' he explained, 'to show that Johnny wasn't exactly "unwelcome company", like Lana said.' One letter 'revealed' that Connery had accompanied both Turner and Cheryl to a London theatre after shooting *Another Time, Another Place*. With some letters innocent, and others full of passion, the press played up the violent aspect of their relationship. 'Ageing Actress Whipped like Dog by Hoodlum Lover!' one headline screamed.

At Cheryl's trial it took a jury less than twenty minutes to deliver, by ten votes to two, a verdict of justifiable homicide. Ominously, for Connery and everyone else even remotely connected with the case, it turned out that Stompanato had warned that if anything happened to him, his friends would 'get even'. Even though Cohen dismissed the notion of a mob reprisal as 'newspaper talk', a feeling of unease lingered.

With the completion of *Another Time, Another Place* Connery had continued to wait in vain for Fox's contract to produce dividends at the studio. He went through what he later referred to as his 'too' period – he was too big, too square, too Scottish, too Irish, too young or too old – too tall for *Boy on a Dolphin*, opposite Alan Ladd, too swarthy for *High Tide at Noon*, too threatening for Marlon Brando in *The Young Lions*. Executives from the Walt Disney organization, on a casting trip to Britain, came to his rescue. After viewing the rushes of *Another Time, Another Place*, they signed him up for *Darby O'Gill and the Little People*, a lighthearted fantasy based on H.T. Kavanaugh's Darby O'Gill tales, to be directed by industry veteran Robert Stevenson. Connery was ecstatic. It was his first film to be shot in Hollywood, the mecca for all screen actors, and it meant third billing, his highest yet, supporting Albert Sharpe and fellow Scot Janet Munro, the cast completed by Jimmy O'Dea, Kieron Moore and Estelle Winwood, Robert Henderson's wife. Unable to place him themselves – 'That damned accent!' – Fox was happy financially, making a handsome profit on the deal after deducting Connery's salary.

The start of shooting, at Disney's Burbank studios in May 1958, coincided with the end of the trial ordeal for Turner and her daughter. It also fitted in neatly with the opening of *Another Time, Another Place*, rushed into release to cash in on the avalanche of publicity the case had engendered. Unfortunately the movie was dismissed by critics as an unconvincing melodrama and plodding potboiler and shunned even by Turner's most ardent fans.

In the US *Time Magazine* derided its 'treacly taste and clumsy structure', while in the UK Philip Oakes in the *Evening Standard* described the movie as 'a brand new film in the bad old style'. Elsewhere it was 'novelettish' and 'diabolically bad'. Connery came off relatively unscathed, variously described as 'handsome and well-spoken' and 'shaggy-looking'. Only one critic, Derek Monsey of Britain's *Sunday Express*, got it seriously wrong when he declared that, 'A newcomer to films named Sean Connery will not, I guess, grow old in the industry.'

Connery himself provided a personal post-mortem on the movie that was considerably understated: 'The script was not entirely satisfactory and we were rewriting as we were shooting. So they started with the end first and I was dead at the end, so by the time they led up to me I was a picture on the piano. The movie wasn't very good. It was beautifully lit by Jack Hildyard, but dreadfully directed by Lewis Allen.'

A sinister coda to Stompanato's murder came while filming *Darby O'Gill and the Little People*. 'Get your ass outta town' was the brief but pointed telephone message Connery received from Mickey Cohen. A friend advised him not to treat the warning lightly. 'You don't know how these boys work out here,' he told Connery. 'They play for real. Anyone who had any connection with Turner and Stompanato in London would be wise to get out of the way.' Connery later confirmed that Cohen had indeed been out for revenge: 'Apparently he didn't believe that Cheryl had killed Stompanato. He thought the killing had been engineered in some way.'

Connery already had a problem: he owed the Hollywood Roosevelt Hotel $600 and was in the middle of a major row at Disney. Thankfully, an accommodation was reached. 'I got up and went to another hotel,' he recalled, 'where I lay low. Nothing did happen, but it was scary as hell for a while.' His new quarters were across the Hollywood hills in the San Fernando Valley, conveniently situated closer than before to Disney's Burbank studio.

'Believe me, it was pretty gutsy of Sean even to stay in the locality,' his friend insists, 'although I suppose if Cohen had been really determined, he could have nailed him back in Scotland in the *Clyde* Valley, let alone the San Fernando Valley. The fact is, Sean defied Cohen.'

Connery provided the last word on the affair twenty years later. 'She was very nice, I adored her,' he said of Turner. 'She was a lovely lady ... a fine woman and a fine actress.' He confirmed the original 'punch-up' with Stompanato at the studio: 'Aye, but that was a long time ago ...'

Chapter 7

'There is nothing more boring, more annoying, more maddening than being told to do something by someone who is incompetent.'

Sean Connery

'Here [in America] there is much more feel for realism [in acting] than in Europe. There there is still a conception of an actor as being somehow divorced from real life. In Britain acting is still associated more with being statu-esque and striking poses and declaiming with lyrical voices.'

Sean Connery

Mickey Cohen's threats aside, Connery's sojourn in Hollywood, filming Disney's *Darby O'Gill and the Little People*, was a pleasant one. Not only was he living the life of an eligible bachelor in bachelor paradise, but his role as Michael McBride, Janet Munro's suitor in the fable of leprechauns and magic, could scarcely be described as taxing. It also yielded a special bonus in the form of an introduction to Walt Disney himself, who seemed to take a paternal interest in him.

Connery danced, fought – even with the studio – and warbled a duet with Munro, 'Pretty Irish Girl', released as a single when the movie appeared in 1959. (Cilento had beaten him to this particular landmark with a single, 'A Fool and His Heart', from her 1955 movie, *A Woman for Joe*.) If there was impatience among the rest of the cast with by-the-numbers director Robert Stevenson's penchant for constant re-takes and script additions, they hardly worried the eager-to-learn Connery. While in Los Angeles he turned down a number of TV series, including the possibility of a leading role in *Maverick*. The steady money on offer was attractive, but he had no wish to be stuck in a series playing the role week after week – especially with a regular slice going to 20th Century-Fox.

Back in London he reclaimed his Wavell Mews flat from house-sitter Ian Bannen and set about converting the garages underneath his three rooms into a thirty-five-foot sitting room. His steady salary from Fox enabled him to acquire a whole succession of cars, albeit of the second-hand variety. When asked why he had traded in one model, he laconically replied, 'The ashtrays were full.'

A third loan-out, back at Paramount this time, was an obvious retrograde step no amount of publicity rhetoric could disguise. Fifth billing as fourth villain in director John Guillermin's feeble-minded *Tarzan's Greatest Adventure* was a blip on Connery's career chart that mercifully went largely unnoticed in a welter of mismatched shots, appalling back projection and unspeakable dialogue. Gordon Scott was adequate as the latest in the Tarzan line after Lex Barker, while seasoned professionals like Anthony Quayle and Niall Mac-Ginnis clearly went through the motions, buoyed solely by the thought of their cheques at the end of the day.

Connery looked physically terrific as drunken sot O'Bannion – 'You cannot reason with an idiot' one of his confrères spouts – but otherwise a curtain is best drawn over the entire episode. 'His acting wasn't very good,' one of his colleagues admitted, 'and unfortunately there was quite a lot of it!' Still, everyone has to learn their craft, as Nick Roeg, the assistant cameraman on the movie, later to emerge as a brilliant director, would testify. Thankfully for Connery, the memory of his Mountain McClintock was still around.

He returned to the BBC for a single play in 1959, *Riders to the Sea*, then headed for the Oxford Playhouse and a season of classics. An invitation to join Joan Littlewood's Theatre Workshop on a tour of Russia and Eastern Europe in a production of *Macbeth* was rejected; Diane Cilento had fallen ill with tuberculosis and Oxford was as far away as he cared to be. He also turned down an offer from producer Samuel Bronston of a featured role in *El Cid*, choosing instead to await Cilento's recovery. When this was complete, they appeared together at Oxford in Pirandello's *Naked*.

Tarzan apart, news on the film side brightened with the release of *Darby O'Gill and the Little People*. Although predictably drubbed by the critics, the public took to Disney's lighthearted blarney in sufficient numbers for Connery to regard the movie as his first hit; in the US alone the movie netted in excess of $8 million. Of equal importance, it brought him to the attention of one of the great unsung British movie moguls.

Nat Cohen's Anglo-Amalgamated, founded with his racing partner Stuart Levy, had made its name with the two Edgars, author Wallace and Scotland Yard's Lustgarten, churning out micro-budgeted 50-minute supporting feature thrillers at a truly alarming and highly profitable rate throughout the 1950s. In 1959, together with *Time Lock*'s team of Gerald Thomas and Peter Rogers, Cohen initiated the record-breaking run of Carry On movies with *Carry On Sergeant*, the success of which emboldened him to finance what he hoped would prove grade 'A' fare.

The first of these attempts was *The Frightened City*, a thriller directed by John Lemont, in which Connery, on loan yet again, took third billing after Herbert Lom and John Gregson. His Paddy Damion, a protection-racket crook operating on the fringes of London's underworld, was a hulking, monosyllabic character not too distant from an urban version of Lenny in

Steinbeck's *Of Mice and Men*. While *The Frightened City* had no such pretensions to greatness, the movie was a decently made, taut thriller that more than adequately filled the top half of a double-bill.

Cohen followed up with a second project that proved a minor landmark in Connery's career, not because the film was successful – it wasn't – but because in *Operation Snafu* he was awarded top billing for the first time on the big screen. Connery's 'Pedlar' Pascoe (shades of his antecedents!) and Alfred Lynch's fellow con-man Horace Pope teamed for what producer Ben (*Hell Drivers*) Fisz hoped would be a riotous wartime caper. Instead, although amiable enough, it was flat, full of self-conscious mugging and pratfalls and a bit of an embarrassment for all concerned.

At least Connery continued to acquit himself well on TV. He impressed as Alexander the Great in director Rudolph Cartier's adaptation of Terence Rattigan's *Adventure Story*, while his Hotspur to Robert Hardy's Prince Hal in *Henry IV*, part of the BBC's hugely successful Age of Kings series in 1960, was another fine piece of work.

Hardy, who had earlier understudied his ex-army buddy Richard Burton in the play at Stratford-upon-Avon's Shakespeare Memorial Theatre in 1951, felt that Connery had the capacity, and the charisma, to be truly great. 'Richard and I knew Shakespeare's history plays backwards,' Hardy recalls, 'and we both agreed that in Laurence Olivier's otherwise great production at the New Theatre during the war Olivier had unbalanced the play by undercasting Hal and cutting out a good deal of his role. It thus became Hotspur's "show", which Shakespeare never intended. The play, after all, is about a young man facing up to the appalling demands of kingship and it takes two plays to get him to the throne.

'I realized that with my playing Hal opposite Sean's Hotspur, I was running the risk of the balance being knocked again, since here was an actor with enormous potential and glamour. Shakespeare shaped the plays in such a manner that as long as you don't cut Hal terribly, the shape emerges and the

Hotspur character is seen for what he is – extremely attractive, but over the top. He has a lovely sense of humour, gallantry and marvellous love for his wife, but his concept of honour is a bit mad compared with the down-to-earth practicality of Hal.

'Hotspur is a difficult character temperamentally, and difficult to capture, and many people expressed their doubts about Sean. They found his accent a bit strange for one thing, not being attuned to strong regional accents, but it didn't take away from the tremendous zest and excitement of his performance. There was an element of untutoredness in the fact that he didn't clarify his speech, but in fact that was one of Hotspur's characteristics. Just to be with him one knew he had great presence. I never had any doubt he was going places.'

As if to confirm Hardy's judgement, Connery was next chosen to play Count Vronsky in Cartier's *Anna Karenina* opposite Claire Bloom. Recorded in June 1961, its November transmission by the BBC was preceded by a brief, truncated run in the West End of Jean Anouilh's *Judith*, in which Connery appeared clad only in a loincloth as the Biblical slayer Holofernes.

The acclaim accorded the production of *Anna Karenina* more than made up for the stage flop. Connery's Vronsky – worlds removed from his wooden Mark in *Another Time, Another Place*, Tarzan's drunken villain, Disney's romantic foil, the taciturn Damion of *The Frightened City* and the fumbling 'Pedlar' Pascoe of *Operation Snafu* – had the power, command and authority that seemed to have slipped from hibernation on the big screen after his television triumph in *Requiem for a Heavyweight*. One thing was clear – when the role called for it, Connery could produce the goods.

Fox's reward was to toss Connery a scrap at the tail-end of his contract, one of forty-three starring roles in *The Longest Day*, their adaptation of Cornelius Ryan's World War II epic of the D-Day landings of 6 June 1941, *Operation Overlord*. It fell to Ken Annakin to direct Connery's Private Flanagan in the Juno Beach sequence. Although tightlipped about the film itself – blink and you'll miss him – friends found Connery con-

siderably more outspoken about his years under contract to
Fox. He had felt 'like a man walking through a swamp in a bad
dream'.

Before *Judith* met its early demise Connery's nearly-naked
figure had served to remind director Terence Young, from his
seat in the circle at Her Majesty's, not only of the actor's star
quality, but also of the promise he had given after *Action of the
Tiger*. Young was already involved in discussions with producers Harry Saltzman and Albert R. ('Cubby') Broccoli and
author Ian Fleming on the possibility of translating Fleming's
best-selling secret agent James Bond from page to screen.
'Watch *Anna Karenina*,' Young advised them. 'I think we've
found our Bond.'

Short, with curly grey hair and a teddy bear face, Harry
Saltzman was a Canadian, born in St John, New Brunswick in
1915, whose showbusiness career dated back to circus and
vaudeville in the States and Canada before a move to Europe
and the legitimate theatre. Following his service in the French
army during World War II he worked for UNESCO before
gravitating to movies in the fifties. Woodfall Films, the
company he founded with director Tony Richardson, spear-
headed British cinema's kitchen-sink drama phase with *Look
Back in Anger*, *Saturday Night and Sunday Morning* and *The
Entertainer*. Blessed with only intermittent financial success,
Saltzman decided to leave Woodfall behind him and pursue the
rights to Fleming's James Bond books.

Having paid the author $50,000 for a six-month option on
007's adventures – with the exception of *Moonraker*, bought
by Rank, which he would later buy back, and *Casino Royale*,
purchased by producer Gregory Ratoff for $6,000 in 1955, then
resold to agent/producer Charles Feldman – Saltzman found no
takers among the major studios. With a month to go before the
option expired he enlisted the aid of fellow independent
producer Albert Romolo Broccoli, another émigré who had
paralleled the Woodfall saga with his own Warwick Films
banner in partnership with American producer Irving Allen.

Broccoli, a large, imposing and dark-eyed individual of Italian stock, was born in Long Island, New York in 1915. As a boy he worked for his uncle on his gardening farms growing vegetables, including the variety named after him, for the New York market. Although the lure of showbusiness proved irresistible following a vacation in Hollywood in 1933, it took seven long years, selling Christmas trees in San Francisco, hairnets in Los Angeles and as an assistant jeweller in Beverly Hills, before he secured a position in 20th Century-Fox's mailroom. By 1941 he was at RKO as assistant director to Howard Hawks on Howard Hughes's *The Outlaw*, with Jane Russell. Following his Navy service he was discharged in 1945 with the rank of lieutenant. A spell with agent Charles Feldman followed before a move to England and the formation of Warwick Films in 1951.

A release deal through Columbia and the signing of Alan Ladd – still hot from *Shane* – got *Hell Below Zero*, *The Black Night* and *Paratrooper* off the ground, Broccoli claiming that 'Warwick's first three pieces of crap turned out $18 million.' *Cockleshell Heroes*, directed by Jose Ferrer, although predictably a hit in Britain, failed to make an impact on the international market; *Fire Down Below*, with Rita Hayworth, Robert Mitchum and Jack Lemmon did better. A low point was reached in the Indian banditry hokum of *Zarak*, starring the over-the-hill actor Victor Mature. By the time Warwick had scheduled *The Trials of Oscar Wilde*, starring Peter Finch – the best film they ever produced, although a failure financially – they had taken over British independent producer/distributor Eros Films from Phil and Harry Hyams, originally cinema-owning brothers now on the point of retirement.

Like Saltzman at Woodfall, Broccoli had reached the end of the road at Warwick; the company was eventually sold off, complete with tax losses, to John Woolf's Romulus Films. Introduced by a mutual acquaintance, writer Wolf Mankowitz, the two men agreed to go 50–50 on the Bond project. Broccoli contacted Arthur Krim of United Artists, who invited the partners to join him in New York for discussions in June 1961.

With their budget argued down from $1 million to $800,000, of which Fleming was to receive $100,000 as well as 5 per cent of the producers' profits, the pair had their backing, largely due, it turned out, to the influence exercised by UA's man on the ground in London, David Picker.

Thunderball was the unanimous choice for the first of what Saltzman and Broccoli's newly formed Eon Productions hoped would be at least a four-part series. When it transpired that the book was the subject of a legal tussle, their attention and that of writer Richard Maibaum focused instead on *Dr No*. Only after rejections from Bryan Forbes, Guy Green and Guy Hamilton, did Eon turn to Terence Young, Connery's director on *Action of the Tiger* and Broccoli's on *Zarak* and *Paratrooper*.

Roger Moore was one of the first actors to be considered for Bond until Saltzman and Broccoli wrote him off as 'too boyish'. Richard Johnson was in the running for a while, with Fleming holding out for an established star such as Richard Burton, Peter Finch, David Niven, James Stewart, Michael Redgrave or Trevor Howard. Saltzman and Broccoli gave Young a shortlist of five names to consider – Connery, James Mason, Patrick McGoohan, Cary Grant and stuntman Bob Simmons. Grant was agreeable, but just for one film; Mason for only two. McGoohan disapproved of the moral stance behind Fleming's hero and declined; Simmons, although a wonderful stuntman, was considered too short at five feet eleven inches and had no acting experience.

Connery's name had edged itself to the top of Broccoli's list after he and his wife Dana caught a showing of *Darby O'Gill and the Little People* in Hollywood. Like Alvin Rakoff before him, Broccoli found himself persuaded by his better half that Connery had the combination of sex appeal and charisma that spelled star quality. With Terence Young's voice added to the chorus, the two producers, having already been introduced to Connery at a party, decided to arrange an interview with their prospective choice in the company of United Artists' Bud Ornstein.

Connery brought an edge to the meeting that none of the three had anticipated, arriving at Saltzman's South Audley Street office casually dressed in sweater, slacks and loafers and sporting designer stubble years before it became fashionable. He breezed in with the 'body movement swagger' Yat Malmgeren had taught – described at one point as 'the threatening grace of a panther on the prowl' – before launching into a dissertation on how Bond should be portrayed. His attitude was clear from the start – 'Take me the way I am or forget the whole deal.' Although he was thinking super-positively and was already Bond in his own mind, Connery was not about to let either of his interrogators into the secret; if Saltzman or Broccoli thought they were seeing someone desperate for their contract, they had better think again. While his interviewers later reported their astonishment as Connery pounded their desk to emphasize his points, Connery himself would discount their version as 'absolute nonsense', admitting only to using 'strong commanding movements, not with weight, but to show how Bond is always in control of a scene'.

As they watched from their first-floor window while Connery cockily made his way across the street below, the partners and Ornstein were convinced they had found their James Bond. 'We'd never seen a surer guy,' said Saltzman. 'Or a more arrogant sonofabitch!' Broccoli agreed: 'He moved like a cat. That did it for us. Harry and I both said, "This is the guy."' They felt that what he undeniably lacked in polish was more than made up for in the sheer animal magnetism of the man and 'his dark, cruel looks'. Broccoli had always wanted 'a ballsy guy' for the role. 'Put a bit of veneer on that tough Scottish hide,' he suggested, 'and you've got Fleming's Bond instead of all the mincing poofs we had apply for the job.' Ahead lay tests – not screen tests, as often claimed, Broccoli and Saltzman having already made up their minds – but camera tests to judge how best to capture Connery on film. Despite Ornstein's enthusiasm, United Artists' head office verdict on Connery's footage was less than overwhelming. 'See if you can do better,' they cabled.

The contract Connery was offered involved a five-picture deal with producer options, expiring in 1967, that would enable him to make one outside picture a year. Weeks of deliberation were spent with Richard Hatton and Diane Cilento before signing. The reasoning was that with US backing and Bond's readership, the film would at least prove a modest success; if it did better, his future would be secure. A negative aspect was Connery's own hard-earned experience of contracts; the five frustrating years with Fox had been rewarding enough financially, but a dead-end artistically. According to Cilento, she pushed the balance in Eon's favour. 'If it were not for me,' she claimed, 'Sean might never have become James Bond.'

In autumn 1961, with *Dr No* still in pre-production, Connery – egged on by Cilento – accepted an offer to appear on Canadian TV in *Macbeth*. In her mind at least, it was a way of balancing the twin books of art and commerce.

In Toronto he found himself unexpectedly brought face to face with his past in the most delightful way. Every morning he was up early, learning his lines before nipping down to the local coffee shop, then walking to rehearsals. During his very first breakfast, *Macbeth*'s soliloquys still ringing in his head, he met two of his ex-classmates from Edinburgh, both of them recent émigrés. It was a small world, they all agreed, as they fondly exchanged tales of 'Auld Reekie'.

Chapter 8

'*Judith* at Her Majesty's was rather a bad production and Sean did very little in it as Holofernes. But he appeared in practically nothing, and with that magnificent body. And out of that came Bond.'

Robert Henderson

Although Ian Fleming might be considered to have delivered an excellent blueprint for *Dr No*'s script in his original book, rewrite followed rewrite during pre-production as the start of shooting approached in January 1962. While Richard Maibaum was given the main credit for the script, it was Terence Young, with his assistant Joanna Harwood and Berkley Mather, who hacked out the final shooting version after Broccoli, who had left script supervision to Saltzman, threw a fit. 'Look, we've paid all this fucking money for this James Bond book and we're not using a word of it,' he raged. 'Terence is a writer, the quickest I know. He's got ten days to put it back. He can take all the scripts we have and bury them and whatever he writes we're going to be stuck with. And Harry – if it's bad, it's *your* fault!'

Young rapidly became Connery's main role model for Bond

in the style, social graces and grooming departments, passing on the benefits not only of his upper-class social background but his Harrow and Cambridge education and wartime service in the Guards. Connery found himself directed to Young's tailor and shirtmaker, told to keep his mouth shut while eating and warned to check his accent when it ran away with him during emotional scenes.

If Young was the teacher, Bond's author was the headmaster. Ian Fleming was the son of Major Valentine Fleming, a Conservative Member of Parliament, and the former Evelyn Beatrice St Croix Rose. A tall, lean man with blue eyes and wavy hair, Fleming's otherwise handsome features were let down by a distinctly bashed-in nose. He credited his expensive education at Eton and Sandhurst, Britain's equivalent of West Point Military Academy, and at the universities of Munich and Geneva, for the accuracy of the manifold pinpoint detail in his books. A service career was abandoned despite the commission he received at Sandhurst, since the army was in the process of mechanization and Fleming had no desire to be what he termed 'a garage hand running a series of tanks'. He tried to enter the diplomatic service and failed, then joined Reuters instead as their correspondent in Berlin, Moscow, then London. A spell as a banker and stockbroker was followed by his World War II service with British Naval Intelligence.

James Bond was created, Fleming claimed, 'as a counter-irritant or antibody to my hysterical alarm at getting married'. He was forty-three when he tied the knot with Ann Geraldine, the eldest daughter of the Hon. Guy Charteris and the ex-wife of Lord Rothermere, the newspaper magnate. Bond arrived 'just out of the air, a compound of secret agents and commando types' Fleming had met during the war. He dreamt up the plots for his thrillers in England at his townhouse near Buckingham Palace, in between playing bridge at Crockford's, the top people's gambling house, and attending the choicest dinner parties – although he claimed to have met more interesting people in the Hamburg stripjoints he had once frequented. Goldeneye, his house on the north coast of Jamaica, was where

Fleming retreated for two months each year to do his actual writing. Here he maintained a strict discipline of turning out between 1,500 and 2,500 words daily, working at a desk in a corner of the study that faced two blank walls.

Friends were aware that his creation of Bond's adventures, with their heady mix of mayhem, sex and sadism, served as a fantasy outlet for the mild-mannered author, who liberally stirred elements from his own experience – fast cars, skin-diving, haute cuisine and fine wines, as well as his Intelligence work – into the formula. 'I think,' he once said, 'that it's an absolute miracle that an elderly person like me can go on churning out these books with such zest. It's really a terrible indictment of my own character – they're adolescent. But they're fun.'

Sparks flew at the initial encounter between Fleming and Terence Young. 'So they've decided on you to fuck up my work,' said Fleming disdainfully. 'Let me put it this way, Ian,' Young replied. 'I don't think anything you've written is immortal as yet, whereas the last picture I made [the ballet movie, *Black Tights*] won a Grand Prix at Venice. Now let's start even.'

Connery unexpectedly established an immediate rapport with Fleming. He found the author a 'terrible snob', as he had anticipated ('He went to Eton and I think that explains quite a bit about that side'), but also discovered there was much more to him than that. He was particularly intrigued that he had once wangled an interview with Stalin simply by telephoning the Kremlin.

'I don't think he approved of me terribly,' Connery confessed, 'but he did have casting rights over the film, so I guess he must have come round to the idea. He had great energy and curiosity and he was a marvellous man to talk to and have a drink with because of the many wide interests he had. What made him a success and caused all the controversy was that his writing was such good *journalism*. He always contrived extraordinary situations and arranged extravagant meetings for his characters, and he always knew his facts. He was always madly accurate and this derived from his curiosity. When he was discussing anything, like how a truck worked, or a machine or a permutation at bridge, there was a brain at work and an enormous amount of research involved; it wasn't just a load of drivel he was talking.' (Connery discovered that he and Bond had at least one tenuous connection, Fleming having included an expulsion from Edinburgh's Fettes College, where Connery had once delivered milk, in Bond's early biography.)

The statuesque Ursula Andress, who would come to be regarded as the quintessential Bond girl, was cast as nature child Honey Rider after Julie Christie's bust failed to meet Broccoli's demanding specifications. Besides, Andress came cheap at £300 a week for the six weeks scheduled, although she was pipped at the post for the title of Bond's first on-screen conquest by the underrated Eunice Gayson's seductive Sylvia.

The movie also introduced several characters who became an integral part of future Bond movies. There was 007's alter-ego and father figure M, played by Bernard Lee; M's eternally patient assistant Miss Moneypenny, adroitly played by Lois Maxwell, an actress well-tutored in the Eve Arden school of wisecracking, and technical whiz Major Boothroyd, 'Q', designer of Bond's gadget-laden weaponry, portrayed by Peter Burton. American Joseph Wiseman's casting as the evil Dr No lent credence to the fantastic goings-on; Jack Lord provided a token CIA presence as agent Felix Leiter (the first of many actors to play this role).

The storyline played on space-race anxiety in its tale of the sinister genius behind the destruction of American rockets launched from Cape Canaveral. Despite the best efforts of Miss Taro and the unfortunate Professor Dent, played by Anthony Dawson – on whom Bond first demonstrates his licence to kill – Bond locates *Dr No*'s Crab Key island sanctum, accompanied by the luscious Andress.

On location in Kingston, Jamaica, Connery discovered that the only man who could keep Fleming in his place was his neighbour, Noel Coward, originally cast as Dr No before a change of mind he later, apparently, regretted. Coward took great delight in describing Bond to Connery as 'a dreary slob'. After filming one night in Kingston's bauxite mines, Connery repaired two hours late, covered with dust, and in the company of Island Records' Chris Blackwell, to Coward's home for dinner. They found their host resplendent in a plum dinner jacket, bow tie, sporting a long cigarette holder and playing the piano, accompanying himself on the album of his live act at Las Vegas. He never batted an eyelid as the two men appeared. 'Come in, dear boys,' he greeted them, then carried on playing while they retired to smarten up. Even when they reappeared, he carried on playing right to the end of the album before giving the signal for dinner to be served.

Connery found himself introduced during the shoot to Eon's accountant, Stanley Sopel, soon to become their associate producer once his union membership was sorted out. Purely coincidentally, it emerged that he was a cousin of Carol, Connery's South Pacific romance. Sopel was an ex-Warwick stalwart, as were cinematographer Ted Moore and production designer Ken Adam, with all of whom Broccoli felt comfortable; the producer was known for endless fretting when new faces were introduced. Soon Sopel and Connery were firm friends, their banter between takes heavily featuring typically male topics such as football and women.

After a month in Jamaica, with the unit poised for a return to England and Pinewood Studios, Connery felt a quiet excitement at the movie's progress. There was something about *Dr No* that was different from any other movie he had worked on – a feeling of internationalism, an innate confidence most of the principals seemed to share in the material, a sense of something special in the making. The day Andress had emerged from the surf and posed provocatively in her white bikini and low-slung hip knife was indication enough to every assembled member of the cast and crew that this was a British film unlike any other. Husband John Derek had come along for the ride with Swiss-born Andress, the first fruit of the star-making process he would continue with Linda Evans and Bo Derek. There was a distinct problem with her accent, but nothing that over-dubbing wouldn't fix.

Ian Fleming visited the unit at Pinewood and admired the miracles production designer Ken Adam had wrought with the interior sets on the minuscule budget of £14,000 he had stretched to £20,000. Nothing like them, he felt, with the possible exception of Universal's sets in the 1930s for *Dracula* and *Frankenstein*, had been seen since the German Expressionist movement. Zena Marshall, playing the deadly enemy agent Miss Taro, found it hard to relax at first in her lovemaking scenes with Connery. After several retakes she described him as 'extremely rough and raw', although possessed of an undeniable charm.

'I don't think I'm meant to be married,' Cilento announced in March 1961. A year later Connery was wholeheartedly singing the praises of bachelorhood: 'There's no one to tell you what to do. I can leave my socks on the floor, play poker all night, come and go as I please. I couldn't ask any woman to put up with that.' Intimate friends read between the lines and interpreted both signals correctly; marriage was in the offing.

Nearing the end of divorce proceedings with Andrea Volpe, Cilento found herself confronted with Connery's acid test – a visit to his family in Fountainbridge. From the beginning she could do no wrong. Although Connery felt considerable trepidation as he introduced his new girl to Effie and Joe, he need not have worried. Cilento plonked herself in a chair, kicked off her shoes and made herself thoroughly at home. As far as Effie was concerned she was 'a wee smasher' who kept them up until two in the morning chatting away in the distinctively husky, down-to-earth Australian drawl she had never quite lost.

She continued to turn Connery's marriage proposals down, even when she discovered she was carrying his child during the summer of 1962. Having made what she described as 'a botch' of her first attempt, she declared that she no longer rated marriage, that she found it too stifling. With her divorce being finalized as she spoke, it still seemed only a matter of time before she gave in to Connery's blandishments. 'He was so sure we could make a go of it,' she later explained, 'while I wanted us both to retain a fair amount of freedom. I don't like ownership in marriage, I don't like too many promises either. There is no way of being sure you can keep them.'

Career conflicts apart, many saw their marriage off to a rocky start even before vows were taken. Basically, Connery was a one-woman man – one woman at a time, that is. That his basic conservatism could never square with Cilento's wild-child persona and concept of an open marriage was a foregone conclusion to many.

Chapter 9

'(James Bond) has no mother. He has no father. He doesn't come from anywhere and he hadn't been anywhere before he became 007. So he was born – kerplump – 33 years old. So I had to breathe life into an idol. I saw him as a complete sensualist, his senses highly tuned and awake to everything. He liked his wine, his food, his women. He's quite amoral. I particularly liked him because he thrives on conflict. But more than that, I think I gave him a sense of humour.'

Sean Connery

At this stage of his life thirty-two-year-old Connery was still struggling to assert himself. The knowledge that he was a late starter and still had a lot to learn often made him appear arrogant, abrasive and remote, as Cilento had discovered for herself that first evening at her flat. Being chosen to play Bond had a far from meliorating effect on this aspect of his behaviour; Bond's licence to kill apparently seen by Connery as a licence to shoot his mouth off. 'We Scots have a tremendous appreciation of the world of the devil,' startled *Sunday Express* reporter Susan Barnes was informed during an interview in the newly converted lounge of his mews home. 'Like people in the northern countries,' he continued, 'James Bond is very much for breaking the rules. He enjoys freedom that the normal person doesn't get. He likes to eat. He likes to drink. He likes his girls. He is rather cruel, sadistic. He takes in a big percentage of the fantasies of lots of people, although it's difficult to get many of them to admit they'd like to be Bond. I have no compunction at all about admitting that I like to eat, I like to drink, I like girls.'

Connery was unabashed when asked if his empathy extended to the cruel and sadistic element in the character. 'I don't think there's anything very wrong with hitting a woman,' he offered, pausing only to top up his tumbler of vodka. 'I don't, though, recommend hitting a woman the way you hit a man.' As if suddenly inspired, Connery leaped to his feet and confronted the startled scribe. 'A right to the solar plexus!' he roared, smashing a huge fist through the air. 'And a left to the jaw that sends her halfway across the room!'

As Connery's mitt whistled dangerously past her chin, Barnes edged further down into the safety of the couch. 'No,' he continued, backing off and settling once more opposite her, 'I wouldn't recommend doing that to a woman.' A glug of vodka produced a wide grin. 'But an open-handed slap is justifiable, or putting your hand over her mouth. I wouldn't think that was being sadistic.'

Easing a cigarette into a long holder, in best Noel Coward manner, he nonchalantly lit up before continuing his train of thought. A proper sadist, Barnes was informed, was never completely passionate, but always aware of what they were doing. And when thinking was removed, the result was passion so pure it became a matter of life and death: 'That's why a little mouse of a wife is able to put the breadknife in her husband's chest.'

Connery then proceeded to lecture the bemused reporter on 'mobility'. As if to remove the cynical look rapidly developing on Barnes's face, Connery fixed her with a gaze. 'I was wondering just now,' he said, 'what you would do if I walked

across the room and kissed you.' His intended victim's terse
reply – that he would be better employed testing his feminine
'mobility' theories elsewhere – drew a resigned shrug from
Connery and the suggestion that one of the first reactions of a
'mobile' person was to cross their legs. At this juncture, Barnes
noticed much to her chagrin, that her legs were tightly crossed.

Spreading his own knees wide apart Connery explained, 'If
you are attracted to someone, you sit like this. A really
confident man's posture is never bound. It is strong and free.
Not like *this*—' Again he leapt to his feet, this time standing
in front of his victim, clenching his powerful arms to his chest
in the muscle-bound crouch of a boxer. Demonstration over, he
sank back on the couch and concluded his dissertation:
'Mobility leads to adaptability, so a mobile woman can be
serene too. They can adapt to a line like this . . .'

As he stretched out horizontally on the couch, Barnes clearly
judged discretion to be the better part of valour and pleaded a
pressing engagement elsewhere. Connery/Bond, the distinction
a trifle blurred by this time, was left sprawling, a tumbler of
vodka in one hand, cigarette neatly tucked in its holder in the
other – and looking enormously pleased with his performance.

Not everyone was so impressed, either with Connery or *Dr
No*. Sue Lloyd, a top model and aspiring actress with chestnut
hair and brown, sparkling eyes, bumped into Ursula Andress
when they both turned up to audition for producer Roy Stark
at Shepperton Studios. 'Dahling, I've just been in Jamaica
enjoying the sun, doing this crappy thriller with Sean Connery,'
Andress informed Lloyd, her ho-hum manner indicating that it
could have been any old thriller, with any old actor. 'It was
ghastly,' Lloyd was assured. 'There were crabs crawling about
all over the place. And everything was done so cheaply –
absolute crap!' Lloyd had never met Connery at this stage, a
situation that would be put right before the opening of *Dr No*.

United Artists were similarly unenthralled with the advance
footage they were shown. Even with Andress's dialogue
entirely dubbed, there was major concern over Connery's own
fluctuating accent. One minute he was 'a limey', the next he

seemed to revert to broad Scots. Or was it Polish? His 'Good evening, *sur'* almost stopped the show at one point. Saltzman for one remained supremely confident about the movie and its prospects, while admitting he had felt the same way about Woodfall's *Look Back in Anger* back in the 1950s before it bit the dust. Connery affected optimism, describing the movie as 'bloody good' to his often sceptical friends, many of whom saw *Dr No*, despite their fondness for him, as little more than a jumped-up 'B' film.

Somewhat defensively, Connery chose to list 007's virtues. 'If you take Bond in the situations that he is constantly involved with,' he suggested, 'you see it as a very hard, unusual field that he plays in. Therefore he is quite right in having all his senses satisfied, be it sex, wine, food or clothes, because the job, and he with it, may terminate at any minute. But the virtues – loyalty, honesty – are there too. Bond doesn't chase married women, for instance. Judged on that level, he comes out rather well. He's dealing with rather sadistic adversaries who dream up pretty wild schemes to destroy, maim or mutilate him. He must retaliate in kind; otherwise it's who's kidding who.'

In Shelley Winters's version both Connery and Cilento were as downbeat as United Artists about *Dr No*. Others were also having second thoughts about their participation in the months prior to the movie's release. Joseph Wiseman, a respected Group Theater player back in New York, was worried that *Dr No*'s 'corny villain' might ruin his career. It was all right to play villains – but only in *important* films.

Between her conversation with Ursula Andress and *Dr No*'s opening, Sue Lloyd, escorted by her actor friend Daniel Massey, bumped into Connery for the first time at the Buxton drinking club behind London's Haymarket Theatre. Under contract to John and Jimmy Woolf at Romulus Films and attending acting classes with coach Jeff Corrie, Lloyd had gained the impression that Connery was popular with his fellow actors without being particularly 'reckoned'; he was just a good working actor without the image of a handsome matinée idol, someone with a good face capable of playing thugs well, but in no way suitable for a romantic lead.

A month later, at one of Jimmy Woolf's parties, attended by Michael Caine, Terence Stamp and other young hopefuls, Lloyd met Connery again; this time they were actually introduced. She knew of his attachment to Cilento, but formed the impression that their tempestuous, on-again, off-again affair was, at least for the moment, cooling off.

Lloyd had a Polish friend, Magda Knopka, a tall, beautiful, titian-haired model/actress known in some quarters as 'the Magnetic Pole', who had often dated Connery, and she knew of several others who had consoled him in between his bouts with Cilento.

She saw all of Connery's women as having one feature in common – they were all strong characters, Cilento included. While no weakling herself, Lloyd was delightfully zany and regarded by Connery as decidedly 'pinkies up' and a bit fey. 'He was very jolly with a good sense of humour,' says Lloyd. 'Very dry humour, and always with a great twinkle, if slightly mickey-taking. Coming from anyone else it might have seemed snide, but not from him. I liked him and made him laugh.'

Connery accompanied Lloyd back to her flat in Upper Grosvenor Street after Woolf's party and spent the night there, innocently curled up beside her in bed. 'We spent some time cuddling,' she recalls, 'and that was all, really. He was very sweet and very lovable, but it was just a matter of convenience, a bed for the night. There was no desire involved. He obviously liked his women, but I don't think sex was a big priority.'

Broccoli and Saltzman, still utterly convinced they had a winner on their hands, were shattered by United Artists' continued lack of enthusiasm when *Dr No* was previewed in answer-print form. Arthur Krim headed the eight-man UA executive team who settled down to watch the complete *Dr No* for the first time, along with the producers, at a 10 a.m. showing. When the lights went up shortly after midday there was silence, broken by the head of European distribution muttering, 'The only good thing about the picture is that we can only lose $800,000.' The rest of the contingent murmured agreement. 'Hammer makes the same kind of pictures for one third the price,' was one scornful comment.

The movie's London Pavilion première, on 6 October 1962, ended the downbeat speculation in the best possible way, at least as far as the UK market was concerned. Every known record was smashed, the movie's take of £69,000 in its first week a new peak that would remain unbeaten for eleven years. 'We played twenty-four hours a day at £1 per ticket,' Saltzman elatedly recalled. 'They never saw such business, and the most surprised was United Artists. They *hated* it.'

Even with this level of box-office, UA dragged its feet on the movie's US release, postponing it to 9 May 1963, and initially on a no-risk two-week booking in Atlanta, Georgia. 'The picture that played before us did $11,000 in two weeks,' said Saltzman. 'We did $44,000 in the first week. The second week we did $46,000 – and we stayed there eleven weeks.'

Variety helped to fan the publicity flames with a tremendous review.

Dr No [they trumpeted] is a high-powered melodrama that crackles with intrigue and suspense and sizzles with romance. There is even some humor of a respectable level to lighten the mixture. The movie has no high-powered names, but this won't matter. *Dr No* is a perfect picture of its special kind and exactly fits that often cited but generally misunderstood category 'pure entertainment'. It should be a hugely popular and profitable attraction. Terence Young directs with style, Bond, played by Sean Connery, is handsome, charming, muscular and amusing. In addition he is Irish [sic!]. Mickey Spillane with class.

There was widespread praise for Maurice Binder's unique main title design, John Barry's distinctive James Bond signature theme, Ted Moore's inspired cinematography, Peter

Hunt's crisp editing and Ken Adams's brilliant sets. If some of the process work was rough and ready, the first fight scene crudely speeded up, and the use of a Connery double in the second scrap blatantly obvious – all this was readily overlooked in the avalanche of praise of the taut plot construction and fluid direction by Terence Young. Connery was judged nothing short of magnificent, every inch the suave, sexy, cultured, sensuous, deadly and gallant superhero.

Although Connery was particularly proud of the humour with which he had ameliorated Bond's mayhem, Cilento felt entitled to share the credit, claiming that they had both realized that Bond needed brightening up: 'The man needed a sense of humour, for God's sake. And that's when we started working on Bond's character, giving him all those silly one-liners. But it worked.'

A visit to Edinburgh to attend the movie's première in the city there brought the nascent superstar down to earth with a bump. Outside his old 'stair' stood the 'faither' of an old drinking pal, the working man's flat cap on his head, contentedly puffing away at a clay pipe. 'Hullo, Tam,' the worthy greeted him. 'Have ye been away?' Connery had occasion to reflect that whatever heights he might reach, there would always be the wry Scots put-down to ground him affectionately.

At the première itself several of Connery's former school and workmates, anxious for a glimpse of their erstwhile pal, gathered round the entrance to the New Victoria cinema. As Connery emerged from one of United Artists' limousines, Eric Boyd yelled, 'Hey, Tam, are you coming for a drink afterwards?' To his astonishment Connery turned and gave him a big grin. 'Hey, boys!' he greeted them. 'Of course! I'll see you after the show.' He did – and stood them a celebratory round of drinks as well. 'He was just the same old Tam,' Boyd recalls, 'although I had a fair bit of bother reconciling him with the "Tich" I used to know.'

As Bondmania gripped country after country it was clear that Connery had made his leap to international stardom. Only the French had a slight problem with his name, which to them sounded exactly like 'sans connerie', slang for 'without balls' – inappropriate, to say the least. And the Japanese had a problem with the literal translation of the title they proposed. This initially emerged as 'We Don't Want a Doctor' – until wiser heads prevailed! To Connery the movie's success spelt the end of what he would refer to as the 'prostitution phase' of his career.

His stage mentor Robert Henderson had a ready answer for his protégé's detractors. 'People said how lucky he was to get James Bond – lucky my foot! He started off with a Scots accent that was so thick it was like a foreign language. He cured himself of that, but think of the study that took! He worked and sweated blood. He always moved marvellously, like an animal, but when anybody says this just came from luck, it's the old thing in the theatre. Everybody gets their chance and the thing is to be ready – like Sean was.'

Connery rejected any notion of simply moving in with Cilento, and argued against the idea of an 'open' arrangement. Soon after *Dr No*'s triumphant opening, he told her that he had splashed out £9,000 on a house in which he was having a nursery built. And there was no need to fear being treated like a *hausfrau*. He appreciated and respected the fact that she had her own career ambitions; their marriage would be a true equal partnership in every sense of the word. Although Cilento declared herself finally sold, friends watched with some amusement. 'She jilted him a few times,' said one. 'He was never too sure of her.'

To avoid the necessity of posting banns and the inevitable press attention their marriage in England would attract, a Gilbraltar wedding was set for November 1962, just one month after Cilento's divorce, with the non-blushing bride seven months pregnant. The choice of location proved unfortunate, with an increasingly impatient and worried Connery being forced to delay the wedding, while Cilento, en route from Spain and travelling on her Australian passport, was held up for hours at the colony's border. Was this the ultimate jilt? Cilento looked back on the delayed registry office ceremony as being 'like a funny TV show, with Sean all feet, all thumbs, frustrated'.

After the wedding, with Connery already in a monumentally foul temper, someone suggested the couple take a romantic stroll up the Rock. In a farcical echo of an 007 adventure, they inadvertently wandered into a military encampment as they made their descent, and found themselves detained for over an hour. A distinctly exhausted and anti-climactic wedding night followed.

The twelve-room deconsecrated nunnery, the ex-Convent of the Order of the Adoratrices Connery had bought in Acton, was still being decorated as they moved in. He constantly haggled with the builders – he had, after all, worked on building sites and knew what corners could be cut – while Cilento's artist sister Margaret pitched in with her contributions. He defended the vivid colours he had chosen throughout, like the huge red carpet with which he covered the lounge, explaining, 'It was gloomy where I grew up.' One room, which would invariably be kept locked, was turned into his 'den'.

In all Connery spent another £9,000 on top of the original purchase price on conversion and decoration of the four-storey house. Set in its own grounds, with a flight of nine steps leading to the front door, 'Acacia House', the name emblazoned in an illuminated sign that could be seen from a hundred yards, was the only dwelling in a cul-de-sac off Acton High Street. By the time their son, Jason, was born, on 11 January 1963, the nursery had been rushed to completion.

Chapter 10

'People sometimes ask me why I act. Well, it's not just for money. You can make money in football too. It's for the fantasy, the way you have to get inside someone else's skin, imagine them, understand them, recreate them.'

Sean Connery

'He's a very natural, basic man. Sometimes he can be quite blunt and even hurtful in the things he says, but you do know where you stand with him. He is no hypocrite.'

Diana Dors

Since *Dr No* had yet to open in the US when Broccoli and Saltzman requested the green light for their second Bond, *From Russia with Love*, the ultra-cautious United Artists, convinced that *Dr No* had been a one-off success, and that this might in any case be limited to Europe, held the budget down to $2 million. The movie began shooting, on the same stage B that *Dr No* had occupied, in April 1963; just one month earlier *Dr No* had finally broken through UA's barrier of indifference in the US, eventually netting an excellent $6.4 million.

Terence Young was back at the helm, fresh from months of

casting sessions in which some bold decisions had been made. Robert Shaw, one of Britain's most powerfully intense acting talents, had been chosen to portray the villainous Red Grant. Veteran Mexican actor Pedro Armendariz was Bond's man in Turkey, Kerim Bey. Even more adventurous was the casting of Kurt Weill's partner Lotte Lenya to portray the wicked Rosa Klebb. A former Miss Universe runner-up, the delectable Italian Daniela Bianchi, was selected from dozens of candidates the suave Young had set himself the task of personally interviewing. Richard Maibaum's richly textured script enlisted Bianchi's Tatiana as the unwitting dupe of SMERSH chief Blofeld – his face never seen on screen – and the fearsome Klebb, in their efforts to put an end to Bond's activities for good and bag a top-secret decoder into the bargain.

Everyone concerned with the movie felt the benefit of the extra budget, not least production designer Ken Adam and director Young, who avidly seized the opportunity to indulge in retakes where he felt it necessary, an option largely closed to him on *Dr No*. The only downside of the spectacular location footage they captured in Istanbul was an outbreak of stomach trouble few escaped, not even super-agent Bond.

On the domestic scene Connery was convinced, as he watched young Jason cavorting amidst the vivid furnishings in his spacious nursery, that he had provided his son with the greatest possible contrast to his own cramped, dingy environment. 'He will grow up,' he predicted, 'to memories and experiences that will be inescapable.' At the other end of the scale he tried in vain to coax his parents to leave Fountainbridge and join him in London. Instead Effie and Joe were presented with an enormous fridge, which they only managed to fit into their tiny apartment with considerable difficulty. Ian Bannen saw it installed and declared it 'quite ridiculous', even while recognizing the genuine thought behind it of the boy wanting to give his parents a taste of the luxuries he could now afford.

From Russia with Love's London première in October 1963 banished any doubts that Bond was here to stay. Terence Young had produced an excellent cold-war thriller that would have stood every chance of being a hit even without Bond as a selling point; with Sean Connery as Bond in attendance, the sky was the limit. *Variety* raved: 'Cannot miss at the box-office. It's a preposterous, skilful slab of hardhitting, sexy hokum. After a slowish start, it is directed by Terence Young at zingy pace. Crisp, wise-cracking dialogue by Richard Maibaum.' The movie went on to exceed everyone's wildest expectations, topping *Dr No*'s net by a massive 50 per cent at close on $10 million. With the rest of the world, sales to TV and later cable and video, the return on United Artists' original $2 million investment mushroomed to bonanza proportions.

Even while praising the movie *Variety* had perceptively delineated what was rapidly becoming Connery's bête noire: 'With these two pix Connery has made quite a name for himself and his only problem now is to avoid being identified entirely with James Bond, whom he has created so well.'

Saltzman and his partner were already rich beyond their wildest imaginings. Not so Connery. Having settled for precisely £25,000 for *Dr No*, the realization that he had sold himself short was emphasized by the increased, but still meagre, advance he received for *From Russia with Love*. At least on this occasion, he consoled himself, he was due a percentage of the profits.

By the time the movie opened, Connery had already completed his first 'post-Bond' project. *Woman of Straw* had been concocted by scriptwriters Robert Muller and Stanley Mann, from a novel by Catherine Arley, and co-starred Gina Lollobrigida and Ralph Richardson. Despite valiant efforts at conciliation by veteran director Basil Dearden, the atmosphere on location in Majorca had been strained from the start, with Connery refusing to buckle under to Lollobrigida's 'inter-pretations' of early scenes. Pointing at Dearden, Connery told his co-star, 'Either *he* is directing this picture or *you* are directing it. If it's *you*, I may not be in it.'

Close to breaking point with La Lollo's temper tantrums, Connery slapped her altogether too enthusiastically in one scene. Although apologies were profuse, Connery pleading that he had underestimated the force of the blow, relations scarcely improved. Perhaps egged on by Cilento to assert himself with the ragged script – he had begun suggesting rewrites while filming *From Russia with Love* – Connery worried that *Woman of Straw* was heading in a direction not unadjacent to the boneyard.

Connery made a conscious decision after *From Russia with Love* and *Woman of Straw* to quit stage work. 'He said he never wanted to do it again,' Ian Bannen recalled. 'All that shouting hurt his throat. He simply wanted to do first-class films – only.' Bannen might have added, 'And for first-class fees – only,' for Connery had been given ample opportunity to compare the salary scales for theatre and movie work. Given a choice, there was simply no contest.

As far as *Woman of Straw* was concerned, Connery's hope that audiences would immediately accept him in 'non-Bonds' proved in vain. His scheming Anthony Richmond, busily framing Maria (La Lollo) for the murder of his rich invalid Uncle Charles (Richardson) was worse than unacceptable to audiences – they were indifferent to it, few even bothering to turn up. The withering critical reception in Britain may not have helped. *The Times* discerned 'glum proceedings'; according to Kingsley Amis in the *Observer*, 'The regularity with which glossily produced, star-studded, two-hour-long packages of rubble come pouring out continues to defy belief.' The *Guardian* detected 'a restless and meaningless cutting style borrowed from the bad old days of British cinema,' while Hollis Alpert in *Saturday Review* deemed *Woman of Straw* 'a slow, solemn yarn'. For Dilys Powell in the *Sunday Times*, 'Connery mistakenly relies on his famous 007 poker face.'

Connery refused the face-saver of apportioning blame. 'I wasn't all that thrilled with *Woman of Straw*,' he claimed, 'although the problems were my own. It was an experience, but I won't make that mistake again. When it was shot down I wasn't entirely surprised.'

*

Before production began on *Goldfinger*, the next chapter of the Bond saga, Connery found he had time to fit in a second outside movie. Wary after the harrowing script problems on *Woman of Straw* he did what few actors had ever dared when approached by maestro Alfred Hitchcock. He asked to see the script. 'If you had been in some of the tripe I have,' he explained, 'you'd know why . . .'

The adaptation of Poldark novelist Winston Graham's *Marnie* had originally been planned as a vehicle to mark Grace Kelly's return to the screen. In the uproar among her subjects that greeted Hitchcock's premature revelation that Her Serene Royal Highness the Princess Grace of Monaco would be playing a neurotically frigid kleptomaniac, as well as his lip-smacking press description of her as possessing 'the finest sex appeal in the world', she bowed out and was replaced by a blonde newcomer Hitchcock was grooming for stardom.

He had discovered 'Tippi' Hedren, as he insisted she was to be billed, during an appearance on television in a soft-drink commercial in 1961. Invited along for an interview with his associates in Hitchcock's office, she was asked to leave behind her photographic file and commercial reel. The result, for the top model with no acting ambition whatever, was a seven-year exclusive contract with the director that added Hedren to the long line of elegant 'Hitchcock blondes' that dated back to Madeleine Carroll in the 1930s and continued through Kelly, Kim Novak and Vera Miles. His need to control every aspect of Hedren's life, down to her clothes, her diet and her friends, was soon bordering on the manic. Associates made the appropriate filmic connection: 'He's playing Jimmy Stewart remodelling Kim Novak in *Vertigo*.'

Fellow cast members squirmed in sympathy as Hitchcock subjected his protégé to day after day of unremitting torture on his adaptation of Daphne Du Maurier's *The Birds*, insisting on real, terrified fowl being hurled at her during the final indoor attack sequence. 'She was alone in that caged room, with the birds beside her, acting for an entire week,' said co-star Jessica

Tandy, 'and with costume changes and all that stage blood she couldn't even go to the commissary for lunch. She lived with that hour after hour and I just don't know how she did it.'

To obtain the frantic pecking close-ups he insisted were necessary, Hitchock arranged that a leg of each bird be tied to a piece of string attached to Hedren's clothing. One bird went for her left eye, gashing her lower lid. Hedren, describing the experience as 'the worst week of my life', was unable to work for a week, confined to bed on doctor's orders, the unit shut down awaiting her return.

With filming completed, Hitchcock began to devote his full attention to *Marnie*. It was a project that seemed to be under a cloud at Universal from the start. Keen as studio chief Lew Wasserman was on keeping Hitchcock happy, especially since he was one of parent company MCA's largest shareholders, he had distinct misgivings about the project and the motivations behind its production. Although Connery declared himself thrilled with the script Hitchcock sent, describing it as the best he'd ever been offered, insiders at Universal doubted that the actor had been Hitchcock's first choice for the ambiguous Rutland. Rightly or wrongly, they detected the fine hand of Wasserman at work, seeking Bond-style assurance – this was before *Woman of Straw*'s opening – to bolster what he saw as, at best, an uncommercial venture.

A few days before Christmas 1963, Connery flew to Los Angeles alone, and was picked up by a pair of Universal VIPs at the airport. He turned down an offer of accommodation at the plush Château Marmont and chose to return to the small hotel at Burbank familiar to him from his days on *Darby O'Gill and the Little People*. He similarly rejected a chauffeured limousine in favour of a modest runaround.

Hitchcock's fixation with Hedren, dangerously mixed with the need to observe, voyeur-style, while pushing her to the very limits of endurance, had already resulted in a falling out with Evan Hunter. Following the year the writer had spent sweating out the first script drafts, their row centred on Hitchcock's insistence on retaining a scene in which Connery's Mark

Rutland, having tried everything else to awaken his frigid bride, violently rapes Marnie. Hunter wanted to at least soften the sequence and lessen the impact of Rutland's horrific change from protector to brutal attacker, arguing that it was out of character and would forfeit audience sympathy.

Hitchcock, determined to portray the scene graphically down to the last lurid detail, would have none of it. 'He comes to her and she tries to resist,' he insisted, 'and then she turns her head away. And you follow her head as he forces her down on the bed – and you *know*...' He went on to pick his way tortuously through the rape that followed; in the end he wanted the camera's focus to linger on Hedren's shocked, catatonic features. When Hunter dug his heels in, he was peremptorily fired.

To replace him, Hitchcock brought in Jay Presson Allen, whose adaptation of *The Prime of Miss Jean Brodie* he had much admired. Allen quickly realized that *Marnie* was 'a somewhat fated project', and that Hitchcock was 'mad for "Tippi" Hedren, just as he had been obsessed with a series of cold blonde actresses before'. (When Connery was asked about Hitchcock's predilection, he retorted, 'What's wrong with that? I mean, it could have been cool, blond men.' Later Hitchcock expounded on the virtues of 'chilly English women': 'They are three dimensional. The other type of beauty – the Italian, big voluptuous dolls, they *look* 3-D, but, believe me, they are just cut-out dolls.' Connery's riposte: 'You've just described my type!')

Many saw Hitchcock's main attraction to the project as the opportunity to explore vicariously on screen the fetish of a man wanting to go to bed with a thief simply because she was a thief. And didn't Hitchcock see *himself* as Connery's Rutland, the half-sighted leading the blind, however misguidedly, to some semblances of sanity, release and fulfilment? Never known as an actor's director – unless they were blonde, female and pliant – Hitchcock declined to spell out *Marnie*'s psycho-sexual implications for Connery. 'If I'm paying you as much as I am and you don't know what you're doing,' he told him at

one point, 'then I deserve what I get in the way of performance.'

Twenty years earlier novice actor Gregory Peck had complained after making Hitch's psychological thriller *Spellbound*,
'He really didn't give us much direction.' Even as Connery was
joining the chorus – 'He gave very little direction, didn't even
look through the viewfinder' – he still claimed to detect method
in Hitchcock's apparent meanness: 'It was because he had
always worked out what he wanted. He could control the
rhythm and tempo of the picture just by being there and making
little adjustments and suggestions.' The main 'adjustments and
suggestions' from Hitchcock to Connery consisted of advising
him to keep his mouth from hanging open when listening to his
co-star, as well as the insertion of 'dog's feet' into his
on-screen speeches. 'Dog's feet?' asked a puzzled Connery.
'Pawses,' the maestro replied.

Despite the darker overtones implicit in his direction, and his
endless concern with Hedren's costume, make-up, hairstyle
and the camera angles, Hitchcock struggled to maintain his
avuncular television persona for much of *Marnie*'s schedule.
Shooting was suspended at 3.30 every afternoon for a teabreak,
during which he would act the genial host, often giving little
speeches and telling jokes.

MCA executives invited to visit the set were promised a
glimpse of 'an Academy Award performance in the making'.
Not from Connery, it turned out, but from the latest of
Hitchcock's obscure and unreachable objects of desire. In the
calm before the inevitable storm, Hitchcock described Hedren
to them as 'the ultimate actress'.

In late February he crossed all boundaries of propriety and
baldly propositioned Hedren in her trailer. When she refused
his advances, he flew into a rage and threatened to cancel a
third picture he had planned for her. He would cut her off
without a penny, Hedren was told, he would ruin her. From that
day forth she became 'that girl', virtually ceasing to exist as far
as her director was concerned. So, for that matter, did the
movie.

Connery was either oblivious to the off-screen drama, or chose to turn a blind eye. He had every reason to feel pleased with his progress. He was being paid a staggering $400,000 fee for his services – well and truly beyond the reach of any theatre in the world – and working with one of the world's top directors. To cap it all, there was an approach from the legendary John Ford to consider the lead in *Young Cassidy.*

His euphoria was clouded only by being tied to what Ian Fleming described as 'that cardboard booby', for despite the fact that his portrayal of Bond had made him one of the biggest box-office stars in the world, Connery was only too aware of the accompanying twin traps. Typecasting apart, he knew that Fleming's super-agent was regarded by his acting peers as a free ride, a piece of fluff, a nonsense role that might have been fine to launch a career – but to repeat it endlessly? Broccoli's conciliatory 'Sean plays Bond and it seems like a cinch, but he is damned clever at it. Bond is a tough assignment' fell on deaf ears, contemptuously dismissed by Connery. He wanted genuine, not self-serving respect.

Expounding on the frustration every typecast actor feels, Connery recalled a casting director who had once asked, 'And what *type* of actor are you, Mr Connery?' Furious, he had walked out. 'An actor *hates* to be typecast,' he declared. 'I don't want to be Bond all the time, it riles me when people call me Bond off the set.'

He pointed out that acting was, after all, merely a job – like carpentry or building roads. 'The trouble with a lot of stars,' he suggested, 'is that they develop heads as big as their posters.' When one interviewer dared to ask if that might apply in his own case, he snapped, 'If I wore hats, I think you'd find I still take the same size.'

His wife's attitude did little to help, her stance as a pure, uncompromised actress considerably boosted by her Best Supporting Actress Oscar nomination for Tony Richardson's *Tom Jones.* When she arrived in triumph halfway through *Marnie* with the children and took up residence in a modest $1,000 a month Bel-Air cabin, where she took to bathing in the nude daily, a few old Hollywood hands sensed an attempted rerun of the all-conquering Oliviers in their halcyon period.

'Sean reacted by coming on as this serious actor for whom Bond was merely a part-time activity,' one studio insider observed. 'Although this was an admirable *goal*, he was then only known and bankable as Bond. The rest was wishful thinking.'

Connery went on to cock a snook at MCA toppers Jules Stein and Lew Wasserman by refusing to attend the cornerstone-setting ceremony of their pride and joy, the new Universal administration building. Instead, he chose to squeeze in an extra game of golf.

Reality began to set in when Cilento lost at the Oscars ceremony to Margaret Rutherford for *The VIPs*; for Connery the moment of truth was the return to London and the resumption of Bond in *Goldfinger*. He was once again, according to another of Fleming's most cutting barbs, 'that labourer playing Bond'.

Chapter 11

'We got in a terrible mess, because Hitchcock was producing *Marnie* as well as directing it.'

Sean Connery

'I wasn't convinced that Sean Connery was a Philadelphia gentleman. If you want to reduce *Marnie* to its lowest common denominator, it is the story of the Prince and the beggar girl. In a story of this kind you need a real gentleman, a more elegant man than we had.'

Alfred Hitchcock

While hardly the damp squib *Woman of Straw* had proved, by Hitchcock standards *Marnie* was considered a let-down from the master. It netted just $3.3m and was judged his 'most disappointing film in years' by Eugene Archer of the *New York Times*, 'his feeblest film since *Rope*', according to John Coleman in Britain's *New Statesman*. Penelope Gilliatt in the *Observer* perceptively detected the tortured undercurrents that flowed beneath the surface action. 'Never has Hitchcock taken more pleasure in physical handicaps and the mannerisms of hysteria,' she felt, noting 'his fascination with physical humiliation and feminine sexual panic'. As for the movie itself, 'Hitchcock has made far better melodramas than this.' 'It creaks,' Alexander Walker reported in London's *Evening Standard*, 'but the cruelty fascinates.' As for Connery, Walker detected 'a nice line in sardonic tongue lashing'. Ian Wright in the *Guardian* went further, declaring that Connery carried the film, while according to *Time Magazine*: 'Connery performs with a pallid competence.' 'If he doesn't suggest a keen intelligence,' Patrick Gibbs wrote in the *Daily Telegraph*, 'at least Connery looks as if he could tame a jaguar.' Philip Oakes summed up *Marnie* as 'a failure only twice as interesting as other men's successes'.

Considering the production difficulties and the amount of the director's attention that was devoted elsewhere, Connery gives a performance of consummate ability, totally exposed as he had never been before as an actor by the admittedly slow, but progessively hypnotic pace of the movie. That apart, it was the outrageously careless process work and painted backdrops that incensed many critics. Theories that Hitchcock intended these effects to be highly stylized are entirely resistible to those aware of his complete lack of interest in the movie's post-production following the Hedren débâcle. It could equally be argued that special effects throughout Hitchcock's movie career have never been state-of-the-art. Those who chose to swim against the almost overwhelming critical tide for the movie have since been largely vindicated. *Marnie* is now widely regarded as one of Hitchcock's most masterful psychological studies, second only perhaps to *Vertigo*.

Before Hitchcock had destroyed his relationship with Hedren, she had joked with her director about Connery being miscast. 'Even if Marnie *was* so screwed up,' she reasoned, 'how could she *not* have been interested in such an attractive man?!' After the movie was in the can, Hedren described Connery as 'marvellous' and bemoaned the fact that she had just played a woman who screamed every time he came near her. 'He practised golf a lot,' she reflected. 'In his free time he always had his golf shoes and clubs out. I guess if I hadn't been interested in somebody else at the time, *I* probably would have played golf!'

Back in England Connery was pleased with the negotiations that had taken place with Saltzman and Broccoli over his return to Bondage with *Goldfinger*. Although the flat £50,000 was a considerable drop from *Marnie*'s $400,000 purse, there was a percentage on top with which Hitchcock's fee might even be exceeded. '[Bond] is going to make me rich,' he now claimed, determinedly putting a bright face on his situation, 'depending on how the tax works out. Rich enough to retire, though, I suppose. I've a contract to do three more Bond movies in the next $3\frac{1}{2}$ years and I'm perfectly happy about it. It gives me security for that time and also leaves me free to make other films for a great deal of money.'

Terence Young had been less fortunate than Connery in his bargaining with Eon and found himself passed over, when he insisted on a percentage of the new Bond's profits, in favour of ex-Carol Reed protégé Guy Hamilton. An efficient but uninspired director of a series of bloodless black-and-white British movies, peaking in 1954 with the POW epic, *The Colditz Story*, Hamilton had noticed Connery in his early stage appearances and been unimpressed, as he himself later admitted: 'I didn't think he'd too much going for him.' Eventually the two men had become nodding acquaintances in Jerry's, a drinking club opposite the stage door of Her Majesty's Theatre.

Hamilton promised a streamlining of what he saw as the retake profligacy Young had practised on *From Russia with Love*, as well as a fresh look at the typical 'Bond girl'. Rather than seek a successor to Ursula Andress or Daniela Bianchi, he cast ex-Avenger Honor Blackman as Pussy Galore, explaining that he wanted an experienced, seasoned actress capable of holding her own against Bond both in and out of the clinches.

Richard Maibaum's script was bolstered on this occasion by Paul Dehn, a former film critic who had already distinguished himself with *Seven Days to Noon* and *Orders to Kill*. Together they worked on Fleming's tale of the ultimate dawn raid on

Kentucky's Fort Knox, the world's gold bullion depository. Mastermind Auric Goldfinger was to be played by veteran German character actor Gert Frobe; the ill-fated golden girl by British ingénue Shirley Eaton; Goldfinger's deadly sidekick 'Oddjob' by Harold Sakata, with Paul Carpenter – one of the stars of Connery's first movie, *No Road Back* – in a five-second bit.

The trend towards fancy props that began with *Goldfinger*, projecting 007 ever deeper into the land of fantasy, would prove a treadmill difficult to abandon. Ken Adam's Aston Martin convertible had everything a super-agent could desire: built-in machine gun and flame-thrower, ejector seat (either for the driver or for an undesired passenger), sliding bulletproof shield, revolving steel blades capable of shredding the tyres of an adjoining car, and a choice of deadly smoke screen or oil slick spewing from the rear bumpers. While these would prove popular gimmicks, many, Connery included, saw them as part of the further dehumanization of Bond, reducing him to little more than an animated cartoon.

As the movie lumbered into production in March 1964, he proved no more eager to suffer fools gladly, or at all, than he had ever been. In the middle of one setpiece a publicity man introduced a French lady reporter. 'First of all she asked what the title of the film was,' Connery recalled. 'I told her. Then what part was I playing? I told her. Then she asked who was starring opposite me. I said a very famous German actor, Gert Frobe. "Well, I've never heard of *her*," she said, and with that I just blew up and walked off the set. So I suppose I'm considered very rude by that person. Well, I consider *her* disrespectful and incompetent, and both are definite sins.' Connery went on to spell out what had become his personal credo: 'If someone treats me rudely or dishonestly, I repay them an eye for an eye. Given the chance, I try to treat everyone, man or woman, as I'd like to be treated myself – honestly, openly and simply. But without being too Machiavellian about it, you have to acknowledge there is no future in turning the other cheek if someone does the dirty on you and sends you down the river when you've been straight with them. You can't be straight with them next time; you have to do something about it.'

US journalist Pete Hamill had already been subjected to a press agent's diatribe in a pub before visiting the *Goldfinger* set. 'Sean Connery's a great big conceited, untalented, wooden-headed ninny!' the worthy had declared. On Stage D at Pinewood Hamill received conflicting advice from a camera operator who had worked on all the Bond movies. 'He is one of the classiest actors I've ever worked with,' Hamill was told. 'This guy's a real man. In this business you don't come across many of them.' The deposed Terence Young added his own two cents' worth: 'Sean could be the biggest star in movies since Gable, but he doesn't give a damn for the ancillary assets of being a star. It's not that he's ungrateful. It's just that he's too concerned with personal integrity. A hell of a lot of people don't like Sean because of this.' Honor Blackman proved another supporter. 'I find Sean attractive and sexy,' she declared. 'I think he's got a pair of the best eyes that have ever been seen on screen, apart from anything else he might have – and there's plenty of *that*.'

To enable Connery to play a convincing on-screen game of golf with Goldfinger, Eon paid for lessons from a professional at a course near Pinewood, firmly hooking their star on a sport that would prove a lifelong obsession. Following completion of the movie in July, Connery joined his wife, mother-in-law and children in Rome, where Cilento was working at the capital's Cinecitta Studios on Carol Reed's Michelangelo epic, *The Agony and the Ecstasy*, with Rex Harrison and Charlton Heston.

The couple had no lack of screen offers, both individually and collectively. Before starting *Goldfinger* Connery had finally turned down John Ford's *Young Cassidy*, both because of an indifferent script and a schedule clash. When Terence Young came up with the idea of co-starring both Connerys in a period romp, *The Amorous Adventures of Moll Flanders*, it was Cilento's turn to cry off. Since there was no stop date on her services in Rome Young switched to the alternative husband and wife team of Richard Johnson and Kim Novak. A second screen pairing was planned by Australian producer David 'Doc' Merman, who had *Big Country, Big Man* – an adaptation of the best-selling *Call Me When the Cross Turns Over* – in mind for spring 1965. To complete the picture Connery was studying the script of producer Kenneth Hyman's *The Hill*, set for an imminent location shoot in Spain.

The shock news of Ian Fleming's death was relayed as Connery relaxed at Rome's Olgiata golf course following a game with Rex Harrison. *Goldfinger*'s première was just five weeks away; Connery was on the eve of flying to Spain for *The Hill*. In what the two men saw as an appropriate tribute, an extra eighteen holes were played, with Connery employing the Penfold Hearts ball Fleming had allocated Bond in his match with Goldfinger.

While the $2.9 million *Goldfinger* was setting box-office records as the fastest money-maker of all time, eventually earning a new Bond record $23 million in US and Canadian rentals, Connery was in Almeria, the hottest province in southern Spain, an area detested even by the Spanish. There he was following in the footsteps of pioneers David Lean with *Lawrence of Arabia* in 1960, Sergio Leone and his spaghetti westerns, and the steady stream of film-makers who had followed.

The clincher for Connery, apart from the useful £150,000 fee he was collecting for *The Hill*, was having Sidney Lumet as the director attached to the project. He had much admired his work on the courtroom drama, *Twelve Angry Men*, then with Brando in Tennessee Williams's *The Fugitive Kind*, and on other contemporary classics like Arthur Miller's *The View from the Bridge* and Eugene O'Neill's *Long Day's Journey into Night*. The puckish director's no-nonsense 'let's-move-it-right-along' approach suited Connery down to the ground.

A graphic tale of military sadism in a British World War II detention camp, *The Hill* had been written first as a TV play before being opened out for the screen. Author Ray Rigby had put his own wartime experiences to work, depicting a punishment devised for detention prisoners in the shape of a man-made hill, a thirty-five-foot mound constructed at an angle of sixty degrees they had to climb repeatedly in full kit under the merciless North African sun. The story focused on five prisoners: Jock McGrath (Jack Watson) a battering ram of a Scot interned after a confrontation with military police; distracted would-be deserter George Stevens (Alfred Lynch); old lag Cockney Monty Bartlett (Roy Kinnear); Jamaican man-mountain Jacko King (Ossie Davies) and Warrant Officer Joe Roberts (Connery) courtmartialled for striking an officer and alleged frontline cowardice. With Michael Redgrave, Harry Andrews, Ian Hendry and Ian Bannen cast as the detested authority figures, Rigby's story explored territories of heroism, cowardice and sadism.

It turned out that Lumet had reasons other than the inherent drama in *The Hill* for his enthusiasm; he had been stationed in North Africa himself during the war and had first-hand knowledge of a prison enclosure, if only from the outside. He gleefully collaborated with cinematographer Oswald Morris in experimenting with visual techniques, using specific camera lenses to enhance the oppressive mood of the movie. Everything in the foreground had to be increasingly distorted, with backgrounds constantly receding, throwing the viewer's perspective and pitching him into the emotional violence on display. To do this Lumet and Morris agreed to shoot the first third of the movie with a 24mm lens, the second with a 21mm, the last with an 18mm. In one prison-cell scene Lumet wanted Morris to move his camera round and round in the cramped interior following the close-to-breaking-point character of Alfred Lynch. When Morris pointed out that his overhead lights would be seen in the shot, the decision was made to go ahead in any case, Lumet judging that the enhancement of the scene's claustrophobic element would more than compensate for the unexplained illumination.

Despite the horrific conditions – 'everything from the trots to leprosy', Connery maintained – he revelled in the production. With his close-cropped hair, moustache and Scottish accent – for once appropriate – he was working with a director totally committed to the material on hand, with his old pal Bannen for the first time, as well as enjoying a reunion with his *Operation Snafu* co-star Lynch. *The Hill*, he declared, was the first occasion outside of the Bond series where he had been given time to prepare and work with the director and producer to ensure they were all about to make the same movie.

'We went off like gangsters,' he enthused during post-production, 'shot the film under time, and it was exciting all the way down the line.' For Lumet he reserved special praise: 'He doesn't waste time or waffle. He knows what a picture costs and gets his money up to the hilt. He works his end. On a scene which needed 350 soldiers, he turned up, actually counted the soldiers, and of course there were some missing. So he said, "OK. We don't go until all the soldiers are there." That's why it's best to keep directing and producing as separate functions, with different people.' Lumet returned the compliment as *The Hill*'s opening date approached. 'Anyone who still thinks Sean can't act is in for one hell of a surprise,' he predicted. Ian Bannen would recall the movie as 'the one picture I was on where there were no yellow, pink and blue script amendment pages. That pleased Sean a lot.'

The entire creative experience had clearly rejuvenated Connery. The next stage, he acknowledged, was how the finished movie would be exploited and received, aspects over which he had absolutely no control. 'I'd like it to succeed, but if it doesn't I shall not lose any sleep over it,' he claimed. 'I am concerned always with the present job. I do not live in the past.'

He conceded that *The Hill* would never have been made without the Bond connection. 'It's the sort of film that might have been considered a non-commercial art-house property without my name on it. This gave the producers financial freedom to make it. Thanks to Bond, I find myself in a bracket with just a few other actors and actresses who, if they put their name to a project, it means the finance will come in.'

Following its unveiling at the Cannes Film Festival in May 1965, *Variety* described *The Hill* as 'a grim, realistic, and sometimes sadistic, study'. While lauding Lumet's daring and commanding tempo, they detected basic flaws likely to handicap, even torpedo the movie at the box-office:

> Its opening sequence runs about 50 minutes, and to an American ear, even one reasonably accustomed to British speech, not more than 20 per cent of the dialogue is intelligible. The rest is a series of sounds. It is not just British speech, but military speech, apt to be as much gibberish from a US drill sergeant as an English one.

When an audience was unable to follow what was going on, they reasoned, they finally wouldn't care what is going on.

Philip Oakes echoed the criticism in Britain's *Sunday Telegraph*: 'Lumet mistakes volume for emphasis and by sheer weight of decibels his film is bawled out of true.' Others detected 'theatricality and glibness', with Lumet expecting the audience to 'clap to order'. Connery's performance was singled out among the superb ensemble cast, with Arthur Knight in *Saturday Review* declaring that he had no cause for alarm in the unlikely event of the Bond series petering out. Director Terence Young was lavish in his praise for Connery, deeming his performance 'one of the best I've seen in my life. It was Spencer Tracy stuff . . . remarkable.'

Although Connery had found a powerful vehicle to do his 'good work' in *The Hill*, *Variety*'s forecast proved all too accurate; at the box-office he had laid another egg. Regardless of his protestations to the contrary, the knowledge that world audiences only seemed to want him as Bond was becoming an increasing source of frustration. 'We were all disappointed,' Ian Bannen admits, 'Sean more than most, I'd say.'

Diane Cilento was experiencing similar identity crisis pangs, engendered by callers asking if she was 'Mrs James Bond'. 'While the idea of being someone I'm not appals me, I usually say "yes" in the end because it's not worth arguing,' she maintained. 'Perhaps the easier way to illustrate the difference between my two identities is to tell you what happens when I ring my bank manager. If I ring as Miss Cilento with a single account and then again as Mrs Sean Connery with a joint account, you can measure the change in attitude because it is in thousands of pounds, even though I was quite well known and could manage quite well before I married Sean. But it is because of him that I am now not just Mrs Sean Connery, but Mrs James Bond at the same time. It's not only confusing. It can be humiliating.'

In a classic confusion of the man with his role, *Cosmopolitan* magazine wondered in print if Bond's compliant on-screen bedmates continued their obedience to the star after the klieg lights were switched off. Connery's declaration, 'Let no man say that a red-blooded Scotsman turns away from a lovely woman's shape,' added grist to their rumour mill, with Cilento's portrait of herself as 'a loner, not heavy on marriage' completing the 'open marriage' picture as far as they were concerned.

Close friends focused meanwhile on the element of competitiveness that had always existed between them. If Cilento was jealous of Connery's ride to fame on the Bond wagon, then he in turn seemed to yearn for the legitimate acceptance his wife enjoyed both in theatre and films, as well as his adoption without reservation by her circle of intellectual friends. So Guy Hamilton had directed *Goldfinger*, the latest piece of Bond nonsense? Why, Cilento was just coming off *The Agony and the Ecstasy* with Carol Reed, Hamilton's 'professor'. Carol Reed? Well, how about Sidney Lumet, at least Reed's equal in the heavyweight division, and in a gritty black and white drama that spurned conventional box-office formulae?

Connery's rapidly developing addiction to golf was another source of dissent. 'There are only four stories you can tell about golf,' Cilento would later declare. 'You played a good first shot, but then a bad second. You played a bad first shot, but then you recovered brilliantly. You played two bad shots or you played two good shots. I've heard them all!'

One way and another, the Connerys' marriage, whether 'open' or not, was rapidly falling apart at every available seam. 'Diane was increasingly annoyed at Sean's Bond success,' one friend maintained. 'Her attitude was "Why do you do that shit when you could be doing so many other things?" She chose to overlook that he was only doing his other projects *courtesy* of Bond.'

'Sean was a fairly faithful type,' another acquaintance offered. 'Diane, though, was a tough egg. When it began to look as if the differences were going to open up into a real split, I guess Diane was the one who wanted to end it.'

Chapter 12

'My view is that to get anywhere in life you have to be anti-social, otherwise you'll end up being devoured. I've never been particularly social anyway, but if I've ever been rude, 50 per cent of it has usually been provoked by other people's attitudes. Though I do admit that, like most Celts, I'm moody. It's fine until people try to cheer you up with gems like "Snap out of it" or "Come on now".'

Sean Connery

'All of his success hasn't changed Sean one iota, subtly or unsubtly, period.'

Terence Young

At the end of February 1965 Connery flew to Paris for the start of filming on *Thunderball*, at $5.5 million by far the most lavish of the Bond sagas to date. Buoyed no doubt by his £200,000 pay cheque, he enthused that it had the best story of them all, 'with wonderful underwater sequences' and a 'wildly exciting' premise. There was, admittedly, the usual side grumble that 007 would never tax him as an actor; all he needed to fill the role was the constitution of a rugby player to get through nineteen weeks of 'swimming, slogging and necking'. He now chose to change tack on the dangers of being typed: 'If you do a weekly TV series it can happen, but not making just one film a year. And I'm doing other things.'

While claiming that he would like to see other actors tackle the role, he quickly added that he thought that anyone who did would be crazy. There had been talk of Richard Burton joining in the fun. 'I think he must be out of his mind,' said Connery. 'It would be like putting his head on a chopping board. Whatever he did couldn't make the films more successful than they are. Even if Sam Spiegel and David Lean made one there is no guarantee it would do any better.'

Thunderball in fact had the usual thin 'plot', with SPECTRE's sinister Largo (Adolfo Celi) and his glamorous assistant (Luciana Paluzzi) behind the abduction of two Vulcan bombers, complete with H-bombs, which they intend to launch on the West unless a vast fortune is handed over.

The unit's move to Pinewood in March acted as the trigger for Connery to move out of the family home in Acton. As news of the 'trial separation' was leaked, it was acknowledged that the couple had been experiencing difficulties for some time. The stage was set for Connery's second encounter with Sue Lloyd, once again at one of Jimmy Woolf's parties. Although Connery had become one of the world's biggest stars since the first night they had spent together, Lloyd detected no difference whatsoever in his demeanour. She was happy for him, glad of the success he was enjoying after his years of struggle, and rather dismayed at Cilento's apparent attitude to it. Although the friendly mickey-taking was again in evidence, Connery seemed to regard Lloyd, after their less than galvanic last encounter, as unfinished business. Now he was James Bond, after all, who never failed to deliver! Lloyd gathered early in their conversation that he had left the family home and would not be averse to a bit of 'consolation'.

After laughing and joking with Connery all the way back to her Upper Grosvenor Street apartment, she found the entire building blacked out by a power cut. This served as a cue for fresh rounds of merriment to accompany the fumbling for candles. Later, cosily tucked up in bed, the couple continued to laugh at the tricks fate plays. Although this time they eventually got their act together sexually, Lloyd smilingly recalls the evening as 'hardly the most passionate I have ever known. We made each other laugh too much – and laughter can be a great passion-killer!' To her Connery was more of a big chum: 'Whenever we met again in the next couple of years he always had a big grin on his face – a "don't know why we bothered" grin!'

Connery was back in Acacia House within a week, Cilento maintaining that their careers had caused the rift, not their affairs. Were they now reconciled? 'Sean spent last night at the house and will spend tonight here too,' newsmen were informed. 'A reconciliation? If that is your interpretation, yes. I leave it to you.' 'Doc' Merman, the producer waiting in Sydney to make *Big Country, Big Man* with the couple, put his own interpretation on the news by swiftly abandoning the project, deciding that if Connery and his wife were having personal problems, it could be utterly futile trying to make a film with them.

Kevin McClory, *Thunderball*'s forty-year-old co-producer, had originally been schooled by entrepreneur Mike Todd before breaking away to make a would-be art house movie, *The Boy and the Bridge*, that left him flat broke. Todd's advice, that he couldn't bank plaques or awards, was immediately taken to heart. Pre-*Dr No* and the advent of Eon, he had gone on to co-author *Thunderball* as a screen treatment with Ian Fleming. When the planned movie fell through for lack of financial backing, Fleming proceeded to convert the plot into book form, eventually selling the rights to Eon. McClory promptly sued, obliging Saltzman and Broccoli to bring him in as a production partner on *Thunderball*. It was either that, they realized, or face the prospect of a rival Bond adventure, an eventuality that the energetic McClory had pursued for a while. Eon's 'let's combine our forces' lure was the services of Connery, whom

McClory hastened to agree was far and away 'the best for Bond'.

Screenwriter Richard Maibaum, hitched this time to playwright John Hopkins, found himself not only with his Eon regulars to contend with on *Thunderball*, but McClory as well. Although socially he found them all affable, amusing, likeable men, professionally they were savagely determined to have their own way. At script meetings Saltzman was abrupt, mercurial, quick-thinking, continually interrupting, spouting ideas like a hot geyser, inclined at first to reject any ideas not his own, but someone open to persuasion in the final analysis. Broccoli he found the more easy-going and genial of the two, usually prepared to accept any idea unless it absolutely conflicted with his own, while remaining subject to infrequent but devastating rumblings of discontent that could develop into volcanic eruptions. He also discovered another huge saving grace – 'Cubby' never held grudges.

Saltzman was the one hipped on Bond's gadgets, Broccoli on Bond's games, both clamouring for plenty of 'bumps, thrills, shocks, surprises' along the way. And both were extremely concerned with Bond's image as a super-sleuth, super-brawler, super-lover. Since many of the plot ideas were his own, McClory's attitude to script changes – his occasionally heroic stammer notwithstanding – was predictably vociferous. The freewheeling Irishman was a skin-diving expert based in the Bahamas whose suggestions for the ideal location sites proved of immense value. Another side benefit was the introduction to the cream of Bahamanian society through his marriage to aviation heiress Bobo Sigrist.

When the unit moved from England to the Bahamas in late March, jets carried 102 cast and crew members, together with over twelve tons of equipment. A full scale fibreglass Vulcan bomber was faked on site, together with a $90,000 facelift on a hydrofoil so it could double as a pleasure yacht. The former luxury pad of multi-millionaire Huntington Hartford, a five-minute sail across the bay on Paradise Island, was pressed into service as a props factory.

Despite their marital differences being painfully out in the open, Connery made it clear from the start that he wanted his wife to join him on location. Cilento finally arrived in April, together with Jason, Gigi and nanny, following a delay caused by a burglary at home, and joined him in a rented bungalow on Love Beach. 'I am through the other side now of being called Mrs Bond,' she informed reporters, 'and although it still happens it cannot hurt me any longer. Sean and I have our own lives to lead in our own way. Neither he nor I mean to allow ourselves to be packaged by this business. The industry can take hold of you and wrap you up like a piece of meat and you are left with about 20 per cent of your time to yourself and your family. It is not enough, and neither of us will allow ourselves to become that involved. We are not going to let ourselves be merchandised.' She went on to claim that she was no longer ambitious, while banking the fires of her 'dedicated artist' persona: 'I have my children and my home and I work when it is *right*. And *only* then.'

Michael Caine witnessed one of Cilento's tempestuous – and hilarious – outbursts when he visited the couple in Nassau. 'Diane was cooking lunch,' he recalled, 'and Sean and I went out. One thing led to another, and we got back home for lunch two hours later. Well, we opened the door and Sean said, "Darling, we're home" – and all the food she'd cooked came flying through the air. I remember the two of us standing there, covered in gravy and green beans.'

At one society party in Nassau Connery suffered a rerun of the French lady reporter episode on *Goldfinger*. 'With all this success as Bond,' a bored guest asked him, 'do you think you'll ever be able to do anything else?' Connery's thunderous expression was a study as he turned away. 'There is all this talk about my image,' he complained to a friend, 'whether or not I'm really like Bond and rather rude and aggressive. What am I supposed to do about it? Go around wearing a sign saying I have played the classics on stage and read books, including the whole of Ibsen and Pirandello and Shakespeare and some Proust?'

Terence Young, happily back in harness, had the perfect answer to one scribe who complained about the surly replies Connery gave out in interviews: 'Why is he being so unpleasant? *He's* not unpleasant. *You* were. *You* started it, after all. Sean's never changed. He's been like this all the time and you're the people who've provoked him. You tried to make a monkey out of him and now he doesn't need you.'

He conceded that Bond was far from being a pleasant hero. One of the roles he would have liked to have seen Connery play was Bothwell, for whom Mary, Queen of Scots, gave up everything: 'He has the physical presence to make her action believable. He can play Hotspur – the British critics compared him to Olivier – and Holofernes. He is a very good comedian with a quick wit, not with schoolboy humour, and he is very well read. Don't ever *unkid* that.'

The Ivan Tors unit, hired by Eon to provide the underwater sequences, harboured few starry illusions and conveyed a healthy disrespect for those who did. Philadelphia-born Frank Cousins, Connery's underwater stunt-double, who resembled the star down to the patch of black chest hair and thinning top hair, and whose physique was even more remarkable than Connery's, admitted he had never read a Bond book in his life. 'I can't imagine anyone wanting to be a movie star,' the thirty-three-year-old asserted.

The subject discussed over dinner by the rest of the crew ranged, in Connery's absence, from the state of his marriage, to his running financial battles with Eon – and bête noire Saltzman in particular – as well as the simplistic nature of the entire series. 'This whole thing is like putting jackstraws together,' one key production member suggested. 'The Bond films are confections so tenuous that they are like cotton candy. There isn't a word of truth in them except the reinforcing of it all by real dandy props, and real hard acting by experts. They're highly entertaining, that's all. And at least half the action that takes people's breath away is created. The film editor is a genius. He takes all these snippets and works a miracle.'

'I hear that Connery has a good case of "thalassophobia", a fear of ocean water,' another of the crew interjected. Any suggestion of gentle derision was quickly played down: 'Skin-diving is something you like or not. Connery doesn't care for it. He might be put off a bit by the underwater team; they are a kind of frightening bunch. Of course he'll eventually have to put on the gear and film the matching shots which show him coming out of the water. But I doubt if he'll ever get much more than his feet wet.'

Visitors to the set of *Thunderball* constituted a regular 'Who's Who' of the island's high society, headed by His Excellency Sir Ralph Gray, the Governor of the Bahamas. The highly expectant Bobo Sigrist had coaxed chums Livvy and Timmy Sullivan into granting the unit full use of their Rock Point fish pool 'for a couple of days' that stretched to six weeks. Then there was Lady Orr-Lewis, with whom Connery daily repaired to the Lyford Cay golf links the moment filming was over.

The tiny blonde figure of Diane Cilento, watchful and intent, was never far from her husband's side. A member of the cast on whom her attention particularly concentrated was the twenty-two-year-old French beauty Claudine Auger, selected as Domino, the latest Bond girl. Auger teased Connery as he flipped through snapshots of his son. 'Get away with you, you French barracuda,' he scolded, dampening rumours of close encounters the two had indulged in prior to his wife's arrival.

With night shooting in progress in what had become Rock Point's deadly shark pool, there was little to concern Connery apart from the endless retakes his director ordered. There was a solid pane of glass between him and the sharks, with his double handling any physical contact scenes with the giant fish. 'Look at that mouth,' Connery still declared with a shudder as a shark was lowered into the pool. 'All right, Barrymore, you're on,' Young cracked. With 007's death-by-shark conveniently foiled by stuntman Cousins, all Connery had to do was surface convincingly. 'That was great, Sean, great,' Young declared, 'but I want a little more of your profile next time.'

The Nassau Development Board was hospitality itself to Eon, even to the extent of restaging its annual post-Christmas Junkanoo parade to fit in with the chase sequence where Bond is pursued by Largo and his gang. The *Thunderball* unit was, after all, pumping large chunks of cash into the islands, quite apart from providing an invaluable travel brochure that would last for years to come. The Bond wagon, it seemed, had become unstoppable. 'Yale has already asked permission to begin a James Bond festival,' a publicity man burbled. 'There are people all over the world who actually believe that James Bond exists and that Connery is Bond. Soon there will be an ABC radio series and a TV Bond. If this thing gets any more out of hand it is going to be way past the peak of manic. There is nothing in popular literature like 007 – except maybe Tarzan.'

Fleming's books, printed in eleven languages, had now sold more than 40 million copies. Jay Emmett, chairman of Licensing Corporation of America, predicted sales of over $60 million in 007 clothing, shoes, cards, toys and toiletries. Bond, it seemed, was blue chip for everyone. Only the man who played the role – and had soared to the top as the No. 1 box-office attraction in the world – still entertained considerable doubts. In *Requiem for a Heavyweight* Mountain McClintock had been drained dry before being sold down the river by his unscrupulous manager. If Broccoli and Saltzman had any such notions about him, they had another think coming . . .

As far as Terence Young was concerned Connery was now in the same league as legends like Gable, Cooper and Tracy. 'Take Sean as a partner,' he urged the Eon duo once *Thunderball* was in the can. 'In future make it Cubby and Harry and Sean. He'll stay with you because he's a Scotsman. He likes the sound of gold coins clanking together. He likes that lovely soft rustle of paper. He'll stay with you if he's a partner, but not if you use him as a hired employee.'

Even as *Thunderball* went on to smash all previous Bond records with a colossal US net in excess of $28 million, Young's pleading fell on stony ground.

Chapter 13

'I honestly believe there's a public life and a private life. On those Bond pictures you'd have the press descending in their hundreds from all over the world, expecting to have dinner with you and watch you limbo. Well, I think there ought to be a balance. I think my public and private lives are very integrated. But I'm secretive by nature.'

Sean Connery

With the cancellation of *Big Country, Big Man* the Connerys went on to separate film projects, he to Irvin Kershner's *A Fine Madness* in New York in September 1965, she to Phoenix, Arizona and Martin Ritt's *Hombre*. Each of them – still together, apparently, although apart – were working with one half of Hollywood's husband and wife team of Paul Newman and Joanne Woodward. In *A Fine Madness* Elliott Baker had adapted his own novel for the screen, with Woodward cast as the despairing but loyal wife of Connery's beat poet Samson Shillitoe, Patrick O'Neal as the archetypal physician unable to heal himself and Jean Seberg as the wife he ignores at his peril – especially with Connery's character on the rampage. The energy Shillitoe devoted to solving the overwhelming problem of a functional artist's survival in an indifferent society was perceptively seen by *Life* Magazine as a metaphor for Connery's attempt at escape from Bondage. True to form, Connery gleefully and fearlessly recalled how he had 'screwed Jack Warner for $50,000' for the overtime payments when the movie ran over schedule.

The sojourn in New York led to a meeting with man-of-the-theatre Sir Tyrone Guthrie. When Connery asked him why he had never directed a movie, Guthrie replied that no one had ever asked him. Even as Connery was bristling at the injustice of this, he began to lay plans for his own directorial debut on Broadway. The play he chose, Ted Allen Herman's *The Secret of the World*, had first been staged at Stratford East, with a hoped-for London transfer failing to materialize.

Connery attempted to explain his altruism, some would say foolhardiness, by referring to the impact his thirty-fifth birthday had had on his psyche: 'I suddenly realized that I was halfway there. And I found that because of the realization I felt younger. I discovered I was choosing brighter colours for my clothes. I was heavier, I weighed 210 pounds compared with the year before when I was just under 200 pounds. And I promised myself from now on, and for the next 35 years, I would do only the things that excited me. *That's* why I want to direct my first play in New York. Of course a lot of people say it's madness, that when 38 out of 44 new productions have flopped on Broadway in the past season, it's hardly the time for an untried English director to be welcomed there. But I'm going because I like the play and I want to do it.'

Pointing out that he was due 10 per cent of the profits of *A Fine Madness*, he added, 'One doesn't do everything for money, but one should be paid what one is worth . . . In the past two years I could have made several million dollars if I had taken on a tame manager to promote me in connection with golf balls or whisky or something like that. But I don't want to sell myself like that. So I make my own decisions – discuss them with Diane perhaps – and then pass them on to my lawyer and agent and accountant. That's the only way to breathe.'

While Cilento was completing *Hombre*, she was also applying the finishing touches to the novel she had begun in the Bahamas, at Ian Fleming's suggestion, as an alternative to twiddling her thumbs. The publication of *The Manipulator* would again put her one up on Connery, whose own 'fine madness' deserted him all too soon; although Shelley Winters was for a time attached to *The Secret of the World*, its Broadway staging never took place. Connery at least took the opportunity to repay Winters's kindess during the 1950s. The duplicate of a fur coat she had particularly admired was delivered with a note that ran, 'Dear Shell, Interest on your money and a belated "thank you". Love, Sean.'

One of the reasons for the play's cancellation was a shift in Eon's schedule. *On Her Majesty's Secret Service*, with Guy Hamilton back at the helm, had been planned as the next 007 adventure. When the essential spring snows in Switzerland were missed, the project became *You Only Live Twice*, from a script by Roald Dahl, with filming set for Japan in May 1966. Director Lewis Gilbert, who had directed Cilento a decade earlier in *The Admirable Crichton*, and was fresh from working with Michael Caine in *Alfie* on a meagre $500,000 budget, initially turned down Eon's offer. He changed his mind only when Broccoli pointed out the huge audience he would be reaching with a Bond adventure, as well as the $7 million budget he would have at his disposal.

Before the trip East Connery took the opportunity to settle a few personal matters. Having set up a trust for his parents he finally, after many discussions, persuaded his reluctant father to take early retirement. As if to confound rumours of a marital split, he bought a Victorian mansion on Putney Heath and placed Acacia House on the market for just under £18,000, more or less what it had cost to buy and refurbish. The decision to vacate Acton was not unconnected with the regular crowds of sightseers hoping to catch a glimpse of 007 'over the garden wall'. Connery acknowledged he would have been found guilty of assault if this had continued. A holiday home in Marbella, Spain, adjacent to the first green of a golf course, was also acquired.

Discovered signing cheques – £15,000 to the Inland Revenue, as well as several bills totalling £800 – he lamented how easy it was to lose sight of the fact that it was real money: 'If you had to pay it all out in notes you'd jolly well see what it is and what it means. I still can't get over the fact that when some producer signs a dinner bill for six people for £80 he is spending in one go more than my father had to live on and bring up our family on for longer than a month. I'm not stingy with money – just careful. And I have respect for its value because I see how hard it is to earn and how difficult to keep.'

He continued to throw slings and arrows at the outrageous fortunes Saltzman and Broccoli were accumulating, declaring himself tired of 'a lot of fat slob producers living off the backs of lean actors'. 'My reason for wanting the money I think I'm entitled to is simple,' he explained. 'Money gives you the freedom and power to do what you want. I want to use the power I have now to be a producer. Not one who merely has some notepaper with his name on the top, but a real one using his power the way Taylor and Burton do to get things done that they want to do.'

After a hard day's play at Wentworth golf course, his handicap now down to thirteen, Connery liked nothing better than to repair to actress Diana Dors's house with golfing pals Stanley Baker, Bruce Forsyth, Eric Sykes and Ronnie Carroll. Dors loved to stage games of Truth or Consequences, where one celebrity would be picked to occupy the hot seat and the others encouraged to question him about any subject they chose; the more personal, probing – and sexual – the better. Ronnie Carroll once asked *77 Sunset Strip*'s Ed 'Kookie' Byrne, 'Have you ever had an affair with a man?', to which Byrne quipped, 'Sure. Hasn't everybody?'

Dors was surprised at the avidity with which Connery entered into the spirit of the game. A private man himself, he seemed utterly obsessed with prising the truth out of every victim of the game. Like a ringmaster, he yelled out instructions and abuse in his Scots accent to all concerned, forcing players to stick to the rules and divulge everything. Dors was fascinated that Connery was so much more interested in this aspect, rather than having the victim face a penalty, which the others saw as the most amusing part of the game.

With Connery and his cronies in tow Dors attended the 1966 World Heavyweight contest between Henry Cooper and Cassius Clay, where all of them cheerfully signed autographs galore until the fighters entered the ring. Halfway through the first round, with Connery hunched forward in his seat, utterly absorbed, a woman pushed her way in front of him, completely blocking his view, and shoved her autograph book in his face. Dors watched apprehensively, holding her breath, aware of the inevitable consequence. 'Get out of my bloody way, woman,' he snarled on cue. 'Do you think I've paid £50 a seat to sit here and look at *you*?'

The reviews of *A Fine Madness* were distinctly ambivalent on both sides of the Atlantic. Connery, in *Time*'s estimation, 'displays some proof of his versatility by shouting a lot'; the movie they judged 'fitfully funny'. Richard Schickel, by contrast, described *A Fine Madness* as 'funny and intelligent, a pleasure to recommend' with

> the most surprising performance contributed by Connery, who demonstrates he can play it hot 'n' hearty more interestingly than he plays it cool and cardboardy as 007. He will never challenge David Niven as a master of light sophistication, but he does have a sense of humour and plenty of raw energy when his Bonds are loosened and his Irish [sic!] is allowed to show.

In Britain John Coleman's *New Statesman* review complained of scriptwriter Elliott Baker's 'leaden language', Kershner's 'boring direction' and Connery's 'ramming, lounging and mouthing'. David Robinson in the *Financial Times*, on the other hand, praised Connery's Shillitoe as 'something very rare in screen or stage impersonations of poets. You feel that this bum actually could write a poem if he tried.' Patrick Gibbs in the *Daily Telegraph* discerned 'much to enjoy, not least in Connery's amiable approach'. Penelope Gilliatt in the *Observer* found Connery's performance 'unexpectedly caustic. He makes the boor self-absorbed, intrigued and appalled by his capacity for havoc and at the same time devotedly attached to it.' The *Guardian*'s Derek Malcolm was unimpressed: 'Its faults are many,' he asserted. 'It is difficult to believe in the casting of Connery.' *The Times* struck a similarly negative note: 'Connery is not the ideal actor for the role ... Sometimes the film has the air of a great joke which no one has remembered to let its hero in on.'

'The critics here are mixed about it,' Connery agreed in London, adding, with at least a modicum of accuracy, 'but in New York they raved. I don't want to sound like a super-egoist, but I think it was worthwhile doing. A film when it is finished is like a young bird leaving the nest. It can be shot down, but if you believed in it in the first place then it doesn't matter. You get detached about it.'

Several years would pass before Connery would concede the movie's essentially non-commercial nature: 'Well, that didn't make a penny, of course. It was a highly successful film, like quite a few of the others I've done. To be perfectly honest, I think it was Garson Kanin who wrote to me saying, "You mustn't be surprised that the public aren't interested in writers or poets." And I think that's probably true, because I don't know of any film that's ever been made that's been a success about a writer or a poet.'

Saltzman and Broccoli had watched from the sidelines as one by one *Woman of Straw*, *Marnie* and *The Hill* had bombed. When worldwide audiences proceeded to ignore *A Fine Madness* as well, the team's negotiating position was further strengthened; Connery's currency, it seemed, was only bankable under their aegis. To add to the star's chagrin, Saltzman had made several outside movies of his own, and with considerable success.

A co-production with Broccoli, *Call Me Bwana*, starring Bob Hope and Anita Ekberg, had been cleverly advertised on

a Turkish hoarding in *From Russia with Love*. Courtesy of
author Len Deighton, Saltzman had gone on to create, in the
decidely phlegmatic Harry Palmer, a grittier alternative to
Bond in *The Ipcress File*, further boosting the career of
Connery's old chum Michael Caine. And a second Palmer
adventure, *Funeral in Berlin*, was about to be followed by
Billion Dollar Brain.

During pre-production of *You Only Live Twice* Saltzman and
Broccoli came close to dissolving their partnership. Their
love–hate relationship, partly engendered by Saltzman's
moonlighting expeditions – Broccoli regarded these as leaving
him carrying the burden of Bond on his own – occasionally
matched the intensity Connery reserved for Saltzman. Associate producer Stanley Sopel still saw the pair as 'a perfect
team' as far as the series was concerned. Broccoli's own
temporary departure from his 'day job' on Bond, the year after
You Only Live Twice – Chitty Chitty Bang Bang – dissuaded
him from further side ventures.

When filming in Japan, Connery refused even to appear on
the movie set when Saltzman was around. Progress was
difficult in any case, largely due to the hysteria of the local
crowds, reporters and photographers who followed 'Bondo'
everywhere from the Tokyo Hilton to locations at Kagoshima.
Connery and Cilento's plan to combine a holiday with filming
in the Far East badly misfired. They had been mobbed by
crowds in Manila on the way out, then followed everywhere by
an army of newsmen and photographers in Japan. 'Everywhere
you go there's always someone coming out from behind a tree,'
sighed Cilento. 'Photographers even follow him into the
lavatory.' TV commentator Alan Whicker watched in dismay
as Connery appeared to abandon his usual fierce professional
concentration and, in a reflexive defence action, affect indifference to the cacophony surrounding his production. 'I don't
believe any of that rubbish of the price of fame,' Whicker was
informed.

Despite the exotic locations, all the usual tired 007 set pieces
appeared to have been brought back into play in the slender

storyline of *You Only Live Twice* with the US and Russian governments blaming each other for the disappearance of their guided missiles. SPECTRE and Blofeld (played on this occasion by Donald Pleasence) turn out – surprise, surprise! – to be behind the hijackings, operating from within an extinct volcano in Japan. Connery found himself sitting yet again in a stationary car mock-up, looking and feeling like a prize chump, his innate acting ability hardly taxed with directions like, 'Look in the rear view mirror. Is he coming after you? You're not sure. Yes, he is! Swerve to the right, now take a sharp left. And keep looking in the rear view mirror.' Enough was enough. 'I don't want to know,' he declared once the movie was in the can. 'It's *finished*. Bond's been good to me, but I've done my bit. I'm *out*.'

Although public reaction to *You Only Live Twice* was enthusiastic, it came in $9 million below *Thunderball*'s record, leading to speculation that Bondmania had finally peaked. At the Royal London première, complete with Zapata moustache, Connery exchanged a few words with the Queen Mother, who asked, 'Is this really your last Bond film?'

'Yes, ma'am, I'm afraid it is,' he replied.

'Did you feel you were typecast?'

'Yes, I think you're right, ma'am.'

Chapter 14

'At the height of his Bond fame he could have had any woman in the world. As far as I could see he often did, because the girls flung themselves at him.'

Diana Dors

In January 1967 Connery made his debut as a theatrical manager, yet another new role and challenge for him. In association with impresario Peter Bridge he presented an Oxford Playhouse production of *Volpone*, with Leo McKern and Zia Mohyeddin, for a six-week run at London's Garrick Theatre. It was not a question of a change of image, he insisted. He now claimed to regret having been unable to return to the theatre since his movie success, and promised that if the venture was a success money would be used to stage other plays. Presumably, since *Volpone* was the first and last in the series, it failed to generate a satisfactory return. His own theatrical plans – amended, it seemed, since his 'movies-only' declaration to Ian Bannen – included acting and directing 'as soon as I get the time' and encompassed a tentative production of 'the Scottish play', *Macbeth*, to be performed in Scotland with an all-Scots cast.

Next on Connery's agenda was a more immediate paying of

dues to his native land. Following a meeting with Sir Iain Stewart at a golfing society dinner in London, he found himself highly impressed with the plans the Scottish industrialist outlined to save Fairfield's ailing Clydesdale shipyard.

Sir Iain's main plank was the abandonment of the 'them and us' syndrome between workers and management that had plagued British industry for so long; he believed that both sides had to become more flexible and less suspicious of each other. How could workers be expected to be loyal to a firm whose bosses treated them like children, as if the future of the company didn't vitally concern the employees whose liveli-hood depended on it? Industrial action, he felt, was too often based on revenge, with memories of the Depression, hunger marches and the means test producing spite strikes. Manage-ment and trade unions had to learn to communicate with each other, he maintained, or British industry was finished. 'Stewart was doing something at Fairfield that hadn't been done successfully anywhere in the world, including England,' said Connery. 'He even had carpenters doing painters' work when necessary and he had union men sitting in the boardroom. It was all working famously and production was up.'

Connery flung himself into the production of a documentary on the Fairfield's 'miracle', writing and directing *The Bowler and the Bunnet* in a few weeks late in 1967. What the documentary did for him in personal terms was to remind him vividly of his own humble origins and demonstrate how unwise it would be to ever turn his back on them. The message he put over in his script was uncompromising and unclouded from both points of view. The bosses' credo, pre-Fairfield's: 'When it's your job to sack one thousand men at the stroke of a pen you can't be sentimental about it.' As far as the workers were concerned: 'The boss takes the gravy when the going is good and when things look bad he sells out and takes his money and vanishes.' Historically the gulf had been complete, Connery summarized, between the manager's bowler hat and the worker's humble bunnet.

Much to his annoyance the documentary was only shown

locally by Scottish Television, before being turned down for subsequent network showing by both the BBC and Independent Television. Even worse, by 1968 the piece was already an anachronism, Fairfield's having been absorbed into the disastrous Upper Clyde Shipyard consortium, and Stewart's bold initiative cavalierly dismantled. Within fifteen months bankruptcy was declared.

Back in the world of movies Connery declined an offer from ex-agent Charles Feldman to appear in a rival Bond movie, *Casino Royale*, the only remaining Fleming property not owned by Eon. Instead, he signed to star in a British western, *Shalako*, opposite 'sex kitten' Brigitte Bardot.

The movie's provenance was inauspicious. Having worked his way up from an ABC theatre circuit manager trainee to personal assistant at Warwick to 'Cubby' Broccoli and Irving Allen, co-producer Euan Lloyd had reportedly been straining at the leash to make a movie since he first read Louis (*How the West was Won*) L'Amour's book. If that wasn't ominous enough, his first independent movie in 1968 had been the virtually unreleasable *The Poppy is also a Flower*, directed by the ubiquitous Terence Young. Producer Dimitri de Grunwald was best known for overblown all-star vehicles like *The Yellow Rolls Royce*. Edward Dmytryk, *Shalako*'s director, had produced excellent work in the past, notably *Crossfire* in 1947, *The Caine Mutiny* in 1954 and *The Young Lions* in 1958, where Connery, so it was claimed, had been bounced by Brando. The 'peak' of his recent work had been Harold Robbins' *Where Love Has Gone*, bizarrely starring Lana Turner in a lurid re-enactment of the Stompanato episode.

Finance from no fewer than thirty-six independent distributors around the world had bankrolled *Shalako*'s $5 million budget. To complete the picture, the Mexican locations originally chosen were switched, when a labour strike threatened, to the dreaded Almeria, where the irrepressible Harry Saltzman was busily shooting *Play Dirty*, with Michael Caine, only a few dunes away.

Connery's Shalako ('Rain King' in Zuni Indian) was an ex-confederate army colonel attempting to save a group of European aristocrats on an ill-fated pleasure safari through New Mexico in 1880 from marauding Apaches. Bardot was the Countess who falls for Shalako, with the party completed by Honor Blackman, Stephen Boyd, Jack Hawkins, Peter Van Eyck, Alexander Knox and Valerie French. Connery's golfing buddy Eric Sykes was drafted in as a quaintly comedic butler, with Woody Strode as Shalako's Indian adversary.

Connery's first encounter with Bardot had taken place in the company of her millionaire husband, Gunther Sachs, following a family holiday with Cilento and the children at Cap d'Antibes on the French Riviera. The atmosphere in Almeria was fraught from the moment Bardot made her delayed appearance, emerging through a swirl of early-morning mistral in her white Rolls Royce, complete with chauffeur, stand-in, secretary and publicist, with a hairdresser, make-up man and photographers following on behind.

The lack of chemistry between the two stars was almost tangible. 'She's all girl,' said Connery, 'but if I must say so, all on the outside.' The constant rows between Bardot and ex-lover Stephen Boyd did nothing to smooth progress on the movie; halfway through the proceedings she threatened to walk out.

Shalako proved a new career low in Connery's post-Bond era, utterly eviscerated by the critics following its world première in Munich in September 1968. Three months later, following its British debut, the *New Statesman*'s correspondent judged the movie 'a waste of time and money', while Alexander Walker in London's *Evening Standard* discerned 'a script of stupefying banality'. In Patrick Gibb's *Daily Telegraph* estimation Connery and Bardot demonstrated the art of 'doing nothing well', while Dmytryk 'just seems to have done nothing'. According to David Robinson in *The Times*: 'The enigma of *Shalako* is whether or not they knew at the time they were making it just how funny it all was. Were these lines written and spoken in all innocence?'

One scene, in which Honor Blackman is choked to death when forced to swallow a diamond necklace, prompted a wag at the press showing to enquire, 'Breakfast at Tiffany's?' 'Almost everything about *Shalako*,' reported the *International Herald Tribune*, 'is embarrassingly bad. So bad that one is staggered by the uniform and unrelieved awfulness. The screenplay is hopeless drivel, its plot manoeuvres awkward, and its acting feeble.' Only *Variety* detected 'quiet warmth and laconic humour' in Connery's performance.

Discussing the subject of ageing with Anthony Quayle, Connery informed his friend that he had reached the age – thirty-seven – when, in a fairly natural extension of his 'halfway there' revelation, he had resigned himself to the fact that one day he was going to die. 'Once you've accepted this,' Quayle replied, 'the next thing is to get your priorities straight.' Connery vowed anew to follow the advice, only doing 'creative things' with 'a few talented people around him'. Maybe *Shalako*'s $1.2 million fee, together with a whopping 30 per cent of the producer's profits – none of which materialized – had proved impossible to resist.

For a rather more modest amount – £30 – he designed the cover for his wife's novel, *The Manipulator*. Intriguingly, this depicted a man suspended by his feet against the background of an orange sunset. 'For Sean', Cilento's dedication ran. The agent to whom she had entrusted her literary affairs, the personable George Greenfield, had become a regular visitor to the Connerys' Putney home. 'She's the brains of the outfit,' Greenfield blithely informed colleagues. 'When I talk to Diane, Sean just sits around watching television.'

During a trip to Oslo in the fall of 1967, Connery checked himself into the clinic of psychiatrist/therapist Dr Ola Raknes, at eighty years of age one of the last surviving pupils of the controversial 'cosmic orgone energy' proponent, Dr Wilhelm Reich. His theories had been widely derided by the establishment and taken up with equal avidity by those attracted to his 'free love' philosophy, in considerable vogue in the 'Swinging Sixties'.

Reich's belief followed up on an early idea of Freud's that undischarged sexual urges would be converted into anxiety, and, left unchecked, neurosis. Orgasm, and plenty of it, was Reich's solution, his formula for a long-lasting sexual relationship consisting of full orgiastic potency, the overcoming of incestuous fixation and infantile sexual anxiety, the absence of repression of any unsublimated sexual stirrings and absolute affirmation of sexuality and joie de vivre. To avoid misery, he believed that all couples should engage in frequent third-party relationships, within the framework of a truly 'open marriage'. Nature, Reich propounded, while Raknes sat at his feet, knew nothing of either monogamy or polygamy. It only knew that powerful sexual impulses persisted throughout every healthy individual's lifespan.

'Sean is not in hospital,' Cilento told enquiring newsmen. 'Not in that sense. He had to go to Oslo to see friends and discuss some business. While he was there he decided to pay a visit to Dr Raknes. He is a great admirer of his work and he's read many of his books. He's certainly not unwell or having treatment of any kind.'

Connery remained incommunicado during the entire visit. If he was absorbing the controversial doctor's theories on sexual inhibition-liberation through vegetotherapy, the knowledge was not about to be notified to the world press. Who knows – maybe he had simply twisted his ankle.

Chapter 15

'I have a great respect for money. I know how hard it is to earn and keep, especially with our diabolical taxes in Britain. I never get over the fact that sometimes I see more money being paid for a meal than my father earned in a week.'

Sean Connery

'Love, work and knowledge are the well-springs of our life. They should also govern it.'

Sean Connery

The first of what was to become two-in-a-row of the biggest box-office disasters of all time was first mentioned as a potential project by director Martin Ritt while Connery was visiting his wife on the set of *Hombre*. The saga of the Molly Maguires, a band of Irish immigrant workers who had banded together in the 1870s to form a secret society in protest against brutal working conditions in the Pennsylvanian mines, carried echoes for Connery of the battle for civil liberties raging in the US. The group had taken their name from an anti-landlord gang in old Ireland in which the men had dressed as women on their raids to avoid recognition. As just as their case may have been, their methods, including beatings and murder, put them beyond the pale; by 1877 thirteen members of the gang had been hanged and the society destroyed.

In Ritt's movie, with a screenplay by fellow-blacklist veteran Walter Bernstein, Richard Harris was James McParland, a detective hired by the pit bosses to infiltrate 'the Mollies', led by Connery's stone-faced, unyielding Jack Kehoe. Samantha Eggar was cast as Mary Raines, a strong-willed local girl who first loves, then leaves McParland.

The Molly Maguires was shot in the small town of Eckley, Pennsylvania, the only coal patch town in America which still existed almost as it had a century ago. The unit painted all of the houses in the tiny community of sixty-two families slate grey, the colour the coal dust from the working mines had originally made them. Shrubs, flowers and trees were temporarily removed and birch trees planted along the streets. All signs of the present, like telephone power lines, were obliterated and rewired underground, a permanent improvement for the isolated community.

Cilento joined her husband on location in May 1968, lodging along with the rest of the cast at Genetti's Motel. Jason was by this time ensconced at Millfield, an English public school where Connery maintained he would be taught 'to appreciate everything about life, not just maths and Latin'. He knew better than most how important the 'right background' was; the economics that had dictated his upbringing were light years removed from what he had in mind for his son.

Cilento's first novel had been well enough received and she was about to start her second, *Hybrid*, for which her stay in Eckley would afford ample opportunity. The fact that the couple were still together was now considered more newsworthy than the rumours of rift that had made headlines years earlier. With friends continuing to assert that they were close to the final split, Connery conceded that the greater the emphasis on the individual's makeup, the greater the dangers of conflict. There could never be complete equality in marriage, either the husband wore the trousers or he was henpecked. Listeners to the formidable Connery were left in little doubt in which pigeonhole he belonged.

An on-screen game of football provided one of the unit's few lighter moments, and a welcome break from the otherwise unrelieved grimness of the script. Twenty-five professional players were brought in from New York and Philadelphia Soccer and Gaelic leagues to augment the acting team of Connery, Harris, Anthony Costello and Anthony Zerbe. With the bulk of the movie in the can the unit repaired to Paramount Studios in Hollywood to add interior shots, leaving Eckley, enhancements notwithstanding, to redig itself into the past.

Although *Time Magazine* found in the *Molly Maguires* both 'great strength and regrettable weakness', they had nothing but praise for the performances of the principal actors: 'Harris, in an intricate role, gives his best performance since *This Sporting Life*, and Connery proves that, after years of Bondage, he's one of the screen's most underrated stars, an actor of controlled power and technical accomplishment.'

Variety found the movie a 'well mounted but sluggish drama' with distinctly 'spotty' box-office prospects. Performances were described as 'professional by all hands. Harris is particularly, and admirably, restrained. But Connery is too much so.' According to Roger Greenspun in the *New York Times*, 'An exceptionally attractive cast does pretty well considering that only a few of its members have real character parts they can settle into . . . Sean Connery suffers most because his role is the most arbitrarily closed. But when he and Richard Harris act together they create a superb and powerful sense of presence that almost hides the absence of anything very meaningful for them to say.' Ritt – whose liberal outpourings were never known to extend to similar quantities of humour, unless inherent in the script – was deemed to have sunk the movie in a series of dour, dolorous tableaux.

Connery was acutely aware of the almost complete lack of humour and responded to one brave reporter who questioned if he was worth *The Molly Maguires*' $1 million fee by snapping,

'Certainly!' Later he was almost contrite, wondering why he had reacted that way – before deciding that he had been perfectly justified and asserting that he was worth every penny he got. It was something he had learned as a youth in Scotland: 'You get damn all for nothing.' In this case, unfortunately, it was Paramount Pictures who got 'damn all' as *The Molly Maguires* proceeded to bomb in the US. With a cost of $11m, the movie returned less even than Connery's fee to the unhappy studio. Although career-wise it was Connery 1, Cilento 1 as far as director Ritt's services were concerned, Cilento had again emerged the victor over her spouse with the highly acclaimed *Hombre*.

Harry Saltzman, noting Connery's continuing box-office plight with what might have been taken as barely disguised glee, decided it was time to pay the star a decidedly back-handed compliment. 'Sean has tremendous animal magnetism,' he declared. 'He could be bigger than Clark Gable ever was if he switched to romantic he-man roles. But poor Sean is trying to be so un-Bondlike that he doesn't know what parts to take any more.' Despite Saltzman's own reported problems with Connery's successor George Lazenby during the filming of the latest Bond adventure, *On Her Majesty's Secret Service*, the producer had no intention of breaking ranks – at least, for the moment. 'That boy George,' he claimed, 'has had more acting training pumped into him in the last four months than Connery has had in his entire life.'

Having dipped his toe in the political water by allying himself with the Scottish National Party, whose stated aims included separation from the United Kingdom and the establishment of its Parliamentary constitution, Connery was invited to go one step further and stand for election as a prospective SNP Member of Parliament. Never having voted in his life for any party, he declined. 'I would not be so presumptuous as to sit for any political candidacy without sufficient work, background and knowledge,' he said, 'and it's not my style to be spoonfed. Besides, I'd get found out.'

Instead, Connery went on to co-found, with Sir Iain Stewart, the Scottish International Education Trust, a charitable foundation dedicated to assisting the young people of Scotland through bursaries, as well as funding a drama chair at Glasgow's Strathclyde University. The formation of the Trust was announced in December 1970 at a meeting of the Saints and Sinners Club, an exclusive group of sixty prominent Scots Connery had joined.

In his travels round the world Connery had met many an exiled Scot who had expressed a desire to 'feed something back into their native heath': for them the SIET would prove the ideal vehicle. Soon there were more events lined up to enrich its coffers, as well as those of the Saints and Sinners, among them a race meeting at Ingliston organized by former world motor racing champion Jackie Stewart, with Paul Newman and James Coburn in attendance, a proposed Celtic and Rangers Select vs Brazil football match at Glasgow's Hampden Park, and the prospect of a fight being arranged for Scots world champion Ken Buchanan in Scotland.

Funds for the SIET's launch would be provided by a golf tournament Connery planned at the Old Course in Troon, Ayrshire, with Bing Crosby, Bob Hope and Andy Williams in attendance. Connery wisely consulted 'the old groaner' while playing in Crosby's own tournament in California; the crooner had been organizing the event for two decades and was happy to pass on a few wrinkles. Although he was putting up all of the organizational money in advance, Connery looked to commercial sponsors to turn the tournament into the richest Pro-Am event ever staged in Britain. At £1,000 for each of the 18 holes the requisite number of backers was soon in place, with a portion of the profits reserved for the SIET, as well as an amount allocated to a survey to be carried out by St Andrew's University to discover the reason why Scots leave their native land. Although he knew the answer in his own case, Connery was determined to solve the mystery on a wider basis.

Next up for Connery was playing the role of Norwegian

explorer Roald Amundsen in a Russian/Italian co-production, *The Red Tent*, in which Peter Finch, cast as Italian general Umberto Nobile, was already toiling away with fellow cast members Hardy Kruger and Claudia Cardinale. He would eventually complete nine months on the movie; Connery, awarded equal star billing, precisely three weeks. The movie recounted the tragic tale of Nobile's dirigible crash in 1928 in the Arctic wilderness, and Amundsen's death in a vain attempt to rescue the marooned party.

Before the journey to Russia he managed to persuade his parents to move from Fountainbridge to Newington, a pleasant residential area of Edinburgh not too far from their old address. He holidayed in Australia with Cilento's parents and planted a few grapevines in Spain. And he had French newspaper *France Soir* busily eating its words. Their suggestion that he had been forced out of Bondage by outgrowing the role, his waistline unacceptably thickened, was not allowed to pass. Pausing only to check that the measurement had increased by precisely one inch since the days of *Dr No*, Connery turned loose his legal eagles. 'It was asserted quite erroneously that the producers of the James Bond movies had dispensed with his services because he was no longer fit to play the role of James Bond,' David Hirst, QC, informed the High Court. *France Soir* duly retracted, apologized for libel and settled out of court with Connery.

In Moscow and Leningrad he found himself in the unusual position of not being recognized. There were times when his anonymity worked against him, as when he was invited over to the British Embassy Club in Moscow for a drink, only to be barred from entry at the door. 'My worst entrance and best exit,' he informed friends. At a restaurant in Leningrad he wryly observed revellers trying in vain to keep in step with a large balalaika band. So much for the myth of the Terpsichorean Trotskyites! 'They wouldn't last ten minutes at Glasgow's Denniston Palais,' he was heard to mutter. Or, he might have added, *five* minutes at Fountainbridge's Palais-de-Danse.

He became acutely aware of the fear element that pervaded

Russia, observing the fast lane painted yellow in the centre of every main road that was reserved for governmental black cars. He marvelled that this was never questioned and began to see everything in Russia as a rather sinister, well-oiled machine, an illusion his hosts did little to dispel. Every day his driver was changed, presumably so that no relationship could be formed. After being driven to Mosfilm's studios, there was the endless ritual of identity checks, invariably carried out by KGB personnel. There seemed to be no sense of urgency in the film unit. Each scene took an eternity to light and shoot, with the Russians displaying a completely different concept of time from Western filmmakers. Any leftist tendencies Connery had entertained received more than a corrective touch on the tiller during his stay.

The Red Tent ran for over four hours in Russia, then was cut in half by Paramount for its brief, belated release in the West in 1970. Connery claimed it was a big success – 'a big *internal* success,' he qualified, 'never a success anywhere else.' There were some respectful reviews, especially for the cast, any sparks on offer being courtesy of the 'strong performances from Finch and Connery', according to the British *Guardian* critic Derek Malcolm, with Patrick Gibbs in the *Daily Telegraph* singling out Connery as 'most satisfying of all' and judging the movie 'a fascinating, if elementary discussion of leadership, responsibility and heroism'.

The adjective most frequently reached for, however, was 'dull', with director Mikhail Kalatozov's deadly framing device of a modern late-night party, with all the ghostly victims commenting on the enfolding action and pointing out where they would have acted differently, judged 'comical' by Gavin Millar in the *Listener*. *Village Voice*'s 'on the whole a likeable movie', was the kindest cut of all. Connery had added another movie, after *The Molly Maguires*, to the list of all-time cinematic losers.

His few weeks on *The Red Tent*, together with tentative discussions on a movie adaptation of *Macbeth*, proved a distraction from his main business of playing golf in 1969. 'A lot of people seem to think I'm wasting my time being out on a golf course when I should be setting up a picture,' he said, 'but I don't see it that way. I like the isolation of golf. I do a lot of thinking when I'm playing. And you meet marvellous people on the course. Golf, food and drink – that's what I enjoy. And the only point of having money is to indulge them.'

To Connery the game was a complete revelation, an expiation of all the shortcomings and problems he acknowledged – his temper, moods and ego. And on top of its therapeutic qualities, he maintained that golf had virtually provided him with a philosophy of life, which he deemed 'a great help to somebody like myself who doesn't have a religion'. It also, he confessed, taught him a lot about his own character: 'When you start there is this big temptation. The ball maybe has a very bad lie and there is no one there to see you adjust it and position it better for you to hit, so you have to surmount that feeling and fight it. And anyone who tells you they don't get that temptation is just full of baloney!'

If his relative life of leisure could be regarded as stepping off the treadmill, the canny Scot was in no way resting on his financial laurels. He acknowledged that Saltzman and Broccoli had turned down a CBS offer of $20 million to show the five Bond movies on television in favour of re-issuing them in theatrical double-bills. 'That gives you some idea of what the re-issues must be worth,' he suggested. That he contractually had percentages on the last four gave him an especially warm glow.

Having abandoned Ted Allen Herman's *The Secret of the World* back in New York, Connery decided on a pitch closer to home for another of Herman's plays, *I've Seen You Cut Lemons*. At Cilento's request, he took over when the original director bowed out and cast the versatile Robert Hardy – Prince Hal to his 1960 Hotspur in the BBC's *Age of Kings* series – as the brother for whom Cilento's character incestuously lusts.

Hardy accepted the two-hander very much against his better instincts. 'I didn't particularly want to do a play at that moment,' he recalls, 'but Sean was very persuasive and I've always been very weak at helping out old colleagues.' Hardy thought that the idea of Connery directing the play was 'interesting' and soon found himself locked into the project.

Shortly after rehearsals began the strains started to pile up. Hardy, forced to adopt a Canadian accent, concedes that he belongs to the generation of actors who have never 'crossed the Atlantic' with any great degree of conviction. That he was never in love, or enticed, by his own sisters, except in the most ordinary terms, also left him feeling wrong-footed with the role.

As he struggled to 'find his character', he began to sense a feeling of impatience on the part of his director. 'I had a mass of stuff to remember,' says Hardy, 'and it's harder to do that when you're not really in tune with the part. Then I didn't get along with Herman, the author of the play, who was around a great deal too much in my view. He was immensely enthusiastic, but distinctly mystical. There was a great deal of Chinese philosophy being spouted, which I didn't think had anything to do with the hard work of actors getting ready for a play. What I thought *was* marvellous was Sean's ability as a director. He was extraordinarily good at analysing the difficulties I was having with the part. He administered lessons in relaxation, which I think Diane found rather tiresome. I felt that having coaxed Sean into directing, she now wanted someone else. I realized that their marriage was pretty thorny. Diane had an extremely powerful personality.'

Prior to the play's Oxford opening, the obligatory provincial tour and the West End opening, Hardy found himself prevailed upon to lodge with the Connerys in Putney for a week. In this way, Connery argued, rehearsal time could be stretched out. Hardy recalls a big, empty house that was attractive enough, but with only the bare necessities of furniture and some interesting paintings.

After rehearsing all day in a church hall in Putney, there were 'words, words, words all evening' before talking long into the night with Connery and Cilento about the play's allegedly metaphysical implications. Young Jason popped in from time to time and announced, 'Hi, *I'm* Jason Connery. What's *your* name?' 'It was a difficult, fraught, testing time,' Hardy recalls with a rueful smile.

Following his first breakfast in the Connery household he found himself introduced in his director's study to an extraordinary zinc-lined wooden 'think tank' of the type originated by Wilhelm Reich and his disciple Raknes, whose clinic Connery had visited in Oslo. Connery believed that isolation in the device protected him from the vibrations of the outside world, enabling him to concentrate his mind and think his own pure thoughts. Other claimed benefits included preventing a leakage of nervous energy, as well as capturing any available cosmic orgone in the immediate vicinity. Urged to try it out for himself, Hardy did so with some trepidation. 'I didn't rush to instal one in my own home,' he confessed.

His initial reservations about the play continued on brief tour as the opening at London's Fortune Theatre in late November 1969 loomed. Mercilessly lambasted by the critics, *I've Seen You Cut Lemons* ran for just five nights. 'It failed because the play simply wasn't fascinating to the public,' says Hardy. 'The set, by Sean Kenny, was magnificent but inappropriate and dwarfed the action.' Connery acknowledged that if he had been one of the actors involved he would have been upset and annoyed by the critical reaction, but declared himself 'more philosophical' from his seat in the director's chair. It was still a major upset, and further eloquent proof that Connery, whatever other assets he might enjoy, was no great judge of material. And the play's failure was hardly the marital cement the marriage cried out for.

Rumours that the Connerys were about to become tax exiles in Spain were gruffly dismissed. 'Scotland would be as far as I considered moving,' he assured everyone.

Chapter 16

'Maybe I didn't exactly hear violins playing, but there were definitely fireworks. Our eyes met in the clubhouse and as far as I am concerned it was love at first sight. And I think there was something in return from him too.'

Micheline Connery

'In the end I walked out on him.'

Diane Cilento

Peter Noble and his wife Mary, Connery's erstwhile baby-sitting benefactors back in the 1950s, received an invitation to brunch in Putney one Sunday. The call took them a little by surprise, even though it was from the Connerys' lodger, director Norman Jewison, and not from the couple themselves. That they had never been invited to Acacia House in Acton they had put down to Cilento, from whom a distinct coolness had been discerned during her visits to their home with Connery. The Nobles gained the impression that a mere journalist and bit-part actress were hardly considered 'suitable company' for thespians in the ascendant.

Cilento certainly looked surprised when Noble and his wife

turned up in Putney; although she did not actually ask 'Who the *fuck* invited those two?' her petulant expression gave the game away. Connery himself was friendly enough, although any sentiment for the dim and distant past was decidedly thin on the ground. As for the future, the Nobles gained the distinct impression that Connery and Cilento's days as a couple were numbered.

In March 1970, Connery left Cilento in Marbella and accompanied Stanley Baker on a side trip to the Moroccan golf championships at Mohamaha. Also attending was Micheline Roquebrune, a petite, vivacious, auburn-haired Frenchwoman and mother of three children. While her second husband had departed in disgust after two days of poor play, to seek a less competitive game with the King of Morocco, it soon emerged that Micheline could hold her own, with her seventeen handicap, with the keenest of the male competitors.

Born in Nice and raised in North Africa, her background could scarcely have been in greater contrast to Connery's. The family's luxurious home in Tunis had teemed with servants and she had gone on to attend a French Catholic boarding school. What they had in common was a relatively strict upbringing, as well as an instant, electric attraction for each other.

Just watching him in action on the green Micheline was particularly struck with the twinkle in Connery's eyes, as well as his boyish smile. She detected an innocence, a complete lack of guile that was enormously appealing and sensed that here was a man who had never performed a mean act in his life, who had never cheated and expected the same of everyone else. She was no movie fan and had seen only a single Bond movie. 'I did not know he was the actor,' she said later. 'I know nothing about the actors. I only knew I liked this man's eyes ... I thought he was big, big ... *whew*!'

That night Micheline had a dream in which Connery took her in his arms. Although she had no way of knowing it, the reality was only hours away. Next day the two met as they were separately awarded medals for their individual competitions. 'In the morning we played golf,' Micheline recalled, 'then we were introduced. In the afternoon we did *something else* ... I think I was madly in love with him from the first ...'

The couple parted after two days, with not a word from Connery about his marital woes and Micheline convinced they would never meet again. An almost unendurable three months later, he called out of the blue and said it was urgent that he see her. When they met, he explained that he had been unable to forget her, that he had fallen in love with her, that he wanted to spend the rest of his life with her. Micheline could scarcely believe her ears, although Connery's vows were exactly what she had prayed to hear. She assured him, in no uncertain manner, that his feelings were fully reciprocated. An idyllic week was spent together before the couple parted to begin working on their respective divorces.

A year after their first meeting, following a golfing holiday Connery spent with Micheline in Spain, Connery moved on his own out of Putney. With the family home put on the market shortly thereafter, there was clearly no going back. 'This time,' Connery conceded, 'it *is* the end. One is always reluctant to admit failure, and a marriage that goes wrong is as bad as anything can be. What we had to do was step back and see just what we were doing to each other, to our lives and to the lives of our son and daughter. Our careers were incompatible, not us. You are offered a part and you want to do it, but suddenly there are a hundred questions to settle: What is she doing? What is he doing? Who will look after the kids? Can they come? Who'll take care of the home? Interminable. Unless you want a travelling circus-life, with travelling manager, domestic manager, base housekeeper, movable housekeeper – it's not my way of living at all. So we finally had to come to terms about what we'd got ourselves into. The children, fortunately, knew the situation. They're great. And it's all coming to some sort of civilized understanding and agreement now. But, you know, I've always found it very hard to discuss. When it comes to these confrontations everything goes out of the window. You start falling into the traps of self-deceit. You get on the defensive because you feel that you've failed. I hate failure – but it's still the only true challenge, isn't it?'

When Connery was a wee lad of five back in Edinburgh, about to share a desk in the front of the class at Edinburgh's Bruntsfield Primary School with Eric Boyd and the rest of the 'thickies', a showman named Robert Weitman was managing New York's renowned Times Square Parliament Theater, offering a combination of movies and stage shows. This was the legendary venue where Benny Goodman, The King of Swing, was re-named The Pied Piper and played to packed audiences for months in the 1930s, while in the 1940s Weitman introduced a young singer named Frank Sinatra to thousands of swooning teenage girls.

With more than a decade of dazzling success at the Paramount to his credit, Weitman detected the writing on the wall; it was time to move on. Television was the next mountain he had to conquer, although it would prove but a lower peak on the way to the pinnacle of Hollywood for the restless impresario. For six years he was production head of MGM before a move from Culver City to Burbank and vice-presidency of production at Columbia Pictures. Following a decision that he would rather make his own movies, he resigned with a long-term Columbia contract in his pocket.

After sifting through many books and plays Weitman alighted upon the galleys of *The Anderson Tapes*, a novel by Lawrence Sanders that described the planning and execution of a daring million-dollar robbery by John 'Duke' Anderson following his release from a ten-year prison term for safe-cracking. The pre-Watergate subplot explored the world of omnipresent wiretapping, bugging and electronic surveillance which gave Sanders's novel its title; as Anderson carries out his masterplan his every move is recorded for posterity by one or other rival agency. Since the movie was set in Manhattan, Weitman could see no one but Sidney Lumet at the helm. Lumet knew the island from end to end, from river to river, and was a past master at combining deft action and nifty characterization with singularly appropriate city backgrounds.

The director went on to land Weitman a big dividend from his previous work on *The Hill* – Connery for the role of 'Duke' Anderson. Both the star and his agent were relieved at the offer. There were others, but Connery in particular had decided that it would take something very special to tempt him back after his last two misfires. Determined to expand the boundaries of his screen roles, he had even approached director John Schlesinger about playing the lead role of the homosexual Jewish doctor in *Sunday, Bloody Sunday*. It was a perfect example of the distance he was prepared to travel to escape the 'Bond booby' image. Unfortunately for him, Peter Finch had already been cast. And with Roman Polanski preparing a rival version of *Macbeth*, Connery had been forced to abandon, temporarily at least, his idea of filming Shakespeare's 'Scottish' play.

Connery was content that in *The Anderson Tapes* he was working with a director for whom he had great respect, and, of equal importance, on what promised to be a mainstream commercial movie. With the rest of a first-class cast assembled – Dyan Cannon, Martin Balsam, Alan King (an old buddy from his early days on *Operation Shafu*) and Ralph Meeker – and with a script by Frank Pierson, Lumet obtained permission to shoot at Riker's Island, the Port Authority Bus Terminal, and the old Otto Kahn mansion that had been converted to the Convent of the Sacred Heart. With a few strings pulled he was even permitted to close off a section of Fifth Avenue to stage a spectacular seven-car pileup. Pyrotechnics and authenticity apart, Lumet was as elated as Connery at their reunion. The actor, he enthused, was 'one of the great naturals'.

'Why is *The Anderson Tapes* less than successful?' asked Tony Palmer in Britain's *Spectator*, before going on to provide his own shock answer: '*Sean Connery*. The double infatuation with being a movie star and being James Bond has sapped Connery's power as an actor both in terms of his plausibility and his technique ... More movies are not the answer. Five years in rep is.'

Elsewhere Connery's performance was variously praised as 'laconic, attractive, beautifully subdued', and condemned as 'no replacement for the cold, complex Kentuckian Sanders created'. Overall *The Anderson Tapes* was judged a disappointment, 'rather slow moving', although 'To Lumet's credit ... about threequarters of the way through ... the suspense gathers and races on to a smashing conclusion'.

Despite the mixed notices, the combined efforts of Weitman, Lumet and Connery resulted in the star's most successful post-Bond outing to date, netting $5 million in the US – hardly phenomenal Bond-type business, but far from a flop either. There was a bonus both for Connery's Educational Trust and for the Saints and Sinners Club with his insistence on a Scottish European Charity première for the movie, held at Glasgow's Odeon Cinema in October 1971.

Connery and the actors he had recruited to make the event an all-star gala found themselves eerily involved in an episode that would not have been out of place in a Bond movie. A delay of an hour in their British Caledonia flight from London's Gatwick airport to Glasgow followed a bomb scare and shooting threats made against Connery, comedian Ronnie Corbett and Stanley Baker. Corbett's agent received a call threatening to shoot both him and Connery, claiming that Connery was giving money to Roman Catholics in Belfast to fight Protestants. Corbett was involved because 'he was supporting' Connery. Baker received a similar call.

Every one of the ninety passengers on board the aircraft was asked to identify their luggage, and was thoroughly searched in a stringent security check by police and aircraft staff. The police presence at the Odeon in Glasgow was also reinforced. 'The whole thing is ridiculous,' said Connery, once the event had passed without incident, 'because I am neither political nor religious.'

'There are three actresses in the world who would be great for Tiffany O'Case,' director Guy Hamilton told 'Cubby' Broccoli one night as they discussed casting for *Diamonds Are Forever*. One by one he began to tick them off. 'Faye Dunaway, Jane Fonda ...'

'You'll have to think hard for the third,' Broccoli butted in. 'Anyway, they cost too much. Let's stop kidding ourselves. What about Raquel Welch?'

'No way,' Hamilton replied, frowning. 'There would be no chemistry between her and Bond.'

'How about Jill St John?'

Hamilton agreed to test St John, the former Mrs Lance Reventlow, an unusual combination of actress, heiress and playgirl best known for her oft-quoted remark, 'The longest period of celibacy for Jill St John is the shortest distance between two lovers.' 'With Connery she'd be perfect,' Hamilton lamented as the test footage was reviewed. 'But we haven't got Connery . . .'

Saltzman and Broccoli had indeed assembled everything they needed for their new Bond, except for the star they wanted. With *On Her Majesty's Secret Service*, George Lazenby had ingratiated himself with neither his producers nor his leading lady, although arguably he had not gone down too badly with the paying public. If the film had been a mammoth hit Broccoli and Saltzman would have been prepared to forgive his on-set behaviour, but with a moderate Bond net, of $9 million, they decided to look elsewhere. Overlooked in the all-round bitterness was the competence with which Lazenby had filled the role, as well as his movie's distinct change of tone, veering away from reliance on special effects and concentrating for once on the human dimensions of the leading characters. Many felt, paradoxically, that this was the angle that had kept receipts low – and not Lazenby at all. Touching moments and a tender love story were not, it seemed, what Bond fans craved.

Was it possible, Broccoli, Saltzman and Hamilton pondered, that they could tempt Connery back, despite his many protestations that Bond was behind him? Was it all down to the size of the purse? The producers dismissed the dread thought that perhaps it was Bond himself the public was getting bored with, regardless of who played him, even though the point was strengthened by the drop in sales of Fleming's books, as well as the dip in takings, with Connery on board, that they had suffered with *You Only Live Twice*. There was, after all, now a host of competition with whom Bond had to contend – Dean Martin's Matt Helm (produced by Irving Allen, 'Cubby' Broccoli's old partner at Warwick), James Coburn's Flint, David McCallum's Ilya Kuryakin in *Man from UNCLE*, not to mention Caine's Saltzman-produced Harry Palmer.

David Picker, by now president of United Artists, decided to take matters into his own hands. The studio was in deep trouble; another Bond smash would ease the pain considerably. Picker engineered a meeting with Connery at Richard Hatton's offices, at which he intended to deliver 'an offer that clearly would be irresistible. The fattest deal any actor ever had in the history of the movies.' $1.25 million in cash plus 10 per cent of the gross was the final figure negotiated, together with $145,000 a week if the movie ran over its sixteen-week schedule. Plus a helicopter flight to the nearest golf course on Connery's one day off each week! Then there was promised development cash and backing for two non-Bonds of Connery's choosing, one of which he could direct. The deal was clinched barely a week before the cameras were set to roll in February 1971. John Gavin, the alternative Bond Broccoli and Saltzman had kept waiting in the wings, was quietly paid off.

Connery's announcement that he would donate the bulk of the cash advance to the Scottish International Educational Trust came as a stunning surprise. While everyone understood the tax break he would probably receive in return, this did nothing to lessen the magnitude of the gesture to the land of his birth. He maintained that he had only agreed to return to Bond so that the Trust, now considered underfunded for all that he wanted it to achieve, would benefit. 'I'm not such an idiot as to forget the money and fame Bond brought me,' he declared. 'It may look like it at times, but I'm not really the kind of man to spend the rest of his life solely on the golf course and in bars. My sort of upbringing gave me the urge to be useful and to contribute what I can. I've been lucky to do a lot of the taking. I'd have been a fool to have turned down that kind of money, particularly after I'd thought of a way to do some good with it ... With a start like that the school has a very good chance. There's no excuse for it not to work.'

'Las Vegas,' declared Harry Saltzman, with a broad grin as he dispensed nickels into a slot machine from a paper cup, 'has to be the spiritual home of film producers everywhere.' Fully recovered from his recent stroke, and pausing only for a brief massage in the Riviera Hotel's health club, 'Cubby' Broccoli returned to the craps table to reinforce his already legendary reputation as a highroller. Michael Caine wryly viewed their partnership as 'good cop, bad cop': 'Cubby gives you the cigarette and Harry knocks it out of your mouth.'

Connery's arrival in town galvanized the production, not least because of the costly overtime payments he would collect if the schedule slipped. '*Diamonds are Forever* is really just another strip cartoon for adults,' he asserted, 'which is why I've never really understood the idea of Bond as a vicious, sadistic killer. There are too many laughs for that. As for myself, I know the image people still have of me – a fellow devoid of intellectual capacity, boorish and aggressive. I reckon I'm a man with a few faults and a few virtues. Among the latter are a sense of the ridiculous, a sense of morality and a sense of the value of money. Among the faults you can count egotism, bad temper, and a little vanity perhaps, seeing that I'm an actor.'

Asked how it felt to be back in business with Saltzman, he shrugged and conceded that he was 'a very clever man in his own way' before delivering the sting in the tail: 'He is powerful because he is wealthy. He is in a strong position, but he makes a big mistake. He presumes people will move the way he would move, jump the way he would jump. That's the trip of all time. Harry will *never* understand me, not as long as he has a hole in his hat. But I understand *him*. I understand him a *lot*.'

With filming completed in Las Vegas the unit moved briefly to Palm Springs, Los Angeles, an off-shore oil rig in the Pacific Ocean, then Germany, France, Holland and Britain, where four stages at Pinewood were taken over. The P & O luxury liner *Canberra* was even shipped out from Southampton dry dock after a quick wash and brush up to feature in the end-title sequence. Obviously bearing Connery's hefty penalty clause in mind, the unit still managed to finish on time. 'It can be done, you see, if there's money at stake,' he pointed out. 'I've been frigged about too much in other Bond pictures. There's so much bullshit that comes from bad decisions being made at the top. I admire efficiency, like watching a good racehorse or the way Picasso works, where everything functions perfectly within its capacity. But talking to some of these moguls about it is like trying to describe to someone who has never taken exercise what it is like to feel fit when you do exercise. They don't understand. Saltzman and Broccoli are not exactly enamoured of each other. Probably because they're both sitting on fifty million dollars or pounds and looking across the desk at each other and thinking: 'That bugger's got half of what should all be mine!'

Ordering a Perrier water after a heavy night's drinking, and with the movie's winter 1971 première only days away, Connery relaxed in a restaurant and watched dyspeptically as writer and critic Kenneth Tynan passed by his table. 'K-k-Kenneth f-f-fucking T-t-Tynan,' he mocked. 'Spends his life criticizing plays from a position of lofty principle and then dives into a show like *Oh! Calcutta!* which isn't half so well presented as Raymond's Revuebar – where I was the other night, even though the Revuebar champagne is so bloody pricey. I'll give Tynan one thing though: I was once at a party he attended and there was this fight between two men over a girl. He helped separate the men and do you know what he said? "Stop behaving like people." He must have been waiting all his life for a situation where he could make a remark like that!' It took all of a dozen oysters before Connery's bile had subsided.

Connery has never tried to disguise his contempt for the Royal Academy of Dramatic Art's voice and house-style. He hates the 'poetry voice' adopted by many thespians, believing that the inherent poetry in the language should be allowed to speak for itself. Because he is Scottish he stresses certain words differently; the Scots say: 'How are *you*?' The English say: 'How *are* you?' He maintains that the Scottishness of the word-stress enabled him to add extra depth to the character of Bond, removing the sting from many of the bad taste jokes he was asked to repeat. 'Poor Lazenby couldn't do that,' he asserted, 'because he just didn't have the experience, even though director Peter Hunt was quoted as saying that he had taught Lazenby all I knew. In three months Lazenby couldn't do a good job because you have to have technique to get the character right. I know he behaved like a prize shit, alienating people from what they tell me – I've never met him – but it wasn't all his fault.'

He reserved his true admiration for fine performers ranging from actors like Sir Ralph Richardson – 'because an audience is never safe with him, you don't know what he's going to do next' – to Scottish comedians. 'People I love like Jimmy Logan just don't seem to travel,' he lamented, 'or if they do, like Andy Stewart, they lose something of their identity. Chic Murray—' his eyes lit up '—now *there*'s a great comedian, the way he can play with words so surrealistically: "I was walking out of the house the other day, putting my left foot in front of my right because that's the best way to walk. I saw my auntie and said, 'Hello, dear!' I always call her dear because she's got antlers!"'

Connery revealed a surprising choice of favourite director in Ingmar Bergman: 'I find I sit through his films absolutely unaware of time. Anybody who can do that for me must have something.'

Like *The Anderson Tapes* before it, Connery insisted on a Scottish European première for *Diamonds are Forever* – free this time of bomb threats, and in Edinburgh's Odeon, with all proceeds going to the SIET to further swell his personal, eventual $1 million contribution. (The SIET first had to be registered as a charity before the cash could be handed over tax free.)

Despite being ill with a virus infection, Connery appeared on stage for fully twenty minutes, welcoming the audience, presenting prizes in a draw and introducing sportsmen Jackie Stewart, Ken Buchanan and Tommy Docherty, the Scottish football manager. 'I won't do another Bond, not even for another million,' he privately vowed after the show. 'If the Trust can't establish itself with all the money already pumped into it, it will have to go under.'

Chapter 17

'On the Bond films I gave my pound of flesh on the set and didn't see why I should be expected to give up my evenings too. What everyone forgets was that whereas an interviewer might have not asked a particular question before, I'd heard it a thousand times. So one had to say "No", or one would have ended up more mentally deranged than one is already.'

Sean Connery

'No film you could do, no matter how good it was, could compete with the new James Bond.'

Sean Connery

Neil Connery, a qualified plasterer with a five-year apprenticeship behind him, met his wife Eleanor in the same Fountainbridge Palais where his brother had once worked as a part-time bouncer. After settling into a council house in Clermiston, a working-class suburb of Edinburgh, the couple were blessed with two daughters, Martine and Leone.

Neil's 'acting' career began in 1967 when his plasterer's tools went missing and his employers sacked him. With the matter referred to the local trade union the affair made the newspapers and caught the eye of an opportunistic Italian film producer who saw a chance to cash in on the Connery name. 007 had a *kid brother*?! A bemused Neil received a telegram first from Dario Sabatello, rapidly followed by a personal visit. A script was soon cooked up which had Neil playing 'a brilliant young plastic surgeon and kid brother of a famous secret British agent' enlisted to defeat the evil forces threatening to blackmail the world.

A concerned Sean Connery appealed to Sabatello not to proceed with the movie. 'By getting my brother to make this kind of picture,' he told him, 'you are exploiting us both.' Sabatello ignored Connery's pleas and went on to snare what was virtually a casting-call of past and present Bond players. There was *Goldfinger*'s Daniela Bianchi, *Thunderball*'s Adolfo Celi, *Dr No*'s Anthony Dawson, as well as Bernard Lee's M and Lois Maxwell's Miss Moneypenny, both playing suspiciously similar roles to their Bond counterparts.

'Sean was only trying to protect me,' his brother told reporters anxious to report a split. 'As brothers we are close and always will be. The feud isn't between us. Sean is not so much worried about what has happened to me as the way in which it has happened.' During the movie's shooting he added, 'You may think I'm trying to cash in on my brother's name, but I can tell you he's sick to death of playing James Bond.' This there was certainly no denying.

Director Alberto de Martino spent twelve weeks putting his cast through their paces for what became *Operation Kid Brother*. It was presented to a waiting world – courtesy of United Artists, anxious in case they missed out on a good thing – in March 1968. Although UA's campaign headline was 'Too Much for One Mother!' their courage failed them before the opening. Wisely, as it turned out, they decided against a press showing. The few critics and customers who did bother to check out *Operation Kid Brother* were rewarded with a violent, noisy, humourless farrago with a hopelessly wooden lead in the totally inexperienced Neil. The movie was chock full of amorous females breathing lines like, 'Your brother was never like this!' *Monthly Film Bulletin* summed up the whole affair as 'a grotesque parody of a parody ... Bad enough to be hysterically funny.'

'It was a dreadful movie,' Lois Maxwell agreed, 'but we [Bernard Lee and I] needed the money. We really weren't paid much for our roles in Bond.' (Maxwell had been awarded just £100 a day for *Dr No* and *From Russia with Love*, with only a two-day guarantee on each movie. And she had to supply her own clothes. Only after *Thunderball* had Eon agreed to provide her wardrobe.)

For both Maxwell and Lee the penalty for accepting their roles in *Operation Kid Brother* was to fall foul of Connery. 'Sean was livid that we were in it,' Maxwell recalled, 'but I think he forgave me finally because I helped his brother handle the Italian press, who were trying to build up a story about a family feud.'

When the movie disappeared without trace Sabatello decided against exercising the option he had secured on Neil's services for seven more movies; Connery's brother had precisely £5,000 to show for his efforts. Although he had returned to plastering before the film opened, the bug had bitten. A spot as 'guest star' in a British cheapie, *The Body Stealers*, was all he was offered as a follow-up, despite letters and photos he sent to producers all over the world. In Neil's version he was turned down for looking too much like his brother. In 1970 he rejected the offer of a TV commercial, plaintively explaining, 'I feel that would be a backward step. I was a *star*, after all.' In the same year someone suggested he should ask his brother to help. 'I would not ask him for a job,' Neil replied. 'Anyway, I think he is more interested in golf than films.' Later he added, in case anyone misunderstood, 'Sean is a great-hearted chap, but I've made it clear to him that I want to be on my own in my acting ambitions.'

His elder brother summed up the situation in typically unsentimental fashion to journalist William McIlvanney in 1970: 'Neil should either shit or get off the pot.'

*

In 1971 Joseph Connery, sixty-eight years old and happily retired for eight years, was given the all-clear by his doctor following a series of tests. A year later his sons were shown their father's latest X-rays – with cancer clearly indicated. Although cobalt treatment was suggested, there was no hope of a recovery. Joe's death in March 1972, relayed in a phone call from Neil, came as a shattering blow.

On his return to Scotland to pick his way through the funeral arrangements, Connery found it difficult to cope. Apart from organizing the burial, there was the death to be registered, a minister to be obtained, and all of the essential details that neither of the brothers had been required to tackle before. He was reminded in his grief of the Masai tribe's belief, 'You're not a man until your father dies.' If that was true, Connery reflected, it was a stiff price to pay for adulthood.

A social conscience, determination to stretch himself as an actor, regret at the irreconcilable differences that had bedevilled his marriage and made his impending divorce inevitable, together with concern for his children's future, all swirled round in the powerful mixture of emotions that beset Connery. The knowledge that he was fortunate in being largely able to sublimate his temper and violence in acting made him question the origin of the pentup rage. Exposure to the outside world had made him aware of what he referred to as 'the unfairness of it all' in his childhood; he still remained uncertain that this was the anger's only source.

He became more and more interested in what would happen to him if he removed the 'safety net': How would it change him? What would it make him? One of the reasons he had gone ahead with the Trust was his desire to avoid the traps, as well as divest himself of the trappings of wealth. With *Diamonds Are Forever* he hoped that had written 'finis' to that part of his life and bought essential breathing space. It was time now to re-examine his priorities afresh and decide what he wanted to withdraw from, what he wanted to reach for – what he really *needed*.

He had his eye firmly fixed on a new horizon in which Micheline Roquebrune loomed large – if friends again read between the lines, that is. 'I don't seem to have the equipment for marriage in terms of the contract that exists today,' he agonized, 'but I'd like more children. And of course I'd want them to be born to a woman who'd bring them up properly. But who knows what will happen? The only difference in my attitude to women today is that now I make my position quite clear from the start. In the past I used to get involved and just let events take their course. I used to fall into the trap of believing that because you thought something regarding the woman it was just like saying it. But it isn't, is it? Where women are concerned you've got to *say* it.'

John Hopkins' work was familiar to Connery through the long-running BBC-TV series *Z Cars*, as well as from his rewrites on *Thunderball*. His play, *This Story of Yours*, in which Connery had turned down the chance to play the lead, had subsequently enjoyed a brief run at London's Royal Court Theatre in December 1968. It was deemed too harrowing for a West End transfer, as well as too stagey for filming when first pitched, but Connery found himself in a position to ease its transfer to film as a result of his two-picture deal with United Artists. His own Tantallon Films – in partnership with Richard Hatton (Connery's agent had decided to move out of representation and into production) and Stanley Sopel (ex-Eon) – would be responsible for its delivery, with United Artists merely supplying the cash and providing distribution.

Connery's third partner in Tantallon was executive producer Denis O'Dell, a blunt, craggy Irishman who had run away from home to join the film industry, starting with George Minter's Renown Pictures in London's Wardour Street. There he had rapidly progressed from tea boy to producer, later helping to put together the Apple organization for The Beatles, produce *A Hard Day's Night*, *Magical Mystery Tour* and *Let It Be* with the group, then *The Magic Christian* with Ringo Starr during his chairmanship of Commonwealth United Entertainment. That he had also worked with Sidney Lumet along the way, on *The Deadly Affair*, made the redoubtable director a logical first choice for Tantallon's first venture.

Connery's role in *This Story of Yours* – which underwent rapid title changes, first to *Something Like The Truth*, finally to *The Offence* – was that of tough, uncompromising, working-class Detective Sergeant Johnson, who kills suspected child molester Baxter (Ian Bannen) while questioning him. When his conduct is investigated, deep-seated problems of his own are revealed. The cast was completed by Trevor Howard and Vivien Merchant as Maureen, Johnson's long-suffering wife. 'Some people may detest his character, others may feel compassionate towards him,' Connery felt. 'The British have always been so anti-analysis in every sense of the word, but this film goes into analysis of why the detective became what he is. It's painful. I'll be interested to see how the public takes it.'

In his usual fashion Lumet organized ten days of rehearsals for the cast. Night locations and a tough schedule of twenty-eight days followed at Twickenham Studios, where set designer John Clark had constructed a London police headquarters that one reporter saw as resembling a legal version of Jean-Luc Godard's *Alphaville*. As far as Connery was concerned a much more endearing fixture at Twickenham was the presence of Micheline Roquebrune.

'We'll make it for under a million dollars, because Sidney's that kind of efficient director,' Connery boasted in mid-production, 'and the people who make the most sacrifices will make the most money ... Like me and (Tantallon's) directors!' As he spoke playwright Hopkins popped his head round the door on his way to see John Gielgud on stage in the West End play *Veterans*. 'Give J.G. a Swiss kiss for me,' Connery shouted, adding with a twinkle, 'If he doesn't know what it is, tell him it's the same as a French one, only with a yodel.'

'It's funny when people talk about stars,' Denis O'Dell mused between shots. 'I never really think of Sean as the biggest box-office star. I find him a totally absorbing actor. He's working a fourteen-hour day on this picture, or it seems like it. He's an absolutely marvellous man. Sean has a great brain and he cares about humanity in a funny way. He's interested in all sorts of things like industrial relations and the Trust he's set up. At Tantallon meetings, if it's getting out of hand he's the one who always pulls it together.'

'Sean is a wonderful actor,' Lumet declared, 'yet even after *The Hill*, so underestimated. He doesn't even get the credit he deserves for Bond. I see the performance as being in the Cary Grant bracket, a first-rate high comedy performance. It involves very complex acting and as soon as you've got a good actor that's half the battle won.'

After the director had shepherded *The Offence* to completion – urged on by Connery, $80,000 under budget – the star had a busy 1972, both sorting out his business life and laying the foundations for his personal future. He read scripts and oversaw the day-to-day workings of the Education Trust. Admission to the venerable Royal and Ancient Golf Club led to his partnering Sir Iain Stewart through to the final round of the Calcutta Cup in St Andrew's before suffering a last-minute defeat. In October he attended a Pro-Am tournament at La Manga in Spain, with Micheline again by his side, before the couple spent an idyllic Christmas together. His return to Britain in the New Year coincided with the opening of *The Offence*.

Although both Connery and Lumet blamed United Artists for the movie's quick box-office demise – Lumet vowing never again to speak to UA company president David Picker, who had served as his best man – the reviews in the main hardly constituted a reason to seek it out. While Connery's personal notices were good – 'He's superb,' said Ann Guarino in the *New York Daily News* – the film was widely slated. According to Francis Herridge: 'It tells the story of a detective who falls apart on his job. The film itself falls apart a lot sooner. With Sidney Lumet in charge of direction and a fine cast headed by Sean Connery, one would expect more. But the plot is a hopeless mire.' Even Connery, it later transpired, harboured a few reservations. 'Sidney made a fantastic job of it,' he declared, 'but I think he got a bit European on us.'

The second film of Connery's two-picture 'anything you want to do' contract with United Artists was never made, despite several tentative developments. John Hopkins was commissioned to write a screenplay based on explorer Sir Richard Burton's life. An idea of Germaine Greer's to capture the travails of Australian Aborigines on film, was turned down by Connery with the rationale: 'I feel the Aborigines have been there thousands of years before us and seemed to have survived – so let them get on with it!' He continued to hold what he saw as his own 'revolutionary' screenplay of *Macbeth* in reserve until he saw how Polanski's version turned out.

Now considered a wealthy man, Connery was asked if he might ever consider giving up acting. 'No, I don't see that happening,' he replied. 'I like the life and I get pretty bored if I'm not working, although I suppose if I could stay on a golf course forever I'd be happy enough. In any case I've no real idea how I'll feel or what I'll be doing even five years from now. I'm eternally concerned with the present.' He ruefully recalled promising himself repeatedly during the 1960s that he would only undertake projects in future that really excited him. They did not turn up every day of the week, he now realized.

Chapter 18

'The early Bond films had such a phenomenal success that, with the exception of *The Hill*, anything else I did counted for nothing. I began to get very tired of being pestered and stared at, I kept being reminded of the Chinese story about the King who was stared to death. Fame turns one from an actor and a human being into a piece of merchandise, a public institution. I wanted to get back to a bit of privacy, to experiment with some other ways of being an actor.'

Sean Connery

In its early days the Education Trust had received mixed reviews from its co-founders. 'We have the funds,' Connery had pointed out, 'but can't find enough young people to whom we can give the cash. The trouble still in Scotland is that a lot of people think there is a catch. The thought of getting something for nothing, or a helping hand when it is most needed, still seems to throw people. I only wish an outfit like the Trust had existed when I had to take a bit part in South Pacific to get into show business.'

Three years later – with the Trust finally registered as a charity, enabling Connery to pass on the $1 million from

Diamonds Are Forever tax free – he was able to report that £180,000 in grants had been awarded. The projects had ranged from the University of Strathclyde's 'drama chair', worth £15,000 over three years, to £3,000 given to a young musician to purchase a harpsichord. He clearly took pride in the Trust dispensing cash to projects other than the highbrow, and was particularly exhilarated in the funding of two Scottish lads who intended to traverse America on a tandem bicycle.

'Having the name of Scotland plastered across America is what a lot of it is about,' he asserted. 'In bringing talented young people to the fore, the Trust will go a long way towards improving Scotland's lot. For example, 23 successful nominees will, in turn, engender another 50 or 75 with their talent in the long run. It will become a progressive thing, involving all skills from the arts to industry and technology. Our problem right now is overcoming this typical Scottish attitude to hang back and let the other fellow do it instead. Scotland is a nation of movers and stayers. And sometimes it is the devil's own job to get the twain to meet. The problem is getting beyond the rigid mind and petty provincialism before you can do anything.'

Despite the critical trouncing and dearth of business for *The Offence*, Connery determinedly set off on a European promotion tour in spring 1973 in a vain attempt to boost the film's fortunes. In March he journeyed to Nairobi for the Kenya Open Golf Championship.

Try as he might, Connery was unable to come up with a second personal project to follow *The Offence*. *Macbeth* was now indefinitely postponed – Polanski's version having turned out all too well – and the eventual screenplay by John Hopkins on the life of Sir Richard Burton proved impossible to mount on United Artists' frugal $1 million limit. In *The Offence* Tantallon had made its first and last film.

By the time Connery had made his Bond breakthrough, Carol Sopel's first *South Pacific* suitor – before Connery swept her

off her feet – had become a top agent with Creative Management Associates (CMA), later to merge with International
Creative Management (ICM). Known throughout 'the business' as 'The Silver Fox' on account of his premature greying,
Dennis Selinger wielded his considerable clout wisely and
well. His philosophy was simple: 'I would never take on
anybody I did not like, or anybody I found too awkward. A
relationship between a client and an agent only works if you
like each other and admire each other's talents. That way you
have total trust in each other. There's no way I would handle
somebody who does not trust my judgement.'

Renowned for his skilful handling of Peter Sellers, his most
recent success had been with Michael Caine, all the way from
subsidizing him in a play in which he was spotted by Stanley
Baker and cast in *Zulu* – to playing Harry Palmer and *Alfie*,
then on to Hollywood.

One night in 1972, while Selinger was playing gin rummy
with Kenneth Hyman, producer of *The Hill* and by now head
of Warner Bros in Britain, Connery popped in with a question
for the executive. A few days later he phoned Selinger himself
to request a formal meeting. At this he came quickly to the
point: 'I want you to represent me.'

'What happened to Richard?' was Selinger's first question.

'He's leaving the agency,' Connery replied. 'He wants to be
a producer.'

Over coffee and drinks Selinger levelled with his client-
to-be: 'Sean, your main problem is that you've made an awful
lot of money out of Bond and since then you don't seem to be
very interested in working. In the last three years you've made
two or three pretty bad movies. Because of that you're going
to find it very difficult to get the good parts. All you will be
offered are Bond lookalikes – which you shouldn't do. We
won't get over this problem unless you make up your mind to
get back to work.'

'So what are you saying?'

'Well, you should do what Mike Caine did. You make three
or four pictures a year. If two bomb out, one of them has got

a chance of making it. It's hard work, but once you get back in, then you can pick and choose.'

While Selinger's system would click in the end, for a while it was touch and go. A script sent to Connery's embankment flat by director John Boorman would provide a rocky start for the brand-new 'launch'. Hot from his triumph in *Deliverance*, Boorman had at first tried to set up a version of Tolkien's *Lord of the Rings*. United Artists, the studio holding the rights, pleaded poverty, claiming that they lacked resources at the time for such a major production. Tolkien, with whom Boorman was in contact, informed him that he had a nightmare of his work being turned into a cartoon – which did eventually happen, in Ralph Bakshi's version. Perhaps mercifully, Tolkien never lived to see it.

Forced to come up with something else, Boorman began to develop a script of his own. *Zardoz* described a techno-commune in the year 2293 whose members, the Eternals, have discovered the secret of immortality. Even with Burt Reynolds committed to his science-fiction fable, Boorman encountered a multitude of problems in raising the budget required, his description of the movie – 'it's about immortality being a fairy-tale' – unsurprisingly counting for little in high-concept Hollywood. After both Warner Bros and Columbia had passed, he gratefully accepted the shoestring support offered by 20th Century-Fox of $1 million. This included no personal fee upfront, but gave him carte blanche to make the movie he wanted without studio approval.

When Reynolds, pleading a ruptured hernia, was forced to withdraw only weeks before filming was due to start, Boorman contacted Connery on a golf course in Spain and briefly described *Zardoz* and the lead role of Zed, mysterious invader of the Eternals' haven. Connery explained that he would be back in London at the weekend; if Boorman could get the script to his flat in Chelsea he would read it quickly and get back to him. The script was duly delivered and read by Connery that Sunday night.

Within two days the deal was clinched, Boorman recalling

their rendezvous, with Micheline standing by, in Connery's distinctly ornate flat. Among the impressive oil paintings, some of which were Micheline's own work, was dotted a weird collection of life-sized statues, one of which struck Boorman as particularly strange. Even stranger was when the emaciated scarecrow figure actually moved, revealing itself to be Connery's *Fine Madness* director, Irvin Kershner. Boorman knew 'Kersh', but had failed to recognize him. The element of surrealism that accompanied the meeting was not entirely inappropriate to their central purpose; Boorman had his 'Zed'.

The director soon discovered Connery was one actor who looked at a script for its total effect, rather than just for his own part. Although the screenplay was in its final draft, several discussions took place with Connery during the subsequent weeks he spent at Boorman's home in County Wicklow, Ireland. After his snap decision to come on board, the star was enormously relieved to find that he and Boorman were on the same wavelength. He felt that *Zardoz* was the most original script he had encountered for a long while, with a sense of mythology about it that held enormous appeal for the Celtic side of his sensibility. 'It seems to say that nature has a potency and you can't screw around with it too much,' he enthused.

Apart from the creative aspect, Boorman found Connery to be a marvellous house guest in the weeks prior to filming, with script discussions, rehearsals and costume fittings the main order of the day. When work was over Connery would make straight for the local golf course, or disappear quietly into his room to write poetry – which he adamantly refused to show anyone. At dinner, although he loved his food, wine and whisky, Boorman never saw his guest the worse for drink, no matter how much alcohol he consumed.

Several days after his arrival, Connery indicated to Boorman that he must be allowed to pay his way. When his director demurred, Connery insisted, and from then on ceremoniously handed Boorman's wife Christine a sealed envelope each week containing – the princely sum of £7! 'It probably harked back to what he'd paid for his digs back in the Fifties,' says

Boorman with a chuckle. 'Now it didn't even cover his whisky, let alone anything else! It was so sweet, really.' Equally endearing was Connery's habit of patrolling the household each night switching off the lights, and turning the thermostat down.

Boorman found his guest willing and eager to talk about his childhood days in Edinburgh. On a recent visit home, Connery recalled, a woman he met in the street had reminded him that they had known each other when they were young. Just looking at her had brought a long-forgotten memory rushing back. Her house had been on his round of newspaper deliveries and when she had invited him to her birthday party her mother had turned him away on the doorstep, declaring, 'You're the boy who delivers our papers. Go away with you!'

'He has this astonishing photographic memory,' says Boorman, 'although I think he has difficulty in learning lines, he has to work at it. But his memory of his childhood is amazing – he remembers all the names of his friends, the numbers of their houses, everything.'

As filming began Connery, like the rest of the cast, prepared to move into a local hotel, where Boorman had arranged for discounted room rates. With Micheline arriving to join him, Boorman was amused to hear that Connery had negotiated the rate down even further.

Ten weeks were spent at Bray Studios and on location in County Wicklow, with cast members Charlotte Rampling, Sara Kestleman and John Alderton. To Connery it was 'a crazy time', spent running round the Wicklow mountains in Arctic conditions, clad in nothing but thigh-high red boots, bandoliers and 'a red nappy', and covered in mud that was actually cement dust and earth that stuck to his chest hair and was agony to remove. The unit had so little money that the Irish extras in the background had their legs painted red instead of boots and their Y-fronts dyed the same colour to match.

'Sean was very sensitive about his skin and with his makeup,' Boorman recalls, 'but apart from that he was great. He'll have a moan, but he'll do his job and doesn't mind roughing it at all. He's so courageous as an actor, so sure of his sexual identity, that he'll take risks that are quite daring for an actor. He's very imaginative and has a wonderful idea of fantasy. His whole feminine side, in fact, is highly developed. He loved this world we were creating and brought reality to it.'

In between takes Connery constantly dispensed solid advice to everyone. 'He was a great support,' says Boorman. 'He's a natural producer and liked everything to be organized. He's a terrific organizer himself and can't bear to see things in a mess.' Creative ways to conserve Boorman's budget were assiduously explored. 'My contract calls for a car and a chauffeur, yes?' he asked his director one day. Boorman nodded. 'What's that costing you? *Really*? I'll tell you what I'll do. I'll drive myself around and split the difference with you.' Boorman agreed, glad of any extra money he could devote to the movie itself. He sees Connery's Irish romanticism as forever at odds with his Scottish frugality: 'He's wildly, impulsively generous in big things, and very cautious about small sums. He's the only friend of mine I'd go to if I was in trouble – say for £100,000.'

Connery brought his mother over to stay during filming. Effie had never travelled abroad before, but had expressed the wish to visit Ireland, the land of her late husband's forebears. Boorman found himself introduced to a large-boned, taciturn lady, who was treated by her son with extraordinary gentleness and deference. Boorman's second encounter with Micheline reinforced his original impression of the contrast between her and Connery, as well as their similarities: 'She's so tiny and he's so large. She's very fiery, a very good artist and a talented all-round woman with tremendous zest and vitality. She's also very shrewd about looking after money.'

When Boorman and Connery played games together, the star displayed an incredible will to win. 'He beat me at tennis several times, and I'm a much better player than him,' said Boorman, 'but he psyched me up so badly! Then we had a snooker tournament during filming. John Alderton was very keen, had his own table, was a very good player, and he and

Sean ended up in the final in a hotel in Bray. There we were, all of us waiting for Sean, and suddenly he appears in full professional gear, waistcoat, bow tie, chalk in his pocket, cue in hand, the *works*! I took one look at John's face and knew he was defeated! Later I beat Sean at snooker playing at Tom Stoppard's – for money, because that's the way he likes it. We got down to where I needed two snookers and the black at the end, and he had me really cornered and said he'd give me 50–10 on this. I got the two snookers and the black and took the £50 off him. He could hardly bear to speak for the rest of the evening. It really hurt.'

The final scene in *Zardoz* called for Connery and Rampling to age rapidly. After hours spent in makeup, with both stars displaying remarkable patience, the scene needed to be re-shot when the film stock turned out to be faulty. The extensive makeup process had again to be endured, rather less patiently this time. After the sequence had been re-shot, a studio trainee accidentally exposed the film, leaving Boorman to explain haltingly why further hours of cosmetic work were necessary. Connery exploded in a manner his director found hilariously frightening. 'If I get my hands on him,' he swore, 'I'll break his fucking neck!' For days afterwards the lad concerned did all he could to avoid crossing Connery's path.

A brief sojourn in Spain followed the end of the *Zardoz* shoot. With Micheline left behind to oversee a beach villa being specially built near Marbella, Connery returned to London and placed his Embankment flat on the market. He explained his decision to sell as 'a pollution thing. After spending all these weeks in Ireland and then being in Spain, London seemed pretty ropey . . . all those car exhausts spewing out muck.' The decision to move abroad, it seemed, was absolutely irrevocable – as was the next, and final chapter of his life with Cilento.

Chapter 19

'When I took him on Sean was only saleable in the wrong
things. What I did to make him bankable again wasn't
brilliant, but it did work.'

Dennis Selinger

Following two years of separation, Connery sued his wife for
divorce. The hearing, at London's Divorce Court in October
1973, brought to an end not only their eleven-year marriage,
but also what many saw as an often destructive career race.
Connery's counsel, Jeremy Tatham, informed Judge
Braithwaite that the couple not only wished for a civilized end
to the marriage, but that they wished to terminate the financial
litigation between them forever. That had been achieved,
Tatham maintained, by capital sums which they preferred not
be spelled out in open court, the first payable to Cilento in full
and final settlement of all her claims; the second put in setting
up a trust for Jason and Gigi.

A decree nisi was duly granted, with Cilento gaining custody
of the children, with reasonable access for Connery, who was
in no mood for any prying questions from reporters after the
hearing. 'I have no comment to make about my private life,' he

snapped. 'As from this day nothing of my private life will ever be divulged to the press. I do not have a particularly good relationship with the press, partly because I do not have a press agent. To simplify matters I am keeping my private life private, which I tried to do in the past without much success.'

A few years passed before Connery relented, just a little, conceding that while their conflicting careers and pressure of fame hadn't helped, they had not been the sole cause of the breakup. 'Love is a matter between two people,' was his final word. Cilento later linked the Bond phenomenon directly with their stormy married life. 'The whole damn thing took over. He really didn't know who he was. People would call over to him things like, "Hey, Bondy, where're you off to next?" or, "Seen any Soviet agents lately?" It became impossible to have any sort of life . . . It got madder and madder with each film. It was a time of huge loves and huge hates. It was the equivalent of going into the fire as a piece of dough. You either come out perfect, as beautifully baked bread, or you are incinerated.'

She went on to offer another, rather more deep-seated reason for the breakup: 'The Scots don't like their wives to work. I virtually gave up my acting career and turned to writing novels. Which was *also* frowned upon!'

After briefly dabbling in a tarot card business that foundered, Cilento decided to give community living a spin, and purchased a derelict farm in Wiltshire. Dubbed 'The College of Continuous Education', it provided a convenient retreat for a variety of hippie types, as well as Roddy Llewellyn when his friendship with Princess Margaret became public in 1976.

She turned up at Cambridge Union on a debating platform with Jonathan Guinness, to oppose his motion, 'Sex liberation has gone too far.' Her argument against any form of sexual constraint was simple – since we know very little about our true sexuality, how can we either permit or deny what we don't understand? She won the day 405 votes to 191.

Following news that her father was ill, Cilento eventually returned to Australia and joined the Queensland Theatre Co. A run-down cane farm bordering the Daintree rainforest was acquired amid predictions that the venture wouldn't last six months. She defiantly named it after the Egyptian temple village of Karnak – the most remarkable religious complex ever built, with 150 acres of temples, columns, chapels and statues – and set about the re-shaping of her life.

Connery's directorship of the Pall Mall bank, Dunbar & Co., was a tremendous source of pride. 'One of the things with having a lot of money is that you have to keep watching it,' he said. 'Being a director I can watch it myself, which I do. Everything I have is deposited here. It isn't easy. Funnily enough, I find I worry much more about small sums than about big amounts. Blood and tears go into parting with £10 on the golf course. Ask any of my friends! But when something like £40,000 is involved, I am much more objective.'

Connery exulted in the image of himself as a businessman/ actor, with prudent investments here, there and everywhere. The illusion was dented with his appointment of a business manager in 1973 to help him 'rationalize', i.e. unravel the situation. 'I reckon if this is at arm's length then perhaps I can get it in some sort of perspective,' he explained. 'It's hopeless having every-thing in one bag – one's emotional life, one's career and one's financial affairs. That way each of them has equal importance, and they're *not* equally important. In no way. And if you have lumped them together in the one bag, they're interwoven. Like a rotten apple, trouble with one means trouble with them all.'

The man Connery entrusted with stewardship of his money was Kenneth Richards, an ex-army major and film production accountant whose first advice to the star was to abandon the bulk of his outside investments. 'It is the easiest thing in the world to start a business empire,' Connery now conceded, 'but it creates a chain reaction of secretaries, minutes, meetings, records of everything, endless correspondence – it just never stops. I found I was a mogul without the structure to support my empire. Every decision had to be mine, and it all became too much. Now I am dropping everything except the Trust and my film interests.'

First to go was the sports and country club he had started with soccer star Bobby Moore and four business friends in sixteenth-century Woolston Hall at Chigwell in Essex. He and Moore retained their share when they resigned as directors; two years later the 'exclusive' club crashed with debts of over half a million pounds, losing both men their entire investments.

Thankfully, Connery also chose to retain the majority of his shares in Dunbar & Co – an extraordinarily fortunate decision in the light of events less than five years later.

While Boorman was busily editing *Zardoz*, Connery followed Dennis Selinger's advice to the letter and plunged into another project. *The Terrorists* was being produced, not entirely coincidentally, by Peter Rawley, an ex-colleague of Selinger's. His role was that of Col. Nils Tahlvik, a security chief in Oslo dealing with political kidnappers. A big attraction was the chance to work with Finnish director Caspar Wrede, whose work Connery had much admired on *One Day in the Life of Ivan Denisovich*, and with Ingmar Bergman's cinematographer Sven Nykvist.

From the start, however, Wrede's disconcertingly pedestrian direction was a source of dismay. Where was the passion that had informed the Solzhenitzyn classic? 'Sold out', one of the crew was heard to mutter. Then problems with weather and catering arose. When the normally reliable northern snows melted ahead of time, truck loads of salt-mix substitute had to be brought in to provide continuity, stretching the budget and elongating the schedule. At one point Connery thunderingly laid down the law about the canteen food, pronouncing it inedible. A threatened withdrawal of his services produced a mysteriously instantaneous improvement.

He returned to London in time for the opening of *Zardoz*, as well as a special gala performance to mark the opening of the Scottish Film Council's £240,000 Glasgow Film Theatre in the shell of the famous old Cosmo art-house cinema. The hopes that both he and Boorman entertained for the success of the movie were largely unfulfilled. While in the main respectful, the British reviews damned the movie with faint praise. Tom Hutchinson in the *Sunday Telegraph* saw *Zardoz* as 'very much a film to be seen, but not necessarily to be believed', crediting Connery with injecting character into a role that might otherwise have been a cypher. Nigel Andrews in the *Financial Times* deemed the plot's confusion as 'unfortunate', since judged purely as a piece of cinema *Zardoz* was 'magnificent'.

Many US critics, on the other hand, detected 'inherent preposterousness'. To Pauline Kael in the *New Yorker* the movie was 'a glittering cultural trash pile ... gloriously fatuous ... Beefy, naked Sean Connery traipses around in a loincloth that looks like a snood.' Andrew Sarris in *Village Voice* commented: 'Connery ... performs with admirable dignity and virility, but in the context of the total casting he resembles King Kong on a rampage through the court of Marie Antoinette.' Jon Landau in *Rolling Stone* saw Boorman's 'stereotyped vision of the future' providing Connery with 'one of the truly thankless roles in recent films'. *Zardoz*, its small, ragged band of supporters notwithstanding, swiftly sank without trace into the nether regions of the imagination from which it had been summoned – taking Connery's profit slice with it.

The star's long-predicted move abroad to join Micheline and her family rendered his private life more harmonious than it had been for years. His career, in contrast, was in deep trouble. *Zardoz* had flopped as resoundingly as *The Offence*, *The Red Tent* and *The Molly Maguires* before it; *The Terrorists*, deemed 'weak and flabby on almost every level' by Derek Malcolm in Britain's *Guardian*, 'shoddily made and incomprehensibly plotted' by Nigel Andrews in the *Financial Times* and 'a thriller without thrills' by Ian Christie in the *Daily Express*, was about to do the same.

Selinger was philosophical about the results – it was a case of two down, plenty more (hopefully!) to go. 'No actor of any quality goes into a picture thinking it's going to be anything other than successful,' he points out, 'but there are a million reasons why it doesn't work out that way. You read the script and it's a good role with a good director and producer, but it doesn't necessarily finish up as the picture you thought it would be. You never go in thinking it's going to be a failure, you just never know what the public is going to think. Nobody can explain why. *Zardoz could* have worked. *The Terrorists didn't* work. All I can say is that it was an interesting script, Sean got paid, and, quite frankly, at the time he wasn't being offered a lot.'

Murder on the Orient Express reunited Connery yet again with Sidney Lumet. The star's handsome, starchy Indian Army Colonel Arbuthnot was completely removed from anything he had tackled before. Like the rest of the stellar supporting cast of Vanessa Redgrave, Richard Widmark, Ingrid Bergman, Anthony Perkins, John Gielgud and Michael York, the role amounted to little more than a cameo, with Albert Finney allowed full rein to steal the limelight with his waxworks Poirot.

Connery's casting was not without controversy. In early discussions with Selinger, he made it clear that he would happily settle for a flat fee. Selinger advised him to stick out for a percentage of the gross; he knew that Lumet was desperate to snare him – had sworn, in fact, that he didn't want to make the movie without Connery. The stumbling block Selinger encountered was with producer John Brabourne, who warned Selinger he would never get a chunk of the gross out of EMI, the movie's backers. Selinger decided to hold out and with Lumet phoning him virtually every hour, on the hour – 'Have I got Sean? *Have I got him*?' – was able to swing the gross percentage because of his long-standing relationship with studio boss Nat Cohen, promoted by now from Anglo-Amalgamated and his early Connery efforts, *The Frightened City* and *Operation Snafu*, via an EMI takeover.

Connery was delighted when the movie went on to become a smash – until, that is, Paramount picked up *Murder on the Orient Express* for distribution in the States. It seemed the studio had negotiated a deal with EMI that allowed them to cream their gross percentage off the top in the US, effectively pushing Connery further down the ladder. He still benefited hugely from the smash US net of $19 million – but not by as much as he'd expected.

'He was unhappy with me,' Selinger confirmed, 'because he thought I should have tied Paramount to his deal. How *could* I? When I did the deal with EMI, Paramount *didn't exist* – they only picked the movie up later! What I'd negotiated was still a great deal for him. He made a great deal of money, probably ten to fifteen times what he would have made had he taken the flat fee he'd first been offered – as he had wanted. I was annoyed that, despite this, he still complained. I felt it was a bit unjust. He just feels he should get his last penny, but it was tough on me. When Sean thinks he's right – my God, just try and budge him! It didn't make me feel very happy, but what the hell – it's part of my job, after all, and water under the bridge now.'

Chapter 20

'While I'm inclined to wing it, I've always had the feeling that Sean's known his lines for weeks. He comes to the set so well rehearsed, it's as if he'd spent hours in his bedroom going through all his moves.'

Michael Caine

'He's a joy to work with, he's a joy to work for. He has a flow of energy, a kind of aura of power and masculinity and humour.'

John Huston

The Wind and the Lion, the next project Dennis Selinger unearthed, purported to be a retelling of the kidnapping in 1904 of an American widow (Candice Bergen) and her children by the last of the Barbary pirates (Connery's Berber Sultan Raisuli), then their subsequent rescue by US Marines acting on the orders of President Theodore Roosevelt (Brian Keith). Bearing in mind that the original incident involved neither a widow, children, an American, even a female, and that the entire affair had been resolved purely by long-distance telegram, historically the movie was bunk.

Almeria's Cabo de Gata, familiar territory to Connery from

The Hill and *Shalako*, provided the ideal Moorish architectural backgrounds. Less ideal was the food, accommodation and other facilities on offer, with Connery complaining loud and long that even after hundreds of movies made in the area, there was still neither a first-class hotel nor a theatre. His co-star Bergen, on the other hand, found no problem in adjusting to life in Spain, having rented her own apartment to give her the privacy she needed to pursue her parallel career of writing and photo-journalism. In all fifty featured players and a crew of 150 were found local accommodation.

One aspect of the movie which did please Connery was working with director John Milius, a thirty-year-old Fidel Castro lookalike and surfing freak whom he saw as 'a very good writer, especially of heroic stuff'. He still expressed concern that Milius seemed to confuse the personal image he wished to project with the movie he was making: 'He is so busy being butch and Hemingway and samurai and all that, it gets in the way of his direction now and then.'

Although Milius was in turn thrilled to have not only Connery, but director-turned-actor John Huston in the cast as the US Secretary of State (describing the experience as being like 'the student directing the master') he went on to complain of suffering from 'battle fatigue' and railed at the attitude of the Spanish technicians and extras, citing the lack of co-operation and the language barrier copout. Connery felt emboldened to take matters into his own hands with the occasionally slow pace of events. After being on call for four days in a row without working, and dressed to kill in his Sultan's robes in the blistering heat, he pushed his way through the horde of extras, climbed into his white Volkswagen and took off in a cloud of dust.

Producer Herb Jaffe struggled hard to find the silver lining, even as his star disappeared into the distance. (Needless to say, Connery was back on time, costumed and word-perfect as usual, for his next shot.) 'Only here could you have made this $4.5 million film so inexpensively or attractively,' he asserted. 'Besides Spain's ideal climate, where else could you find terrain that has plains, mountains and ocean? We could never have done this film on so vast a scale in Hollywood.' Despite Jaffe's optimism, shooting stretched, everyone's best efforts notwithstanding, from ten to thirteen weeks.

A varied reception awaited the finished movie. 'Connery scores one of his major screen impressions,' *Variety* maintained. 'Milius has crafted a superior film ... *The Wind and the Lion* looks like a very big summer money film.' Less enthralled was Vincent Canby in the *New York Times*, who saw the movie as 'an elaborate, expensive-looking, ludicrously jingoistic historical adventure that comes out so firmly in favour of Teddy Roosevelt's "Big Stick" policy, 70 years later, that it could also be a put-on. Sean Connery is the courtly desert brigand who often sounds as if he'd taken a degree in fortune-cookie philosophy at the University of Edinburgh.'

Pauline Kael in *New Yorker* magazine was having none of what she saw as Milius's nonsense: 'When the actors begin to talk, which they do incessantly, the flat-footed dialogue and the amateurish acting take one back to the low-budget buffoonery of Maria Montez and Turhan Bey.'

'It has been a long time since Hollywood has produced an adventure as sumptuous as *The Wind and the Lion* or a fantasy as rich,' Jay Cocks countered in *Time Magazine*, adding, 'Sean Connery, who has become a superb actor, makes a funny, dashing Raisuli.' 'A performance from Sean Connery to rank among his best,' Tom Hutchinson agreed in Britain's *Sunday Telegraph*, before adding the zinger, 'considering that his role is among his clichéd worst.' Director Milius had come 'a resounding cropper', Nigel Andrews in the *Financial Times* insisted, describing the movie as 'a sad waste of time, money and proven talent'. To David Robinson in *The Times*, however, it was 'as heady and irresistible an entertainment as we have seen for months'. Although far for the smash *Variety* had predicted, the $4.5 million production still returned $4.9 million in US net rentals, enabling Connery to claim a second post-Bond starring role in what amounted to at least a modest success. *The Wind and the Lion* remains one of his favourite movies.

*

Originally director John Huston had envisaged Clark Gable and Humphrey Bogart in the leading roles of his adaptation of Rudyard Kipling's *The Man Who Would Be King*, but had been unable back then to find a script to his liking. It was producer John Foreman's suggestion that Huston write the movie himself, with support from Gladys Hill, that led to the $8m production being greenlighted. When he approached Paul Newman, with the idea of a rematch with Robert Redford in mind, Newman had some pithy advice for the veteran director: 'For Chrissakes, John, get Connery and Caine!'

Connery's encounter with Huston on *The Wind and the Lion* helped to clinch his participation, although it took a meeting between Selinger, Caine, Connery and Huston at London's Burke's Restaurant to clinch the deal. 'We needed someone to play the Indian at that run-through,' Selinger recalls, 'and I got my old friend and client Graham Stark, who had a good Indian accent, to do it. We read it through and it was hysterical, we all fell in love with it. My only later regret was that we couldn't give Graham the part in the movie, he himself said it had to be a real Indian.'

With Connery and Caine toplined as Danny Dravot and Peachy Carnahan, the two rough and ready ex-sergeants in the British Indian Army turned soldiers of fortune, Christopher Plummer was cast as Kipling, with 'real' Indian actor Saeed Jaffrey set to play Billy Fish, the ex-Gurkha soldier who teams up with Dravot and Carnahan. Doghmi Larbi, one of Morocco's foremost character actors, was Ootah, a local chieftain; Patricia Neal's seventeen-year-old daughter, Tessa Dahl, initially cast as the native princess Dravot wishes to marry, was later replaced by Caine's wife Shakira, a former model and runner-up in the Miss World contest. Her role represented the sum total of the movie's glamour quotient, since part of the bargain struck between Dravot and Carnahan for undertaking their adventure was to swear off both women and wine, their chief weaknesses. Huston saw the movie as a great adventure story with excitement, colour, spectacle and humour drawn from character, as well as contemporary significance.

The team selected Morocco for the twelve weeks of location filming because of the country's cosmopolitan mixture of races and tongues, including Arabian, African, French and Berber. They also utilized to the full the variety of scenery on offer – the deserts, plains, forests, hills, lush green countryside and mountains, each of them essential, since the locations were standing in for no fewer than three different countries: India, Afghanistan and Kafiristan. Happily for Connery, he was only a matter of a forty-five-minute sea trip from the Spanish coast for much of the shooting.

He had already been introduced by Micheline to Morocco's King Hassan. Although the monarch was keen to encourage filmmaking in his country, his tenuous hold on power brought about a discreet change in the movie's working title to *The Man Who Would Be Alexander*, after Alexander the Great, allegedly the last westerner to enter Kafiristan.

Following completion of the sequences set in Rudyard Kipling's newspaper office in Lahore, India – actually filmed in a large and picturesque villa on the outskirts of Marrakesh – the filmmakers transformed Marrakesh's railway station into Lahore's as it was in Queen Victoria's time. Travellers arriving by scheduled trains were astonished to step off their 1975 carriage into the crowded India of nearly a century ago. A large open square in Marrakesh was turned almost overnight into the teeming Kumharsen Serai, the packed market-square area of 1880s Lahore, with myriad native stalls, fruit and vegetable sellers and even the occasional snake-charmer and performing monkey.

On his way by car to Marrakesh one day Connery saw an old man limping along by the roadside, weighed down by the enormous pack on his back. 'Stop the car!' he shouted to his driver. 'Offer that guy a lift.' The traveller kept glancing at Connery as the offer was made, pressing his hands together and making jerky bowing motions. Slowly the driver made his way back, smiling sheepishly, 'He thanks you, but he prefers to walk,' he explained. 'He says he's not due in Marrakesh until tomorrow. If he accepts the lift he will arrive early and have nothing to do!'

The unit next decamped to the foothills of the Atlas Mountains, where the Kafiri village of Er-Heb was brought to life, centred around the actual village of Tagadirt-el-Bour, its rugged landscape selected for its resemblance to India's Northwest Frontier. The long processions of trucks, coaches, vans, trailers and cars became a familiar sight to local inhabitants, many of whom had never even seen a motion picture in their lives, let alone a movie camera or star.

After Connery, resplendent in his turban and muttonchop sideburns, and Caine, wearing a jaunty Afghan cap, had strode across the dusty parade ground – in character – issuing commands to hundreds of soldier extras, Huston decided he wanted a retake. 'Quiet,' the assistant director shouted, his instructions immediately echoed in French, Arabic and Berber through a series of loudhailers. 'Action,' Huston breathed, giving his shaggy beard a rub, followed by a sharp tug.

'All right, you bloody muckers,' Connery was to bellow, drill-sergeant style, 'we're going to make bloody soldiers out of you so you can go and get slaughtered like *civilized* men.' In a rare miscue he stumbled on the line. '*Bloody damn*!' he exploded, then turned to his director and crew. 'Sorry, gentlemen,' he apologized. 'How was it up there, John?'

'Really darn good, Sean,' Huston replied, breathing in the smoke from his panatella. 'You're doing just fine.' The director's reaction visibly reflected his delight at how smoothly the movie had progressed. 'Sean and Michael are marvellous,' the sixty-eight-year-old enthused as a third take was set up. 'They are quick and intelligent. They give me ideas. It's like watching a polished vaudeville act – everything on cue, with perfect timing. And hell, I've come to think of them as Danny and Peachy.'

With Foreman predicting that their pairing would equal the success of the Newman/Redford team, Connery squinted at the sun and looked around the set with its 116 vehicles, 150 actors and close on 500 extras drawn from the local Moroccan population. The reason for the chemistry everyone detected between the stars was easily explained. 'I've been friends with Michael for twenty years,' said Connery, rolling up his undershirt and exposing his tattoos. 'But this is the first chance I've had to work with him. He's great fun, a grand bloke. In this movie there are a lot of rich, well-drawn characters and it's a good story at many levels, with fantasy, size and scale. And lots of twists and turns. There's something wild here, but also a great deal of sense. The character I play is obsessed with the idea of power and overdoes it once he gets it.'

Often Connery and Caine would block their scenes out between them, Caine recalling, 'If John said, "I'm not going to cut on this, I'm going to do six pages," we would arrange the movements so that we worked each other round, so that each time you got the best bit of your part you'd be facing the camera. Unlike a lot of actors who'd have tried to hog it, it's very easy with Sean, there's no sense of evil intent in his acting. A lot of actors spend a great deal of time working out how to screw the other actor, which of course screws the scene, usually screws the picture and *definitely* screws them! They don't last very long, but if you happen to meet up with them it's very wearing and boring.'

One particular evening was spent in Connery's company in a little town on the edge of the Sahara where there was nothing to do at night except trip round to the local disco. Unfortunately it was men dancing with men, since women weren't allowed out at night. As the two stars took in the scene from the bar, Connery leaned over to Caine and said, 'Do you mind if I dance with your driver? Mine's too ugly.'

The interaction between Connery and Caine had the unit constantly in stitches, belying the basically serious nature of much of the script, and lightening the rigours of working in the hot and dusty location. Ready to mount their trusty steeds for one scene, attired in scarlet British Army tunics, both actors looked for Huston's signal for them to lead their column of troops through the town gates. 'Michael, old boy, didn't you wear one of those uniforms in *Zulu*?' Connery asked as they waited. 'Bloody right, luv,' came the reply. 'Me first film. I was a lieutenant then. Twelve years later and I'm demoted back to sergeant. No bloody justice!'

When Dennis Selinger visited the set he was delighted at the rapport between two of his biggest stars. 'The pair of them were falling about on the set!' he recalls. 'Michael's very funny and Sean can be too. He just needs somebody to start him off. I think he spent more time in Mike's trailer than in his own.'

Spotting one of the extras in the line of march swinging his sword dangerously close to the soldier behind him, Connery suggested he keep the weapon closer to his side. 'You're about to castrate your mate behind you,' he pointed out. 'He wouldn't like that, now, would he?'

The star himself almost had a nasty accident along similar lines a few days later, when a wire attached between his legs to pull him off a horse turned out to have been badly strung. The French, with their 'sans connerie', could well have been ahead of their time. 'It was close,' unit doctor Len Petrie confirmed. 'He nearly lost his balls.'

Soon the entire unit was flown high into the Atlas Mountains to Quazarzate where, at nearby Tifoultout, the battle between the rival communities of Er-Heb and Bashki was fought. By this point in the tale Dravot and Carnahan had crossed Afghanistan into the wilds of Kafiristan, established themselves with a local chieftain and trained his army to defeat his rivals; Dravot was about to be elevated to ruler and begin to believe, tragically, in his royal destiny. The Gorges du Todra at Tinghir became the Khyber Pass for film purposes in a sequence involving a hundred camels and many hundreds of extras.

The filmmakers created the spectacular Holy City of Sikandergul on a hitherto virgin hilltop, bulldozed to erect the massive stone and plaster of Paris courtyard. Behind the parapets of the courtyard, against an unbelievably beautiful background of distant snow-capped peaks, 1,200 shaven-headed monks waited patiently under the blazing sun for filming to start, ready to collect the $5 a day that was on offer.

Since *The Man Who Would Be King* was the first film in which he was playing completely *au naturel*, with neither toupee nor hairpiece, Connery himself was virtually unrecognizable as he sprawled on the steps leading to the courtyard. With his sun-bronzed bald head he looked a million light years removed from the suave Bond as he lay in his white and maroon robes, assiduously studying the financial pages of *The Times* while his sandalled feet clip-clopped against the steps. The sight was anachronistic, to say the least, especially with his white Volkswagen minibus parked close to Caine's trailer.

One evening Connery drove alone into town to explore. Wearing just an old T-shirt and chinos, and with several days' growth of beard, he was stopped by Moroccan police as he made his way back to the unit in the early hours. He had no identification on him and for a while the situation looked extremely dicey – until a certain character from his past came to the rescue. On the point of being escorted to prison and at least held overnight, Connery stared determinedly at the two policemen who confronted him and blurted out, 'Oh, oh, *seven*!' at the top of his voice. Initial incomprehension changed swiftly to disbelief, then all the way to utter glee as the magic numbers were understood. The crisis was over.

Lunch breaks produced a mixture from the London catering crew of exotic local Moroccan dishes as well as traditional British fare, like shepherd's pie, washed down by gallons of hot tea. Connery was completely caught out during a feast organized by local sheiks. Having been assured it would cause great offence if he refused, he was obliged to eat the special treat of two sheep's eyes he was offered. As he chewed on the second, the 'sheik' whipped off his robes. It was Connery's golfing friend from England, comedian and prankster extraordinaire Eric Sykes.

During a visit to the set by Micheline, Connery laughed somewhat ruefully as he denied rumours that he was already worth $10 million. 'That's rubbish,' he protested, 'I wish it were true. But I do intend to be worth $3 million after I've finished getting my affairs sorted out. I mean, I've earned enough money for other people. If you work your arse off the way I have, there has to be some reward.'

When asked about his current marital status Connery was quick to remind the scribe of his ground rules, that when he and Cilento had separated, he had vowed never to speak again about marriage or any other aspect of his private life. One deep breath later, he caused considerable puzzlement by claiming that he had recently re-married.

In his refusal to confirm or deny that the ceremony had taken place in Casablanca several months earlier, he had good reasons for his reticence – the couple did not in fact finally tie the knot until filming on *The Man Who Would Be King* was complete.

As with Connery's first wedding, the ceremony took place in a registrar's office in Gibraltar; the date was 6 May 1975. 'If you take my picture, I'll knock your head off,' he threatened the solitary photographer who turned up. The happy couple then departed for their home in Marbella. 'He divorce! I divorce!' Micheline later told a reporter. 'We get married in Spain. No, not in a church!' Hands were thrown up. 'We are *sinners*!'

Although *The Man Who Would Be King* was one of the best-attended entries at the Teheran Film Festival, the movie was judged by many to be one of the event's biggest disappointments. *Variety* referred to the 'poor performance' by Caine in particular, blaming him for the too-broad comedy touch in the movie. Connery they judged to have given a 'generally credible, but not very sympathetic' portrayal of the simple man thrust into potential greatness, only to throw it away. For them the most redeeming aspect of the film was Plummer's Kipling, a portrayal they saw as completely impressive, both physically and dramatically. Then there was the 'delightfully warm and often comic' performance by Saeed Jaffrey. Maurice Jarre's approach to Eastern music was considered 'misguided'. Box office was seen as initially good, on the strength of the marquee names, but with shaky legs.

John Simon in *New York* magazine disagreed, viewing the

epic as nothing less than John Huston's best movie since *The African Queen*. While conceding it was not a great work, more a happy piece of hokum, derring-do and entertainment, he took issue with *Variety* on the merits of Caine's performance, judging it 'gutter gallantry at its juiciest'. Plummer he described as one of the screen's most versatile actors, while Connery was deemed to have effected 'a good, blustering Dravot'.

'Worth the wait,' Jay Cocks maintained in *Time*, 'the best work Huston has done in a decade. Caine and Connery make a splendid couple of cronies, full of bluff and swagger.' 'It is Connery who continues to be amazing,' said Margaret Hinxman in the British *Daily Mail*. 'With every film he grows in stature, discarding all the vestiges of James Bond, to become a truly fine character actor.' Patrick Gibbs in the *Daily Telegraph* disagreed. 'Caine makes something of Carnehan,' he argued, 'but Connery can do little with Dravot, certainly not suggest an overweening ambition.' Of the movie itself: 'What is entirely missing is the terror and the tragedy, the blasphemy and the sense of evil.' To Tom Hutchinson in the *Sunday Telegraph*, however, the film was 'simply magnificent'.

The $7 million production returned a handsome-enough, but still less than hoped for $11 million in net rentals in the US. 'It wasn't handled at all well,' Selinger maintains. 'It should have taken more. Now it's become a cult movie.' Although *The Anderson Tapes*, *The Wind and the Lion* and *The Man Who Would Be King* still looked like small beer compared with *Dr No*'s $6.4 million, back in 1963 – and smaller still compared with *Thunderball*'s $28.6m in 1965 – Connery had still managed to break his long, dry spell. And Selinger's 'pile 'em high' policy had been vindicated.

By registering as a resident in Monaco while basing himself in Marbella, Connery had taken steps to ensure that Britain's Inland Revenue would no longer receive the vast bulk of his earnings. A fond hope that the Scottish National Party would sweep the board and lead to the creation of a Scottish tax haven had been well and truly dashed. 'I was paying 98 per cent tax,' he complained. 'I was making all this money and making movies and I had nothing. People said you should have two cars and three secretaries, because they're deductable.' An anguished pause. 'But they're not *constructive*.'

Many friends, like the fiercely nationalistic Stanley Baker, were shocked and saddened by Connery's departure; Baker's philosophy was that the privileged should pay the taxes of their native land as a return of dues. Although the rift between them was mended before Baker's untimely death in 1976, it was a close-run thing.

Chapter 21

'The death of my father had an absolutely devastating effect on me.'

Sean Connery

'One of the qualities Sean projects well is sexual innocence.'

Richard Lester

When you're hot in Hollywood, you're hot. And Richard Lester was hot in 1974 following the success of *The Three Musketeers*, hotter than he'd ever been. Just how hot he found out when he was traced to his den at Twickenham Studios by an emissary from David Begelman, the head of Columbia still several years before his embezzlement activities hit the headlines. Acting as Begelman's deputy was the future apple of Sony's eye, Peter Guber, full of vim, vigour – and, to Lester's delight, offers. 'Here are seven cards,' Guber told Lester, spreading them out on the desk in front of him. 'On each of them is a story idea that Columbia owns. Pick the one you want and make it for us. I'm not going to leave this office until you agree.'

For Lester, who had always been obliged to fight tooth and

nail for every penny for his previous movies, it was a golden moment. He still drew a blank on six out of the seven 3 in × 5 in cards Guber proffered. It was on the seventh that his imagination seized, where just six words were inscribed: 'Robin Hood as an Older Man'. *'That's* what I'd like to do,' Lester declared, enthusiasm positively bubbling over. 'You got it,' Guber assured him.

With the speed of light a dinner meeting was arranged at London's Berkley Hotel with Begelman, Lester's agent Judy Scott-Fox and a full supporting cast. James Goldman was writing the script; Lester would produce and direct *The Death of Robin Hood*, a rough budget was agreed, casting was discussed. With Begelman declaring himself 'thrilled' and the entire package 'terrific', the deal was concluded on a handshake. He was off on holiday, Begelman informed the assembly, but as soon as he returned papers would be written, contracts drawn up.

Six months later he was refusing to return phone calls. During a visit to independent producer Ray Stark's office on Columbia's Burbank lot, Judy Scott-Fox discovered a script lying on Stark's desk headed, 'The Death of Robin Hood, a Ray Stark production for Columbia'. Thunderstruck, she tracked Begelman down and reminded him of the meal in London and their deal. 'How could you do this?' she asked. 'You shook hands with Dick Lester at the Berkley.'

'I have *never*,' said Begelman indignantly, 'been in the Berkley Hotel *in my life*!' It took Lester a year to get the project back, with Stark now on board as executive producer. Stark also introduced a friend, Richard Shepherd, to the project: *The Death of Robin Hood* was now a Ray Stark/Richard Shepherd production. The movie had acquired not only a hefty overhead, but an eventual change of title, opposed by Lester, to *Robin and Marian*.

By a strange coincidence Lester's first contact with Diane Cilento had roughly coincided with Connery's back in the late 1950s. The US-born director's career had started in Britain in association with Peter Sellers, Spike Milligan, Michael Bentine and Harry Secombe – the ground-breaking Goons. While directing a TV show hosted by Bentine, Lester engaged Cilento as a guest. Driving from London to the studio in Birmingham together, they were involved in a minor car crash and ended up in a tangle on the floor, shaken, but relatively unharmed.

Lester's introduction to Connery himself was made while *The Offence* was being filmed at the director's home base of Twickenham. Being small and intimate, filmmakers working there are almost bound to meet; the ebullient Denis O'Dell, whose association with Lester dated back to *A Hard Day's Night*, brought the two together in the studio commissary, and would continue the association as producer of *Robin and Marian*. At first Lester had Connery in mind for the role of Little John until the idea of his playing Robin took hold. After Dennis Selinger had forwarded the script during the shooting of *The Man Who Would Be King* in Morocco, a trip to Marbella for Lester was necessary to confirm the star's participation. Audrey Hepburn was next to be signed as Maid Marian, then Nicol Williamson as Little John, Robert Shaw as the Sheriff of Nottingham, Richard Harris as King Richard, the supporting roles also filled with top British actors Denholm Elliott, Ian Holm, Kenneth Haigh and Esmond Knight.

At a party in Paris during pre-production with Connery and Hepburn, Lester was introduced to Micheline. He found her 'a very, very lively lady – in the good sense, a strong person with a lot of energy and a quite unique personality'. He also sensed an inner strength that was obviously good for her husband.

'Innocence and simplicity are the key to the movie,' Lester spelled out. 'In the end everyone around him has to treat Robin in a childlike way. Marian and the Sheriff turned out to be the sophisticated ones, while he never grew up. He's been forced to try to come to terms with a legend he didn't understand, and that confuses him. He's still living the way he thinks he should behave – if you want something, you go clattering over the fields to get it. Marian, meantime, has come to terms with her life.'

When the two men relaxed together, Lester discovered, like

John Barman before him, that Connery was a hard man to play tennis with. Although they were both pretty poor, mere amateurs, to Connery it was still a Wimbledon final.

At age forty-five Connery found himself being asked by the insurance company to submit to a full medical check-up. As he proceeded to dress following the examination he casually asked to hear the verdict. 'You're in good shape for a middle-aged man,' he was advised.

'Middle-aged! I'm not middle-aged!' Connery protested, completely shocked. The doctor looked at him with some amusement. 'How long do you think you're going to live?' he asked. 'Till I'm ninety,' Connery replied. 'Right,' said the doctor, 'you're halfway there. You're *middle-aged*.'

Ageing, and any accompanying attempts to combat the process artificially, has never been an item on Connery's agenda. Once he was reconciled to thinning hair way back in his late teens, the process has held few terrors. 'The fascination for looking young,' says Connery, 'is the joke of all time. Age is as inevitable as tomorrow.'

Way back in *Diamonds Are Forever*, his hairdresser had confirmed his impatience at having hairpieces fitted that had been specially flown from London to disguise the balding forehead. 'He would prefer to play Bond as a balding hero,' she said. 'He keeps telling me to thin out his wigs until there is almost no point in his wearing them at all.' Connery later explained the incidental disadvantages of his series of 'rugs'. 'I get credit for taking off my hairpiece, but I never did like to wear one. I don't like them; they change the sound of my voice, like wearing earmuffs. The sound reverberates in my head.'

As filming on *Robin and Marian* began in the Plain of Urbaza near Pamplona, the same Spanish location where Lester had shot *The Three Musketeers*, the director quickly sensed how utterly straight Connery was in his dealings – and how he expected everyone else to behave in the same manner. 'His attitude was always to be ready on time,' Lester recalls. 'And if others weren't he'd threaten to do their scenes with a stunt double. He felt that if his name was above the title he had a responsibility to the production. Sean set the example, always ready to rehearse on time no matter how hot it was, or whether he'd had a drink the night before. You can't ask for more than that.'

There were problems during the six weeks of filming, with Audrey Hepburn reportedly nervous about how she would come over on screen at forty-six. Coaxed back from semi-retirement, Lester's one-take method was not the type of filmmaking she was used to. His habit of working with several cameras, shooting simultaneously from different angles, was unnerving to her at first. And before she had always been dressed by Givenchy – now she had just one costume, and it was made out of coarse, oven-glove material.

Lester's policy of not showing rushes also bothered Hepburn at first. Then she relented. 'I trust him,' she declared. 'If he is satisfied I'm not worried.' Connery agreed: 'It doesn't bother me as much as I thought it would. Lester hasn't seen them either. You just go ahead and do the job and hope we get what we want. One thing I know is that I won't have to play Robin over and over again. He dies at the end of this picture, so that's that!'

Some members of the crew complained that Lester was driving everyone too fast in a race to finish ahead of schedule. Connery, desperate for some time off, had positively encouraged the notion. He had, after all, gone from the arduous locations on *The Wind and the Lion* and *The Man Who Would Be King* to *Robin and Marian*. 'I'm not even going to the cast party after the work is over,' he assured everyone. 'If I did I'd probably get drunk and spend a whole day recovering. As soon as the last scene is shot I'm jumping right into my car and driving home to Marbella.'

Connery was spotted standing in the blistering sun at one point in front of an old castle being used as a backdrop, clad in just a simple tunic with nothing underneath, unlike the armour-clad majority of the cast. When a rare breeze blew the tunic's rear slit to one side, exposing his naked behind, an assistant discreetly ordered onlookers away, groaning and protesting.

For a movie Lester describes as having been shot 'in six weeks under a tree', *Robin and Marian* should, in his view, have been brought in for $1.5 million. Instead, it cost close on $5 million. Stark and his producer visited the set just once, together with three reporters and their wives, the whole party having been jetted from California to Madrid and met by a fleet of limos. After a brief lunch with Lester and his stars, the contingent motored to the Palace Hotel in Biarritz. A week later it was back to Madrid by private plane and a jet home. 'It's a perfect example,' says Lester, 'of how justified Sean is in insisting he gets every penny of his money. His neck is on the line, his career is up for grabs, yet he is forced to watch money being spent that will never appear on the screen.'

Towards the end of shooting the formidable Connery was asked if he ever felt intimidated. 'At my age now,' he replied, 'by very few people.' Had there been occasions in the past? 'Oh, *yes*,' he admitted. 'I can't imagine anybody who isn't occasionally intimidated. I don't know why everybody gets in such a fuss about it, because it's normal.'

Questioned about the 'coming of age' roles in which he now seemed to specialize, he shrugged off any significance. 'It just happens that the scripts I read and liked were *The Wind and the Lion*, *The Man Who Would Be King* and *Robin and Marian*. I'm aware that there are a great many actors who wouldn't play characters those ages, though I don't know why. To my way of thinking, not only are these roles marvellously written, but also, if a character is fifty-odd, there are greater chances of making him more interesting.'

With *Robin and Marian*'s release it seemed that each of the main participants had reached a professional watershed. According to Frank Rich in the *New York Post*,

Of all the wonderful things about *Robin and Marian* the most wonderful of all is what the picture means in the context of the careers of its stars, Sean Connery, Audrey Hepburn and its director Richard Lester. The film has more to do with fresh beginnings than swan songs. While each of the three talents flared brightly in a single end-of-decade project – Hepburn in *Two for the Road*, Connery in *A Fine Madness*, Lester with *Petulia*, they were at creative crossroads with no clear directions to take. With *Robin and Marian* all three return to the forefront of our movies ... It's the work of people who have come to terms with themselves and their talents.

Connery's he described as 'an ironic, reverberating performance ... there's a tenderness of a kind this actor hasn't revealed in years'.

Andrew Sarris in *Village Voice* agreed, describing *Robin and Marian* as 'one of the most affecting moviegoing experiences of recent years'. Vincent Canby in the *New York Times*, on the other hand, judged the movie 'curious and contradictory', and 'ultimately most appealing as a story of mismatched lovers who found too little too late. The film depends almost entirely on the presence of Connery and Hepburn to generate responses that are not otherwise supported.'

John Simon in *New York* magazine had no such reservations: 'Perfection,' he asserted, 'is unattainable, but this film comes close.' The movie, he added, had two assets so genuine as hardly to deserve them. One was David Watkin's cinematography, the other was the acting: 'Can you ask for more than Hepburn and Connery? More than Williamson, Harris and Shaw? And each of them better than morning prayers or peace or food to eat? In fact, almost as good as food for thought.'

Despite a mass of favourable reviews, *Robin and Marian* accrued just $4 million in rentals. 'The title should have been left as *The Death of Robin Hood*,' Lester maintains. 'In changing it we were inviting the kind of mindless technique many critics have of evaluating the movie by the last one you made. To me the movie was not a "comedy adventure", but people kept asking me where the jokes were. Sean is an actor who looks for humour in his parts, to humanize his character, which is quite right. But Robin was straight, I always saw it like that, and because of the connotations of the changed title, it prompted the wrong reaction.'

Connery agreed that the original title should have been retained: 'That's what it was about, and people were disappointed because from the new title they expected some stirring adventures. The whole thing was very much antimythic. This guy comes galloping back after eighteen years away in the Crusades and he shouts, "Hey, I'm back." And of course no one much cares any more. And he's getting up each morning in the forest, creaking and groaning and coughing and having a leak in the bushes and it's all too much for a man of his age. They hated that idea in the States. They can't take the idea that their hero might be over the hill and falling apart. Also, we never anticipated the resistance from the Catholics. They protested about Marian being a nun, and helping me to die and then committing suicide.'

He still felt that if Columbia had opened the movie with a selected release and allowed word of mouth to build, they might have had a winner rather than a loser. Or there again: 'Maybe you just can't tamper with myths that way.'

One observer who remarked that the series of movies he had just completed – *The Wind and the Lion*, *The Man Who Would Be King* and *Robin and Marian* – had conferred upon him the 'legitimacy' he had always sought, recognition as an actor, was treated to one of Connery's most revealing and thoughtful replies. 'In a way that's true,' he agreed, 'but all the time I've been working I've only had my own yardstick to go by. And the yardstick should be in terms of material. Some assholes make demands about all sorts of things that have nothing to do with the real problem. That is, you get a good script, and a good director, producer, actors and technicians. Then there's a good percentage chance you have a good film. I must assume that the more work I do and the better the subject matter and people involved in the project, the better I shall become. Otherwise, what's the point in going on?'

*

By September 1975, when Connery travelled to Ireland to confer with Kevin McClory in his County Kildare home, the Bond saga had been rolling on without him since his avowed swan song in 1971 with *Diamonds Are Forever*. Roger Moore's maiden outing in 1973's *Live and Let Die* had pulled in an impressive $15.9 million net. 1975's *The Man with the Golden Gun*, on the other hand, at $9.4 million, had emulated the lowest of the series, George Lazenby's *On Her Majesty's Secret Service*.

McClory's proposition was simple. He owned the remake rights to *Thunderball* and basically wanted to rehash the story, with Connery and Len Deighton roped in to join the writing process. The purpose: to emerge with a brand-new Bond adventure, *James Bond of the Secret Service*. The diminishing returns of the series were dismissed; McClory and his associates, after all, intended to revamp the most successful Bond of them all. How could it miss? The inevitable reaction from Eon was awaited with considerable trepidation. Rightly so, it later emerged.

Chapter 22

'He's as professional an actor as I've ever met. He's not afraid to take the responsibility of being the leading actor in a film. I have enormous respect for Sean.'

Richard Lester

'As far as being legitimized as an actor, to be perfectly honest I think it's a case of the chicken or the egg. Which comes first? Frankly, image isn't of genuine concern for me because it's something determined by the public and critics.'

Sean Connery

It was the idea of appearing in something modern again, after *Murder on the Orient Express*, *The Wind and the Lion*, *The Man Who Would Be King* and *Robin and Marian*, that first attracted Connery to *The Next Man*. Then there was the concept, as he saw it, of posing an attempted solution to Middle Eastern problems in his role as a far-sighted Saudi-Arabian visionary, Khalil Abdul Munsen. His Scottish accent? No problem – the script blithely introduced an Edinburgh college education to explain it away.

The Next Man's producer, Martin Bregman, had developed

the script for the political thriller over six months with his director Richard Sarafian and co-writer Mort Fine. A former agent, Bregman had turned to film producing with *Serpico* and followed it up with *Dog Day Afternoon*, starring his friend and client Al Pacino. When both movies became Academy Award contenders Bregman was transformed overnight into one of Hollywood's most successful producers, all the while remaining determinedly based in New York. 'I chose Sean,' he explained, 'because he's a marvellous actor who has style and a huge presence on screen, a bigger-than-life glamour. And he is an artist.'

Connery's three-time collaborator Sidney Lumet, who had also directed *Serpico* and *Dog Day Afternoon* for Bregman, had praise of his own for the producer, describing him as 'a totally positive force in production, completely supportive of the creative elements. He fights for the money to go on the screen and has a genuine instinct for drama. All in all the best creative producer I've ever worked with.' Because this came from Lumet – although he was not involved in *The Next Man* – Connery was most impressed.

Following a spring vacation in the Bahamas, he journeyed to New York with Micheline to shoot several sequences for the movie. The leap from Lyford Cays to the Big Apple left him gasping at the rudeness and insensitivity he encountered. While moving into an apartment they had rented on First Avenue and 56th Street, Connery found himself sharing a crowded elevator. One woman watched intently as he pushed his floor button and said to her friend, '*Twenty.* He's on floor *Twenty*' – as if he wasn't there. The second woman turned and eyed him up and down. 'Does nothing for *me*,' she snapped. 'Silly bitch!' thought Connery, thoroughly offended. Later, one of the film crew was heard to remark, as Micheline walked by with her husband, 'He didn't marry a young chick, did he?'

One scene at the Waldorf Astoria was shot in the hotel's blue and gold room, with seventy-five extras in formal dress milling around an enormous oval table waiting for Connery to arrive. When he did, he was in his street clothes, brown shirt unbuttoned to the waist, sleeves rolled up and faded tattoos clearly visible on his right arm. After chewing over a problem with director Sarafian and cameraman Michael Chapman, he nodded at the gathered reporters before repairing to his dressing room, and quoted the late jazz master Eddie Condon's response to critics of his music: 'Those cats tell us how to play. Us cats don't tell them how to write.'

When Connery re-emerged, resplendent in a tuxedo, Micheline chatted happily to reporters while glancing in his direction. 'Oh, he is impressive, no?' she asked. 'The tuxedo, it was specially made in Paris.' She went on to explain that she accompanied her husband whenever possible: 'If we are not together, what is the point? I go with him to Europe, Morocco, New York, Pamplona . . .!' She paused. 'I have a wonderful life, no? I paint, but I do not call myself an artist. Only a painter. Sean comes first to me. Oh, God, yes. He is a beautiful man, no? He doesn't care how he looks. He is unpretension himself, that is the way he is born! He is not one whose head cannot pass through the door, no? He does not care. Not even in the scene in *Robin and Marian* with Audrey Hepburn, where he wakes up, forgets Audrey is there, and starts to make pee-pee in the woods.'

She revealed that her favourite Connery film was *The Offence*. 'But for the way he look, *The Wind and the Lion*. Oh, he is so romantic in that one.' She acknowledged his attraction for the ladies: 'Yes, the women follow him. In the supermarket, the women chase him, so he has to run. Also they write him letters – but they can save their stamps! I have the fantasies, I grow crazy. I shoot myself. I try not to think about it.' Another pause, then a shrug. 'But it is not that bad. Sean, he is the man-man. What I love is that he is so Anglo-Saxon, not like the Frenchman . . . I *hate* the Frenchman. Always *cherchez la femme*. Sean like to be more with other men. He has many men friends . . . I love that. He does not like so much to be friends with women, with wives. He talks to men. He plays golf with men. And when he plays, that is all he wants to talk about – his game. He goes over and over it. If I did not play golf myself, I would go crazy.'

Between scenes a giggling wardrobe lady vouchsafed that

Connery only wore undershorts when scenes called for them. 'He's the greatest thing since Coca-Cola,' his co-star Cornelia Sharpe remarked. 'We were playing a heavy emotional scene and he did the most incredible thing. I'm not really experienced and I'd forgotten to check the camera. Sean did what no other actor would do, he touched my cheek and turned my face towards it. Any other man would have turned my face away! And not only that, Sean's so smart. Most stars have dead flashlight batteries upstairs. Sean has a brain.'

When Connery met one female reporter who expressed concern at his reputation for roughing up the press, he wasted no time in blaming the Bond publicity machine. 'Basically I'm a private person,' he informed her, 'and the Bond producers wouldn't let me be that. I'd work six days a week, all day, with much of the work physical, then have to spend every free moment answering stupid questions like, "Do you like to beat people up? Slap women around?"'

Questioned about the 'new' *au naturel* Connery image he retorted, 'What they mean is an *old* Sean Connery! I'm forty-six and don't mind playing my age, or even older, unlike in Hollywood where they won't play a man of fifty even though they *are* fifty! They scratch out fifty and say thirty-five. This having to be young forever – that's America, that's Hollywood. I find most people are most interesting when they've lived a little bit more. And although I'm a chap who likes all the girls, I don't necessarily have to *have* all the girls.' As for the bout of insomnia that had struck him since his arrival in the States: 'New York has its fingers in me,' he explained. 'That's why I can't sleep.'

Despite the on-set harmony, which continued on locations as far apart as Nassau, Ireland, Munich, Nice and Morocco, Connery had inadvertently involved himself in another grade 'A' turkey. Vincent Canby in the *New York Times* described *The Next Man* as

a suspense melodrama made by people whose talent for filmmaking and knowledge of international affairs would

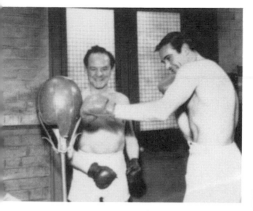

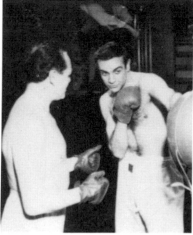

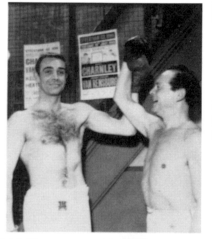

Selection of shots taken during production of *The Frightened City*. *(British Film Institute of London)*

Double-bill poster for *Dr No/You Only Live Twice (British Film Institute of London)*

Connery with 'Tippi' Hedren in Alfred Hitchcock's *Marnie (British Film Institute of London)*

Connery as rebellious prisoner Joe Roberts in *The Hill. (British Film Institute of London)*

First wife Diane Cilento in her Oscar-nominated role in *Tom Jones*. *(British Film Institute of London)*

Connery as the Berber Sultan in a scene from *The Wind and the Lion*. *(British Film Institute of London)*

Connery in *The Man Who Would Be King* with co-star Michael Caine. *(British Film Institute of London)*

The all-star cast of *Murder on the Orient Express* (Connery, second bottom left; others, left to right, Albert Finney, Lauren Bacall, Martin Balsam, Ingrid Bergman, Jacqueline Bisset, Jean-Pierre Cassel, John Gielgud, Wendy Hiller, Anthony Perkins, Vanessa Redgrave, Rachel Roberts, Richard Widmark, Michael York). *(British Film Institute of London)*

In a distinctly unglamorous portrayal of Robin Hood with co-star Audrey Hepburn in *Robin and Marian*. *(British Film Institute of London)*

Connery as Agamemnon with Craig Warnock in *Time Bandits*. A HandMade Picture/Avco-Embassy release. *(British Film Institute of London)*

Top Left: Connery with Betsy Brantley in Fred Zinnemann's *Five Days One Summer. (British Film Institute of London)*

Top Right: Diane Cilento and son Jason Connery in *The Boy Who Had Everything. (British Film Institute of London)*

Center Right: Connery as the sleuthing friar William of Bakersville with Christian Slater in *The Name of the Rose. (British Film Institute of London)*

Bottom Right: With co-stars (left to right) Charles Martin Smith, Kevin Costner and Andy Garcia in his Oscar-winning role in *The Untouchables. (British Film Institute of London)*

Top Left: Connery and Harrison Ford, in a scene from *Indiana Jones and the Last Crusade. (British Film Institute of London)*

Top Right: Connery in a scene from *The Hunt For Red October* with co-star Alec Baldwin.

Center Left: Connery, Matthew Broderick and Dustin Hoffman in *Family Business. (British Film Institute of London)*

Bottom Left: Connery with Christopher Lambert in *Highlander II: The Quickening.* An Interstar release. *(British Film Institute of London)*

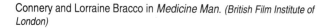

He turned his back on civilization.

Only to discover he had the power to save it.

Medicine Man

Connery and Lorraine Bracco in *Medicine Man*. *(British Film Institute of London)*

both fit comfortably into the left nostril of a small bee ...
[This] is the first film I've ever seen that is so acutely bored
with itself it tries to go away. Who is responsible for
mindless moviemaking of this magnitude I've no idea. There
have been more expensive films this year, and more foolish
ones, but *The Next Man* must be the most foolish film of
such expense.

Andrew Sarris in the *Village Voice* mitigated the assault just a
little. '*The Next Man* has received some of the worst notices of
the season,' he acknowledged, 'and though it is not even a
passable movie, it is not as bad as all that.' He was particularly
struck by the critical overkill directed at Cornelia Sharpe, soon
to marry producer Bregman, for 'parading around as a blank-
faced clotheshorse':

One would think that this was the first big glamor buildup in
movie history. Most of the reviewers seemed to have availed
themselves of some private gossip about the actress's close
connection with the producer. Horrors! Someone is trying to
make a new female star. Call out the police! The male stars
only outnumber the female stars by 10 to one. How dare a
producer try to disturb that ratio. It is interesting to note that
she had previously gotten some good notices for docile
bedmate roles in *Busting* and *Serpico*. Her part in *The Next
Man* makes so little sense that her acting deficiencies are
overemphasized. Still, I wonder if her biggest crime with the
critics is putting on airs.

Connery's response to the attacks on Sharpe proved that
gallantry, at least on his terms, was not yet dead. To the
astonishment of one female scribe, who had baldly stated that
Sharpe had landed the role only because 'she was the girlfriend
of the producer', Connery personally called her up. 'She didn't
say anything,' he wryly reported. 'She was speechless. She was
perfectly entitled to say what she liked about Cornelia's
performance. But *not* to comment on why the girl got the part.'

What many considered far more apposite was why Connery himself had taken the role. Artistic elements and a sense of high purpose, however misguided, could be detected in many of his post-Bond flops, especially *The Hill*, *A Fine Madness*, *The Molly Maguires*, *The Offence* and *Zardoz*. *The Next Man*, however, unashamedly joined the ranks of *Woman of Straw*, *Shalako*, *The Red Tent* and *The Terrorists*, all of them busts both commercially and critically. Connery may have 'liked the concept' of *The Next Man*, he may have been beguiled by Marty Bregman's excellent track record, but he had landed himself with another lulu, a movie condemned as totally unreleasable in his native Britain and only given a belated airing several years after its production on late-night television. Selinger's multi-picture plan was certainly keeping Connery's name to the fore – but it wasn't selling too many tickets on his client's name.

A planned follow-up collaboration between Bregman and Connery of his old Sir Richard Burton project, *The Devil Drives*, was eventually shelved.

Early in 1977 Connery signed to appear as Major General Urquhart in producer Joseph Levine's $25 million World War II epic, *A Bridge Too Far*, to be directed by Richard Attenborough. Like the equally star-studded *The Longest Day*, the screenplay was adapted from the book by Cornelius Ryan and told the story of the near-disastrous military operation that had taken place in Holland in the autumn of 1944. Codenamed 'Operation Market Garden', General Montgomery's plan had been to seize the three bridges on the road to Arnhem, thereby enabling Allied troops to cross Holland and enter Germany. Urquhart, leading 10,000 of the troops involved in the attack on the third bridge at Arnhem, found the Germans lying in wait; in the bloody battle that followed many British soldiers lost their lives.

Having signed on for $250,000, Connery was shocked when Micheline read in a newspaper a few weeks before filming was due to start that Robert Redford was collecting a cool $1 million for his contribution. There were also hefty chunks for Ryan O'Neal, James Caan and Elliott Gould. 'At first I thought it must be a mistake,' Connery recalled. 'But then I learned it wasn't. Now, considering the size of my part in the picture, the salary I'd agreed on was fair. But when I found out how much the others were getting – for the same amount of work and with no more ability – it became unfair.'

The individual on whom Connery again vented his wrath was Dennis Selinger. 'We had done a deal which was acceptable,' says Selinger, 'but – and here I was in full agreement with Sean – not when we discovered what the other stars were getting. All hell broke loose when Sean found out. He's not a bully, there was no table-thumping, but unquestionably there was a great deal of raised voices. I had rows with Dickie Attenborough and finally we negotiated a substantial increase with Joe Levine. I don't mind admitting the whole episode gave me a few heart attacks!'

A few weeks later, on location in Holland, Connery impressed everyone on the set with his democratic ways. He refused to accept any of the privileges of rank and stood in line with the rest of the unit, including the still photographer's children, for the Dutch treats of chips and mayonnaise.

Although *A Bridge Too Far* was not well received critically, it garnered over $20m in US rentals, edging just ahead of *Murder on the Orient Express*. It was ironic that these two movies, in which his total time on screen amounted to less than many a single supporting role, represented Connery's biggest hits in the 1970s outside of his last James Bond adventure.

One reporter, turning a blind eye to Connery's lengthening string of flops, decided to tackle the star about his apparent lack of satisfaction with his success. Frowning, Connery asked, 'What do you want me to do, make a speech about myself? We both know what I've achieved. Why should I elaborate on that? If it's about work you're asking, I don't think anyone doing anything creative is ever completely satisfied. By the time an old project appears, you're deep in the problems of new ones – and when you do see the earlier thing, its weaknesses stare you in the face. I have no illusions that anything I'm going to do will give me this completeness that you're implying I'm in search of.'

Connery sees golf as the archetypal loner's game and maintains that it could only have been invented by the Scots. A series of photographs in a Costa Del Sol magazine perfectly served to illustrate the monumental rages that he can conjure up when things go wrong at the game. He was shown exploding in fury over a missed shot, hurling the club into the air, shaking the tree in which it lodged, then collapsing into helpless laughter at the sheer ludicrousness of it all. Acquaintances noted that the ability to step back and see the joke was a fairly recent characteristic.

'He is an awesome sight when his ire is up,' says John Boorman. 'It is as if his entire being, bone, flesh and sinew are contracted into pure energy. When it reaches a kind of critical mass, all his frustrations and irritations erupt in a magnificent volcanic rage.'

Chapter 23

'He's a straightforward guy. He could have made millions sticking to James Bond, but he didn't want to be typed. Now he's one of the few actors, who, it doesn't matter how the films do, they'll get their $1.5m tomorrow. In two seconds I'd let him play in anything I've got.'

Joseph E. Levine

'I would never cheat anyone, and I expect that from others. It's very unpleasant to discover otherwise. Michael Caine always says that in Japan being a lawyer is a very dishonourable profession. If the Japanese break their word to each other, they don't call a lawyer, they commit suicide.'

Sean Connery

It began quietly enough. *The Man Who Would Be King* had been released domestically by Allied Artists in 1975, having been financed via a complicated arrangement including Columbia Pictures, which had distribution rights in foreign territories. On 23 January 1978, Connery and Michael Caine jointly announced they were suing AA for residual payments for their services on the movie. According to them, *The Man Who Would Be King* had achieved $8,207,998 in rentals as of 30 September 1977. (According to AA, the figure was $6.5 million; *Variety* eventually revealed the figure to be $11m.) Caine and Connery claimed they were each entitled to receive $410,400, representing their $250,000 fee and 5 per cent slice of the rentals, but had received only $301,254 each.

In the week after the suit's filing, Connery unwisely chose to mount a solo attack on AA, describing his situation as 'just the tip of the iceberg' as far as Hollywood money was concerned. 'I've never cheated or stolen from anybody in my life, and I would be quite happy to stick anyone who steals from me in jail,' he declared, before going on to lash out at 'the mastodons, the Bel Air crowd, who never dirty their feet ... Everyone has a suit going against someone or the threat of a suit, but none of them ever seems to come to anything. It's as though if you ignore it long enough it will fade away.' A report in the *Los Angeles Herald Examiner* linked Connery's comments to the David Begelman embezzlement at Columbia.

Within days AA had mounted their defence, claiming that Connery and Caine had hatched a scheme to damage the company through 'publication of false and defamatory statements as to the honesty and integrity of Allied and its officers'. The 'scheme' was designed to hold down the stock price of parent company Allied Artists Industries, they alleged, and otherwise hurt the company on the eve of the release of its major 1978 movie, *The Betsy*.

They further claimed that Connery and Caine had filed their suit 'to give Connery a purported excuse to attack Allied through the press'. As to why Connery would do that in the first place, AA maintained that the whole scheme had been hatched 'for the benefit of Connery and others in furtherance of the plan announced by Connery to enter into production of films in competition with Allied'. (The suit neglected to specify Connery's supposed production plans, nor whether those 'plans' included Caine in any way.) 'Allied has been seriously prejudiced in its efforts to obtain new product', they alleged, 'in its negotiations with third parties and in its dealings with suppliers, dealers, employers, exhibitors, bankers, other lenders, television media, authors, publishers, musicians and recording companies. Among other things, Allied has been obligated to put up additional security with respect to obtaining prints of *The Betsy*, and its executives have been forced to spend an inordinate amount of time dealing with problems created by Connery and Caine.'

Connery was about to discover the first law of court action in the US – sue and be sued. In the defamation response AA mounted, however, there were two crucial differences. One was its main focus on Connery. Following his remarks to the press, the company claimed that the quotes attributed to him had been calculated to 'defame the company and its officers by imputing to them the commission of criminal acts', as well as providing evidence of the Connery/Caine 'scheme'. The second crucial difference was in the amount of money AA sought in compensation – a staggering $21.5 million from Connery alone, as well as $10 million in punitive damages from both actors.

For months on end Connery stared absolute ruin in the face. 'Film companies don't spend any sleepless nights,' he declared. 'It's just another assignment for their battery of lawyers. When you stand alone against those huge legal resources ... you realize how easily the law can strip you of everything, even when you're totally in the right.' He admitted to not having 'a good business head': 'I fall into two traps. One is believing things people tell me, the other is I find the people who are really good at business are betting with the bookies' money. I find the sharpest are the quietest. I'm not very good at delegating. I'm trying to learn that. In America, I've got two good lawyers now. American lawyers, I find, give you straightforward advice. British ones, when you say you're in the shit, tell you, "There are two ways of looking at that. Yes and no."'

He cited the parable of the Mau Mau in Kenya, where their particular tribal society had been based on oath and word of honour before the British had corrupted them and forced them to go back on their word. 'Of course,' Connery concluded, 'that society didn't have lawyers.'

John Boorman at first misunderstood Connery's main motive in the action and tried to offer his friend what he considered sound advice. 'Sean, you could do two pictures in the time you spent on this, and make more money than you'd get if you won.'

'You miss the point, lad,' Connery replied. 'Someone's got to stop them – or we're just vassals, performing monkeys.'

The two stars went on to win their case, agreeing to settle out of court, while AA's suit against both of them was thrown out. Connery was left to reflect on the cost in shredded nerve-ends: 'I said one sentence and it cost me $37,000 for lawyers and I got sued for $22 million!'

It was also something of a pyrrhic victory in that AA, the company described by John Huston during production of *The Man Who Would Be King* as 'dismal assholes', went bankrupt before any payments were made, leaving Connery and Caine on a long list of creditors. 'We don't even have alphabetical billing,' Connery joked. He devised a simple rule for future participation deals: 'If it's something simple and I can understand it, then I'll do it. If I can't understand it, then something is wrong.'

Even before the tussle with AA had begun, Connery was already embroiled in another financial nightmare, a horror from which there would be no escape for close on seven years. It began in September 1977, with Micheline's feminine intuition telling her that all was not right, either with Connery's financial affairs or with Kenneth Richards, the man to whom they were entrusted.

When the Connerys had moved from London to Marbella the removal of the furniture was left to Richards. His explanation as to why a new washing machine had failed to turn up was that he had given it to his son as a wedding present. After all, he explained to Micheline, it would have been useless to them in Spain since the power supply was different. The explanation struck her as being odd, to say the least. Later she discovered that Richards had ransacked her desk and removed private papers and letters, some of them from Connery. Totally shocked, she concluded that Richards had been trying to find some evidence of scandal he could use against them, perhaps that she had had a secret lover.

Since Connery was in Holland working on *A Bridge Too Far* at the time, Micheline flew alone to Richards's home in Switzerland to beard the accountant in his den. When she asked to see the books he kept for her husband, Richards blithely informed her that there were none. What rapidly emerged, despite his initial protestations that he knew nothing about such deals, was that Richards had systematically ploughed all of the Connery fortune with which he had been entrusted – over $3 million – into property deals in the South of France. Specifically, he had 'loaned' it to one Jean Canela.

Micheline described the discovery as the worst moment of her life. Richards, whose salary had been raised by Connery from £4,000 a year + 1 per cent of his earnings, to £12,000 + 2 per cent between 1973 and 1977, was summarily dismissed. Although Connery followed legal advice that the best way to pursue him for a return of the money was to institute proceedings through the Swiss courts, by the time the case was filed his ex-financial adviser had temporarily fled the country.

While developments lumbered on in Switzerland, another bombshell was exploded when Richards, in an attempt to seize the initiative, brought an action against Connery in 1978 in London's High Court, claiming a 2 per cent share of his ex-employer's retrospective earnings in thirteen films, including the Bond movies *Goldfinger*, *Thunderball*, *You Only Live Twice* and *Diamonds Are Forever*, as well as damages following his dismissal. Connery promptly filed a countersuit alleging negligence in the handling of his financial affairs and breach of duty.

Following a full year of Micheline working with French lawyers to unravel the mystery of his missing millions, Connery was finally able to confront Richards in open court in

1981. Eight days of hearings and four days of cross-examination followed before Richards decided to abandon his action and concede Connery's counter-claim. He had little choice. Connery's defence counsel described one of Richards's letters, alleging that the actor might go to prison if certain matters came to the attention of the Inland Revenue, as nothing less than blackmail.

'It was written in the heat of the moment when emotions were high,' Richards's counsel, Mr Roger Buckley, QC, maintained, denying any intent to blackmail. In Justice Talbot's summing up it was made perfectly clear that there was never any likelihood of blackmail, as all of Connery's accounts had been fully disclosed to the Inland Revenue. 'I have never witnessed a party's case so thoroughly destroyed,' he declared, going on to describe Richards's action as 'wholly without merit'. The accountant was ordered to pay court costs of over £100,000, together with a sum for damages and breach of duty to be assessed.

'Connery near to tears as he wins Bond film fight,' Britain's *Daily Telegraph* reported. 'I am absolutely delighted,' he confessed as he and Micheline held hands outside the courtroom. 'It's been going on since 1978 and I am thrilled that eventually justice has been done ... If I had lost I'd have had to pay him more than £100,000 and continue to pay him. But the truth came out. It was certainly an ordeal I don't want to go through again. His claim against me was for a trivial sum compared to what he owes me. Now it is up to the courts to decide how much he is responsible for, and for me to take steps through the courts to get it back.'

When Connery went on to petition for recovery of the fortune Richards had squandered, the High Court awarded him an interim £1 million in 1982. 'I'll only be happy when I see the money,' said the ever-pragmatic Connery, elation tempered by the knowledge that he was unlikely ever to see a penny of the money. 'Who knows? He may surprise everyone.' In February 1984, in a final judgement, Connery's award was increased to £2.8 million, a record for a single individual.

'The irony,' he pointed out, 'is that had Richards not started proceedings against me in England, I would probably still be awaiting the outcome of proceedings in Switzerland seven years after these started.'

Bankruptcy proceedings were duly instituted against Richards, who professed insolvency. In October 1985, the 63-year-old informed London's Bankruptcy Court that his only asset was £36 in cash and his sole income came from teaching English literature in Switzerland. Questioned by the official receiver, he agreed that he had placed around $3,250,000 of Connery's money with Canela. He acknowledged that he had no written authority to advance the money, but claimed that both Connery and his wife had known all about the deal. He also claimed to have entrusted Canela with £250,000 of his own money, without security.

When asked what the attraction of the project had been, whether he was perhaps to have received a share of the overall profits, he replied, 'Not at all. This was purely for Mr Connery.' As for his own investment: 'I thought what was good for Mr Connery was good enough for me, in my humble terms. I was getting on the bandwagon.' Richards was made bankrupt for a total of $2,879,731.

Although there was no monetary consolation, Connery's 'constant nightmare' of seven years' litigation had ended. 'I was betrayed by a man I trusted,' he summed up. 'What made matters worse was that when the case finally came to an end, the man I had thought of as a friend tried to blame my wife and make her the villain of the piece.'

Understandably, there was no question of forgiveness. 'Richards is alive and well and living on the hog in Switzerland,' Connery bitterly maintained. 'He professes to be broke, and there doesn't seem to be much I can do about it. It seems that the law inevitably protects the crook ... I'd like to wring his neck. It's very nice to be awarded money on paper, but that man should pay in flesh.'

'Sean rang my wife during the case and told her that I had $4 million,' an apparently far from contrite Richards informed the press. 'It's not true. All the furniture is my wife's and we rent our flat.' He went on to allege that Connery had once threatened him with his life. 'If I had a knife,' he maintained the star had told him, 'I would kill you.' From the protection of Lausanne he offered his ex-employer what was clearly the hollowest of open challenges: 'I'll fight him man to man!'

Connery was at least fortunate in that at least one of his pre-Richards investments had been left intact, and doubly fortunate at the appreciation it had enjoyed. Although he had resigned his directorship of Dunbar & Co in 1979, he had wisely retained the majority of the 102,857 shares he had held since the bank had begun operations a decade earlier. In December 1980, a block of 100,000 shares in the Dunbar Group, representing 10 per cent of the Company's capital, was placed with investors at 300p each. First time dealings on the City's Unlisted Securities Market produced a rise to 380p, then a further surge to 420p.

At that level Connery's original holding was worth £432,000 – £223,000 more than the placing price. It was a welcome ray of sunshine amongst the gloom of the Richards affair. A year later the situation was even brighter when the Hambro Life Assurance Group made an agreed takeover of the bank, offering a share swap of forty ordinary shares in Hambro for every thirteen of Dunbar's. The deal, worth over £10.5m, effectively valued each Dunbar share at around 812p each, boosting the worth of Connery's original holding to £835,198.

The need to replenish his depleted coffers – the fruits of years of struggle – was still pressing. 'Of course Sean was terrified of losing his money,' John Boorman confirms, 'as who wouldn't be? And he came close to being completely wiped out. He was devastated by it, deeply depressed and enraged by his whole sense of security being threatened. To make things worse, his career was uncertain at the time. He'd had very little from the Bond pictures, and he wasn't getting any younger. It just happened his looks got better and better as he grew older. Many actors reach fifty and they're no longer convincing as heroic figures. Sean was about to turn that notion on its head.'

Chapter 24

'Had they not been so greedy, today United Artists could belong to Connery, Broccoli and Saltzman.'

Sean Connery

Dennis Selinger was in Lapland in 1977 with Michael Caine, busily filming *The Eagle Has Landed* for Lord Grade, when he was astonished to receive a phone call from Connery in the early hours of the morning. 'Dennis? This is Sean,' the voice boomed.

'Sean who?' Selinger asked groggily, rubbing his eyes.

'*Sean Connery*!'

As Selinger attempted to focus on his client's concern – it seemed he was again on the receiving end of something he considered unfair – he was at the same time aware that the increasingly protracted, one-sided conversation must be clocking up a record amount of international call charges. All of a sudden Connery stopped talking, leaving just an eerie silence on the line.

'What is it, Sean?' Selinger finally asked.

'Dennis—' Connery sounded in shock— 'Dennis, I've just realized *I'm* paying for this call!' The next sound Selinger heard was the 'click' as his client dropped the phone like a hot brick.

Connery had already committed to a project to follow *A Bridge Too Far* in 1977 when news of Kenneth Richards's conduct was relayed to him in Holland by Micheline. The plot of *Meteor*, propagated on the premise that at any moment a large meteorite, or major earthquake, could strike and demolish any city on earth, would turn out to be a true disaster movie in every sense of the word.

'Here's the meteor,' English director Ronald Neame explained in his best headmaster style, almost as if he were trying to convince himself, 'five miles wide, flying at the earth at 30,000 miles an hour, and a chunk of it has hit New York's AT & T building, driving the population under the Hudson River. If the rest of it hits the land the impact would be ten times the greatest earthquake ever recorded. Earth's scientists have exactly six days to divert it from its course.' Neame, the self-styled arthouse director of movies like *The Prime of Miss Jean Brodie*, had been offered *Meteor* after his success with *The Poseidon Adventure*. 'Now I get nothing but disaster blockbusters,' he complained, decidedly tongue in cheek. After turning most of them down, he had chosen to do *Meteor*, 'because it says more than most'.

It certainly said plenty about the raising of finance and the screenwriters' lot in Hollywood. From the beginning the name that sparked interest among potential investors was Connery's; eventually the stage was reached when the movie's production became absolutely contingent upon his participation. 'Get Connery,' Warner Bros – who would stump up $4 million for the rights to the bulk of foreign territories – had urged. 'He's a hero. We need a hero-type. He's a star round the world.' Nippon-Herald, paying $1.5 million for Japanese rights, agreed, as did American-International, stumping up $2.7 million for the US and Canada. In all, $15 million was raised, in a repeat of the *Shalako* fund-raising operation.

Edmond North's first script draft was completed in the fall

of 1976. It was promptly passed on to a second writer, Steve Bach, for 'restructuring'; the result was then handed over to Connery's friend Stanley (*Woman of Straw*) Mann for a further draft. Connery responded to Mann's script by indicating that he was interested in principle and would meet with the producers, Mann, and Neame, in Los Angeles.

At Neame's Coldwater Canyon home, it quickly transpired that Connery was not wildly enthusiastic about the script as it stood, or, for that matter, any of the characters, situations or dialogue as they were presently constituted.

Neame reacted by putting a proposal of his own to Mann: 'Start with me from scratch and write an entirely new screenplay from fade-in to fade-out.' Two days later Mann dutifully reported to Neame's home; over the next six weeks a lengthy treatment was hammered out. 'If the script ends up as good as the treatment,' Connery responded from Spain, 'I'm in.' Eight weeks later, in July 1977, Mann and Neame forwarded their completed script to Marbella. (The Writer's Guild insisted, over Neame's protests, that the final credit read 'Screenplay by Stanley Mann and Edmond H. North. Story by Edmond H. North'). Connery declared himself satisfied and laid down only one stipulation – that shooting must begin by the beginning of November; if they wanted him, they had precisely twelve weeks to get their act in order.

American-International promptly rented space at MGM's Culver City studios, including Esther Williams's old swimming pool on stage 30, and frantically began construction of the elaborate and vastly expensive sets that involved a replica of part of the New York subway system. Then there was the casting to complete. Natalie Wood received her script from Guy McElwaine, who also happened to be Connery's Hollywood representative at ICM. Donald Pleasence was on board briefly, then was obliged to duck out, since he was still involved on Universal's ill-fated musical, *Sergeant Pepper's Lonely Hearts Club Band*; Brian Keith filled the breach as the Russian scientist equivalent of Connery's Dr Paul Bradley, to whom Wood's astrophysicist acts as interpreter. Karl Malden was the NASA chief; Trevor Howard the Jodrell Bank professor, Henry Fonda the US President.

The gap that often exists between studio publicity versions of stars' salaries and the real thing was amply demonstrated by a leak of how much each of the principals was pulling down. In place of Connery's alleged $2 million was a contract in the 'high six figures', albeit with his usual percentage on top, with Miss Wood in the 'low six figures'; the stars' total budget stood at $1,428,526. Neame was set to get $250,000 plus $1,000 a week in expenses, plus 7 per cent of any profits.

Before flying to Los Angeles, Connery had made a nostalgic trip down memory lane, accompanied by his mother, Micheline, Jason and stepbrother Stephane, to have a last look at 176, Fountainbridge before the demolition squad moved in. Micheline pronounced it 'dreadful', Stephane 'awful', Jason 'interesting'. Effie just looked on and smiled as the memories came flooding back. 'I wanted them to see it,' Connery said later, 'but it really *was* a dump, a terrible place, no hot water, gas mantles on the landing...'

In Los Angeles Connery's keep-fit routine included attending classes in Japanese Aikido, considered the most difficult and spiritual of martial arts. For this he enrolled in Steven Seagal's 'dojo', impressively named 'Ten Shin' (Divine Spirit of the Heart). Here he was following in the footsteps of other actors like James Mason, who had imparted a modicum of advice to aspiring actor Seagal: 'The secret is not to act, but to *be*.' Mason apart, action man Seagal credits Connery with influencing his approach to acting.

Although *Meteor* began on schedule, Neame was in a perpetual state of anxiety as one calamity followed another on the huge sets that had been constructed: roofs collapsed, scaffolding buckled, one technician tumbled thirty feet on to a concrete floor and lived to tell the tale. 'I don't want to spend my life directing great big buggers like this, but it's easier to find $15 million than it is to find $2 million,' said Neame. 'A movie has got to be bloodthirsty and brutal, or sexy and provocative, or contain some kind of shock value to get an audience. It's always been like that in Hollywood. The whole thing is a comment on the decline of the movie industry. *Meteor* won't be rubbish' – here he looked round quickly to make sure his producers weren't listening – 'but it won't be *The Prime of Miss Jean Brodie* either!'

The simulated clouds of dust that were used to give the collapse of the communications system under Manhattan an air of reality soon affected everyone's sinuses, Connery's worst of all, including a respiratory ailment that halted shooting for two days.

Following his recovery, he announced that he would do no more interviews on the movie, since he was too busy preparing the suit he and Michael Caine were bringing against Allied Artists over *The Man Who Would Be King*. During every break, he rushed back to his trailer and called his lawyers in New York. The crew was acutely aware of what was going on. 'It's you people, the distributors,' the unit publicist informed an American International representative, 'who are robbing everyone blind. As a group, you're the biggest bunch of crooks in the world. Everyone knows it. It's high time *someone* sued.'

'That may be true,' the AIP man responded, 'but the exhibitors are robbing the distributors as well. They have to make such ridiculously one-sided deals to get a hit movie that they need to skim off the ticket sales to stay in business. It's insane. The whole business has gone crazy. They're paying Marlon Brando $3 million for a few weeks' work on *Superman*. And Ryan O'Neal gets $2 million per movie. *Ryan O'Neal*! Who goes to the movies to see Ryan O'Neal for crissakes?!'

The most difficult scene of all to capture was the flooding of the subway, which began shooting on 11 January 1978 and continued for eight days – at a total cost of $1.5 million. About one million pounds of Bentonite, a jelly-like mud substance normally used by oil drillers, was trucked to MGM's stage 30 and pumped through ducts into the swimming pool to be protruded through flumes seventy feet above the subway stage. The original plan, to heat the mud to seventy degrees to make it more comfortable for the actors, was immediately abandoned when the cameras fogged up. It remained unheated at fifty-five degrees, too thick to swim in and so slippery the crew found it well nigh impossible to control.

There were considerable worries about what the mud might do to the actors if it were less than skilfully controlled. Connery was expecting the mud, but *after* he had finished saying his lines, not *during* them. Instead, when a technician mistimed the opening of the ducts, globs of wet slime hit him in the mouth while he was talking. Off he stalked, understandably upset. The problem as he saw it was not how to *act*, but how to *survive*. Neame spelled it out even more graphically: 'These sets cost millions of dollars and once we blow up the pipes and the mud collapses we've got to do it in one take. We can't go back and do it again.'

Each day the actors performed their scenes with cotton balls stuffed in their ears, having their eyes washed out after every shot. Wood, who had already pronounced the ordeal as 'like wading through pudding. When it pours down it's like being buried alive in a Mixmaster', discovered a huge shard of glass floating in the mud, then was hit by two accidentally dislodged shovels. 'We have a fine line safety factor,' one of the crew admitted, deadpan. 'We're trying to supply as much mud as possible without actually killing Sean Connery.'

The star relented during a break to discuss with the press his feelings on being back in Los Angeles and making a movie again in the States, his first since *The Molly Maguires* ten years earlier. 'I'm learning to like Los Angeles again,' he told them. 'I have more energy here. I get up at 6 a.m., drink half a gallon of milk and I'm on my way. Then when I get to the studio they cover me with a ton of stuff that stays wet, slimy and colder than hell. It looks like chocolate pudding, but it tastes like shit. Normal mud dries and takes body temperature. This stuff has oil in it and stays wet, slimy and colder than hell.'

He spelled out the advantages he had found in returning to the film capital of the world: 'This is where it's all happening as far as films are concerned. And it's nice to hear good talk again. Since I moved to Spain three years ago that's something I've missed – conversation and stimulus. But this is only a good place to be if you're working.'

The sixty-five days of shooting on *Meteor* ended on 27 January 1978, only three days over schedule. Or was it? Not for the special effects, with which the producers expressed considerable dissatisfaction. Re-shooting was scheduled, none of which, thankfully, involved the main players. 'There's an old saying in this business,' one of the producers pointed out. 'If you are going to flop, flop big. What *Meteor* will do is just make my next four or five "swindles" easier. Nobody will know for another year whether this picture is going to flop. By that time I'll be involved in a couple of other things.'

Delays in post-production put *Meteor*'s release back to Easter 1979, then October 1979, by which time the massive special effects had inflated the budget to almost $17 million. Now, after paying for prints and advertising, a net of $30 million was required just to break even, let alone make a profit.

For once the US critics were united in their appraisal, deeming the movie 'idiotic', 'hare-brained' and 'lunatic', descriptions that were echoed across the Atlantic. 'Not so much a disaster movie as a disaster,' John Coleman maintained in Britain's *New Statesman*, with Philip French in the *Observer* agreeing that director Neame 'gets it all wrong', and Derek Malcolm in the *Guardian* asserting that '*Meteor* would lose out to a firework display on a very rainy night'. 'The year's most unnecessary scare picture,' Alexander Walker summed up in London's *Evening Standard*. The movie netted just $6 million in US rentals, overall recording almost a 100 per cent loss.

Like *The Molly Maguires* and *The Red Tent* before it, *Meteor* easily captured a niche on the list of all-time cinematic flops. It also unarguably – and understandably – marked Connery's return to working purely for money, his vows after *Diamonds Are Forever* and the heady days of donating $1 million to charity superceded by Kenneth Richards' investment acumen.

*

Connery's penchant for sharpening his dialogue and working with directors in a manner approaching collaboration was in evidence once more on *The Great Train Robbery*. In adapting his own best-selling book for the screen, director Michael Crichton had gone back in time from his previous successes, *Westworld* and *Coma*, all the way back to 1855 and what was for the nineteenth century a criminal first, the daylight robbery of gold from a speeding train, the heavily protected London to Folkestone express, its bullion destined for the Crimea. With a budget set at $7 million, the movie was produced, in the summer of 1978, by John (*The Man Who Would Be King*) Foreman for hardy Italian entrepreneur Dino de Laurentiis.

With eight weeks of shooting originally scheduled at Pinewood, Connery at first declined the venture on the basis that it would use up a large chunk of his ninety-day tax window beyond which he would be obliged to pay British taxes. Only when the majority of filming was moved to Ardmore Studios in County Wicklow, John Boorman's 'manor', and Dublin, with Pinewood cut down to two weeks, was his participation confirmed. A trotting course in Phoenix Park, Dublin's largest, was the scene of an encounter between Connery's Edward Pierce and his fellow conspirators Agar (Donald Sutherland) and Miriam (Lesley-Anne Down). Blane Castle, once the home of George V's mistress, served as Pierce's London townhouse as well as an elegant bordello. The courthouse in Naas, County Kildare, and the Georgian building on the quadrangle of Trinity College, Dublin, stood in for the courthouse where Pierce was tried.

Connery agreed to do a series of particularly hazardous stunts on top of a moving train, on the understanding that the speed would be restricted to 35mph. 'When we came to do it,' he recalled, 'I knew the train was going faster and faster because we had a helicopter following me all the way out and back. When I got off the train the pilot landed in the field next to us and said I was bananas, I was doing 55mph. The pilot and I walked down to the Irish train driver ... he said 35mph was all the train could do. We looked and there was no speedometer, no gauge, and we asked how he knew it could only do 35mph. He said, "We count the trees!"'

'It wouldn't have looked nearly so effective with a double,' was still Connery's rationale. Luckily for him and for the hapless production team, Micheline was absent during these carriage-top sequences. 'Really, I was mad,' she later declared, 'because if I had been there he would *never* have ridden on the train!'

In England the requisite period splendour was beautifully recreated, notably in a reconstruction of the Crystal Palace Queen Victoria had erected in Hyde Park, as well as a section of The Strand as it was in 1855, with shoppers strolling and horse carriages moving on dirt streets, the vista culminating at St Clement Dane's Church at the Aldwych.

Dedicated 'with love and respect' to the memory of Geoffrey Unsworth, the brilliant British lighting cameraman who died shortly after completing the movie, the critical reception for *The Great Train Robbery* ran the gamut. For Frank Rich in *Time* it was 'a mediocre movie' that 'looks gorgeous but lacks bite and narrative rhythm', while Nigel Andrews in Britain's *Financial Times* found it 'hugely enjoyable'. For Derek Malcolm in the *Guardian* it was 'a bit of a disappointment', with 'the finale thrown away like a cheap farce', while, according to Philip French of the *Observer*, 'neither Connery nor Sutherland has the requisite style'.

The lukewarm notices were matched by the movie's net return of just $5 million, indicating at best a break-even at the end of the day. With a little more pace, snap and wit the result could have been very different. As it was, Connery's film fortunes had begun to echo the financial upheaval in which he was involved.

Chapter 25

'As for the producers of the Bond films, I wouldn't piss on them if they were on fire.'

Sean Connery

'All I ever did to Sean Connery was make him an international star and a very, very wealthy man.'

'Cubby' Broccoli

The renewed frenzy of activity for Connery between the start of litigation against Kenneth Richards in 1977 and the final outcome in 1985 continued unabated after *The Great Train Robbery*. With unthinkable financial catastrophe – perhaps even worse for a proud man, the bulk of his financial arrangements and misplaced trust held up to public ridicule – his back was well and truly to the wall. Fortunately, a well-known Scottish trait is for the position to reveal the race at its most resourceful.

Putting the 'missing' millions to one side, what were Connery's assets? Financially there were other investments, notably the shares he had retained in Dunbar's. On the personal side Micheline was a tower of strength, as adept at soothing a fevered brow as she was at massaging an ego. As for his stock-in-trade as an actor, he was still well-regarded despite the string of 'difficult' movies, misfires and outright flops he had endured almost non-stop since abandoning Bond. Work was the answer – *more* work, *more* movies, and for new money that would not be flung into the black hole of the past.

Incredibly, or perhaps not so incredibly, considering his track record of only scoring major successes outside of Bond in what amounted to guest spots, the only movie that clicked at the box-office in the next few years was one in which he again played a cameo. First up came an unfortunate reunion with Richard Lester. The director had never ceased looking for a new project to reunite them from the moment he had finished work on *Robin and Marian*. It was a process he had never undergone before with an actor, and something he was normally against in principle. But their first collaboration had gone so well. . .

Cuba emerged from discussions with producer Denis O'Dell; in 1960 a mutual friend had witnessed Castro's takeover of the country. Scriptwriter Charles Wood was contacted to create a personal drama set against this backdrop; Lester felt it would be fascinating to watch a culture and society changing from a sleazy, half-Mafia fascist dictatorship to a society run by a rigid set of principles, all within a matter of three days. What would the experience be like for an ordinary person? 'We set out to show just that,' says Lester, 'but soon discovered we were making a film about a whole bunch of extras, with no star role. So we developed this character who was hired as a mercenary by Batiste and then realizes he's on the wrong side.'

With Connery signed as soldier-of-fortune Robert Dapes, teamed with Brooke Adams as his old flame Alexandra Pulido (replacing Diana Ross, an early choice), and with a strong supporting cast boasting Jack Weston, Martin Balsam, Hector Elizondo, Denholm Elliott and Chris Sarandon, the start of shooting in Spain was delayed several times in a vain attempt to iron out script problems. September, which would have been ideal weather-wise, became a far from ideal 27 November 1978. Quite apart from the deadline, imposed by Connery to suit his schedule, Lester became extremely concerned that he might be seen as trivializing a vital period in world history.

Some aspects of the character Connery was to play became less appealing as Lester and Woods wrestled with each new draft. 'Sean was playing a man who was dumbstruck with the political machinations and sophistication, as well as the cynicism of his former girlfriend, who had been fifteen when they had had their affair,' says Lester. 'He started out as a soldier, then a soldier of fortune, then a mercenary, then a parasite, but he was still doing the same job and didn't understand the change. His girlfriend is the one who has to tell him that he doesn't understand anything. That's the quality of innocence that Sean produces on the screen. It's a wonderful skill and I think there's an element of truth in it. Sean is one of the easiest people in the world to live with, he's uncomplicated and I don't think he wants complications in his life. He's a pussycat – and I mean that in the best way, there's nothing better than innocence in personal relationships. Not for politicians, though, and this is where his character became lost in *Cuba*.'

Enormous technical problems plagued the unit's eventual progress in Spain. Three days before filming was due to start all army bases were placed on alert following the assassination of a Spanish general. The *Cuba* unit was promptly declared out of bounds, and all the military equipment immediately withdrawn. The boiler of a locally hired train blew up on the first day. A DC-5 on loan from its base in Malaga hit a tree on the rehearsal lift-off and was declared hors de combat. With no train, no plane and no tanks for the crucial evacuation scenes in the last reel, Lester was forced to ad-lib frantically. Mock-up tanks were improvised that were little more than piles of hardboard mounted on Landrovers; extraordinarily skilful use was made of the stationary train; the fuselage of the grounded DC-5 was made to look determinedly airborne and matched with the rehearsal shots. That the script stubbornly remained unresolved was even more difficult to camouflage, while the freezing cold made it well nigh impossible to give the movie the look of stifling hot Havana; four little black children brought in from Cadiz cried their eyes out when asked to remove their tracksuits.

'You can never foresee these things,' Lester contends. 'I mean going in, I always expect each movie to be as good as anything before, because you just continue hoping and intending that each draft will be an improvement on the last. And nothing ever comes out exactly as you want anyway. Anybody in life will tell you that.'

During the shoot Connery and Lester largely dispensed with the niceties of social evenings. This was convenient in one sense since neither are particularly social animals. 'While I'm shooting,' says Lester, 'I might only have a drink once a week in the evening. I have a bath and think about tomorrow. I work on my nerves, pulling the crew along. On the occasions when Sean and I have spent evenings together I've found him someone who likes to relax and have a laugh. I think he's very much aware of money, all the stories are true, but he's a far more interesting man than that implies.'

Signs of Connery's disgruntlement with the production were soon in daily evidence. On location in Seville and with a weekend break looming up, he spurned one reporter who had waited all day for an interview. 'As soon as I get this stuff off,' he growled, pointing to his dark make-up and hairpiece, 'I'm off. I can't hang around, I'm driving home to Marbella and it's a long drive. That's *it*.' Then he looked at the reporter with a half-pleading expression. 'Give me a break,' he suggested with a smile. 'I've done my bit.'

As he drove off Denis O'Dell gave a helpless shrug. 'That's Sean,' he said. Then, perhaps in reference to the star's ongoing financial litigation, as well as his immediate concerns on the movie, he added, 'The man has a lot on his mind right now.'

Although nervous and considerably overawed by her co-star, Brooke Adams watched as Connery spent considerable time happily rehearsing with the cast, including those with much more formal training. 'Most actors like to keep secret what they do and how they do it,' said Adams. 'Not Sean. He taught me how to psychologize a character. He left the room and walked in like two different men simply by altering his relationship to space; the difference was incredible. But mostly I'm in awe of his never trying to *inspire* awe.'

The shop-floor acclaim for Connery remained rock-solid despite all the problems. 'He never throws his weight around, and always treats everyone with respect,' one of the technicians testified. 'I truly think he regards himself as a member of the crew, and maybe, because of his background, is more comfortable with technicians, electricians, grips and gaffers than with big shots. I've heard that he uses his fame and power to get what he wants from front offices, but when he's working, it's almost as if he's unaware of both.'

Cuba was wrapped after ten weeks of filming on seventy-eight locations from Seville to Jerez to Cadiz. Although there was little joy on the set, Lester says that Connery's apportionment of the blame for the production débâcle was never made known directly to him, even after a viewing of the assembled footage. The star's later view of the movie as 'a fatal error . . . a case of patchwork', that 'Lester hadn't done his homework', was relayed second-hand.

The movie was mercilessly lambasted by the critics, the pack led by Stanley Kauffman in *New Republic*: 'The picture begins by *telling* you it's going to be bad . . . Every line of *Cuba* could have been written by a good film-writing student who had made a close study of *Casablanca*. Connery is more flexible than usual, but still a bit of a stodge. *Cuba* is, in the perspective of Lester's accomplishments and talent, a bitter reminder of filmmaking realities.' Pauline Kael in *New Yorker* joined the attack: 'Lester has pinned everything to a plot that is so unconvincingly presented and so imperfectly worked out than we are not simply bored and disappointed but almost affronted at the misuse of so much promising stuff.' *Variety* wrote: 'Cuba displays uniformly unsympathetic characters enacting a vague plot amidst a splendid recreation of Havana at the very end of the Batiste regime. Of no help either is the ineffectual interloper played, with unusually uncertain footing, by Sean Connery.'

The *Boston Phoenix* gave both Connery *and* his hairpiece a bad review: 'I didn't know so much eyewash could exist in one screenplay, but writer Charles Wood has me flummoxed ... Nor does Lester make much effort to wrest a decent performance from the usually masterful Connery, who appears terribly preoccupied with his toupee here.'

Cuba's box-office fate was sealed; a perfect example of 'Suppose they made a movie and nobody came? ...' At a press conference in 1981, Connery added his two cents' worth. 'I haven't made too many mistakes,' he claimed at a press conference, 'but I made one with *Cuba*.'

Lester was shattered by the reception afforded his movie and still struggles today to put his finger on where the project went so wrong. 'I think we got over-interested in Sean's character and his love affair and shunted the revolution into the background. Then we tried to balance it with the strength of Sean's personality. I think he wanted *Cuba* to be a more romantic film than we did. But the film kept shifting back and forth and we all failed to get it right in the end.'

Considering the miracle of symmetry the same team had wrought with *Robin and Marian*, Connery and Lester might have been expected to put *Cuba* firmly behind them and forgive and forget. Instead, the unforgiving side of Connery's personality was starkly revealed. 'I haven't heard from Sean from our last moments on *Cuba* to this day,' Lester admitted more than a decade later, regret etched on his features. 'Oh, I walked into a golf club once and bumped into him and we exchanged a few pleasantries, but that's all. He is a very strong character and things come out in a very black and white way.'

Chapter 26

'I've been screwed by more people than a hooker.'

Sean Connery

The parting of the ways from ICM's Dennis Selinger, for Michael Ovitz's thrusting Creative Artists Agency (CAA), was amicable enough. 'I think he wanted to make a clean break from everybody,' Selinger rationalized in 1991. 'Basically, he fell out with my people who represented him in America. He doesn't have anyone here in Britain now to represent him and seems quite happy with that arrangement. We didn't part enemies. We still see each other, I last saw him during the summer in Monte Carlo. Six or seven years ago I had something written for Sean and Michael and Roger together, in which they all played sea captains, an old-fashioned action drama. We finally got a deal with Joe Levine. Then Joe died and it fell apart and I've been unable to resurrect it. *All the Tea in China* it was called; Sean was a bit worried about working with Roger, that it would be seen as two Bonds working together, a bit of a gimmick, but it was a bloody good story and one day I'll get it made without Sean.

'He can be enormously charming, he can be enormously

difficult, he's almost a person of extremes. That middle lane thing almost isn't there at all, except maybe at home. I'm very fond of him and I'm proud to have done something in his life. I think I helped him at a certain time in his career, whatever he may say, and I'm glad to have had the opportunity to do it. I miss him.'

Terry Gilliam seldom consciously thinks about the filmmakers who have influenced him, but when put to it he will mention the names of Kurosawa, Kubrick, Fellini, Bergman – and Buster Keaton. Disney was a huge influence on him as well; not only his cartoons, but elements of *Herbie Goes Bananas*, *Treasure Island* and *20,000 Leagues under the Sea*.

Gilliam's theory is that truly creative people are freaks whose genes failed to click together in the accepted mode. On the one hand he has a need and a desire to create work that will excite, stimulate and shock the world, on the other, he longs simply to entertain, just for the fun of it. It is a balancing act he constantly seeks to perfect.

A chance meeting with John Cleese in New York led to Gilliam hiring him to appear in a photo-story for *Help!*, a satirical magazine he was editing. In 1967, when he decided to move to Britain, he renewed contact with Cleese, who gave him the names of several television producers, one of whom was Humphrey Barclay of *Do Not Adjust Your Set*. Eric Idle recalls his first glimpse of the émigré: 'Mike Palin and Terry Jones didn't like him at first, but soon came around. He arrived wearing this strange goatskin coat from Afghanistan. For me, it was love at first sight. I fell in love with that coat at once!'

A soulmate was found in Terry Jones during the Monty Python years, for the two of them were frustrated directors. Together with Cleese, Idle, Palin and Graham Chapman, they worked on the Pythons' first cinematic outing, *And Now For Something Completely Different*. The movie flopped; it seemed that no one was ready for a big-screen version of what could be seen for free on television. They tried again with *Monty Python and the Holy Grail*, this time directed by both Terrys.

It was shot in just five weeks, and for £250,000. 'Don't ask me how,' says Gilliam.

Gilliam has what he sees as a fairly modest aim in making movies, that of encouraging his audience to perceive the world a little differently. He understands and shares the element of security all of us crave. The walks on the wild side he frequently encourages represent his antidote to the everyday anodyne. Like most artists he enjoys life 'on the edge', while admitting that living in constant chaos would be his personal worst nightmare. Gilliam has always been intrigued by the artist René Magritte, who lived a typical middle-class life, wore a business suit and bowler and went to work each morning, even as he was twisting and turning the world in his art. Like Magritte, Gilliam requires frequent doses of the routine and commonplace to ground him.

The broad dark streak that he also encompasses is another, perhaps less obvious side of his own personality. In a quiet, reflective moment, he admits to thinking about mortality almost every day since childhood. He used to fantasize about his own funeral when he was twelve years old.

The idea of making a movie out of a poem, *Jabberwocky*, held enormous appeal. Eric Idle maintains that 'a typical Gilliam con' raised finance for the movie – the claim, utter nonsense of course, that the entire Python team would be participating.

When EMI pulled out of the next *real* Python movie, *Life of Brian*, as the crew were heading for Tunisia, George Harrison bounded to the rescue, establishing HandMade Films with his manager Denis O'Brien. After the movie proved a huge success, a large assortment of different projects were discussed with HandMade. Gilliam tried to sell *Brazil* to O'Brien at the time and got nowhere. Then, over one hectic weekend, he came up with the idea for *Time Bandits*, six dwarf former employees of God.

It was Connery's participation – following a record sixteen-month lay-off after *Cuba* – that lifted the enterprise off the ground. With his name attached the canny Gilliam was soon able to put the rest of his package together, including cameos from Sir Ralph Richardson (as 'The Creator'), David Warner, Ian Holm, Michael Palin, Shelley Duvall, John Cleese and *Soap*'s Katherine Helmond. A schoolboy, Craig Warnock, who had never acted before, was cast in the leading role of the time-traveller.

Connery saw the movie as 'a child's picture about a kid's fantasy, as well as being about the kind of modernized, contemporary parents who are much more interested in Green Stamps and toasters and that kind of thing than their son. In the boy's fantasy he goes into a dream that takes place all over the world; he's with Napoleon and he runs around with the six dwarfs. I'm his sort of father figure, Agamemnon, whom he discovers fighting this man with a bull's head on in Ancient Greece, and I start to teach him about life and what have you.'

Connery revealed that he had always been a fan of the Python school of humour, to the extent of having the pro-grammes taped and preserved for repeated viewing. Without that admiration he probably would not have agreed to do the few days required on *Time Bandits*, thereby excluding himself from his biggest box-office involvement since the heady days of Bond.

For his part Gilliam had been impressed with Connery since his first sight of him coming ashore on the screen in *The Longest Day*: 'He stuck out in my mind as someone who was exceptionally good at comedy. His timing was excellent. Then what impressed me was his choosing movies like *A Fine Madness* and *The Hill* after the Bonds that were really dark, intelligent, dangerous, non-commercial films. He did a lot of work which basically failed. In Bond he had that twinkle and that's what I wanted in *Time Bandits*.'

Gilliam had dinner with Connery every night during the star's brief stint on the movie location in Morocco, shot next to a golf course where Connery played with racing driver James Hunt. He recalls two topics dominating their conver-sation – golf and money. 'Talking to him every night, there was just less and less to talk about,' he recalls. 'He's obsessed with money, and he's got this deal with CAA – he was one of their first clients – where he gets money direct from the studio and pays *them* their 10 per cent because he says otherwise they tend to hold on to the money and why should they be earning the interest? He says he's the only one in Hollywood to have this deal. His being very big on litigation is this thing about not wanting to be screwed. He feels that it's morally wrong they should get away with all this crap. He's big enough to fight it and he will. The other side is that I keep hearing all these stories about these Scottish charities he supports.'

Shooting in Morocco overran after Gilliam had promised to release Connery a day earlier than originally planned. When it looked as if he wasn't going to be able to make his departure with a day to spare after all, the star was not a happy man and did not hesitate to communicate his distress.

Despite being alternately addressed by Connery in his roughly humorous manner as either 'Boy' or 'Quasimodo', Gilliam sees Connery as one of the most impressive men he's ever met: 'He is what every star should be, a gentleman. His voice just booms and he knows how to use his voice and stature. In Morocco he was great. He didn't demand special treatment, he really pitched in, he's a real pro. We had this scene when he had to mount a horse and he refused, because he said he couldn't do it gracefully anymore. He wouldn't let me shoot it, although I said I wouldn't use it without his approval. He didn't trust me. He *doesn't* trust people. It's a defensive thing. He's been screwed, and feels he's going to be screwed again and he's going to protect himself at all costs.

'Impressive as he is, he doesn't *give* as much as he could because of this defensiveness. He knows what he can do and does it very economically. In a strange way there's not a great generosity of spirit, but I think there could be with someone he trusted completely. He'd never worked with me before, after all. He did some great things, though. We were shooting on a mountain top with this little boy who'd never made a film before and was scared stiff. Sean saw me floundering a bit and refused to waste time. He said I should shoot his stuff quickly and then I could spend time with the boy and shoot him separately.'

Gilliam throws an interesting light on Connery's motivation for accepting his role in *Time Bandits*. 'I think the surrogate father in him was intrigued by the role. Maybe he felt guilty that he hadn't been the father he should have been, which is the standard guilty thing of most actors. He asked for scenes where he could shout at the kid and not just be a goody-goody, and that impressed me. He wasn't trying to be lovable.

'He also came up with the ending, that Agamemnon should reappear after the dream sequence as the present-day fireman. We were shooting in England by this time and because he only had a certain number of days he's allowed, we ran out of time with him. I had to write him out of the big battle scene and then had to beg him for a couple of hours when he was next in London on other business. I put him in a fireman's outfit and took two shots with him, one pushing the boy down and saying, "Are you all right?", the second in the fire truck looking back and winking at the kid. Then we wrote a scene around that and it worked beautifully. But it was entirely Sean's idea and it was nice to be forced into using it. He knows so much about filmmaking he really should be a director, he's so well organized. And he simply *exudes* sex. When he lifts his bull's head up in the movie and his short Greek skirt rises, every woman in the audience goes "*Woooo*!"'

Despite the time the two men spent together on *Time Bandits*, Gilliam felt he never got to know Connery all that well. 'Sean somehow scared me a little,' he readily admits. 'Not that we've ever had a fight or anything, but I felt that I didn't want to ask him favours, to impose on him. You have to know where the boundaries are with him. His wife keeps him on a tight rein. I'm intrigued by the man – men generally are in awe of him, but aren't threatened by him. That's because he's bigger than any of us!!'

HandMade released *Time Bandits* in America through the tiny Avco Embassy company, with the $5 million prints and ads bill being guaranteed from England. Some of the reviews were less than overwhelming, Richard Corliss in *Time* deeming *Time Bandits* 'a ragged film that misuses Holm's talents, underuses Cleese's and doesn't use Connery's at all'. Carrie Rickey in *Village Voice*, however, described the movie as 'part kiddy adventure, part grown-up wit and all enjoyable'. Britain's *Sunday Times* found it 'the most thoroughly satisfying, frightening, comical – even educational children's film in ages'.

To the astonishment of everyone, with the possible exception of Gilliam, his $5.5 million movie went on to net over $20 million in the US, equalling the combined income from Connery's last three flops – *The Great Train Robbery*, *Meteor* and *Cuba*, together with the next three – *Outland*, *Wrong Is Right* and *Five Days One Summer*.

Connery was working, but the lead roles he was choosing were refusing to work for him. 'My financial track record hasn't been too good,' he admitted. 'I have to accept responsibility for that . . . The unsuccessful ones started before the script was completed. In the last fifteen years the business has gone arse over face. You get two names on a piece of paper between two dates and you go ahead with nothing else ready . . . which proves that because a so-called name is starring in a film doesn't guarantee its commercial success. But it's really a two-stage experience. First you make the film you want to make, and then after it's completed you see it and realize you've done what you wanted to do in the first place. But then comes the period when the public and critics see it – and how they accept it.'

For Connery and all concerned with his movies, that moment of truth was becoming increasingly painful. At least the family coffers were being significantly replenished; after years of camping out in John Schlesinger's pad while staying in Los Angeles, Connery finally purchased an apartment of his own, and, as further evidence of his returning confidence, an investment for the future in the shape of a 600-acre pig and cattle farm in Iowa.

Chapter 27

'A lot of actors, myself included, have pushed for all manner of change in films, like taking salary cuts in return for a piece of the profits. It's a thankless effort. When a film is a success, actors who have gambled like this are obliged to bring auditors in and fight court cases for money they should be entitled to without question. It's a joke, and the future of the movie industry will depend upon management accepting equal responsibilities.'

Sean Connery

Among several projects Connery chose to turn down in the early 1980s was an adaptation of *Taipan* offered by Dino de Laurentiis; in view of how that turned out, in the version starring Bryan Brown, it was an extremely wise decision. Then there was another project emanating from author James Clavell, the ABC-TV mini-series, *Shogun*.

Anxious to get back to work and continue to rebuild his fortune, he seriously considered producer Ray Stark's offer of Daddy Warbucks in the film version of the smash stage musical, *Annie*. During the course of singing lessons he undertook, however, Connery began to feel pressured by the daily phone calls from the extraordinarily persistent Stark. 'I was bugged,' he admitted. 'I wouldn't make a decision until I was sure I could do it well enough. I didn't want to take it on and then find I was going to be dubbed.' In the end, possibly because the vocal calisthenics were too much to contemplate, Connery changed his mind and cleared the way for Albert Finney to take over.

He signed instead for *Outland*, a science-fiction movie scripted by director Peter Hyams, despite the fact it was to be shot in London. This was partly because he felt that the technical facilities there were superior (the unit would utilize much of the *Star Wars* equipment) but also because he hadn't made a complete film there in Britain since 1974. Needless to say, the movie still had to be produced within his ninety-day tax window.

Hyams's stated goal was a specific intensity, an attempt to make a movie set in the future that was charged with emotion. Following a series of unexplained deaths among the Con-Amalgamate titanium mining colony on Io, the third moon of Jupiter, Connery's Marshall O'Neil is dispatched to sort things out. Deserted by his wife (Kika Markham), O'Neil's only friend on the colony is an elderly unit doctor (Francis Sternhagen) as he locks horns with the dastardly mining boss Sheppard (Peter Boyle), nefariously intent on 'frying the brains' of the miners as a side effect of the drugs designed to boost their productivity. When Sheppard flies in a killer elite led by the deadly Montone (James B. Sikking) the stage is set for O'Neil to face the final shootout alone. In Hollywood shorthand *Outland* was soon dubbed '*High Noon* in space'.

The $14 million movie was the first real flowering of ex-20th Century-Fox chief Alan Ladd Jr's own Ladd Co., following a bridging release of Bette Midler's concert movie, *Divine Madness*. His unprecedented run at 20th Century-Fox had been the envy of Hollywood, as he scored not only with spectaculars like *Star Wars* and *Alien*, but smaller, intimate movies like Fred Zinnemann's *Julia*, Peter Yates' *Breaking Away* and Herbert Ross' *Turning Point*.

Connery conceded that even with a good script he normally had difficulty identifying with futuristic tales, partly because of the technological paraphernalia involved that to him was so much gobbledegook. With the colony's mines in the movie constantly under surveillance by a complex video camera/computer system, he struggled at first to get a handle on the technology involved, realizing that skilled access would be second nature to O'Neil. In time, however, he reminded himself that the mechanics were only as good as the information fed to them, that it still came down to people. This made the hardware seem much less intimidating; as long as the down-to-earth Connery could see a human hand involved, the problem vanished.

It was a field day for Connery watchers as the star chose to throw some light on the increasingly mysterious selection process he used. *Outland*, it seemed, had struck a personal chord. He saw O'Neil as a decent man, but one with a big mouth that had landed him in trouble before; now he was in a classic confrontation with greed: 'I never have any specific thing in mind in advance. What does impress me is the writing and you can always tell by the first few pages whether you like what the writer's about. Of course it's always difficult to find an original idea, but it's even harder to find really good dialogue, and if somehow there's a combination of both original ideas with good dialogue ... well, that's what it's all about ... The picture also says something important about what people have to do if civilization is to survive. Very few things fall at once. Whether it's a society or an individual, decay is a slow process, and it's caused by people. Sometimes they may not even know they're causing it, which is really tragic. Little discourtesies that cause a chain reaction – someone cuts you off on the road, and when you get home, you yell at your kids. Someone in the press misrepresents you, so you're wary about doing a lot of interviews. It's a slow and relentless process that we have to reverse somehow. That's a theme in our picture.' Inadvertently or not, much of it could also be taken as a theme in the continuing Connery saga.

In mid-shooting at Pinewood a futuristic bar room, not dissimilar to the way-station in *Star Wars*, was assembled. 'When Sean comes in,' Hyams informed the dozens of extras dressed as mine workers, 'I want everyone to look at him. All eyes on Sean.' Unsurprisingly, since they were all in complete awe of him, none of the extras seemed to have the slightest problem following this particular instruction, their reaction spilling over spontaneously in the studio canteen a couple of hours later. During lunch Connery grunted courteously enough at the fairly constant stream of visitors to his table, but leapt to his feet when Sir Ralph Richardson tottered over; he venerated the actor and did not hesitate to show it. The feeling, it turned out, was reciprocated. 'My dear boy,' Sir Ralph greeted him, '*wonderful* to see you.'

'Wonderful character,' Connery said later. 'He still rides a motor bike to work. At his age! Can you imagine?' He was less enamoured with the occasional antics of fellow-cast member Boyle. The previous afternoon, after half an hour's rehearsal together, it had become obvious that Boyle's mind was elsewhere. Connery had arranged for a further rehearsal early in the morning and arrived at Pinewood punctually at 9 am, raring to go. Boyle finally showed up two hours later. In a scene completed a couple of days earlier Connery's O'Neil had been filmed striding through a crowd and punching Boyle on the mouth. 'You can't help feeling,' one of the crew now remarked, 'that Sean might have put more feeling into that scene if it were being filmed today!'

Enveloped in his spacesuit, Connery later found himself suspended from a harness to simulate weightlessness. When the cameras failed to roll on cue, he angrily signalled to be let down. 'Get everything set to shoot before you put that harness round my balls again,' he sternly instructed.

If all was not sweetness and light during *Outland*'s filming this was mainly, though not entirely, due to outside factors – like Britain's tax laws. Here he was, Connery railed, responsible for bringing a $14 million production to England, and having to fly off every weekend to conserve his precious ninety-day allowance. The period, he contended, should be a personal allowance and exclude working days, although he conceded that tax might legitimately be levied on British earnings.

To many it sounded as though Connery wanted to have his cake and eat it too, his ninety-day window having already been narrowed by his insistence on regularly attending pro-celebrity matches for BBC TV ('There's no matching Scottish courses'), rendering even more imperative his regular weekend flights.

As far as Hyams was concerned Connery's contribution to *Outland* was all-encompassing: 'When there's a leading role in a film for a man who has to portray a sense of strength as well as a sense of intelligence and vulnerability, Sean is one of the few people who spring to mind. He is an extraordinary actor. His emotions seem very close to the surface of his skin. You have the sense that you can truly sense what he's feeling. He's wonderful, and he's a remarkable craftsman. He raises the level of everyone around him.'

At fifty Connery was at the stage where he felt entitled to hold a mini-review of his life. He contrasted Jason's attendance at Gordonstoun, where Prince Edward was a fellow pupil, with his own 'street' education. 'You could argue for his style of upbringing,' he agreed, 'and you could argue for mine. But each cannot know the other, so we talk from two different viewpoints.'

He admired young people and claimed to enjoy their music enormously – even punk rock. 'The lyrics are much more interesting that any we had,' he suggested, chuckling as he recalled the Fountainbridge fare of the 1940s and '50s. 'Remember the one that went, "I'm Going to Buy a Paper Doll To Call My Own?" I ask you! Youngsters of today are looking for a reason for living, in a much more direct, refreshing way, and I approve of that.'

He rued a few legacies from his own misspent youth: 'I have terrible knees from all the soccer I played as a kid. I have a cartilage in one knee and it's like iron filings in the other. I can still sprint around a bit, mark you, though I'm pretty crook at the end of a strenuous game of tennis. I think it has a lot to do with all the delivering of milk I did as a child, in the rain and going straight to school in wet clothes.' A pause. 'I don't think the whisky helps either.'

Without naming names, he listed what had become his bête noire: 'There's nothing worse than being directed by someone who's incompetent – nothing more boring, annoying or maddening. As far as I'm concerned people can make a multitude of errors, as long as they're enthusiastic. Enthusiasm is the most important quality of all in my book. I hate negative people, and those who are not prepared to take risks . . .'

The topic of money – the earning of it, the keeping of it, even the losing of it – was never far away from Connery's mind. 'If there's any advice I'd give anyone,' he said, 'it's get a good lawyer . . . I had a period when I was involved in all sorts of business transactions – you name it, I was in it. And all these operations should have been put through a lawyer. But it never occurred to me. The trouble is, most people believe mistakenly that everybody's like themselves. That's especially true of people from my kind of background. Man to man, that was good enough for me for any deal. But I've found, having seen both sides, that one can certainly be over-trusting. I've also found, the older I get, the more so-called "experts" there are. It gets kind of spooky.

'Money helps,' Connery hastened to concede. 'I remember when you didn't call the doctor to your house but went and sat in a freezing waiting room instead because calling the doctor out cost fifteen bob! I'm still not entirely used to having money. I still go around the house putting out all the unused lights.'

As John Boorman is the first to testify . . .

As *Outland*'s première approached, with Connery predicting the film would take 'a fortune', he saw that his screen work occurred in cycles. His last run had been with *The Wind and the Lion*, *The Man Who Would Be King* and *Robin and Marian* – all of them made entirely on location. Since shooting *Outland* he had already completed Richard Brooks' *Wrong Is Right* and was preparing for Fred Zinnemann's *Five Days One Summer*. 'It's like coming across three good pieces of material again,' he enthused.

As Alan Ladd Jr and his associates prepared to sweat their way through *Outland*'s crucial preview in Texas, Laddie confided that every preview he had ever attended had been terrifying. 'But we feel *Outland* has the potential to do something extraordinary at the box-office,' he added. 'That only increases the possibilities and the tension. What if we've been fooling ourselves?'

Tickets began selling at 1 pm in the 1,100-seater theatre in Dallas's North Park Shopping Center and were sold out by 7 pm. As the lights dimmed Laddie was still heard to fret: 'The ending doesn't work. The last third of the picture has no punch.' A sigh. 'But it's fixable.'

Variety kicked off with a reasonably encouraging review, even while detecting several mile-wide plot holes and one key under-developed main character: 'The film emerges as a tight, intriguing old-fashioned drama that gives audiences a hero worth rooting for . . . Connery delivers a stellar performance . . . overall *Outland* is a fine picture. The real problem is that it could have been better.'

From then on it was downhill all the way. Richard Corliss in *Time Magazine* had no doubt as to the film's major asset: 'If *Outland* has anything besides familiarity going for it, it is the presence of Sean Connery . . . He is perhaps the one genuine romantic hero in the movies now. He is strong; he is soft. He can be hurt physically, and take it; he can be hurt emotionally, and show it. *Outland* gives Connery every chance to strut and smoulder and sends him off on one splendid chase sequence. The rest is strained silliness.'

Rolling Stone was no more encouraging: 'Connery himself, though fitter than ever and still able to command an audience with his charisma, looks glum. Perhaps this big bruin of a man knows that in a shoddy sideshow like this, he's just another dancing bear.'

Comparisons to *High Noon* were superficial, according to Jack Gelmis of *Newsday*, who saw *Outland* as 'A ludicrous updating of the morality tale starring Cooper and Kelly. Connery and Boyle give rote performances. Their dialogue is so banal you expect them to blush as actors, or the movie to suddenly reveal itself as deliberate parody – like Mel Brooks turning the western genre inside out with *Blazing Saddles*. But *Outland* is no comedy. It's a *travesty*.'

Back home in Scotland, with Connery again organizing an Edinburgh première for the movie, there was little relief from the critical onslaught, Tom Hutchinson in the *Scotsman* detecting 'no real glow of illumination' beneath 'Hyams' surface flash'. He saw the movie as populated by 'two-dimensional cut-outs', with only Connery amplifying O'Neil into a credible human being. 'Certainly, he isn't helped by the script,' Hutchinson maintained. 'It seems more than an instinct with him, shaped by years of professionalism.'

If only, many wished, all the 'years of professionalism' could be put to better use than the ill-conceived projects Connery continued to choose with almost unerring frequency. *Outland*'s US net of $10m reflected not only the movie's lack of impact – the lame ending that Laddie had spotted at the preview was never properly fixed – but also a misguided campaign to continue selling the film as '*High Noon* in space'.

'It was ill-advised and wrong,' Fred Zinnemann, *High Noon*'s original director, declared. 'I saw *Outland* and naturally observed similarities in isolated incidents, but the pictures were *totally* different in mood and meaning.' Connery was unrepentent. 'What was clever,' he insisted, 'was setting it in space – a frontier town. *That* was what appealed to me in the first place.'

Chapter 28

'Sean's a great big pussycat, a rare animal. He talks to you
like a person. He doesn't put on airs.'

James B. Sikking

Richard Brooks route to the director's chair had been forged as
a writer on such classics as *The Killers*, *Brute Force* and *Key
Largo*. As a director he had known disaster before, notably
when failing to do justice to Joseph Conrad's *Lord Jim*. On the
other hand there was his groundbreaking *Blackboard Jungle*,
riveting *Elmer Gantry* and arguably the best-ever Tennessee
Williams adaptation, *Cat on a Hot Tin Roof*; somewhere in the
middle came the controversial, over-the-top *Looking for Mr
Goodbar*.

When Connery accepted the role of an on-the-spot international reporter in Brooks' *Wrong Is Right* – personally adapted
by the director from Charles McCarry's novel, *The Better Angels*
– circumstances were unusual, to say the least. The rest of the cast
received just an outline and their script pages. Connery was the
only one to receive the final script; according to Brooks, previous
work of his had been zeroxed and stolen, and he had no intentions
of inviting a repeat performance.

Set in 'the near future', the plot involved political dirty tricks, hidden microphones, spy satellites, two missing nuclear bombs, paranoid CIA chiefs, treacherous oil tycoons, exercise bikes in the Oval office – and assassins lurking round every corner. Connery described it as 'a kind of thriller story, a kind of satire, and it touches on terrorism. I think it's a terrific subject and it's got terrific stuff in it.' So badly did he want to make the movie that he agreed to film in the US, with 70 per cent of his salary going to Uncle Sam. He admired Brooks's track record and viewed the rough-hewn crew-cut director as an extremely complex individual, even as they worked in harmony together on the material.

Although previous endeavours had raised serious questions about Connery's artistic judgement, *Wrong Is Right* would qualify as the ultimate finger-pointer. According to Stanley Kauffman in *New Republic*: '*Wrong Is Right*'s only distinction is that, besides being *basically rotten*, it's also rotten on the surface. I'll spare you the inanities of the plot and the stupidities of the characters ...' Carrie Rickey of *Village Voice* found the movie, 'Sadly, miserably unfunny' while Robert Garrett of the *Boston Herald* exclaimed, 'What a dog of a movie this is! *Wrong Is Right* is all wrong. The editing is incredibly sloppy, the feel of the film is cheap and tinny, the jokes are zeppelins which self-destruct prior to laughter ... Sean Connery is totally wasted.' Alan Brien described the movie in the *Sunday Times* as 'an incredible hodge podge'.

'Brooks wants to be Stanley Kubrick,' David Denby attested in *New Yorker Magazine*, 'but his satirical thrust at the craziness of international politics rapidly degenerates into clownishness ... Sean Connery is miscast and distinctly uneasy.' Vincent Canby in the *New York Times* agreed with the Kubrick comparison: '*Wrong Is Right* is Mr Brooks's attempt to make a black comedy, something on the apocalyptic order of Kubrick's *Dr Strangelove*. He has a couple of major defects to be successful in this kind of project. He is a man with no great feeling for comedy of any sort and his reaction to the lunacies of contemporary life are trivial. Mr Brooks's screenplay is supercharged and uniformly silly. The star is Sean Connery, giving his first uncertain performance of an otherwise exemplary career.'

'Apocalyptic' turned out to be a good way of describing *Wrong Is Right*'s performance in the US, where it netted just a few hundred thousand dollars. In a desperate attempt to boost business on its British release Columbia Pictures changed the title to *The Man with the Deadly Lens*, an allusion to James Bond that probably outraged Connery as much as it did Saltzman and Broccoli. The company need not have bothered; the title change fooled no one.

Some years later, towards the end of the Reagan era, Connery stubbornly continued to stand by the movie. 'It's full of guys using that kind of double talk which Larry Speaks, the White House press spokesman who has just resigned, used over the Irangate business. "Are you saying that the President said that?" "No, I didn't say that the President said that." "Are you saying the President *didn't* say that?" "No, I'm not saying that the President didn't say that either." And the film was about people who were giving terrorists weapons on the one hand so as they could bomb New York and hold it to ransom, and then they're giving the public statements about never giving in to terrorism. Very topical.'

Dilys Powell, the doyenne of UK-based film critics (perhaps, in all fairness, unaware of just how thick and fast the flops were piling up) chose to defend Connery's track record. 'All artists make terrible choices,' she pointed out. 'If you look at any of the great stars they suddenly appear in some perfectly awful film. Luckily it doesn't always affect their career. I don't think it affected Connery's career. *Shalako*, for instance, is rather a terrible film. But never mind, he gets away with it, and because he has this great quality of command I don't think it matters. I don't think he's made a great number of bad choices. If you look back over his career it's an interesting and exciting one. It hasn't fallen, really. It's remained on a good, commanding, steady level, or now and then it's risen to considerable heights, as in *The Man Who Would Be King*.'

Allied Filmmakers' Jake Eberts pointed out that most stars go through periods of unfortunate judgements. Many of Connery's failures, he suggested, can be attributed to his scramble to escape the Bond image, together with the concurrent reluctance of major studios to cast him in non-Bond roles.

Richard Lester, in exile from Connery country, chipped in that he saw the star's average as no worse than that of many others. David Picker, he recalled, had once told him that if he had cancelled all the films he made at United Artists and made all the films he cancelled, he suspected that he would have come out about the same. 'I'm certain Sean doesn't choose frivolously,' Lester added.

As T.S. Eliot once put it: 'Between the reality and the idea falls the shadow.'

A greater contrast between the rambunctious, gung-ho Richard Brooks and the genteel sensitivity of director Fred Zinnemann would be difficult to imagine. An Austrian emigré, Zinnemann had arrived in Hollywood in 1929, having studied cinematography in Paris and worked in Berlin as assistant to Billy Wilder. He is fond of recalling that he arrived on the day the stockbrokers were jumping out of windows after the market crash. Basically, he reasoned that matters could only improve.

Zinnemann served a hard apprenticeship during the 1930s, first as an extra – he was in Lewis Milestone's *All Quiet On The Western Front* over at Universal – then as a script clerk in the mills of MGM. At last, together with fellow-trainee Joseph Losey, he was entrusted with the direction of short subjects, including several episodes of the famed *Crime Does Not Pay* series. All the while he was learning his craft and preparing for full-length features.

In 1946 he scored at his home studio with *The Search*, the movie that launched a new star in Montgomery Clift; in 1950 the trend continued with Marlon Brando in *The Men*, the two outings firmly establishing Zinnemann's reputation as an actors' director. In 1952 he enjoyed his first smash hit with the epoch-making *High Noon*, giving Gary Cooper his greatest-ever role and providing an acerbic metaphor for the shame of the Hollywood blacklist.

One year later his powerful film version of James Jones's *From Here to Eternity* exploded on the screen, not only furnishing Columbia Pictures with its biggest success to date, but re-launching Frank Sinatra's career and shattering over-night Deborah Kerr's long-time good-girl image. Audrey Hepburn had the advantage of Zinnemann behind the camera on *The Nun's Story*; his film version of Robert Bolt's *A Man for All Seasons* proved another Oscar-laden triumph. With *Julia* having earned Alan Ladd Jr kudos as well as cash during his tenure as studio head at 20th Century-Fox, it was natural that Laddie should turn to Zinnemann to provide more of the same for his own Ladd Co.

Music, women and mountains had been Zinnemann's pre-occupations as a young man in Austria, making it only a matter of time before he got around to capturing the themes on celluloid. Way back in 1950 he had been impressed by a short story from Kay Boyle entitled 'Maiden, Maiden', a tale of a young girl's obsessive love for a married man twice her age. With a background of the Swiss Alps thrown in, only music seemed to be missing until scriptwriter Michael Austin sug-gested making the older man the young girl's uncle, adding a twist of incest to the tale, as well as a rival romantic interest in the form of a young guide.

Zinnemann then incorporated a folk tale that had haunted him for years, in which an old woman retrieves the perfectly preserved body of her bridegroom from the ice into which he disappeared on their wedding day forty years earlier. Before setting up the movie the director went hiking in the southern Swiss Alps, a jealously guarded area of natural beauty. As he retraced the steps of his youth, he knew he had found the ideal location to recreate the atmosphere of the Alps of the 1930s in the days before ski lifts and tourism.

Zinnemann had particularly admired Connery's work in *Robin and Marian*. 'Sean was my first and only choice of actor,' he said, 'because no one else could undertake the hazardous exercises required, and yet was mature – and yet again could act.'

A fresh-faced newcomer, Betsy Brantley, was cast in *Maiden, Maiden* – which underwent a fairly swift title change to *Five Days One Summer* during production – opposite Connery's earthy Scottish doctor, with French actor Lambert Wilson as the guide. Connery seized the chance to work with a director he had long admired, someone he saw as 'a living legend'. The unsympathetic light in which his character often appeared was of no concern. 'Liking and disliking a character is entirely the prerogative of the people watching the film,' he suggested. 'You have to be indifferent to the reaction of the audience. Some actors will send little signals indicating "I am not really like this." I can't bear that ploy. I took on the character with all its plusses and minuses.'

Three months of location filming in the Bernina range of mountains, stunningly captured by famed Italian cinematographer Guiseppe Rotunno and a team of daredevil climbing technicians, was not without its fractious moments. In particular, Connery's ever-present concern about being taken for a sucker was thoroughly put to the test by the practised Swiss. 'They take you for every penny,' he complained. Nor, for that matter, was he at all enamoured of the endless snow and freezing cold.

Secure in the knowledge that Zinnemann had employed the best climbers in the world as technical advisers, Connery refused a stunt man for his sequences, arguing, as he had in *The Great Train Robbery*, that the contrast between the closeups and long shots would break the vital communication with the audience. Never having understood the science of climbing, the techniques he learned from the experts proved an eye-opener: 'I thought you were tied together so that if one fell you all fell. It was a total revelation to me how well it was worked out how one climber would create an anchor for the other.' The full-time mountaineers he found 'an interesting bunch, but I think in most cases they have a screw missing. All of them have had to climb down at some time with a broken arm or leg, or suffering from frostbite. It's not my idea of a good time.'

Zinnemann had his heart in his mouth during one particular scene shot in Pontresina, in which Connery dangled perilously on the end of a rope, a two-hundred-foot icy crevasse yawning beneath him. 'There he was,' the veteran director recalled, 'this *marvellous* man, this superstar worth millions, just *hanging* there. Although he had insisted on doing the stunt himself, I felt *totally* responsible. It was a tremendous relief when we were all back on level ground!'

The difficulty, Zinnemann admitted before the movie opened, had been in finding a story that was not about mountain climbing but said something valid about the human condition: 'Our story is not terribly overt, because I like to leave things to people's imaginations. Maybe this style is considered out of date, but it's curious how public taste changes. Concepts like discipline and responsibility – words that were almost proscribed ten years ago – are what many of my films are about, which is perhaps why some of them have not found acceptance at various times.'

Kathleen Carroll in the *New York Daily News* confirmed the worst fears of many when she described *Five Days One Summer* as 'a movie clearly out of step with these explicit times. Zinnemann has been so discreet and tasteful in uncovering the true relationship of his two lovers that *Five Days One Summer* appears to be a movie frozen intact in the '30s, emerging in a remarkable state of preservation ... Connery is still so magnetic and vigorous that it's easy to understand why a woman in her twenties would find him impossible to resist. But, although he is well cast and plays the part with just the right mixture of paternal concern and sexual longing, he seems uncomfortable with the restraints Zinnemann has imposed upon him ... a disappointingly frigid movie.'

The reception afforded *Five Days One Summer* from the ultimate arbiters, the ticket-buying public, was similarly frosty, so few people deciding the trip was worth it that the movie disappeared faster than snow in summer, and with less than

$1m in the till. Nearly a decade after its release, Zinnemann adamantly refuted the theory that Warners had 'failed to promote the movie properly' – the standard cop-out for many artists whose movies have bombed. 'One mistake I made in the casting,' he reflected, 'was in anticipating audience reaction to Betsy's character leaving Sean to take up with a younger man. Despite Sean's wonderful performance, this, it seems, was just not feasible!' He still cherishes the memory of working with Connery, whom he describes as 'utterly professional – and utterly straight in his dealings'. Not since the days of directing Gary Cooper in *High Noon* had he come across a man like him, 'not only a great natural actor, but a hell of a man'.

The three movies Connery had just made back to back in a gruelling eighteen-month stretch had gone a long way to replenishing his depleted fortunes. Not so, alas, those of the movie companies involved. Following *Outland*, *Five Days One Summer* and several other flop movies, the Ladd Co. ceased production.

Connery was philosophical about it all, and well aware of the frantic pace he was pushing: 'In Marbella we have an excellent garden, and I've recently found myself looking at it more. Perhaps it was trying to tell me something. To slow down? I don't know. When I was twenty-five I thought everything would be perfect when I reached the age of forty. Now that I'm fifty I'm putting my state perfectly in order and I don't know whether that's a preparation for living or dying . . .'

Already, during the filming of *Five Days One Summer*, possibly under the influence of the role he was playing, there had been autumnal reflection inherent in Connery's declared schedule for the future: 'A little living, a little work, support my children and die quickly and without pain.'

Chapter 29

'I couldn't be with someone *all* the time. The best relationships are probably those when you spend a lot of the time apart and there are times, even when you're at home when you have to be alone. I have a room in my house in Spain, a sort of study that I can go to and just lock the door. My wife understands that's the way I am.'

Sean Connery

'Positively, definitely, beyond a shadow of doubt, the last Bond.'

Sean Connery (on *Diamonds Are Forever*)

Back in 1975, when Kevin McClory had first contacted Connery about the possibility of a *Thunderball* remake, the star was interested enough to accept the producer's offer to work with Len Deighton on a script. Initially unaware they would have to stick to the same basic plot, it was a process he thoroughly enjoyed. 'We had all sorts of exotic events,' he said. 'You know these airplanes that were disappearing over the Bermuda Triangle? We had SPECTRE doing that. There was this fantastic fleet of planes under the sea – a whole world of stuff had been brought down. They were going to attack the financial nerve centre of the United

States by going in through the sewers of New York, which you can do, right into Wall Street. They'd have mechanical sharks in the bay and take over the Statue of Liberty, which is quite easy, and have the main line of troops on Ellis Island.' There he was content to let it lie, leaving it to McClory to find someone else to portray 007 in what was then known as *James Bond of the Secret Service*, later *Warhead*. He reckoned without the producer's perseverance.

Only after much prodding did Connery begin to come round to the idea of personally updating the character. 'I don't know where or when it came to me,' he claims, 'but I thought it might be an intriguing idea to play Bond ten years on. There might be a different kind of humour to play, the sort of sexual athletics or whatever else was involved could have been quite amusing. So I said, "All right, let's see what we can do", not understanding that when there is so much money involved, suddenly people come out of the woodwork, including the lawyers.'

On his own, after Harry Saltzman had sold out to concentrate on theatrical and other interests, 'Cubby' Broccoli, flanked by United Artists, moved swiftly to create a mountain of litigation. Arthur Krim, UA's boss, insisted that a new script would be illegal; absolutely nothing must be added, nothing short of a note-for-note remake of *Thunderball* was allowable. Faced with this, Connery decided to withdraw tactically. The freeze with Broccoli even reached the stage where the producer tried to prevent clips from the early Bonds being shown at Connery retrospectives in London and Paris. 'It was petty and pathetic,' the star argued. 'But Broccoli, what is he? He's seventy-five and down to his last $100 million. What's he going to do with it?'

McClory ploughed on; as far as he was concerned the movie, with Connery back as Bond, was far from being a forlorn hope. His confidence proved justified; with the threat of litigation receding early in 1980 he sold the rights to ex-lawyer Jack Schwarzman, the producer husband of Talia Shire, Francis Coppola's sister. It was Micheline, with a fine sense of irony, who suggested the name change to *Never Say Never Again*.

With his mother hospitalized in Edinburgh Royal Infirmary after suffering a stroke, Connery broke his arm while rehearsing a fight sequence in Los Angeles. Back in Britain for five days, and with his arm in a fibreglass cast, he discovered that Neil had a broken wrist and cracked pelvis after tumbling fifteen feet from a ladder. His younger brother warned him to expect no sympathy when he flew up for the weekend to see Effie; she had burst out laughing when he had hobbled in to visit her.

The accident spelled the end of Neil's days as a plasterer, the trade to which he had returned after his fling in the movies. The attempt to crash into showbusiness on the back of the Connery name had signally failed to drive the wedge between them that some newspapers had inferred. Neil watched the career of 'The Brother' as he often referred to Sean, with unbounded pride, the family living room at Clermiston a shrine to his sibling's career. As for 'The Brother', he was only too aware how differently events might have unfolded. 'We're two quite different people coming out of the same environment, but going different ways,' he acknowledged. 'Once you make your own momentum, your own direction, you evolve in an entirely different way. I could have made coffin polishing a career – yes, why not? If you're within a framework of an accepted society like my brother is, for example, then he's got all the basic compass points of reference to build his life from. But if you branch out on your own you evolve with a different culture, with different friends. And you must have to change within yourself.'

Never Say Never Again began shooting in September 1982 in the last of the summer sunshine in the South of France before the onset of the annual mistral. Simultaneously, through his executive producer stepson Michael G Wilson, Broccoli joined the Bond race in tandem with Roger Moore, filming *Octopussy*. Both movies, it was reported, had budgets of $25 million.

Broccoli had excellent reason to believe that, with Moore at his helm, the rival challenge could be successfully met. Although in the public consciousness Connery would forever be the quintessential Bond, Moore had done astonishingly well after the $9.4 million nosedive with *The Man with The Golden Gun*; in 1977 *The Spy Who Loved Me* bounced back to $24.3 million; in 1979 *Moonraker*, at $33.9 million, even outpaced *Thunderball*'s old record of $28.6 million; in 1981 *For Your Eyes Only* captured a still-stunning $26.5 million – all three outpacing Connery's $19.7 million 'swan song' on *Diamonds Are Forever*. 'It's been a long time since the last one, and there's room for two Bonds,' Connery stoutly maintained. 'I'll be ten years older and greyer than I was in *Diamonds Are Forever*, but Bond's an interesting character. There's a lot more I can do with him.'

He dismissed what he saw as 'the trumped-up rivalry' between him and Moore: 'Roger plays it his way, I play it mine. I don't want to make comparisons. But one newspaper did. It was flattering to me and unjust to Roger. I don't appreciate that kind of flattery.' When he and Moore had recently met, Connery had suggested that they squash all the rumours and speculation once and for all by posing for a picture together and issuing a joint statement. With both men off to their respective locations, however, the desired communiqué was never issued.

'A pity,' Connery pondered. 'In a sense it's a no-win situation. Whoever comes off best, we both lose because we're being set up against each other.' He was aware of the difference as seen by outsiders: that Moore, egged on by the increasing role of hardware in the movies, played Bond increasingly for parody, using this as a character lifeline, where Connery aimed for a more rounded character study in which humour emerged as a natural, unforced ingredient. Rather tumbling into the media's lap, he asserted that 'the trap with Roger's way' was the overwhelming hardware: 'You get the feeling they dreamt up the stunts first, then built the story round it. I try for a more realistic, credible film within the realms of possibility.' Moore, his $5 million upfront fee safely tucked away, had the last word, asking, doubtless accompanied by the well-known flicker of the eyebrow, 'Does John Gielgud complain because Laurence Olivier is playing *Hamlet* at the same time?'

With a financial return negotiated that he felt was in ratio to his own investment of time and talent, Connery endeavoured to ensure that the film would in no way be an embarrassment to him. As all the world knew, he had criticized Broccoli and Saltzman often enough for what he saw as their greed and ineptitude. Schwartzman had certainly posited the required ideals as they had shaken hands on the arrangement. 'Let's be honest with each other,' he had suggested. 'If at any point we see the quality of the film suffering, let's call it off. Let's go for something of a very high quality and start by casting it in a way that we'll be proud of.'

To this end Connery had personally enlisted Edward Fox for M, Klaus Maria Brandauer, whom he considered one of the ten best actors in Europe, to play the villainous Largo, and Max von Sydow for SPECTRE's mastermind Blofeld. He also had control over the choice of director, Irvin Kershner, and cinematographer, Douglas Slocombe, as well as the casting of his leading ladies.

Apart from the movie's title, and her active encouragement that her husband make another Bond, Micheline helped to spot one of his female co-stars during a stay at London's Grosvenor House. 'She pressed the elevator button for the seventh floor,' she whispered to Connery as Kim Basinger made her way up to her room. Basinger found herself duly cast. 'If I were the jealous type,' said Micheline with a chuckle, 'I would already be dead.'

Connery's idea from the start was to update Bond's character to 1983, with a view to how both he and the world had changed, as well as how international opinion of secret agents had shifted. M, for instance, had been transferred into a cost-conscious, arrogant technocrat. 'Look at Britain today,' Connery suggested. 'The Thatcher government is making all these cutbacks in government services. We've used all that kind of stuff in the script and given the film a new edge.' Schwartzman confirmed their common purpose: 'Our approach is to have Sean play Bond at fifty-two, not go on pretending he is thirty-two. He's not playing it bald and paunchy, but he's not a cardboard figure either.' Connery worked on the finished script with Lorenzo Semple Jr before Dick Clement and Ian La Frenais added a final polish.

In the race to build up a new fortune by returning as Bond – a move seen by cynical observers as born of pure desperation – Connery was acutely conscious of the brand new treadmill he might be creating for himself. 'I have to be in the public eye for a fairly large part of my life,' he agonized. 'You don't go into show business in the first place if you're an introvert. But my family life is private and well away from the spotlight. I've a terrible feeling that it's just all about to start up again. But I've only myself to blame for that ... And, in any case, I can handle that kind of thing better now. I'm older, for one thing.'

The movie crew energetically worked the Riviera from their base in Nice, capturing on celluloid the opulent Monte Carlo casino, where the main gambling salon was temporarily shut to facilitate filming. Then it was on to Antibes and Menton, where a spectacular motorcycle chase was filmed. Ahead lay several days at the magnificent Villa Rothschild at Saint Jean-Cap-Farrat, the Riviera's Millionaire's Row. There the Rothschilds' museum was transformed into Palmyra, Largo's plush domain where Bond and Domino (Basinger) are brought as captives.

Already the schedule had begun to slip, prompting Connery to take personal charge of several scenes. At other times he issued a series of crisp, no-nonsense instructions to Kershner. 'Well, I'd done seven Bonds,' he tersely explained to justify the move, 'and this was his first.'

A visiting reporter sensed the rapidly developing tension on the set between the star and his director. He could see that Kershner was under a black cloud even as he tried to claw back the schedule, Connery's humour and creative interest transformed to vociferous anger. With ten minutes of rehearsals lost when Kershner changed his mind about a key feature of one scene, then forgot to tell anyone, Connery exploded with rage. Meantime, Schwartzman seemed to have done a disappearing act, leaving the weight of frustration sitting heavily on Connery's shoulders.

Further along the coast, in the old fishing village of Villefranche, the Citadelle became another part of Palmyra. The locals watched, awestruck, as an enormous portcullis was erected in the courtyard of their seventeenth-century fortress. Even more impressive was the appearance of one of the largest private yachts in the world, billionaire Adnan Khashoggi's *Nobila*, sailing into their tiny harbour. Access for filming aboard had been granted for the very first time. By mid-November the unit had moved to McClory's home turf of Nassau in the Bahamas, where sequences featuring live tiger sharks were shot; unlike on *Thunderball*, Connery now felt qualified to perform many of the underwater scenes on his own.

Like Diane Cilento before her, Micheline seemed to know when to visit the set in Bermuda and when to stay away – at least on most occasions. 'I study the script and the call-sheet,' she explained, 'and when I know Sean has a sexy scene coming up I stay away. These scenes are very hard work, you know, and Sean doesn't want me around embarrassing him.'

She misunderstood the nature of one day's work in the Bahamas and arrived on the set just as Connery was heavily engaged in a love scene with 'Fatima Blush', Barbara Carrera: 'Oh, it was *very* hot, my dear. My first instinct was to turn and run, but then I thought that if I did the film crew would go around saying, "Ha, ha. Did you see how upset Mrs Connery was today?" So I made myself sit down coolly for an appropriate length of time before leaving.'

By this time Micheline was well used to watching her husband's animal magnetism working its magic off the set as well as on. One beautiful young creature had swooped on him at the airport, only to be brushed aside as if she were a piece of luggage. Although Micheline just laughed, knowing better than anyone the effect her husband has on women, Connery was absolutely furious with the girl. 'She's not interested in me,' he snapped, 'she's only interested in the image.'

As Scotland's world-famous poet, Robert Burns, once said, 'The best laid schemes of mice and men gang aft agley'. So it turned out with *Never Say Never Again*. As the production rapidly descended into bedlam, Connery's romance with Schwartzman quickly evaporated. What a difference a few months can make! 'In the middle of everything he moved to the Bahamas with an unlisted number,' the star later protested. 'It was like working in a toilet. I should have killed him.'

At a National Film Theatre lecture Connery chose to elaborate further: 'I hate parasites, I hate incompetence. There's nothing I like better than a film that really works, providing you don't have to deal with all the shit that comes afterward in terms of getting what you're entitled to. But when you get into a situation where somebody who is totally incompetent is in charge, a real ass, then everything is a struggle. There was so much incompetence, ineptitude and dissension during the making of *Never Say Never Again* that the film could have disintegrated ... What I could have done is just let it bury itself. I could have walked away with an enormous amount of money and the film would never have been finished. But once I was in there I ended up getting in the middle of every decision. The assistant director and myself really produced the picture.'

Hoping against hope that the finished movie would at least play respectably despite its troubled passage, Connery arranged for a charity première in Minneapolis in aid of the SIET.

He personally emerged well enough from the notices, David Edelstein in *Boston Phoenix* first pointing out what was good about the movie:

> *Never Say Never Again* resonates with the personality of Sean Connery. And the actor has so much élan, so much spiritual largesse, that he gives 007 more than license to kill: he gives him poetic license. It's a charming comedy that enlarges our fondest memories of the series' highlights, with a beneficent offhand style that almost never slips into archness. Connery and Kershner don't send up Bond, they enlarge him.

Then there was the bad:

> Some scenes are dim, confusing and poorly timed; although overlong at more than two hours, the film appears to have been heavily cut. It's hard to believe that a movie whose first sequences are so meticulously worked out can end so crappily and half-heartedly.

David Denby in *New York Magazine* noted that the production had Connery either rolling about on the floor or wrestling with sharks.

> Am I projecting my own boredom and unease on to others, or did I sense some discomfort in the audience? [he asked.] Much of *Never Say Never Again* is clunky and second-rate. Connery seems more courtly with women than before – the suave menace is gone – which only makes one long to see him in sophisticated comedy. In every other way, he's as indomitable as ever ... But by not taking any interesting notice of Connery's age or special quality, they let him look foolish. When he makes Bond's usual dirty puns, you feel a bit sorry for him.

After a head-to-head battle was wisely resisted, *Octopussy*, released first, managed to pip *Never Say Never Again* at the box-office post, netting an all-time Bond record of $34 million. Connery's $28 million a couple of months later was still an excellent result, considering the sudden glut of agent 007 on cinema screens.

Even with $5 million stashed away from the experience, he was said to be despondent and jaded with acting in general. Having done what he had always sworn he never would, the return to Bond had to be considered a career watershed. After his next movie, which would involve just one week of his time, the future was a gigantic question mark.

Chapter 30

'He's not the kind of person that will call his agent if he's not happy with his dressing-room. He'd just go up to the producer and say something like: "I'm not going in that shithole, thank you very much. You get that changed by the afternoon otherwise I'm not coming back."'

Joy Jameson, agent

It took six months for British director Stephen Weeks to persuade Connery to appear in the crucial supporting role of the Green Knight in his projected *Sword of the Valiant*. The reason for Weeks's patience was simple; without the star's participation there would be no movie. Weeks had already directed an earlier version of the same story, *Gawain and the Green Knight*, without conspicuous success. Now, it seemed, his fascination with the tale had made him determined to 'get it right' second time around.

The first meeting with Connery took place at Ardmore Studios while *The Great Train Robbery* was being filmed. Weeks found him extremely polite and attentive to his pitch, although the subject of the fee was never raised. Instead, Connery seemed genuinely intrigued by the project itself, as well as by Weeks's enthusiasm. The director decided, after subsequent months of battering his head against CAA's door, that offering an enormous fee for the work involved – four days that eventually stretched to six – was the only way to grab the agency's attention. They were totally dismissive when an interview was eventually granted, arguing that although the Green Knight was the pivotal character in the movie, he was not the real star. Weeks agreed, but exited on the line that CAA's attitude was a great shame – since he was prepared to offer $1 million for four days' work!

By the time he got back to his hotel there were messages galore urging him to call the agency back; the deal was then closed in incredibly short order. Armed with Connery's agreement, and with muscleman Miles O'Keefe toplined as Gawain, Menahem Golan and Yoram Globus of Cannon Films were approached by Weeks to fund the project, and to cough up the $500,000 deposit necessary under the terms of Connery's contract. Anxious to expand their burgeoning empire with a star of his magnitude, the 'Go-Go boys' signed on the dotted line.

Demands followed for script rewrites to strengthen Connery's character and maximize his star presence. Golan's attitude was simple, and, under the financial circumstances, reasonable and practicable: 'If we're paying $1m, we might as well go for six days' worth of work.' Faced with this, Connery's and CAA's answer – equally practical and reasonable – was to demand $250,000 for each day in excess of six.

To avoid what he saw as shortchanging the public, Connery had insisted on a clause that he would not be misleadingly billed as the movie's star. In flagrant disregard of this, word filtered back from the Cannes Film Festival that Cannon was touting the movie as 'Sean Connery in *Sword of the Valiant*'. The star's fury at being exploited almost killed the deal stone dead before it was signed. Weeks was required to fly to Los Angeles to calm everyone down; thereafter he detected little love between Connery and Cannon's bosses.

Although he agreed to shoot everything outside of the UK to

suit Connery, the star came to Britain on occasional visits, notably to Elstree Studios to have a cast of his head taken for his decapitation scene. What Weeks discovered afterwards, to his absolute horror, was that the same experts, in casting an actress's hand a few weeks earlier, had inadvertently left a ring on her finger, and that due to the metal's reaction to the chemicals involved, her finger subsequently had to be amputated.

The Pope's palace in Avignon was used for one of the most elaborate scenes in the movie, with hundreds of extras and extraordinarily complicated set-ups involved. In one of them Connery's Green Knight was required to burst into a crowded hall on his horse, ride up to Trevor Howard's King, dismount and throw his axe into the dais of the throne, narrowly missing Howard's head. The scene and its follow-up, the beheaded Knight strolling away with his head tucked under his arm, required 142 set-ups spread over two days.

With the $250,000 a day bounty awaiting him, Connery could hardly have been blamed for, at the very least, failing to force the pace. Instead, he was the one who constantly did this, encouraging everyone to move right along. He supported the worthy veteran Howard, who was going through what Weeks diplomatically refers to as a 'dull patch', unable to work too easily after lunch.

His equilibrium was shattered, not by his star, but by the unit's dependence on Cannon's finances. Halfway through shooting the production accountant was told to collect money in a suitcase from an individual in a Paris street one particularly fraught dawn. When Weeks opened the case he found it contained no fewer than five different currencies. Then there was the refusal by Cannon's chiefs to reimburse Connery's make-up expert for $80 worth of cosmetics. Frantic, Weeks warned the duo that denying the cosmetician her $80 could end up costing them $250,000 if the movie ran into overtime. The last day of Connery's schedule involved his crucial transformation scene, changing from the green of spring into summer, autumn, and winter hues before disintegrating completely, each stage swallowing three hours. Weeks's solution was to recompense the $80 out of his own pocket; even then he had to assure the cosmetician the money came from Cannon, not him.

Connery had already let it be known that if he caught a plane to Malaga an hour earlier than the last flight, he could squeeze in a game of golf that night. Incredibly, even with the champagne celebration he attended to mark the end of shooting that afternoon, he made it.

Weeks was fascinated to contrast Connery's behaviour with that of his lead actor, Miles O'Keefe. With a track record of only *Tarzan, The Ape Man* behind him, he found O'Keefe a prima donna in the making, constantly attended by a personal manager and agent. In complete contrast, Connery had no minions and stayed in the same Sofitel hostelry with the rest of the cast, with Micheline his only visitor for a couple of days. Weeks recalls him walking across the town square in tweeds and cloth cap, a modest, workaday, practical Scot with none of a 'star's' trappings or airs.

Sword of the Valiant was dubbed 'an unsatisfactory mixture of realism, fantasy and deadly seriousness' by film encyclopaedist Leslie Halliwell, one of the few critics who saw it. Although the director ended up deep in financial litigation with Cannon over what he saw as their eventual mishandling of his movie, Weeks retains warm memories of Connery, and of one pre-production meeting in particular, where he saw himself as the undisputed object of envy of countless Connery fans.

Following a discussion on the necessity for his star's chest hair to be dyed green, the option was aired that the dye uptake on his white hairs might be different from that on the dark. Leaning over and carefully picking his way through Connery's luxuriantly hirsute chest in an attempt to gauge the extent of the potential problem, Weeks had the sudden, and not altogether irrational thought, that if only he could capture the experience and market it to millions of eager women around the world . . .!

Scottish writer William McIlvanney, intrigued by the notion of the Edinburgh milk roundsman who had 'become' James

Bond, had first interviewed Connery at London's Dorchester Hotel back in 1970. As they sat chatting in the foyer a handsome couple approached, to be greeted by the star with some embarrassment. Although he had recently spent a month at their ranch in Spain, it seemed he'd completely forgotten their names! His whole manner struck McIlvanney as authentically charming. There was a sense of integrity that constantly communicated itself, leaving the writer in no doubt that Connery could never have been content to be trapped in the Bond scene, no matter how lucrative it became. He was also made aware of the hard, unsentimental, unforgiving side of the star's nature. He asked him about a recent tale that had circulated in which Connery was playing cards in a casino when someone had tapped him on the shoulder and informed him that 'Cubby' Broccoli had just suffered a massive stroke that left him paralysed down one side of his body. 'Fucking good,' Connery had apparently replied, without so much as skipping a beat. 'I hope he's paralysed down the other side tomorrow.'

Connery admitted that the story was true and that he had no wish to retract it, even with hindsight; McIlvanney was free to use it. His next remark, that Neil should 'Either shit or get off the pot', was equally straightforward and carried not the slightest undertone of resentment. The only implied caveat was that while there was any amount of room on the wagon, it was only for individuals capable of grasping the reins by themselves. The opening line of the article McIlvanney intended for publication cut straight across 007's 'Sean Connery is James Bond' catchline. 'Sean Connery is Sean Connery' it ran.

Seven years passed before a second meeting took place between the two. It started with a phone call from Connery suggesting a rendezvous at Edinburgh Zoo. Once they were settled in the coffee shop there, Connery revealed that he was interested in developing McIlvanney's highly acclaimed Glasgow-based detective novel *Laidlaw* for the screen, as a project both for him to direct and star in. He suggested that McIlvanney should write a script while he tried to raise the money and get the production set up. Although no option deal or other financial arrangement was mooted, McIlvanney was struck by Connery's obvious enthusiasm. The distinct air of surrealism that threatened to pervade the meeting, preceded as it was by a wintry walk past lion cages and monkey houses, came into its own as McIlvanney spotted a woman watching them. Eventually she came over and said to Connery, 'Excuse me, are you who I think you are?' Fixing her with a fish-eyed gaze, Connery replied, 'No', leaving the woman with little alternative but to make a reluctant retreat, murmuring, 'Oh, sorry . . .'

A year later McIlvanney was offered an option deal for *Laidlaw* – for money this time – by a US agent. Connery had been unable to raise backing – 'At the money end,' he informed one reporter, 'they decided it was too Scottish to be of worldwide interest.' McIlvanney reluctantly signed the deal, advising the agent to let Connery know in case he still thought it was available. Three years later, with the option acquired by the Scottish production team of Mike Alexander, Mark Littlewood and Iain Smith, Connery was brought back into the picture – briefly, that is. According to one report, the proposed shooting schedule in Glasgow would have overrun his ninety-day tax window. 'Now that we have the rights, and with McIlvanney writing the script, things could be different,' Alexander argued in January 1981. 'We have sounded Connery out. Leave it at that.'

Three months later the project, with Connery apparently on board, was on ice until 1982 at the earliest. 'We cannot make it this year with Connery,' Littlewood confirmed. 'As a tax exile he would not have enough time in this country to film. With his other visits there is no way he can do it this year. He is now in Los Angeles reading the second script written by McIlvanney. We could do it this year without Connery, but who has Connery's worldwide appeal? Not very many, and certainly no other Scot.'

In 1982 Connery bumped into McIlvanney at a Hampden football final and still expressed interest in playing Laidlaw.

McIlvanney, attending the match with some friends from the Glasgow Crime Squad he had met while researching the book, together with his son Liam, was greeted with a cheery, 'Hey, Bill, how're you doing?' In turn Connery was hailed by people in the crowd with, 'Hello, big yin, how are you?' He told McIlvanney and his companions that he'd been sitting at 2 am that morning in Tramps nightclub in London when Rod Stewart informed him he had tickets for the game. Undaunted, one of McIlvanney's crime squaddies replied, 'Aye, it's a small world, big yin. I was sitting in a house in Muirhead this morning surrounded by tramps as well!'

After the game Connery asked McIlvanney to accompany him to the airport in his taxi, with young Liam proudly perched on his knee. During the pint before the plane left the other occupants of the bar lined up for autographs. Connery signed what he considered a dutiful amount before calling a halt and returning to his pint.

Disappointingly, *Laidlaw* never took off. At one point, just when the money seemed to be there, it turned out to be Mafia-sourced. For a while discussions were held with Scottish Television, before they came up with a rival detective series of their own in the long-running *Taggart*. (In which, incidentally, Neil Connery appeared in a bit part and daughter Leone – most impressively – in a featured role.)

Over the years Nicol Williamson, Michael York and Maurice Roeves have all expressed interest in portraying Laidlaw. Perhaps one day it will get the big screen treatment it so thoroughly deserves.

Chapter 31

'He's an interesting handknitted commodity in an industry of synthetic fibres.'

William McIlvanney

'The trouble with the British film industry is that there's all these marvellous plans for reforming it, but catch any of those producers foregoing their posh suits in luxury hotels and company limousines and extravagant luncheons. *That's* where the money goes.'

Sean Connery

Connery's expressed concern about the film scene in Britain in the early 1980s stemmed from the decline in cinemas and cinemagoing clearly evident since his departure for Spain. Instead of the four cinemas in Putney he had been able to choose from, now there was only one. 'It needs Margaret Thatcher in the middle of it,' he contended, puzzling some friends who had always seen him as decidedly left of centre in his political views. He recalled an initiative he had tried to get off the ground years earlier in which the British film industry would have been reconstituted as a public company that owned the studios. Then the talent exodus, of which he was part, might have been stopped.

'A different approach now would stop the drain of talent and give people a closer interest,' he maintained. 'There's no question that areas of the film industry could be enormously successful in terms of overseas prestige.' He stipulated one essential condition – there would need to be legislation passed on tax relief that could not be overruled by successive governments. He characterized as 'disgraceful' the pittance with which the industry was subsidized compared to the amounts handed out to the National Theatre and the Royal Shakespeare Company.

If Connery had really been of a mind at that point to take an active role in marshalling the British film industry, he could hardly have picked a better man to partner him than Jake Eberts, the brains behind Goldcrest Films. Eberts has backed a whole series of winners, from *Chariots of Fire* to *Gandhi*, by putting his company's money on a combination of proven talent and astute hunches.

In 1983 he had initiated what was to become an annual pro-celebrity tennis tournament in aid of muscular dystrophy. With Richard Attenborough as its president Eberts' role was to persuade actors, rock stars, and indeed any personality whose name held marquee value, to play doubles tennis on stage with the leading lights of the Wimbledon circuit. The whole trick to attracting audiences, he quickly realized, was to offer at least one superstar. For the first tournament he managed to fill the David Lloyd Tennis Centre with a thousand ticket-paying supporters. The following year his sights were set considerably higher – on the 6,000 seater Albert Hall. On the professional front he had McEnroe, Connors, Amritraj and Gerulaitis lined up; from the world of showbusiness he had Andy Williams, John Forsythe and Bruce Forsyth.

Just six days before the event his principal star bowed out. Eberts was in deep trouble; he had promised the crowd a superstar and still hadn't managed to sell all of the tickets. In desperation he called Attenborough and explained the situation.

'Well, Sean's more of a golfer than a tennis player,' Eberts was informed. 'Maybe so,' he replied, 'but I've been told by a friend of mine, Gary Hendler, who just happens to be Sean's lawyer, that he's a pretty keen tennis player as well.'

Armed with this information, Attenborough agreed to call Connery. When he got back, it was to inform Eberts that Connery was interested and awaiting further word in Marbella. With the situation explained to him, the main problem now lay in the timing. Eberts was calling on a Sunday evening – with the event set for the following Friday! Connery paused on the line for just a few seconds to digest this information, then, 'Well, boy, I'll be there,' he assured Eberts.

A few days later he called from his hotel in London to ask precisely what he was expected to do. 'We have a photo call today, Sean,' Eberts explained, 'with some of the MD sufferers. They're all young boys and they're going to die. It would mean such a lot—'

'Where's it being held?' Connery asked.

'At the Albert Hall.'

'I'll be right over.'

'Will I send a car to collect you?'

'No, I know where it is. I'll make my own way there.'

With the photo session complete a grateful Eberts approached his star attraction and asked if he would like a practice game before the event. 'No, I'm OK,' Connery assured him. 'But I haven't got a tracksuit with me. Can you lend me one?' Without further ado Eberts repaired to the nearest sports shop and bought one.

Unknown to him, Connery had a special surprise up his sleeve for the event. At 7 p.m. the first and second teams kicked off with short matches. It was all done with great good humour, with raffles and lots of money-raising showbiz flourishes along the way. Connery was due to appear in the third match of the evening and was introduced simply as '007'. Eberts had explained in advance that he would be unable to greet Connery personally before his 'turn', since he was required to sit in the audience with the trustees. He was therefore as surprised and delighted as everyone when 007 made his entrance, wearing a bright tartan tam-o'-shanter and carrying golf clubs! The capacity crowd completely broke up. Connery had risen splendidly to the spirit of the occasion and set the whole tone of the evening in the most delightful fashion. After playing his set – extremely well, Eberts recalls – Connery thanked him for his invitation and disappeared into the night.

Eberts phoned him the next day to express his gratitude for making the evening such a resounding success. The new-found friendship between the two men flourished further over a lunch and continued to blossom during another get-together in California several months later when Eberts discovered later that he and Connery had many interests in common. 'He's a gregarious kind of guy,' he says, 'the type I like a lot. He gets right to the issues, he's very direct, very intelligent, he's always got good ideas, good, sensible plans – and *no pretence*. I found him a delightful, charming friend. Micheline? She's what the French call an *animatrice*, someone who brings a sparkle to any occasion.'

A bizarre combination of their meeting and a series of bullets pumped into a French film producer in an underground car park in Paris was about to provide Connery with arguably his greatest-ever role.

The death of Euphemia Connery in Edinburgh's Royal Infirmary in April 1985 came as a terrible blow to her family and a whole host of friends. With the grief-stricken brothers standing by, her ashes joined those of Joe, interred in Newington Crematorium's Garden of Remembrance. Their wreath of pink orchids had 'Mum' picked out in red carnations, accompanied by a simple card inscribed, 'From Sean and Neil'.

Years later Micheline was still crediting the indomitable Effie as the source of her husband's sense of purpose and inner discipline. 'She was very strong,' Connery agreed. 'I probably have got it from her.'

In the meantime there was a numbing sense of desolation to

contend with, as well as yet another shattering reminder of mortality.

$1 million for what amounted to a brief but telling cameo spot was the lure that brought Connery to the hokum of *Highlander*. In this he played Ramirez, an ancient Egyptian aged 2,437, in the year 1536, serving as chief metallurgist at the court of King Charles V of Spain, before being called upon, in his capacity as an immortal, to help out one Connor MacLeod, a character up to his sporran in a spot of bother in a Scottish glen. 'Haggis? What is haggis and what do you do with it?' Connery was called upon to enquire, in a ripe Scottish burr detectable several glens away. 'You eat it,' MacLeod (Christopher Lambert) explains. 'How revolting!' Connery splutters, setting the stage for 'the Quickening', when special effect lightning pours down after one immortal beheads another, and 'the Gathering', with Lambert still roaming the earth in modern New York, acting out his tale of love and revenge.

Highlander had its demented start as a final year UCLA student film school thesis; with Razorback and music video director Russell Mulcahy roped in, the stage was set for a sword and sorcery epic, partly shot in Scotland, that almost, but not quite, displayed the courage of its convictions. 'What's the film like?' Connery was overheard asking one journalist at the Edinburgh Film Festival in 1986. While he appeared to display only the minimum of curiosity, he was in fact keenly interested in the box-office take of the movie in which he had his obligatory percentage.

Although a hit in Europe, the movie failed completely in the US market – so much for all the beautiful location work at Ballachulish, Lochaber, Ben Nevis, Glencoe, Morar, Loch Duich and Doune Castle – and so much for Connery's peacock-cloaked high-camp performance, a rare and welcome departure for him.

'All style and no content,' harumphed Victoria Mather in Britain's *Daily Telegraph*, while Philip French in the *Observer* railed at the 'harebrained fantasy that bounces off the eyeballs like a laser beam but never gets near the brain or the heart ... half-baked'. Connery had no regrets, apart from the movie's demise in the US. After unrepentantly describing the making of *Highlander* as 'great fun', he participated a few years later in the sequel, *Highlander II: The Quickening*.

First published in Italy in 1980, Umberto Eco's monumental best seller *The Name of the Rose*, with its portrayal of homosexual and criminal monks, was barred in several monasteries. Producer Gerard Leibowitz, a man with known connections to the Paris underworld, snapped up the rights and planned a movie version. He saw Michael Caine as the fourteenth-century Franciscan monk-cum-detective Brother William of Baskerville. With Leibowitz's assassination in a hail of bullets in a parked car, his estate auctioned the rights to another French producer, Alexandre Mnouchkin.

Jake Eberts had read the book and loved it, and noted in passing that Caine was attached to the project. He left Goldcrest in 1984 and briefly joined a US company, Embassy. Soon he was back in Britain, avowedly independent, setting up his own Allied Filmmakers outfit. Just before the Cannes Film Festival in 1985 he received a call from Bernd Eichinger, head of Germany's Neue Constantin, the company behind the hugely successful *Christiane F* and *Never Ending Story*. Eichinger informed him that he had bought the rights to the movie in France.

In Eberts's new capacity at Allied, Eichinger asked if he would help achieve a US presale for the $21 million movie with a major studio. 'We'll need a major star to achieve that goal,' he pointed out. 'Well, the previous producer had Michael Caine in mind,' Eichinger replied, adding, 'He's a good actor, but I personally think he'd be miscast as William.'

Eberts, in a flash of inspiration, made an on-the-spot suggestion: 'How about Sean Connery?' At first Eichinger demurred; only when Eberts kept up the pressure did he begin to see how Connery might fit the role. Eberts was convinced that the star was virtually a latter-day William exactly as Eco had described – a very direct character, with people all round

him playing games. William, like Connery, consistently stuck
to what he believed in.

Apart from the strength of the role it was the element of
incongruity in the casting that held enormous appeal for the
star. 'Larry Harvey was once accused of being such a bitch he
could play Hedda Gabler,' he recalled. 'Larry replied, "Well, it
is a good part!" It was something like that. If something is
interesting and stimulating for me – and it is obvious from
some of the choices I have made that not everyone is of the
same opinion – then I do it.'

It certainly took a good few turns of anyone's imagination
to contemplate Connery running the gamut from Bond, without
doubt the screen's most notorious sexual adventurer, to playing
a medieval monk sworn to lifelong celibacy. 'With the Bond
thing people sometimes tend to forget that I've made other
films,' Connery lamented. He regarded himself as fortunate to
have landed the role, which he saw as a mixture of Sherlock
Holmes and Thomas More all wrapped up in a habit. He saw
William as far from an ordinary monk, someone both arrogant
and a loner, his instruments of intellect and reason leaving very
little room for faith. He saw the movie as being about the
suppression of information; only the select few in the cloistered
society had access to the classical writings that were anathema
to medieval church training.

Connery detected twentieth-century parallels galore, not
least in the Soviet Union and Eastern Europe. He felt a pressing
need to prepare himself by understanding the religious beliefs
of the period. Although he had never been interested in
religion, he still found it intriguing that others had unshakable
beliefs. He visited a monastery just outside Madrid to see what
he could learn. Not much, it turned out – they had never heard
of the book. At least, though, they knew of Connery.

A handsome fee was negotiated – not huge, since Eichinger's budget was unable to stand it – but with Connery's usual
piece of the gross included as an extra incentive. A conversation that began between Eberts and Andre Blay at Cannes led
to a video deal being concluded for the US; eventually Eberts

also interested 20th Century-Fox in acquiring the US theatrical rights for the project. Shortly after the festival Eberts found himself called back by the distraught Goldcrest management; in his absence the company had been brought to the brink of collapse. Eberts awarded the balance of the movie's foreign rights to the company while performing a holding operation. His own Allied Filmmakers, meantime, waited in the wings for his return.

He visited Connery on the huge *Name of the Rose* monastery set outside of Rome, clearly visible to drivers making their way along the autostrada towards Florence. The crew had just arrived back from five weeks of shooting in a series of cold, damp cathedrals in Germany at Kloster Eberbach, overlooking the Rhine near Wiesbaden and Stuttgart. The shaven-headed star had bronchitis; the young French director Jean Jacques Annaud was sparing his cast nothing and demanding take after take. Connery was moaning about the cold, the damp, his terrible cough, but all with a roguish twinkle in his eye. 'You could hang meat on this set,' he was heard to mutter. As for playing a celibate – 'That side of it is very easy at my age,' he cracked. It was the first time Eberts had actually seen Connery in action.

'I'm wearing a monk's outfit, thermal underwear and space boots and my ass is still freezing,' he informed all and sundry. From the beginning he had made a whole string of comments on the script and had clearly thought out ideas on how the role should be played. Even now, three months into shooting, he was constantly discussing changes he could make to improve his character and the narrative's flow. 'Some people,' says Eberts, 'would find this difficult and would want him to shut up and take his pay cheque. The script had already been through five writers at this stage. The difference with Sean is that he's *worth* listening to.'

Annaud discovered a hitherto unsuspected side to Connery during the filming. 'He's so entertaining at dinners,' the director revealed, 'that we made a tradition of them on the set. During the feasts he'd do magic tricks and sing Spanish songs, while I danced the flamenco.' There was a feeling in some quarters that this was the disarming flipside of the loner who spent most of his time off the set with his make-up man and chauffeur. 'Yes, Sean protects himself,' Annaud confirmed. 'He's afraid of emotions, so when he opens the gate it's really something to see. I guess it's all because he's a star.'

Seventeen-year-old Christian Slater, playing William's apprentice Adso in the movie, watched apprehensively at first as Connery lived his role, before finally realizing that William only shows compassion to Adso toward the end of the movie; Connery was simply following the storyline.

The Name of the Rose proved an enormous success throughout Europe, watershed proof that a movie could approach a gross of $100 million (about $48 million net) without dependence on the US market. A corresponding success in America, of course, would have been the icing on the cake. Alas, it was not to be. '*Name of the Rose* has taken more money in *West Germany* than in the whole of America right now,' Connery raged upon its release there in 1986, 'and that's because they don't know how to market it. They just trot it out, without thinking of the right time, the right climate, the right size of cinema, and they have dumped it. The other problem, of course, is that *Name of the Rose* is dealing with a period of history before America existed. In America they have all been weaned on vitamins since the Revolution and they all look wonderful. Here's this film full of medieval monks who look hideous, like gargoyles, and I don't think they can take it.'

There was also, of course, the small matter of the critical notices, which were less than glowing. David Edelstein in *Village Voice* described the movie as a 'sludgy, narcoleptic horror show'; David Denby in *New York Magazine* said, 'Like a cheap horror film, *Name of the Rose* exploits religion for morbid kicks.' In Britain the reception was no warmer, Alexander Walker in London's *Evening Standard* describing it as a 'stodgy, plodding whodunnit', while Nigel Andrews in the *Financial Times* found the film 'flatfooted'. Only Connery emerged with total credit – for making chastity look appealing, as well as for his 'deft performance' and 'commanding presence'. Overall, however, it was not simply a case of the wrong theatres and poor promotion – although 20th Century-Fox's US posters are unquestionably among the most diabolical ever seen.

When the movie had been first released in Europe, Eberts was utterly staggered at the energy with which Connery flung himself into the publicity whirl: 'He was absolutely terrific at promotion. He called me constantly about posters, release details, went to Rome and did a TV programme. All these things interested him, even though he was already in the middle of another picture. When the movie opened in the UK he did another few days of arranging publicity for it, with a non-stop stream of people calling. It was far and away the most impressive performance I've ever seen by an actor involved in publicity, with incredible attention to detail. In the States it was a joke, there was no campaign at all, it should have done at least $20 million at the box-office.'

During interviews in Britain journalist Iain Johnstone deigned to ask Connery how important money was for him. '*Very* important,' was the swift and unsurprising reply. 'Having been ripped off so many times, and down to the wire a couple of times with mismanagement and things, all because of altruistic, trusting reasons, I hope not to get caught again. It's *very* important.'

Chapter 32

'I've always chosen the projects on my own. My wife reads the script, and I've listened to what she has to say. But the final decision, whatever I do, rightly or wrongly, is always mine . . . I think it's the only way you can do it, personally. Otherwise, I don't think there can be a developed body of work, where you can see where it's going – or where it should have gone.'

Sean Connery

'When you're with Sean you learn pretty quickly what your own place in the galaxy is. And it pales.'

Kevin Costner

Michael Caine recalled in 1981 being asked to dinner with his wife, Shakira, together with the Connerys, by 'a very fine actress who shall be nameless'. (Purely for the sake of argument, let's call her Barbra.) The subject over hors d'oeuvres was *The Man Who Would Be King*. Natural enough since the movie had featured both star guests. By the time the main course was served 'Barbra' had a question for Connery: 'Would you be directed by me if I gave you a part in a film?'

In a blinding flash of insight Caine realized that he had been asked along purely to ensure Connery's presence. ('She knew that if I came, so would Sean, but he wouldn't have come on his own.') Drawing in his breath in the moment of palpable tension before his friend's reply, he thought of all the excuses he might have made in his place – like 'I'll have to speak to my agent' or 'Well, my wife's having a baby.'

Instead, Connery came out with a typically straightforward, 'Good God, *no*. Why should I? I've made more pictures than you.' He then proceeded to turn the tables on 'Barbra': 'Would *you* be directed by *me*?'

'No,' she replied, looking decidedly crestfallen.

'Well, why on earth would you even ask me the question?'

Caine later learned that the lady, more than slightly stunned, was still up at dawn talking about the encounter. Connery's uncompromising brick wall of down-to-earth Scottishness had once again proved impenetrable.

The Untouchables began its life as a one-shot television docudrama set in Chicago in the 1930s prohibition era. Based on crimefighter Elliott Ness's autobiography, and starring Robert Stack as the Federal agent pitted against Al Capone, the show featured breathless 'you-are-there' narration by Walter Winchell. Its popularity spawned a weekly series that ran on ABC television from 1959 to 1963, with Ness and his band of agents – The Untouchables – battling not only Capone, but 'Bugs' Moran, Ma Barker, 'Legs' Diamond and 'Mad Dog' McColl, among many others. The show seemed to succeed because, rather than despite the fact that, it contained something to offend everyone. To begin with all the gangsters looked and sounded Italian, infuriating and alienating the large Italian-American audience. Then there was the violence – mind-numbing, relentless and served up with lip-smacking relish in the form of gangland bloodbaths at least once per episode, sometimes twice, with the producers desperately sheltering behind 'historical accuracy' placards that fooled no one. Nor did they care, as long as 'a rattling good yarn' was served up in which good triumphed over evil and corruption was cleaned up – until the following week's mayhem was unleashed.

The genesis of the revived *Untouchables* was a meeting over dinner in a Greenwich Village restaurant between producer Art Linson and playwright David Mamet. Linson had a three-year production contract with Paramount Pictures in his pocket; Mamet had just won the Pulitzer Prize for his play, *Glengarry Glen Ross*. As soon as Linson had finished pitching his idea of a big screen remake of the TV series, Mamet declared himself in. Kinson would claim that the quality of Mamet's delivered script 'makes me look as if I know what I'm doing'.

Armed with Mamet's work Linson and his recruited director Brian De Palma together picked the relatively unknown Kevin Costner to play Elliot Ness, Connery for seasoned Chicago beat cop Jimmy Malone, Andy Garcia for Italian immigrant Stone, diminutive Charles Martin Smith for Wallace and Bob Hoskins for Al Capone. Hoskins became an early casualty, paid off with a cheque for $200,000 to cover his bruised feelings when Robert De Niro, an obvious scoop, became available.

The twin problems with De Niro, that he had to complete the run of his play *Cuba and his Teddy Bear*, and that he wanted the production delayed so he could put on thirty pounds for the part (shades of his *Raging Bull* avoirdupois, which he'd sworn never to repeat) were solved by agreeing that all his scenes be filmed at the end of the movie's seventy-day schedule. Even though Linson and De Palma had commissioned Giorgio Armani to design all of the movie's costumes, De Niro sought out his own regular tailor, eighty-five-year old Richard Bruno, in his Little Italy workshop. And he went to Park Avenue's swank Sulka & Son for the same silk underwear Capone himself had favoured – presumably so he could 'feel the part'.

Costner had worked as a movie set technician for six years before a series of small roles in B-movies that made little impact. Following what might have been his breakthrough, *The Big Chill*, where his contribution landed on the cutting room floor instead of neighbourhood theatres, he resurfaced as part of the ensemble cast in the modestly successful western, *Silverado*. Despite being sponsored by Steven Spielberg's Amblin Entertainment, *Fandango*, in which he starred, proved a box-office no-no. A movie for Orion, *No Way Out*, awaited release. Still he had managed to make enough impact to impress both De Palma and Mamet. 'Robert Stack's was a great portrayal,' Mamet conceded, 'a stoic Gary Cooper, a Superman. But the character of Ness in this movie is a young fellow, full of ideals, desperately in need of an outlet and a mentor.'

Costner fitted the bill perfectly, except in his own mind. He saw Mamet's upright, uptight junior lawman as far too much of a boring Boy Scout. Only when he began to grasp the subtle changes Mamet imposed as the lessons of violence sunk in did he see how far he might take the character. De Palma saw Costner as a 'basic American boy' as well as an extremely fine actor, with the same Gary Cooper innocence that Mamet had pinpointed as central to the original Elliott Ness.

As for his mentor, there was but one choice. Like De Niro's Capone, the part of the disillusioned Irish street cop Malone was in the nature of 'a major cameo', but a crucial one. A meeting with De Palma clinched the deal as far as Connery was concerned. 'I see so few scripts of this calibre,' he enthused. 'Mamet has a great gift.' He saw the choice of the Chicago-born playwright as doubly inspired, since he had the advantage of being knowledgeable about the city's ethnic problems, together with the endemic police corruption.

While he had previously admired De Palma's technical expertise and sense of style, and always enjoyed elements of his movies, his feeling was that they were too detached. When he talked to De Palma, however, he became aware that this time the director intended to operate on what was for him an elevated emotional level. 'You set up Capone,' De Palma explained, 'you set up Elliott Ness's dilemma, and then the first third to half of the movie is the assembly of the Untouchables. It's like *Seven Samurai* – each one's got his own little story.'

Connery's 'method' came as close to being defined on *The*

Untouchables as it ever will be. First, he familiarized himself with the shape of the story and his part as a whole, noting other characters' attitudes to him. Then he turned down the top corners of the pages in which he appeared and read only those. Then he went back and read only the other parts in which he was absent. In this way he absorbed not only what the character was aware of, equally importantly what he was *not* aware of: as far as Connery is concerned the trap that bad actors fall into is playing information they don't have or playing scenes before they get to them.

He believes strongly in maintaining his character at all times, even when alone on the screen and unobserved. 'This is something not fully explored in films,' he maintains, 'but when someone believes that they're unobserved they're often more revealing about themselves than when they're with others. It's a marvellous thing to be able to show their reality.' Connery saw Malone as 'a guy who is worldly-wise, streetwise, knows the score with the crooks, is frightened for his life, and had just planned on staying alive until he met Ness'.

He viewed the movie himself as being about natural justice, whether upheld by the police and judiciary or not: 'There are times when the law's enough, and times when it isn't. Times when it falls over backwards to be fair and favours people like Capone, and sometimes when you've almost to overstep it.'

The role gave him the chance to overlay and contrast Malone's gruffness with his own qualities of innocence, gentleness, even tenderness. He saw Marlon Brando as one of the best early examples of the art; powerful and dynamic as he was in *On the Waterfront* and *A Streetcar Named Desire*, there had been touches that bespoke inner sensitivity. Robert Henderson's advice back in the 1950s to 'speak one thing, look another' was still being well-heeded.

A full week of rehearsals preceded filming, during which time Connery got to know his fellow actors. Even when they were rehearsing together, however, he tried to remain in the character of the old teacher, giving the 'fledglings' a bit of a rough time, saying slightly anti-American things to annoy them, while they in turn tried to top him. The unit publicist often noted Connery in a huddle with Costner, Smith and Garcia, all three gazing like schoolboys as he laid down his feelings on the day's shoot. 'He was always so respectful toward me,' says Costner, 'but at the same time he was always taking little shots at us, keeping a little tension going.' After doing one scene with Costner, Connery loudly enquired, 'Is that the best it's going to get?'

By the time the cameras rolled entire scenes had been reworked based on the new-found rapport between the characters. The process also ironed out one of Connery's main complaints about American film actors; in their desperation to be 'liked', even 'loved', he felt they were apt to give signals that they were not *really* the unpleasant characters they were being asked to portray.

He worked hardest of all on Malone's first appearance as he encounters Ness during a routine patrol. After watching him throw a scrap of paper into the river, Malone rebukes him for littering. Connery decided to be absolutely nit-picking in the process. 'I decided to have an unnecessarily strong go at this guy. So I talked to him like a child or an idiot. And that created humour, because the audience knows he's a police investigator who's just had a terrible day. But after all, *I* don't know that, and I'm in a job I'm not happy or satisfied with ... With Malone, I tried to show at the beginning he could be a real pain in the ass, so that you wouldn't think he could be concerned with such things as Ness's family, and *then* show he was someone else underneath, capable of real relationships.'

At Connery's suggestion the scene in which Malone delivers his speech on Chicago tactics to Ness was shifted to a church from its original street setting. He loved the eye-for-an-eye Biblical elements of Mamet's sermon, and unerringly sensed the sinister resonances the church setting would add. 'You want to get Capone, here's how to get him,' he whispers. 'He pulls a knife, you pull a gun; he sends one of yours to the hospital, you send one of his to the morgue. *That's the Chicago way.*'

At the start Connery stuck in a few extra 'ands' and 'buts'

into his dialogue, until he learned just to repeat what he saw as Mamet's 'beautiful lines' the way they were written. As filming progressed he felt able to relax, convinced that all the elements of a grade A production were present, fully confident of his director and co-stars. He and Costner worked particularly well together. 'The casting of Kevin was as good as you could have,' says Connery, 'because he has a very elemental openness and directness that I frankly don't see in a lot of the younger American actors. They have a tendency to play the angles much more, be oblique and inside. They would probably find this sort of thing a bit too exposing, wouldn't want to appear that vulnerable.'

Impersonations were the order of the day as the cast bantered their way through the schedule. Connery noticed mud on Andy Garcia's boots as they prepared for a riding scene. 'Where have you been with those boots?' he asked. 'I went fishing,' Garcia replied.

'Didn't you have a rod?' Connery riposted. Choking back a smile, Garcia launched into a spot-on impression of Connery's Scottish burr: 'Aye, I went trampin' in, kickin' the fish. Nothin' a drop o' mink oil won't fix!'

Later it was Costner's turn, reciting scenes from one of his favourite movies, *Hombre*, with Paul Newman and Richard Boone. 'You got a lot of hard bark on you, mister!' was delivered in an authentic Boone rasp, then, 'What do you suppose hell is gonna look like?' Obviously unaware that Diane Cilento was in the movie, Costner then went on to describe one of her scenes. 'This bitch gets in front of Newman and she won't move. She ends up getting him killed. Hey, who *was* that woman?'

'That bitch,' Connery crisply informed him, 'was my first wife.'

'That was your wife?' Costner echoed disbelievingly. After faltering for a few seconds he was back on track. 'That's great,' he declared. Then, 'Jeez, Sean – you're *something*.'

During production Connery managed to take several evenings off, once to see Liza Minnelli at New York's Carnegie

Hall, another to have dinner with his old friend Sidney Lumet. He even arranged to set one afternoon aside for a game of golf as filming drew to a close. After that every day was marked out; at the end of production a few days in London were followed by a return to Spain 'for a look at what we've got in the pot'.

Overall *The Untouchables* was well received critically, albeit with the inevitable dissenting voices, such as John Gross in the *New York Times*: 'For all its virtuosity it has something hollow about it.' Janet Maslin saw it as 'by far the most complete and most successful film Brian De Palma has made'. For Richard Schickel in *Time Magazine* it was 'a densely layered work, with confident, compulsive energy'. Pauline Kael found it 'not a great movie, it's too banal, too morally comfortable – but it's a great audience movie'. As for Connery: 'At 56 this grizzled Scot has an impudent authority that's very like Olivier's, except that Connery is so much brawnier. His performance here is his most sheerly likeable since *The Man Who Would Be King*.' In Britain the bulk of the reviews were favourable, with Philip French in the *Observer* proclaiming it a 'rich and operatic movie', Charles Spence in the *Daily Telegraph* 'an absorbing thriller', with Connery's performance described by Alexander Walker in London's *Evening Standard* as 'a gale force of moral integrity'.

At last, whether in a 'major cameo' or not, Connery was back in the big time US hit league, without reliance on Bond, with *The Untouchables'* $37 million net. And 1988 turned out to be the year of the awards. In February he was nominated for an Academy Award for Best Actor in a Supporting Role for the movie; in March he was honoured at BAFTA as Actor of the Year for *The Name of the Rose*; in April he won his Oscar against stiff opposition from Denzel Washington, Vincent Gardenia, Morgan Freeman and Albert Brooks, and was given a standing ovation as he left his seat to collect the award from Cher. 'I first appeared here thirty years ago,' he cracked. 'Patience is a virtue!'

Many felt that the Oscar ceremony had yielded a long-service medal, and one that was thoroughly deserved. Although

Connery himself, taking a leaf from his mother's book, tended to downplay his delight, Michael Caine recognized the occasion as a turning point in his friend's life. He had not only cast off forever the burden of Bond and been accepted by the establishment as a fine actor in his own right, but had caught, in the unprecedented ovation, just a hint of the warmth and affection with which he was regarded by his peers.

Chapter 33

'I don't like the idea of being ripped off and nobody's been ripped off more than me.'

Sean Connery

'My strength as an actor, I think, is that I've stayed close to the core of myself, which has something to do with a voice, a music, a tune that's very much tied up with my background experience.'

Sean Connery

Like his poetry, which he refuses to discuss, let alone have published, Connery's feminine side seems destined to remain his dark continent. 'I'm not very good at reading my feminine side,' he claims, before adding that he doesn't see himself 'as macho as the image. It's something that got built up.'

If and when his poetry does finally see the light of day, the general public may be permitted a glimpse of this 'highly developed' aspect of Connery discerned by John Boorman back in the 1970s. For now, even having the subject brought up sparks the suspicion that the question is critically, derogatorily angled. Perhaps the substitution of 'sensitive' for 'feminine' would be more appropriate, and certainly more acceptable than 'touchy', another way of describing Connery's occasional outbursts. 'People treat him as if he has no sensitivity because of the way he looks,' says Michael Caine. 'But there's an extraordinarily sensitive man behind that, *extraordinarily* sensitive, more sensitive than you could ever imagine – so sensitive that I wouldn't even embarrass him by describing it.' (Memo to MC: 'Good grief, how much "sensitivity" can one man hold?')

Over the years interviewers have also referred to Connery's apparent lack of appreciation of his 'glorious luck', referring to the leg-up being chosen for Bond provided. As an article in Britain's *Telegraph Magazine* pointed out early in the 1980s: 'He still attacks the exploiters, rather pointless since he's as rich as any [of them]. It is the puritanism again, informed by a slightly left-wing sympathy. But actors are made to be used, and if they want to be stars, exploitation of their qualities is essential.'

Connery, of course, would certainly take leave to object to the last assertion. He would probably underplay the 'leg-up' as well, even though Bond's constant revivals in cinemas, on television and on video kept his name in the forefront, together with his cameos, throughout an almost unprecedented string of flops.

Connery saw *The Presidio* as a study of 'marvellous conflict' and flung himself into reworking Larry Ferguson's script with *Outland* director Peter Hyams. Together they concentrated on paring down dialogue to leave as much as possible 'to basic acting'.

The illustrious Presidio, the 1,400-acre army compound situated at the base of San Francisco's Golden Gate Bridge, was the setting for a joint murder investigation between crusty Provost Marshal Lt Col. Alan Caldwell (Connery), forced against his will to work with civilian police inspector Jay Austin (Mark Harmon), the two men already having gone through an earlier confrontation when Austin was an MP under Caldwell's command. When Austin and Caldwell's daughter

Donna (Meg Ryan) begin an affair, the situation becomes even more confused. Connery was interested in exploring the human side of the American soldier, including the fellowship involved in the military that seemed to have been obscured since the Vietnam War. Fair enough, many felt, but was an action director like Hyams the man to look to for introspection? Or did Connery know something that no one else did?

The Presidio's shooting in the late fall of 1987 at Paramount was a relatively trouble-free affair, with Harmon describing Connery as 'a guy's guy, tell-it-from-the-hip, who wants to work, to prepare a scene, to rehearse ahead of time, to do his homework. He works and he listens. It's a real lesson being with him.' Rick Zumwalt, who played Connery's three hundred pound adversary in a bar-room brawl scene, was approached by the anxious star after every fall to make sure there was no damage. 'We had some shots there where I came real close to punching him,' Zumwalt admitted, 'and he said, "Hey, put it right there. It's my job to move." He's no prima donna.' Connery cheerfully obliged old pal Alan King, busy shooting *Memories of Me* across town, when the comedian requested a walk-on appearance in his movie.

During the shoot Harmon found himself voted 'World's Sexiest Man' a year ahead of his co-star. The next time they met Connery hailed him across a crowded lobby with, 'Hello, ducky. *God*, you are sexy. Any chance of dinner tonight?'

Connery was visibly high on the project. 'It's difficult to know what reactivates you,' he mused, 'what gets you going again. Invariably it's the writing in a screenplay and a good part. You never lose touch – but suddenly you find something that really works and the more diverse the work is, the more fun it can be.' Once again, with the critical pasting that awaited the movie, his confidence turned out to be misplaced.

Janet Maslin in the *New York Times* wrote that Connery was 'a fine actor under normal circumstances, but he doesn't do much acting in *The Presidio*. What he does is recite his lines over Mark Harmon's shoulder.' As for Connery's dialogue-paring exercise: 'Larry Ferguson's screenplay overstates and overexplains everything.' The *Boston Herald* described the movie as 'action-packed, but pointless … Pointless scene follows witless scene.'

Harmon, it seemed, had proved yet again to be a small-screen actor, although it would have been difficult for anyone to shine in such dross. (Connery: 'I suppose he could have been stronger. You know, like Costner or that chap Don Johnson'); Meg Ryan was cute to the point of charmlessness, especially in a decidedly uncomfortable sex scene, and Connery's timing – and judgement – was off in a thoroughly pedestrian outing. Maybe he took the movie so he could play in the rooftop scene with Jack Kruschen in which he delivers an earth-wisdom soliloquy; if the scene had been half-decently written instead of doggerel, it might have been worthwhile. On the other hand maybe he took it just for the money. If he did, the movie's less than $10 million US net denied him his customary percentage.

'The movie's about lies,' Terry Gilliam enthused. 'It's about the greatest liar the world has ever known. It's about flying to the moon and meeting sixty-foot-high people with detachable heads. It's about falling into the centre of the earth and meeting Vulcan and Venus. It's about being swallowed by whales and riding on cannonballs. It's about dancing in the sky. In other words, a normal, everyday sort of film!'

Before Gilliam could proceed with *The Adventures of Baron Munchausen* he first had to raise $25 million or so to get the project off the ground. Although securing Connery to play the Baron would undoubtedly have helped – and his German-born co-producer, Thomas Schuhly, who had worked with him on *Name of the Rose*, argued that he would turn Munchausen into a sexy, romantic hero – Gilliam had his mind on someone less well known, and older. 'Sean's great, but he's not our Baron,' he flatly declared.

Schuhly was unconvinced. He had listened all too well to Gilliam's version of the running joke on *Time Bandits* which had Connery addressing him alternately either as 'Boy' or 'Quasimodo' and had read 'umbrage' between the lines. 'Sean can be very mean with directors,' he maintains, 'and maybe Terry has never forgiven him for the slight ... Sean is the typical leader of the gang; when he is angry you can see death in his eyes. Only the law holds him back. He has an enormous presence and if you feel insecure as a director, he can become very ironical. I know how to handle him, you have to humour Sean. If you don't have the weight to withstand him, it can get nasty.' When he next proposed Connery for the key cameo of King of the Moon, Schuhly rather spoilt his case. 'Now you're talking,' Gilliam immediately agreed. 'Sean would be *terrific* as the King.'

Allied Filmmakers' Jake Eberts, Gilliam's vital seed-money backer for the project and the man behind Connery's renaissance in *Name of the Rose*, was present when the star arrived in Rome to discuss the role. He recalls a sparkling dinner party with his friend in top form, animatedly discussing the project with Gilliam and guests Ursula Andress and Valentina Cortese, the veteran Italian diva scheduled to play Queen of the Moon to Connery's King. Everything seemed set ...

The problem with Connery's participation was that he had agreed to play the role *as originally written*. When the worried money men behind the movie, completion guarantors Film Finances Inc., insisted at the halfway stage of *Munchausen*'s production in Rome that Gilliam depopulate the Moon from two thousand to just two people – the King and Queen – doubts were raised as to whether Connery's enthusiasm level would be sustained. And even as Schuhly was frantically trying to confirm that he was still on board, CAA was penning its own missive to Film Finances, seeking clarification of the movie's fiscal health. The big question was whether Connery was in any way obligated to play a 'half-assed' version of the original script.

Early in December 1987, Schuhly despondently relayed the information that Connery had called him to say he was bowing out, despite what the producer referred to as their 'gentleman's agreement'. By 17 December, with the moon scene due to be shot in six weeks' time, Schuhly flip-flopped following a personal visit to California and informed Gilliam that Connery was prepared to 'fulfil his obligation in principle' – but only if the role were 'improved dramaturgically'. 'I feel the credit "Sean Connery" will certainly be an asset to the different national distributors when they launch the picture,' Schuhly urged, 'therefore, why should we not at least *try* to get him?'

A thoroughly puzzled Gilliam wrote to Connery, setting out the facts in the most honest and forthright manner he could. While he still wanted the star, he was not about to pretend that the King of the Moon was the part it had been; as for being 'dramatically improved' Gilliam was busy *cutting* scenes under constant threat of being fired by Film Finances. Headed 'From the Wooden Box that Terry Gilliam sits on when on location', his letter ran:

Dear Sean,

Confused as I am about many things, I find that, as predicted, [Schuhly's] return from his L.A. conversation with you has added to my predicament. I thought you were a definite 'No', but Thomas claims you are a less definite 'If'. I'm not exactly sure what the 'If' is, but since (my co-writer) and I have just had some new thoughts concerning the Moon sequence, we thought you should see them straight away. As you will see, the King is quite a different animal. I'm not sure he will appeal to you, but I'll leave that to you.

It would be very useful to get your response quickly to ease my mounting confusion.

Thanks, Happy New Year, Bon Année, Terry.

The day after Gilliam penned his missive, with which he also faxed a copy of the latest script, co-writer Charles McKeown bumped into Schuhly at Cinecitta Studios. After expressing the hope that Connery would take on board Gilliam's 'no-bullshit' message he was startled when Schuhly replied, 'No, he won't ... Sean will never *see* Terry's letter. Film Finances read it before it was faxed and decided it should be suppressed. They told me not to send it. Their worry was that if Sean got the impression he was being said "No" to, CAA would have legal grounds to claim his money anyway.'

Soon after the turn of the year Schuhly made a further attempt to secure Connery and claimed to emerge triumphant. 'In a long telephone conversation on January 9,' he trumpeted, 'I finally succeeded in eliciting a clear "Yes" from Sean as to his revised part. He accepts the role as it now stands.' Two weeks later he had a different story to tell: 'He called me yesterday and *definitely* withdrew his acceptance of the "King of the Moon". I am so thunderstruck by this sudden about-turn that I am at a loss for words. As to the reason for his decision, Sean stated that he cannot match the dates . . .'

Schuhly later offered another explanation for Connery's withdrawal, claiming that Gilliam had been quoted in the US press as saying that he didn't particularly want the actor, that he had someone else in mind. 'Once that was published,' said Schuhly, 'Sean phoned me immediately and his agent at CAA explained that the article had been their topic at their 11am meeting. They decided then that Sean would *never* do a film for a director who was less than 100 per cent keen on his participation. Sean called me and gave me 2,000 excuses about preparation for the new Indiana Jones movie, all of that. Because he likes me a lot, he was willing originally to do me this favour. But he can't do it when he thinks the director doesn't want him.'

With Robin Williams an inspired last-minute choice for the role, Gilliam sought to place the whole episode in perspective. 'I first tried to talk Sean into playing the part before the film started. Even then I told him the part wasn't much, but it was a chance for him to play the big floating head that he didn't get to play in *Zardoz*. I needed an anchor and he was that. It would have made the scene really work with somebody as majestic as him. Also the idea that the Baron could steal Sean Connery's woman was very important. That's what it was all about. When we reworked the thing there was just no part for someone of Sean's stature any more.'

Following the unfortunate series of misquotes, misunderstandings, suppressed correspondence and diluted scripts, few would take issue with the star's final decision.

*

Connery was pissed off. While the *Munchausen* fracas was rumbling on, and despite the approaches made by Steven Spielberg and his producer George Lucas that he consider the role of Harrison Ford's father in *Indiana Jones and the Last Crusade*, the team was adamantly refusing to hand over the script. Connery's antennae began to relay the message that at least one of them was less than keen on his casting. He was correct. 'George wasn't thinking in terms of such a powerful presence,' Spielberg later admitted. 'His idea was for a doting, scholarly person, an older British dramatic actor. But I had always seen Sean Connery in the role. Without a strong illuminating presence I was afraid Harrison would eradicate the father from the movie. I wanted to challenge him. And who could be the equal of Indiana Jones but James Bond?'

One of the reasons behind the making of *Indiana Jones and the Last Crusade*, it turned out, was the fulfilment of a commitment Spielberg had made to Lucas that a trilogy would be completed. 'I wasn't happy with the second film at all,' said Spielberg. 'It was too dark, too subterranean and much too horrific.' The other reason, therefore, for *Last Crusade* was 'to apologize for the second one' and 'make a movie I could stand naked on top of'. It was writer Jeffrey Boam's 'brainwave' to award Indiana Jones a screen father in the first place, a concept both Spielberg and Ford preppily considered 'far out'.

Connery turned down the first script he was eventually shown. After the months of teasing secrecy, the whole thing seemed an anti-climax. He cared not at all for the way his character had been conceived. When the trio eventually met for a discussion, Lucas flinched at Connery's idea of basing the character on the explorer Sir Richard Burton, someone who would have been totally indifferent to his son's growing up and who would have disappeared into uncharted jungle for months on end without so much as a by-your-leave, and with no feelings of guilt. It was the sheer un-Americanism of the concept that shattered Lucas. And it was the same with sexual mores. Both Spielberg and Lucas initially vetoed the idea of

Connery having enjoyed a relationship with the film's heroine before his son appeared on the scene and repeated the honours. 'Why?' Connery asked. 'It's been done before, you know. Some of the old Greeks were ahead of you.'

He was stunned at the producer's puritanical response, the way Spielberg and Lucas seemed to regard Indiana Jones as some kind of ethereal creature straight from the scriptures. It took considerable persuasion before they began to see matters his way – and only then did he sign on the dotted line.

Although Spielberg had been Connery's chief supporter for the role of Professor Henry Jones, the director was unprepared for the way he continued to pour his own ideas into the development of his character from day one of shooting, 16 May 1988, back in the familiar territory of the Almerian desert. Originally, the Professor had been introduced on page 70 of the script – until, that is, Connery came up with so many extra scenes that he was moved up to page 50. 'He was instrumental in all the rewrites,' Spielberg confirmed, 'and when he gets a good idea, which is about twenty times a day, he's such a child, his face lights up. He's from the old school of the complete professional. He has to say his lines word perfect.'

Connery speaks with lightly qualified praise about Spielberg. While bowing to no one in his admiration for the director's visual sense, he feels that he is on less secure ground when dealing with actors' motivations. 'He understands what he wants to try and get, but he's not absolutely certain about how to get it in terms of performance,' Connery maintains, before flashing his trademark grin and adding, 'But then he's young, eh?'

In between maintaining the on-screen father and son banter with Ford when the cameras stopped rolling, Connery relaxed in his usual uninhibited manner, removing the lower half of his Harris tweed suit in order to let the breeze blow freely around his nether regions. He stayed that way when only his top half was required on camera. During real-life son Jason's visits he detected the interaction between his father, his screen son and Spielberg. 'There was a real buzz when they were working out scenes,' he recalled. 'Things were being thrown in the whole time and it came off the page. Dad had a great time on that movie.'

'The biggest thrill,' Spielberg claimed, 'was putting Harrison and Sean in a two-shot and calling "Action!" and trying not to ruin the take by laughing. I think it helped Harrison to have such a venerable screen force to compete against. And I think Harrison being Indiana Jones, with Sean a visiting star, kept Sean on his toes. So together their mojos were working.'

Without Connery and his injection of sly wit into the proceedings, who knows how successful *Indiana Jones and the Last Crusade* would have been? A different movie would certainly have resulted from Spielberg's and Lucas's original strait-laced ideas. *Raiders of the Lost Ark* had netted $116 million back in 1981; the sequel, *Indiana Jones and the Temple of Doom*, had dipped just a little to $109 million in 1984; with *Indiana Jones and the Last Crusade* the take was back to $116 million in the US, and proved an even greater hit round the world than either of its predecessors.

'Sean is not like anybody else,' Spielberg acknowledged. 'He's an original. He's never been stronger or more sought after and he's finally been recognized as the movie star he's always been. Hollywood has at last admitted to itself that Sean is one of the great movie stars; he will be remembered throughout recorded film history.' Few disagreed in essence with the sentiment.

Having Harrison Ford as a fictional son was one thing; discovering the existence of a second quite another. 'Dennis Connery' had already fooled quite a few people in England, mainly gullible young women, by claiming to be working for his 'famous father'. When the imposter resurfaced in the States, Connery admitted that technically he didn't know what he could do about the situation. 'I mean, apart from physical damage if I get my hands on him,' he growled threateningly.

The warning was enough to make 'Dennis Connery', the phantom son, do a nifty overnight disappearing act.

Chapter 34

'When Dad walks into a room the atmosphere changes. He's incredibly muscular and strong and bulky, with a deep, heavy voice he uses to maximum effect to get a point across. Even now, when someone shouts at me like that it hurts much more than if they'd actually hit me.'

Jason Connery

'Dad is so straight. He never believes anyone is going to do him down, because he would never think of behaving like that himself. When people do cheat on him he is always amazed.'

Jason Connery

Jason's impression that his father thought him 'a flipping ass' dates back to his coming home from school with reports like 'Jason has ability, but doesn't use it.' Concerned that his son had no centre and little purpose, Connery would shout with rage and produce a stream of oaths. Jason was painfully aware that he was the prototype 'boy who had everything' who 'couldn't make it as a person' in his father's eyes, the backlash from his parent having made his own way out of the ghetto. 'I worried him and made him angry all my life,' said Jason in the mid-1980s, describing his father to reporter Corinna Honan as 'an aggressive man' who 'used to hit me – but not without reason'.

Jason was well aware of the conflict and aggression that existed between his parents during his childhood. Even though he was on the upper floor of their house he could still hear them arguing four floors below. Recalling these occasions he would refer to his father's 'powerful voice' and 'presence like a thunderstorm'. 'I didn't know what it was like to come back home and find my mother and father round a TV set,' he said. 'We didn't go in for any little family suppers after they'd finished work. But because I didn't know them I didn't miss them.'

'Wild kid' was a reasonable description of young Jason. At the age of four, swinging an axe, he smashed up a greenhouse. After watching an episode of *Superman*, he dived off the top of a staircase and split his head open on a radiator. 'I've always been dramatic,' he cheerfully admits, dismissing his parents' domestic problems as the reason behind his own: 'I didn't trust anyone, and I enjoyed being alone. I'd get pig-headed, even when I knew I was wrong. And I was always fighting at school.' Belying his tearaway nature, Jason looked like the archetypal blond chorister. Being teased by fellow classmates as 'a pretty boy', and nicknamed '$003\frac{1}{2}$' served only to make him aggressive. ('Maybe one day I'll overtake him and they'll make me 008,' he was still able to joke.) Aged ten, he bit through his best friend's wrist because he had nabbed the seat next to his girlfriend in school. With his victim bleeding profusely, Jason was ordered to vacate the classroom in disgrace.

He found it impossible to maintain his enthusiasm level for longer than five minutes in subjects that were of no interest to him, like history, geography and mathematics. The diatribes from his father evoked vows of trying to do better. 'I've got to work. I've *really* got to work,' he would say to himself over and over again. Somehow, it never lasted: his years at Millfield are not exactly packed with fond memories. Gordonstoun, following in the footsteps of two royal princes, and in the company of a third, Edward, was an altogether happier experience, despite his new nickname of 'Bowlegs'. He felt much more at home, despite the cold showers, early morning runs and general air of stringent regimentation – although he still declines to quantify some of the 'dreadful things' he got up to. Instead, he laughingly claims that at least some of the masters 'thought he was OK'.

It was Micheline who decided that Jason and his father were not close enough, and took the initiative in encouraging frequent visits. At first Jason felt distinctly uncomfortable watching his father with someone other than his natural mother; Micheline was 'just someone who was staying with us'. The nervousness that she shared at their first meeting established an initial rapport, although a major barrier was her inability to speak English all that fluently. Then there was a gradual, mutual acceptance.

Due to his stepbrother's inability to communicate at all in English, Stephane Cosman Connery was bombed out as far as Jason was concerned. 'I can't be bothered with this guy,' he thought to himself; all the two of them did until Stephane departed for boarding school was make stupid faces at each other.

A year later, with Stephane's language ability enhanced, a great friendship developed between the boys. Jason revealed a touching protectiveness of the new family unit in 1983, when he declared, 'The only people my father sees are the people he plays golf with. Apart from them, he doesn't have many friends. He doesn't need them. *He's got us.*'

Through his stepmother Jason was at last able to experience the simple delight of belonging to a family – with all its attendant joy, as well as drawbacks. 'I never felt homesick until my stepmother brought the family together,' he declared. 'Unlike my mother she's not an actress, so she is the stabilizing force. Now I love her like a mother.' Although his relationship with his father had also improved out of all proportion, he still admitted, as late as 1983, 'he can shout at me now and I would be reduced to tears.'

Until he was sixteen Jason had wanted to be a vet. It was hanging around listening to the conversations between his father and showbusiness friends that brought about the change, as well as the recognition that the hunger his father had known, to get out and make something of himself, existed in him too. Different though it was with his privileged background, the similarity lay in wanting to be the best he possibly could at whatever he took up, and to succeed on his own, rather than ride on his father's coat-tails.

There was one major hurdle to overcome with Jason's decision to take up acting; he was terrified what his father would think, and was completely nonplussed when a favourable reaction was evinced. 'I thought you wouldn't like it,' he managed to stammer. 'Why shouldn't I?' Connery asked. 'I think it's terrific!' He had just two pieces of advice for his son: 'If you have enthusiasm, you will progress', followed by: 'Look out for sharks!'

Connery put Jason in touch with agent Joy Jameson. 'What that boy's got to realize,' he told her, 'is that life isn't going out to lunch every day, it's having a bowl of minestrone on the back burner.' After securing him the job of 'gofer' on *Five Days One Summer*, he stood back and – despite several famous names from Connery's past that are sprinkled among Jason's early 'opportunities' – let his six-foot-tall son make the rest of the running himself. 'Nepotism I abhor,' Connery declared, just in case anyone put two and two together and made an inaccurate five. 'There's no question that his stint in Perth was helped because of who I am, but once he got there it was clearly up to him.'

Jason initially applied to join several repertory companies and had actually started at Bristol Old Vic before hearing there was a place at Perth Repertory in Scotland. Off he went, officially as 'assistant stage manager', unofficially a dogsbody. He played in the company's Christmas '81 pantomime *Aladdin*, as 'Who Flung', probably the first-ever Chinaman with corn-coloured hair and grey-blue eyes. He followed up with the plays *Spider's Web, Night and Day* – and *The Man from Thermopylae*, in which his father came to see him. 'I was proud of you,' he assured Jason afterwards.

His film debut came in 1982 in Paramount's *Lords of Discipline*, directed by Franc Roddam, a drama set in America's West Point Academy, shot mainly at Sandhurst and Wellington Colleges in England. After having his hair closely cropped and undergoing strenuous training for the role, there was considerable disappointment when most of his performance ended up on the cutting room floor. He moved into a flat in London rented from one ex-Gordonstoun friend, with another college pal, Geoffrey Moore, together with brother Stephane, then working at Christie's the auctioneers. A bachelor paradise for ladykillers? 'I would love to be a ladykiller, but I can't find any ladies to kill,' Jason claimed, adding, 'I *hate* London girls. All they seem interested in is how much money you've got, who you are and what car you drive.' He looked back fondly on his stay in Perth: 'The girls in Scotland were much nicer and more genuine.'

Jason was out of work for six months after filming *Lords of Discipline*, his £5,000 fee for the movie spent in record time on the assumption that more work would be forthcoming immediately. Instead, there was the dreaded round of auditions that confronts all aspiring actors. 'When I fail I get terribly depressed,' he said. 'But if there's one thing my father taught me, it's not to be soft. If you want something, go out and get it.' To confound expectations he defiantly declined to ask his father for help, financially or otherwise, and was hurt when he was treated as 'son of Sean' by some in the profession rather than as an individual in his own right.

'Had I looked like my father,' says Jason, 'I would have changed my name. As it is in this business, people know who you are however you try to hide it. I found people wanted to meet me to see if I looked like my Dad. I'm always asked if I get jobs because he is my father. But at the end of the day it is up to me to prove I can do the job, regardless of why I was offered the part.'

Having developed his first ulcer at nineteen, Jason admits he is a born worrier: 'I worry when I'm working and I worry when I'm out of work; of the two working actually worries me more.'

A lifeline came along in the shape of an offer to appear in a fantasy movie to be shot in France, *Dream One*. 'You weren't any great shakes,' was his father's verdict on this occasion, a ruthlessly honest judgement that still hurt Jason deeply, although he tried desperately not to let his feelings show. The film, for the record, was no great shakes either, a surprisingly amateurish affair from producer John Boorman, Connery's *Zardoz* director, before his triumphant rebound with *The Emerald Forest* and *Hope and Glory*.

Much more successful was a co-starring role Jason landed in the ironically titled *The Boy Who Had Everything*, an Australian movie that remains by far his best screen outing to date.

As a student refusing to buckle under to his new school's disciplinary tactics, he appeared in every shot, including a drunk scene, a stand-up fight and a nude scene with a prostitute. Playing her son's mother, both on-screen and off was Diane Cilento – resident since the mid-seventies on the edge of the Daintree rainforest in far North Queensland, with daughter Gigi happily domiciled in Adelaide. She coached him to expand the flat timbre in his voice that to her screamed 'Gordonstoun', but acknowledged the difference the college had made in her son: 'He was given a lot of responsibility, and that is what he needed.' She listened sympathetically as Jason explained the mixed blessing and curse of the Connery name. 'It must be ghastly,' she agreed, bittersweet memories of her own doubtless flooding back.

The movie, it quickly transpired, was based on director Stephen Wallace's own rites of passage. 'While we were shooting,' Jason recalled, 'you suddenly saw him reacting, especially to the scenes with my mother. I wanted to be slightly more overt, but he said I had to keep it inside me, which tensed everything up. That, he said, is how it was. But I felt very much at ease with my mother playing my mother. I learned a hell of a lot from working with her.'

Back in London, after inviting his father round for spaghetti bolognaise, Connery asked to see the video of *The Boy Who Had Everything*. Jason nervously clicked it into the machine and immediately repaired to his bedroom. There he lay with the door open, watching his father's reactions while the movie played. His heart was in his mouth as the verdict was pronounced. 'You were very good,' Connery told him. 'It was good work and I enjoyed it. And *believed* it.' Thrilled as he was, Jason still felt a 'less matey' relationship with his father than he enjoyed with his mother. Honest as his father was, there seemed to be a reluctance to demonstrate his 'caring' side, a lack of emotional openness. Aware that he occasionally rang Joy Jameson behind his back to ask if he was working hard and being professional, Jason bridled at the implied mistrust. 'The best thing Dad has given me is a sensible attitude to life,' he rationalized. 'I respect him and want to be like him, except as an actor, where I want to go my own way. I hear a lot of superstars' sons end up committing suicide. It isn't easy measuring up to my father. But no way am I going to jump under a train.'

Despite his appealing combination of ruggedness and sensitivity, twenty-two-year-old Jason still regarded himself as hardly a good bet for any girl. He had formed a romantic liaison during his stay in Australia, but somehow back in England found himself tongue-tied when confronted by a pretty girl, and far from adept at picking up the signals from a female that fancied him. Although he loathed 'macho men', a remark from someone asking if he was gay had the effect of bringing out the macho in him. He came close to punching the questioner on the nose.

Early in 1984 he played a hurdler in a five-hour mini-series, *The First Modern Olympics*, directed by Alvin Rakoff, Connery's original *Requiem for a Heavyweight* champion. In August of the same year he tested for Robin Hood, the role Michael Praed had just vacated in the ATV series. The producers were looking for someone of similar 'teen-appeal', together with qualities of leadership, a solid screen presence and boundless enthusiasm. They informed Jason that they would 'let him know'.

Christmas that year was spent in Queensland with Cilento and playwright/screenwriter Anthony Shaffer, the couple having met in 1972 while filming the off-beat horror movie, *The Wicker Man*, scripted by Shaffer, then at Cilento's 'College of Continuous Education'. Jason described their two-hundred-acre tropical fruit farm, a paradise of whistling ducks, exotic birds and brilliant butterflies as the 'Garden of Eden', crocodile-infested rivers notwithstanding. Despite everyone's direst prognostication, Cilento had created a new lifestyle for herself that many would envy.

While mucking out the goat shed one morning, a call came through from London to confirm that Jason had landed the role of Robin Hood. When the elation died down he thought soberly about how he intended to tackle the role. He decided to play Robin true to his character as he saw it; whether that made him attractive to women or not struck him as immaterial. Ironically, he was adamant that the assignment was in no way destined to make a sex symbol of him. That was the last thing, he swore, he wanted to be.

The few problems that inevitably arose in joining the established crew as a 'new boy', albeit as the star, were soon overcome. At first Jason was teased relentlessly by the regular 'Merrie Men', all of which he took with immense good nature. When he found himself being pelted with a couple of dozen empty Coke cans, scriptwriter Michael Carpenter explained, 'They wouldn't do that to anyone they didn't admire.' In fact the 'Merries' were just as daunted with the prospect of working with 'Son of 007' as Jason was of joining their company. Casting director Esta Charkham sensed that Jason was 'riddled with insecurity' when he came to the unit. Acceptance as the new Robin by viewers worldwide eventually helped, exemplified as this was by two thousand letters a week, mainly from teenagers across the States.

In a change of pace in 1985, Jason starred in an Italian movie directed by Mauro Bolognini, *La Venexiana* (*The Venetian*), based on an anonymously penned seventeenth-century play. He played a foreign student arriving in Venice and falling for a beautiful young girl and her neighbour, a widow; although he has but one night in the city he manages to spend it making love to both of them. Laura Antonelli was the sexually unfulfilled Angela, Monica Guerritore the married Valeria. A lush score by Ennio Morricone underlined the movie's high erotic content, with Jason coming over as perfectly at ease in the frequent nude scenes, his athletic, but hitherto slender frame having filled out impressively. 'Jason Connery projects the kind of raw masculinity of his Dad, Sean,' *Variety* proclaimed following *Venexiana*'s 1986 première at the Cannes Film Festival, 'and his acting fits smoothly into the Italian ensemble.'

The call of the stage brought about a short run in *The Three Musketeers*, followed by the journey from London's fringe to the West End in a unanimously acclaimed revival of R.C. Sherriff's *Journey's End*. After the impersonal atmosphere and short takes on film and TV sets, Jason felt as if he had come back home to the stage, and in a role he could really sink his teeth into. He created an indelible impression as the tragic, drunken twenty-one-year-old Stanhope, a man brutalized by war. Connery gave his son a congratulatory hug backstage after the first night, with tears of joy, pride and delight unashamedly shed by both men; for the first time Jason had sensed that kind of openness from his father. Equally gratifying, he collected his best-ever notices and began to be treated like a serious actor for the first time. John Boorman sent him a letter of congratulation after watching the play early in the run, adding one or two notes that he felt would enhance his performance even further. 'I saw him a couple of weeks after that,' Boorman recalls, 'and he thanked me for the note and told me he kept it in the breast pocket of his battledress every night when he was on stage.'

So totally wound up was he in the play that he spent hours every night trying to find where he had parked his car. Invited to present an award at the BAFTA ceremony he decided to do it in character. 'I *became* him, pretended I *was* Stanhope,' he said, 'because on these sort of showcase occasions I hate being myself. Personal appearances freak me out. I feel such a tart standing there.'

Even with this success the insecurities Esta Charkham had sensed back in Jason's *Robin of Sherwood* days were far from being dispelled. By the time he was twenty-five a second ulcer had developed. 'I may look relaxed, but internally I'm a mass of anxieties,' he confessed.

There was a faint sense of embarrassment when Jason knew he was being considered for the role of Ian Fleming in the TV-movie, *The Secret Life of Ian Fleming*. Was it just too close to home – and was he being used by the filmmakers, hoping to trade on the Connery name? When he telephoned his father for advice it came straight and simple: 'If the script's good, do it.' Jason wittily and sardonically summed up the implications inherent as he took the role: 'Freud would have had a field day. Fleming created Bond, Dad played Bond, Dad created me and I'm playing Fleming!'

This brush with Bond was as close as Jason cares to get to the saga, for he thinks deeply about the implications behind the books. 'I wasn't even born when Dad made the first Bond,' he points out, 'and only nine when he did the last in the series. I didn't think too much about it at the time, but these days I do. The phrase "licence to kill" is just horrific. It's immoral. You *can't* give someone a licence to kill. Who *says*? But take it in the context of the movies and there has to be an overriding element of humour. You can't play "licence to kill" without it, otherwise it is very dangerous territory. Fortunately Dad was always well aware of the humour potential of that role, and he was brilliant, he played it to the hilt. He delivered 007 with a hefty helping of salt. It was never something you would take too seriously.'

When his father was honoured with a special Lifetime Achievement award at the British Academy of Film and Television Arts (BAFTA) in 1990 – presented by Princess Anne 'to a British actor who has made an outstanding contribution to world cinema' – Jason gave the best speech of the night. 'I'm often asked,' he said, 'if my father is a good actor.' He paused.

'I tell them no, my father is *not* a good actor.' In the few seconds during which Jason paused again and stared into the sea of faces in the audience, before alighting on his father, a pin dropped would have gone off like a hand grenade. Then, to thunderous applause, he added, 'My father is a *great* actor.'

Later that same year Jason helped break box-office records during a run at the Greenwich Theatre in *Cyrano de Bergerac*, playing lovestruck Christian de Neuvillette as less of a dullard than usual. A television mini-series followed, *Mountain of Diamonds*, based on twin Wilbur Smith novels *The Burning Shore* and *Power of the Sword*, in which he played a Second World War fighter pilot. Then came *The Sheltering Desert*, another World War II epic shot in Namibia with Joss Ackland and Rupert Graves. In this Jason describes his character as 'a bit of a wimp'. In the future he wants to tackle Shakespeare, and to play a homosexual on screen: 'I'd like *for once* to see a gay man who isn't portrayed as either over-the-top effeminate, or a wonderful human being who happens to be gay.'

Jason seems to have no immediate plans to marry, although he came close in 1990 before his romance with blonde actress Lucinda Fisher foundered. He sees romance as 'nice when it's working. When it doesn't go well, it can be bad news.' He leads the campaign for totally feminine women: 'I'm probably going to sound like a total sexist here, but I really hate it when women abandon their femininity because they feel it makes them more modern or stronger. What's worse is that you can't even talk about it without people blowing their lids. Girls do seem to be over-under-compensating, or whatever it is. But I don't understand why. If I were a girl I would certainly wear red lipstick.'

Ideally he would like to be able to move between the worlds of radio, TV, film and theatre. He grabbed the chance to play a villain in the actors'-co-operative movie, *Tank Malling*, a doomed project. 'If they knew how things would work out,' he said philosophically, echoing, no doubt, his father's sentiments on the subject, 'actors would never make bad movies. I have read good scripts that turned out to be a load of old rubbish and then there are films like *Saturday Night Fever* which were full of clichés, but caught the imagination.'

His preference for the moment seems to be for the theatre and the exhilaration of working with a like-minded group, as well as the intimate communication with an audience. A television mini-series shot in the Cook Islands in 1991, *The Other Side of Paradise*, confirmed his potential yet again, both as an actor and matinee-idol. That none of his movies has yet achieved a significant release is naturally a source of disappointment. There is one consolation: in 1993 he will still only be thirty years old; his father was thirty-two when he hit his stride as Bond. There is time enough yet, as there is for the further consolidation of the bonds between father and son. This may well emerge, ironically, when Connery loosens up on the traditional 'heavy Scottish father' role he often adopts, and pays his son the compliment of allowing him to make his own decisions.

'I often think he is jealous of my privileged background,' said Jason. 'But then he gave it to me!' A shrug. 'I just get on with being an actor. If you're bad, then you're bad. If you're good, nobody can actually say, "He's very good because his father's Sean Connery."'

Chapter 35

'I hope he has a good lawyer.'

> Sean Connery, commenting on Timothy Dalton's
> assumption of the James Bond mantle.

Producer Lawrence Gordon spent four exhausting years developing the script for *Family Business* with novelist Vincent Patrick, author of *The Pope of Greenwich Village*. The project was shopped to every studio in Hollywood, and rejected by them all. 'It's too good a yarn not to get made,' Gordon kept assuring Patrick. When Sidney Lumet declared the triple-generation theme 'charming' Gordon was elated; a year later, when Lumet snared Connery, he was ecstatic.

Connery was less than thrilled with the first script he was sent, deeply concerned that his character was neither harsh nor tough enough; the whole approach struck him as over-sentimentalized. It turned out that Patrick agreed with him; he had been ordered to make it more saccharin to please studio chiefs. Since Lumet also agreed with Connery, the acerbic note Connery wanted was soon injected.

With Matthew Broderick also signed, TriStar adopted the movie and gave the green light. The addition of Dustin

Hoffman to the all-star cast brought the actors' salaries to close on half the movie's $25m budget. 'Obtaining the three leads after the years of uncertainty,' said Patrick, 'was beyond my wildest dreams.'

Genetically the improbability of Connery playing Dad to Hoffman's diminutive son and granddad to the compact Broderick – three generations of thieves – never fazed Lumet for one moment as he contemplated his fifth collaboration with Connery and his first with Hoffman after a couple of almost-rans. The tragi-comic McMullens, he conceded, were 'a strange family, God knows, but a wonderful one. And I just couldn't see anyone else but Sean as its head.'

Connery's Jessie McMullen, unsurprisingly of Scottish origin, is an unrepentant ex-con married to a Sicilian, whose son Vito (Hoffman) is encouraged to follow in father's criminal footsteps. This he does, before a rethink in the cooler. Back in circulation, he marries a Jewish girl, moves uptown and sends his son Adam (Broderick) to college. Blood tells, however, when Adam sides with granddad shortly after his graduation and goes on to mastermind the heist of DNA gene-splicing secrets from a bio-engineering laboratory.

Someone remarked that Connery – at fifty-nine – was a little young to be playing father to Hoffman, only seven years his junior. Wasn't this quite a feat, even for the ex-James Bond? 'I think I look old enough,' Connery growled. 'I simply do what's interesting to do, and all of a sudden I seem to have become a kind of teacher/father figure.'

Producer Gordon's concern, that moviegoers would suspend disbelief and swallow that his trio of stars were related, disappeared as the shooting got underway. 'There was no question that Dustin is Sean's son and Matt is Dustin's,' he declared, 'I think this is a combination that will intrigue the movie-going public'.

The movie was shot in the streets of New York with which Lumet was so familiar – uptown, downtown, in Hell's Kitchen bars, on the docks, at Rockland County and on Route 59, where the three stars converged in the Spring Valley Market Place to acquire the sledgehammer, drill bits, screwdrivers and chain-saw needed for their raid. 'I don't know any other director who could do it this fast,' producer Gordon marvelled between shots. 'We bop along, we get it done,' Lumet agreed, with a quiet smile of satisfaction that the movie was edging ahead of schedule. *Family Business* was in fact wrapped in a super-efficient 31 days, partly attributable to the generous rehearsal time Lumet organized for the stars ahead of shooting.

Any doubts Lumet and Gordon might have entertained that Connery's no-nonsense acting style might clash with Hoff-man's notorious Method adherence soon vanished. 'Sean and Dustin interacted wonderfully,' said Lumet. 'Yes, they have two different styles – Dustin loves to improvise and Sean, normally, hates it. Sean is extremely disciplined and Dustin is very improvisational, all over the place with his lines. But they got along so well that Sean tried improvising. And he turned out to be *brilliant* at it! Dustin was perfect – creative, contributive, funny, he worked his ass off. I didn't know where it would end up, but Sean met Dustin improvisation for improvisation.' A private showing of the upcoming *Rain Man* brought an assurance from Connery that Hoffman would be in line for an Oscar. Dustin modestly demurred, although clearly elated by the possibility.

Matthew Broderick, not unreasonably, felt just a little intimidated by all the high-power camaraderie going on around him: 'Sean just kind of lets you know he doesn't want some kind of smart-ass kid in his face all the time.' Soon he took to doing side-splitting imitations of him behind his back. When the cause of the hilarity reached Connery's ears, his reaction was an amused but cautionary, 'Well, why doesn't Matthew do it for me?'

'I think he might be afraid to,' an assistant replied.

'Good,' said Connery. '*He should be*!'

During the shooting Lumet addressed Broderick as 'Pussy-cat' and Hoffman as 'Dusty'; Sean remained 'Sean'. 'Most people think of him as a legendary star,' he said with a broad grin. 'I don't – but only because we go to the toilet together.'

News of the death of his eighty-three-year-old uncle Jimmy was relayed to Connery during the shooting. The memory that came flooding back, of sitting contentedly by Jimmy's side on his cart while being clip-clopped through the Canongate, was just too sweet at first to share. 'What's up with Sean?' was the unspoken question on the minds of Hoffman and Lumet.

Casting apart, *Family Business* became the first to feature a Sicilian vendetta, a Passover Seder and an Irish wake, all in the first thirty minutes. Unfortunately, even following Connery's newly regenerated career heat, Hoffman's triumph in *Rain Man* and Broderick's teen-appeal, *Family Business* proved a dispiriting box-office bust, despite several favourable reviews. 'Connery is self-effacing charm as Jessie,' wrote Carrie Rickey in the *Philadelphia Enquirer*. 'Hoffman is a generous ensemble player. Broderick, surprisingly, is the movie's revelation. Lumet has made his best film since *The Verdict* and his most seriously funny film since *Dog Day Afternoon*.'

Lumet was gloomy when asked why he felt the public had stayed away. 'The only thing I can work out,' he offered, 'is that with that cast they wanted something with more weight. I think people are spoonfed now as a result of television. They're impatient and won't do any work, and I think it will get worse.'

'I like the film,' Connery chipped in. 'I think we succeeded in what we were trying to do, apart from the end. I have some differences with Sidney about how we resolved the end. But the film was a *disaster*. And it's hard to know why, because it had a very good cast. Everybody says, "It was timing, it was Christmas, it was all the rest of it." Well, that's the beef factor. I've done five films with Sidney; he's the type of director I really like to work with because he's very fast, professional, no nonsense, we get on with it, and it's hard work, but rewarding. And, needless to say, he gets depressed about that result. I liked the script. I liked the characters that were in it. I think they're marvellous actors, and I thought it all worked. The detail I'm talking about is nit-picking. But the picture hasn't had *anything* like even a curiosity success – you know, a measure of "Well, let's go and see it, because ..." It's just what I was saying to Sidney – you would go round the bend trying to resurrect it and do some more work on it.'

One individual who had mixed feelings of his own about *Family Business* was director John Boorman. His production of *Where the Heart Is* had been scheduled for filming in London in September 1988, with Connery in the lead, after *Indiana Jones and the Last Crusade* was in the can. Until, that is, the star cried off, explaining that he was 'knackered'; *Indiana Jones* had run a few weeks over to the end of August and proceeding with Boorman's movie would have backed into Tom Stoppard's *Rosencrantz and Guildenstern Are Dead*, already on Connery's busy schedule for early '89.

Disappointed as he was, Boorman was left with no alternative but to bow gracefully to the inevitable; it took him another year to set up a deal for *Where the Heart Is* with Connery's replacement, Dabney Coleman. His reaction when Connery signed for *Family Business* instead, just a few weeks later, was predictable. '*Of course* I was upset at the time and did speak to Sean about it,' Boorman confirmed. 'I think he was stressed out, he said he needed a break and pulled out, but after he'd rested for a couple of weeks he obviously felt OK again and did *Family Business* instead of my film. I didn't see him for quite a while after that, then I bumped into him in a restaurant and we had a lovely chat. Work with him again? *Of course* I would.'

Hoffman's Oscar for *Rain Man* produced a pleasant coda, the presentation briefly reuniting him with his *Family Business* pater. 'I'm there holding the Oscar,' Hoffman recalled of the evening, 'and there's this amazing standing ovation. And I'm looking out into this sea of faces and the only person I saw was *Sean Connery*. I'm not kidding. He's in the fifth row, looking like a leprechaun on steroids with those pointed ears and that sweet smile of his. And I could read his lips: "I *told* you!"'

Recurring discomfort Connery had experienced with his throat throughout 1988, and in particular during the shooting of *Family Business*, was eventually traced by X-rays to three tiny white dots on his left larynx. Before surgery to remove them was undertaken, one specialist suggested thirty days of silence in an attempt to cure the problem and avoid a biopsy. Connery took to wearing a pen round his neck and scribbling messages on the backs of old scripts; hundreds of pages were soon covered in this way. He also had cards printed saying, 'I'm sorry, I cannot speak. I have a problem with my throat. Thank you.' This had everyone looking at the card, then asking, 'Why, what's the matter?' When Connery had finished writing, he found that half the people grabbed his pen and wrote their answers back. 'I realized very quickly,' he said, with a roll of his eyes, 'that the world is full of idiots.'

He returned to Los Angeles in February 1989 to the news that he had to have the biopsy anyway. Connery admitted to being absolutely terrified; like most people he found medical matters a complete mystery and began to imagine all sorts of scenarios. Close friends were aware that he had a phobia about hospitals and had even been known to faint at the mere sight of a hypodermic syringe. With a pipe containing a camera inserted into his throat and showing up the three white dots, the decision was made on the spot to combine the biopsy with an operation to remove the nodules. Under Californian law Connery first had to sign a statement certifying that if he woke up under the anaesthetic he wouldn't sue the doctor.

The tabloids had a field day, some suggesting that Connery had had cancerous tissue removed from his throat and might never speak again, except though an electronic voice simulator. Jason, busy on stage in London, moved quickly to dispel the notion. 'If he had cancer I wouldn't be in Britain,' he declared. 'I'd be by his side. These rumours are very hurtful, and totally untrue. My dad's career is not in any jeopardy ... I was shocked but Dad reassured me that everything was all right. He had a wart which was found to be benign and it has been cut out. He is not allowed to speak for four weeks which is normal after a throat operation, but he will be as right as rain.'

A cancer specialist, Andrew Swanston of St Bartholomew's Hospital, London, spelled out the details of Connery's operation: 'A benign nodule looks just like the kind of wart you get on your hand and is caused by the vocal chords rubbing together in a way they don't like. You can burn it off with a laser, freeze it or cut it off. Connery will have to have three or four sessions of speech therapy so he can get his muscles back to normal. It will also teach him how to use them without causing the problem again.'

During visits to his 'voice doctor', Dr Lillian Glass, a former Miss Miami and university professor, Connery discovered he had developed bad habits in the way he spoke and breathed. For film acting he had deliberately refrained from using enough breath, aware that everything was measured minutely by the movie camera, that too many facial movements or a projection in his voice would be picked up as overdoing things. He visited his speech therapist at her Beverly Hills surgery for several weeks, learning how to breathe properly and how to marry his breathing to his speech by opening up his throat muscles.

With these sessions behind him, Connery looked forward to total recuperation. Within weeks he was in London, and set to defy his doctor's orders to rest his vocal chords by agreeing to host a TV special in aid of the Princes Trust. The Royal Gala was being held at the London Palladium in the presence of Prince Charles and Princess Diana and was due to be screened by London Weekend Television. Connery finally got the all-clear from doctors only hours before he was due to take the stage. 'He didn't speak during rehearsals and kept gargling medicines,' a spokesman later noted. 'But even if he hadn't got the go-ahead I think he would have carried on. He was so keen to do it.'

Unknown to London Weekend Television, or to anyone else outside of the surgery, Connery had received a considerable shock during the routine checkup in London – the three white dots were back and required further surgery. Even when the all-clear was delivered for a second time after this operation, he was cautioned to have further checks carried out every three to six months. One thing at least had changed – the fear had been banished. 'My attitude is entirely different now,' Connery disclosed. 'I know the problem and it can be treated. I have no worries.'

Micheline recalled how the period of enforced silence had affected her husband's golf. 'Yes,' he smilingly agreed. 'I couldn't express myself on the course.'

'You mean you couldn't swear!' she retorted. 'You should *hear* his language!'

Klaus Maria Brandauer threw Paramount into a fair old tizzy when, running late with a movie he was acting in and directing in Europe, he withdrew from the lead role of the Russian submarine commander in *The Hunt for Red October*, just two weeks before filming was due to start. The response director John McTiernan got when he contacted Paramount's chiefs and mentioned Connery as a replacement was an incredulous, 'What, are you out of your mind? How are we going to have a Russian sub captain with a Scottish accent?'

They had also absorbed the British tabloid reports that had Connery practically on his deathbed following the throat operations. Even with this nailed, they had heard he had backed out of Tom Stoppard's *Rosencrantz and Guildenstern*, as well as turning down an offer from Steven Spielberg to appear in *Always*. Would he be up to the physical demands of *Red October*? With Connery's stamina reaffirmed, McTiernan soon had the studio talked round, not only because of what he described as Connery's 'great control of his acting and of his accents', but also because of his box-office pull.

At their client's behest, CAA managed to extract a safety net clause from Paramount that compensated Connery in the event of the dollar falling against European currencies. 'I don't think the studio had heard that argument before,' the elated Scot declared, 'but funnily enough they came round to my way of thinking.'

Connery's withdrawal as the Player King from Stoppard's

movie, just one week before it was due to start shooting in Toronto in February 1989, was attributed at first by the author's agent to 'conflicting dates'. Only later did it emerge that Connery had handed over $300,000 to settle with the movie's producers.

At the beginning of October 1990, he gave his version of events: 'Stoppard was the person I had contact with. I didn't even know who the producers were, I never met any of these other people, but I had given my word that I was doing it. And eventually I gave them $300,000 to get out of the contract.

'I couldn't tell anybody about my throat and I was on a month's silence. Then they came round with a lawyer and they wouldn't believe it, they thought I was on some sort of dodge. I've since had four operations. I couldn't have gone into court on it. Normally I would have sued Stoppard out of the country. He and my wife were privy to what the whole thing was about . . . No, Stoppard behaved very badly.'

One week later, in a letter to the press, Stoppard weighed in with his account: 'When Connery let me know, a month or so before shooting, that he might have a problem with his throat, I told him in so many words that a film was only a film and he must put his health first. A few days later he confirmed that he would not be fit to film in February. I flew to LA with one object, which was to tell him that we would wait for him. He didn't want to meet me (he wasn't allowed to speak), so I had to convey my message by way of a phone call to his wife. Through her, Connery replied that he didn't want us to wait for him.

'I explained that if there were any chance of his working later on (we only needed him for three weeks) we had little choice but to wait, since on his signing the contract we had committed ourselves to delivering "a Connery film" and had accordingly been spending much of our budget in preparing it. Connery then got cross on paper (read out by his wife) and that was that. Next day I was told that I had "harassed" him. Happily, he recovered in time to make *The Hunt for Red October* in the spring.

'Meanwhile the producers of *Rosencrantz and Guildenstern* had an obligation to substantiate the reason for their being unable to deliver the Connery film as contracted, and it was their unsuccessful attempt to get Connery's co-operation on this which he now characterizes as "they thought I was on some dodge". Connery says that, but for his throat, "I would have sued Stoppard out of the country". He's confusing different parts of his anatomy. Connery paid up because he didn't have a leg to stand on.'

Part of the settlement between Connery and the producers was a clause committing both sides not to divulge or discuss the outcome. The above exchange between Connery and Stoppard might be seen as effectively ending the uneasy truce. The biter had been well and truly bit. By the writer.

The front page was missing when Connery first read the script of *The Hunt for Red October*, the producer Mace Neufeld reasoning that he might be put off if he saw that the manuscript pre-dated the advent of Gorbachev's glasnost. The star admired the side of ex-insurance executive Tom Clancy that could deal with the minutiae of US and Soviet missile drill and cabinet strategy, and was overwhelmed as well by the sheer scale of the Red October submarine author Clancy described – seven storeys high, five hundred feet long, with a score of nuclear warheads aboard, a monster capable of vast long-range destruction.

While dubious that the effect could be convincingly captured on celluloid, even with the most up-to-date technical wizardry, he still saw that it was the human element that carried the story, how the reactions of the opposing American and Russian submarine crews revealed aspects of their differing personalities.

The motivations of the Lithuanian-born commander of the Russian submarine, Marko Alexandrovich Ramius, he found less clear. What, Connery wondered, would make Ramius defect, complete with the mighty *Red October* and a complete crew, after giving his whole life to the Navy? In the original script, by Larry (*Presidio*) Ferguson and Donald (*Missing*) Stewart, Ramius's wife had died and he was unhappy with her treatment at the hands of the authorities. John Milius, whose work Connery had admired on *The Wind and the Lion*, was brought in, uncredited, to inject additional motivation.

'Milius made it all make sense,' Connery declared. 'Here was a man who's been sailing for forty years with no real war, no monuments, but a lot of casualties, and then he receives a blueprint for a ship that has only one use, as an offensive weapon. Suddenly, he's facing the path to destruction. *That's* what we needed to know about him.'

Shooting began in May 1989 on the adaptation of Clancy's best-seller, with Connery's salary set at well in excess of *Rosencrantz and Guildenstern*'s entire budget – and with a healthy percentage on top. He quickly established a good working relationship with co-stars Alec Baldwin and Scott Glenn, as well as with director McTiernan. Producer Neufeld maintains that Connery 'brought discipline to the set and respect from other actors. Nobody wanted to screw up in front of him.'

Connery bridled when this was put to him, maintaining that if any of his co-actors felt intimidated, their feelings were 'self-inflicted'. Or was it a case of life imitating art in his authoritative portrayal of the commander? Not entirely. 'I don't know if it was the character of Ramius, or whatever, but there was a certain lack of order and discipline that I like on a set,' he conceded. 'There were sixty-two of us on the submarine set. Everybody was on top of everybody and most of the kids there were Russian and half of them didn't speak English. What was lacking was a very co-ordinated routine. It was rather loose and they would get false starts. I find that very difficult for an actor.' McTiernan gratefully acknowledges the sphincter-tightening Connery produced in synchronicity with his character: 'He affected a formality even when he wasn't shooting. The minute he stepped on the set, he became unapproachable. Everyone else around him involuntarily straightened up and stood a little straighter.' He admitted he would have been 'blue in the face' if he had tried to get the young Russians to act that way through interpreters.

With filming complete, the only reservations Connery continued to harbour were over the special effects. He need not have worried; Paramount's team did a state-of-the-art job, mixing their scale models with glimpses of the real thing, or close facsimiles, to produce stunningly seamless shots that truly conveyed the awesome scale of *Red October* and her pursuers. Nor did the drama become lost at sea, as in so many waterlogged epics; although far from gut-wrenching, the tension was gradually tightened by McTiernan and his skilful team editors to produce, after a longish wait, a tremendously exciting finale.

It was Paramount's turn to worry following a series of disastrous previews held in the months prior to the movie's release. Following a bit of fine tuning, however, the studio regained its nerve and made a calculated decision to give the $40 million movie a blanket release, backed by a massive print and ads campaign rumoured to have cost close on $20 million. The reviews were excellent, covering everything from 'Connery's incredibly commanding presence – who would have *dared* countermand him' to McTiernan's 'watertight direction'.

Paramount's campaign landed Connery – after a monumental thirty-year wait – with his first certified *solo* smash in the US outside of Bond, *The Hunt for Red October*'s gross smashing the magical $100 million barrier, and returning a net of $58.5 million to the studio. With the rest of the world and television and video rights still to come, everyone was happy – Connery, with his dollar-insulated percentage, most of all.

Chapter 36

'Sean is always shocked by people. He has such high ideals; he's a totally genuine man. I have tried to teach him cynicism. "Don't be shocked," I say, "the world is like that."'

Micheline Connery

'Dozens of beautiful women made themselves available; he doesn't give them a chance. What a compliment to Micheline and their relationship!'

Princess Hohenlohe, Marbella

While Scottish scribe Ian Bell once jocularly maintained that Connery memorizes his contracts before his lines, the star contends that his screen choices can be traced to his inherent puritanism. He is interested in work that poses moral questions, especially if he perceives it as well-written, when it's not so much what's *said* that matters, but what's *revealed*.

Micheline's benign influence on Connery has been evident from the beginning. 'At the start of the relationship he had a lot of problems,' she recalls. 'Everything about Sean was dramatic. My first job was to calm him down. It was like undoing a knot. He was, and still is, a very emotional man, because he is an artist. But I can see things very clearly and I'm not fooled by promises or flattery.

'He was surrounded by people who wanted to take from him. Many were telling him, "Everything you touch turns to gold." It flattered him that people were saying how fantastic he was. But I would say, "Sean, you *are* fantastic. A fantastic *actor*. The rest? *Forget it.*' He was good at making money, but not so good at keeping it. Not that he was stupid – just too open and honest.'

'Many people have been caught in the same situation as me,' says Connery. 'The difference is that I admitted it . . . Everyone loses at some point, because they are actors and not business-men.'

Security considerations apart, possessions were items that never concerned Connery until he planted roots with his wife in Southern Spain at San Pedro del Cantara, originally a fishing village along the coast from Marbella. And even here there are few. What does characterize their sprawling and comfortable, rather than lavish villa is a deep sense of informality and ease, epitomized by the lived-in clutter and huge open fireplaces that distinguish home from hotel room. Privacy at Casa Malibu, complete with tiled murals hand-painted by Jean Cocteau and a biscuit-marbled ground floor, is granted courtesy of a bougainvillea-covered white wall that separates their property from the beach, as well as a sign near the fountain in the drive announcing 'Propiedad Privada'. On a clear day Gibraltar can be seen from the verandah; on a crystal-clear day the coast of Africa is visible.

As a birthday surprise, and bowing to her husband's need for regular bouts of seclusion, Micheline designed a self-contained study at the rear of the property, complete with its own bathroom and kitchen bar. Her quid pro quo is her studio, a few steps across the terrace from the master bedroom. Two magnificent choc-olate-point Siamese cats, Hector and Luna, perform regular sentry duty of the premises, assiduously checking out each and every visitor to the low-slung stucco and tiled villa. Connery's established routine in the precious weeks he spends there is to take it easy following some tennis in the early morning, then nap after lunch before repairing to the golf course. No wonder Micheline calls their home his 'Sanitorium Rancho'.

Over the years Connery has been constantly invited to paint a verbal portrait of the 'type of woman he prefers'. One answer has been that there is no such thing: 'I find most women attractive, all age groups ... I don't like one special type, blonde hair, big bust, or tall, dark with long legs. No, that doesn't work with me. It's chemistry. I find some women repellent, just as I find some children or men repellent. You're either drawn to someone or you're not. The fact of their being male or female is interchangeable – except when you get down to having sex.' The eyebrows rise, the grin broadens. 'But if you're asking me what type of face I find attractive – well, I think my wife has a *very* attractive face.'

He has admitted to finding foreign women more attractive either than British or Americans; the latter he accuses of taking relations 'too seriously' and having a tendency to be 'over-analytical'. He also has no patience with women who 'whine or go into hysterics', or for 'women dictators who don't understand there are times when you want to be alone'.

What offends Connery most about a woman? 'Incompetence and dirt,' he answers without hesitation. As for unpunctuality: 'If a woman's late, she won't find me there.' The only circumstances under which he would give in to a woman would be if he were clearly in the wrong. Being approached he still finds pleasurable: 'I don't think I'll ever get to the stage where I won't enjoy it. But it doesn't have the same excitement for me as it did when I was young and there was the challenge to have all the girls like you.'

As for the mysterious quality he would find irresistible: 'That depends on the woman. There are many different levels of attraction and it needn't be just on the surface. But it's either there or it isn't. It's not something that a woman can fake. And it doesn't necessarily disappear with age. Some old women have it.'

One of the secrets of Connery's across-the-board appeal lies in the sexual attraction he has for women, while remaining either 'one of the boys' as far as men are concerned, or a father figure either sex can look up to. He was almost speechless when told of *People Magazine*'s 'Sexiest Man Alive' accolade. 'It'll be all downhill from here!' he cracked. Barbara Carrera, one of his *Never Say Never Again* co-stars, points to the longevity of his reign: 'He's one of the few men who've stayed sexy with age. All over the world women ask me about Sean Connery. They stare at me with their mouths open: "What's he like to work with??"'

'Old flame' Shelley Winters agrees. 'He was sexy at 26 and at 60 even more so. He makes a woman feel sexual chemistry. To be his leading lady I'd lose fifty pounds and get my face lifted. As a matter of fact, I'd get *everything* lifted!'

Agent Joy Jameson wishes he'd 'stop banging on about how old he is. After all, he's only two years older than Joan Collins.'

Lois (Miss Moneypenny) Maxwell offers an intriguing combination; here's one woman who wants to have her cake and eat it too: 'I'd like to be married to Roger Moore, but have Sean Connery as my lover. He has a cross between menace and humour in his eyes. And he has a chewable bottom lip.' Why not the other way around – Connery for a husband, Moore as lover? 'He *is* very moody. I can imagine his sinking to the depths of despair. But Roger would always try to lighten the bad times.'

Diamonds Are Forever co-star Jill St John, on the other hand, points to Connery's 'natural sense of humour'. 'What I like about Sean,' says *Dr No*'s Ursula Andress, 'is that he's still the same down-to-earth person he was when he was unknown.'

Critic Pauline Kael considers his appeal from a historical cinematic perspective: 'Connery looks absolutely confident in himself as a man. Women want to meet him and men want to *be* him. I don't know any man since Cary Grant that men have wanted to *be* so much.'

Safely out of Micheline's hearing, Kim Basinger revealed that she had always had a crush on Connery: 'I fantasize about riding bareback with him, on an Arab horse along a sandy beach. We fall naked on the ground and make passionate love in the moonlight. It always leaves me hot and bothered. I just love the man!'

Micheline deserves the last word, offering as she does the *definitive* secret of her husband's universal appeal: 'Sean *is what he is*. He's not trying to *hide* anything. That genuineness by itself is sexy in a man.'

Connery normally refuses to play golf with his wife (he occasionally makes an exception for television cameras), an arrangement Micheline is happy to go along with – provided *all* women are excluded. 'She thinks it quite sweet actually,' says Connery. 'She reckons if I'm out on the course all day with three other men there's not very much I can get up to or down to, unless we're all queer, of course. But she thinks the business of a bar for men only is very funny. In France men like to be with women much more than we do. She likes the company of men, British, rather than French. Her English has improved enormously. It's had to, mark you, because I don't speak French.'

The charge of male chauvinism has often been levelled at Connery over the years. In the mid-eighties TV interviewer Barbara Walters cited an old quote from *Playboy* in which Connery had apparently said, 'It's not the worst thing to slap a woman now and then.' (Her research obviously stopped there; had she gone further back, to Susan Barnes's *Daily Express* interview in the early 1960s, she would have discovered that nothing much had changed.)

'You surely don't think that's *good*?' Walters pressed her guest.

'I don't think it's *good*,' Connery replied, without batting an eyelid, 'but I don't think it's *bad*. It depends entirely on the circumstances ... (When) you give them the last word, but they're not happy with (it), they want to say it again ... they can't leave it alone – then I think it's absolutely right.'

'Do you ever slap your wife?'

'She doesn't provoke it.'

Walters then came straight out with her challenge: 'You *are* a male chauvinist, aren't you?'

'Am I?' Connery replied, completely unruffled. 'What *is* a male chauvinist?' The riposte apparently threw Walters, who moved quickly to round up the discussion by inviting Connery to complete the sentence, 'Sean Connery is . . .'

Grinning, Connery replied, '. . . *almost* a male chauvinist pig!'

The reaction of the public to the interview was instantaneous, as Connery discovered the following day as he drove along Melrose Boulevard to Paramount's studios. Men jabbed their fists in the air in 'Right on!' gestures; one woman at a red light gave him the finger. A reader answered *People* magazine's 'Sexiest Man Alive' accolade in 1990 with 'Try – *most dangerous*'. Another suggested taking the 'e' out of 'sexiest', making Connery the most *sexist* man alive. ('There aren't too many of them in the graveyard,' was Connery's wry response to the *People* award. Then he looked back unflinchingly to his youth: 'I remember spending most of my adolescence chasing women, trying to find them. I don't think I was successful with women at all. I was shy in those days. Everybody in adolescence has these insecurities, no matter what they profess to be, even if they appear to be the epitome of confidence with women. Most men would agree if they were truthful with themselves. With success, certain things come easier and confidence emerges. That's why I'm in favour of sex lessons and the biological factors being taught in school to save a lot of problems later on. I was stuck with all that doctor and nurses stuff.' To 'Sexiest Man Alive', add 'Most Honest Man Alive'?)

'I'm talking about a slap in the face,' Connery, more than a trifle on the defensive, later clarified the Walters encounter. 'And that you could do much, much worse damage to a woman, or a man, by totally demoralizing them, by taking away their whole identity . . . I'm saying that if one of the couple is intent on having a physical confrontation, it's impossible for it to be avoided. It's emotional, it's passion. And passion lacks thinking. Therefore it will explode. And that's all I'm saying without getting into a three-act play ... but if we had discussed it for four hours or fourteen Barbara wouldn't have got the answer she wanted.'

Confronted with her husband's 'chauvinism', Micheline's answer was to shrug her shoulders, throw her hands in the air and say, 'I just happen to like male chauvinist pigs!'

Although Micheline has always accepted, however reluctantly, the situation with Connery's ladykiller image, and the attendant non-stop parade of women ready to throw themselves at his feet, she would not be prepared to stand helplessly by if the situation got out of hand. 'If Sean was responding to temptation,' she spelled out, 'if he was giving me any real reason to be jealous, I would take it very badly. I wouldn't wait around. I am not one of life's victims – and Sean knows that.'

The ever-practical Micheline can also see beyond the warmth of the reception afforded her wherever she goes with her famous husband. 'There are so many advantages being married to Sean but I always remember who I am – *Mrs* Sean Connery. If I were in Hollywood I'm taken care of not because of my beautiful eyes, but because I'm Sean's wife ... I don't forget that.'

Micheline also claims to be happily resigned to all aspects of their marital relationship, reasoning pragmatically that her husband's good points far exceed the bad. When he comes back to her tired and fractious after a day's work, she tells him to 'be as nice with me as you are with your producer'. He is told to sit, listen, and only make his comments when Micheline is through. 'There are some things in the house that Sean thinks he can do,' she laughs, 'but he obviously can't. He thinks, for example, that he can cook. Every time he goes into the kitchen, he just has to be gently led out of it!'

Once, when Micheline had a lingering tooth infection, Connery informed her she had been 'very boring' for several months. 'Oh, really!' she retorted. '*You're* sometimes boring and you're *never* ill!' He was horrified.

Micheline makes no bones about how she has worked to keep their home life as tranquil as possible. 'Fights don't bring anything good,' she maintains. 'In a relationship you have to be careful with words. They can be killers. We have "discussions". If Sean raises his voice, I raise mine. But it is very limited. If I have to let him know he's getting overweight and needs to slim, I leave a note where he can find it. And then I get out of the way!

'He is not the sort of man to tell me I am the most gorgeous woman in the world,' she admits. 'The most I'm going to get is, "You look very good tonight." Surprise presents? Never. He's a very generous man, but not in that way. Flowers from Sean? It would be like ... my God ... like a *miracle*. But he will write little words like "je t'aime" – spelt badly! – pinned on clothing or in drawers. I keep these bits of paper from over the years like a treasure.'

Connery once left a message for his wife at their London hotel that read simply, 'You are the best.' 'To me that's the best kind of gift,' she says. 'I just *melt*!'

One compensation for Connery in his sixties is the contentment that increased wisdom brings. He has flashes of what he takes to be wisdom, while making no great claims to have learned a great deal. Like many others he went through the 'searching' phase of the I Ching, Ouspensky's *In Search of the Miraculous*, Gurdjieff and *The Tibetan Book of the Dead*. What he found was not dissimilar to the contents of the Bible.

'I'd like to think one gets better,' he says, 'but it only correlates with how much enthusiasm you invest in it. I know how hard I work. As long as you're inspired by the material you don't measure the time. If I felt, "This is it, kid, it doesn't get any better than this," I wouldn't bother ... The main thing for an actor or writer is not believability, but the removal of time. Because I think the only occasions you really are enjoying yourself, being happy, swinging, as they say, are when you don't know what time it is — when you're totally absorbed in something. When an artist can suspend time like that for an audience, he has succeeded.'

Despite the acknowledged changes Connery has made over the years, there are certain fundamental elements that remain constant. 'I've learned a great deal from my wife,' he happily admits. 'She is very intelligent about so many things and makes a very good sounding board. Had I been educated a different way, I would never have been caught up in all the things I was. Having said that, my two boys are pretty naive as well. *And they'll probably get screwed too!*'

Although *Rosencrantz and Guildenstern* had fallen through amidst considerable acrimony, Connery remained destined to work in collaboration, no matter how distant, with Tom Stoppard. A month before starting work on the playwright's adaptation of John le Carré's *The Russia House*, he startled his admirers with the news that he was ready to quit films. Asked if the threat was made in all seriousness, Micheline replied that only her husband could answer the question: 'If he continues to be offered excellent scripts, I don't think so, but with Sean, you never really know. He is very much his own man and makes his own decisions.'

Connery was the first and last choice for the leading role of Barley Blair, the drunken, burned-out publisher pushed into playing a pawn in a sinister East–West game. 'When you think of someone of the right age to play this part,' director Fred Schepisi mused, 'someone who is considered box-office, someone who will attract attention and will possibly be surprising in the role ...' Producer Paul Maslansky chipped in that Connery deserved every bit of the success he had achieved: 'He is much more than a brilliant actor, he is a brilliant technician too. He involves himself at every level, without being selfish or an egomaniac – like so many other big stars I could mention.'

Not least of the supporters was Connery himself, who thought it was a marvellous idea to play a character around his own age: 'Like him I'm fond of jazz and I like the idea that this guy is in the toilet, he's washed up and that's as much as we know about him at the beginning of the movie ... He's a bit like a gelding, a horse with no future, and he's having no success with his publishing. He's obviously well educated, but he's a real mess. Out of all this, through the association with Katya and the events they become involved in, he suddenly finds himself in a situation where his actions can be measured in almost heroic terms. I find that almost optimistic and it's really, I think, how I'd like to see things.' Given virtual carte blanche on casting, Connery chose Michelle Pfeiffer for Katya, James Fox as Blair's inscrutable spymaster and Klaus Maria Brandauer as the elusive Russian scientist.

It was back to Moscow and Leningrad to film *The Russia House*, the first time for Connery since his involvement a quarter of a century earlier in *The Red Tent*. The main difference he detected on this occasion sprang from the knowledge that everyone knew the full extent of the rampant inefficiency, how the entire infrastructure was geared to the military and State Police rituals and bureaucracy. 'The artisans don't even know how to hang a door,' Connery scoffed. 'There's no sense of apprenticeship, and they are totally indifferent to standards. Nobody knows, because nobody cares. You can see that it's rotten. The general level of health is pretty pathetic. Teeth bad, skin not great, soap rubbish. It's like wartime Britain. Long queues. And they are outspoken to an extreme in criticizing Gorbachev; they don't seem to be conscious of how big a leap they've taken compared to when I was here before.' One particular improvement Connery did find in the still-present KGB was that they seemed younger, looser, more outgoing – and had considerably more girls in their ranks. And the anonymity that he had enjoyed during his last visit had gone with the winds of change – or, more specifically, the advent and proliferation of largely black market VCRs.

During the tight five-week shooting schedule in Russia Connery constantly made suggestions very much in his usual manner, rushing to watch the action replay on a six-inch screen after completing a take, fretting about losing the light when delays threatened to make this inevitable. His by now familiar

– and formidable – expression of irritation at any sign of inefficiency or non-co-operation was regularly in evidence.

The spark that was struck with co-star Pfeiffer afforded a rare intimacy in their scenes together. Connery, the consummate professional, recognized dedication when he met it. And as someone never known to work particularly at accents himself, he was still full of praise for Pfeiffer's efforts in that direction.

Following the gruelling spell in the Soviet Union the unit whistle-stopped to London, Portugal, London again and finally Vancouver. 'I worked ridiculously hard on *Russia House*,' Connery claimed, adding, 'We *all* did! We just did overly long hours there. I started thinking I should move into the Gulag! We were overly ambitious in what we tried to shoot. There are sixty churches outside of Moscow and I think we shot near all of them. No one will ever get the visuals we got.'

During all of the frantically overlapping pre- and post-production on *Family Business, The Hunt for Red October* and *The Russia House*, Connery managed to squeeze one twelve-day break in which he returned to Spain. This provided little respite, the visit being marked by the worst storms to hit the country in two hundred years.

Schepisi had a tough job on his hands transmuting Stoppard's version of Le Carré's best-seller to the screen. There were no villains for audiences to boo, only a mass of 'grey men'. Connery himself maintained that the only 'villain' was the lack of understanding on both sides. And how to convey the folly of spying through a love story and a man's rehabilitation?

Despite better-than-respectful notices when the movie was released as MGM/Pathe's Christmas package in 1990 – David Ansen of *Newsweek* called it 'A marvellously literate, ravishingly good-looking adaptation ... dense with detail, packed with wit, laced with layers of deception ... director Fred Schepisi's impeccably crafted film hums with intelligence' – *The Russia House* caused no stampede at the box-office, netting a highly disappointing $10 million in the US. Beautiful it may have been, but for 'dense' read 'baffling' and for 'literate' read 'wordy' – to all but hardcore Le Carré and Stoppard addicts, that is.

Knowing her husband's aversion to big parties, Micheline took a chance in organizing a surprise sixtieth birthday bash in Hollywood. Although at first he almost turned and ran for the door, the occasion proved a huge success, not only because of the star-studded guest list, including Spielberg, Donald Sutherland, Clint Eastwood, Sidney Poitier, Liza Minnelli, Sylvester Stallone and Harrison Ford, but also because of the warmth of the occasion – as well as the banner Micheline unfurled: 'The 60th for the Sexiest!' And what could top a gypsy violinist to bring tears to Connery's eyes? Micheline had the answer even for that – two Scottish pipers to regale her husband with memories of the old country.

Two months later Connery followed up on his original plan to revitalize that not-so-magnificent invalid, the British film industry. He was undaunted, it seems, by a meeting in Salzburg a few years earlier with Prime Minister Thatcher in which she had dismissed the idea out of hand. Now he proposed that a £50 million fund be set up via a share structure that would have directors pledging either their time, money, or both. The snag with the latest version of Connery's scheme, as with so many others of similar ilk over the years, was its central reliance on the British government to stump up a portion of the funds. Bearing in mind that they had pledged a paltry £5 million earlier in the year, a more significant contribution looked unlikely, as did the prospect of a political all-party ten-year plan that covered government ownership of Pinewood Studios.

There were a couple of original quirks in Connery's plan, notably the allowance of foreign investment. His suggestion of a powerhouse to head the operation – the figure he mentioned was seventy-three-year-old John King of British Airways – was countered in the *Sunday Times* by a more novel idea from business editor Ivan Fallon. What, he wondered, would it take to tempt Connery himself into the job? Not only was the star much younger than King, but he possessed the combination of shrewd business brain and personality that might just make the plan work.

While Connery is able to carry on collecting millions of dollars per movie, Fallon's proposal seems like a distinct non-starter. Besides, Micheline is probably correct in her judgement of her husband as a 'fantastic actor'. The rest? *Forget it!*

Chapter 37

'I think the success of his recent films has made him relax and he seems to be enjoying life more. The roles he's taking now are more flexible and enable him to show his talents to a greater extent. Being suave and sophisticated and powerful and macho and so on is rather limiting. I think he is really excited by what he is doing and he is having fun doing it – and it shows.'

Jason Connery

'I don't think I'll ever reach the stage, however old I get, that I won't turn to look at a see-through blouse.'

Sean Connery

The list of movies Connery has turned down, or let slip through his fingers, is revealing. The photographer anti-hero of Antonioni's *Blow Up* in the Swinging Sixties would have been an interesting departure – and is the one part he regrets not doing. The director asked Connery if he was interested, but was only able to produce a script four pages long. Highly offended that he should be asked to produce even this, he handed the part to David Hemmings.

Although Connery felt it was the best script he'd read in ten years, he turned down the role Nigel Davenport went on to play in *Chariots of Fire*. Many projects, like *Taipan* and *Shogun*, were probably best passed over; his King of the Moon, however, in Terry Gilliam's *The Adventures of Baron Munchausen*, would have been a lark – at least in its original full-length conception – to which he would undoubtedly have brought the sense of fun he handed Spielberg on a plate in *Indiana Jones and the Last Crusade*. The list goes on and on, all the way from Daddy Warbucks in Ray Stark's *Annie* to Boorman's *Where the Heart Is* and Stoppard's *Rosencrantz and Guildenstern*, and even the mighty Spielberg's *Always*.

Before Peter O'Toole assumed the mantle, Connery was in line to play the Scottish tutor in Bertolucci's *The Last Emperor*. A reunion with Michael Caine in *Travelling Man* was on the cards for a while at George Harrison's HandMade Films. With Kim Basinger pencilled in as the battered wife in Joseph Ruben's *Sleeping with the Enemy*, Connery was slated to play her husband. His desire to try directing after Tantallon's fizzle led him to eye a lapsed Orson Welles project, *Dead Calm*, under the impression that Warners held the rights. It turned cut that they didn't.

The way Connery tells it, he is prepared to look at any project, including one movie he was offered in which he would have played a schoolteacher in Venice who becomes involved in a drag act and discovers his own gayness. The script, apparently, didn't come up to scratch. The degree of his proclaimed sexual sophistication can be judged in his reaction to another query. 'Why *not* play someone who is impotent?' he asked. 'If it's indigenous to the story, I see no reason why not. The fact is you could be so enamoured with someone, you could become impotent – or the person could play such a severe game with you that it could make you impotent.' What a pity, one can't help feeling, that John Schlesinger had already cast Peter Finch back in the seventies in *Sunday, Bloody Sunday*...

As for some of the roles for which he has been considered

and turned down, Connery points to his long history of litigation. 'If a big role was between me and a couple of others,' he suggests, 'I think the attitude has sometimes been to dump me. It has a lot to do with Hollywood political strategy, which I have never been privy to. I have never understood how it worked.'

One aspect of any projected venture that may weigh heavily in Connery's decisions is the country in which filming is scheduled. In the same way that *Outland*'s locations in Britain were contained within his ninety-day tax limits by dint of regular weekend flights abroad, US-based movies face similar restrictions.

In 1987 Connery's old friend, showbusiness scribe Peter Noble, was in Vancouver to attend the annual film festival. There he met director John Boorman, in town to promote *Hope and Glory.* Together they were sitting down to dine in a Chinese restaurant one Friday evening when, to their astonishment, Connery breezed in alone and quietly sat down at a corner table. Until he recognized them, that is. 'What the hell are *you* doing here?' asked an astonished Boorman, leaving Connery to explain that while filming *The Presidio* in the States he had to fly to Canada every weekend to avoid paying US taxes. And even as he greeted Noble warmly he felt it necessary to tick him off for being a little too open to one writer about his early babysitting activities back in the starving fifties. 'Who wants to read that old stuff?' he chided.

In Scotland Connery eventually passed – or was forced to pass – on McIlvanney's *Laidlaw*, together with a cameo in Bill Forsyth's *Comfort and Joy*. A third Scot, filmmaker Gareth Wardell of Jam Jar films, had dealings with Connery, father *and* son, that proved stillborn. Wardell first met Jason late in 1989 to discuss one of two junior male leads in *Greenyards*, his projected movie retelling of the infamous Scottish Highland clearances.

Over dinner at Ayrshire's Turnberry Hotel, Wardell, accompanied by his partner, the painter Barbara Rae, was thrilled to have Jason's interest not only confirmed, but intriguingly quantified. Jason had sussed out the two roles on offer – the female lead's suitors – and had already dismissed in his own mind the Byronic 'broth of a boy' in favour of the dark, sullen, repressed alternative character. 'Much more me,' he assured Wardell, now busy picturing him with his blond hair dyed black, and imagining how good he would look in his uniform. A year later, after the project had survived a false start, Wardell was astonished when Jason announced he was turning the role down, arguing that his character 'hadn't got anywhere' in subsequent drafts.

Wardell's initial skirmish with Connery père dated back to 1988 and his submission of a potted biography of Scots-born detective Alan Pinkerton. After being sent direct to Connery in Marbella, the piece was referred to CAA, who eventually turned it down. A guest appearance as a drunken judge in *Greenyards*, which would have involved two days' filming, was similarly rejected. Finally, Wardell submitted his *pièce de résistance*, a script by John (*Zulu*) Prebble, recounting the *Glencoe* massacre of 1692, a work he describes as being 'of Shakespearean proportions'.

Months later, with no reply from CAA, Wardell began to count the cost of the faxes and phone reminders, and wrote a sharply worded letter direct to Connery pointing out the lack of courtesy on his agents' behalf. Within forty-eight hours CAA was in touch, apologizing for the delay, their excuse being that the script had been temporarily lost in the move to their I.M. Pei-designed headquarters on Wilshire Boulevard. Soon afterwards Wardell was informed that they had decided to pass on *Glencoe* 'because of Sean's other commitments'. The Scots entrepreneur decided this wasn't good enough; it was one thing for the project to be turned down because it wasn't interesting; if it truly *was* 'other commitments', he was quite prepared to wait.

As a response to repeatedly hearing that Connery 'would only respond to big bucks', Wardell pointed out to CAA that he had already raised up to $3 million for their client's fee, and that once a US distributor was in place it would be possible to top this up even further. 'Look, don't dismiss this lightly. It's quite special,' he pointed out to Jay Maloney, Connery's man at the agency. The finale came in a telephone message from Connery personally in mid-1991. Describing himself as 'up to my armpits here' in Mexico during the filming of *Medicine Man*, Wardell was informed: 'I've read it and it's not for me, but I wish you the best of luck with it.'

While extremely grateful that Connery had taken the trouble to call, Wardell was left thinking, 'What do you have to do to get Sean Connery involved in a film that might be made in part or wholly in Scotland?' The cynical answer seemed to be: '*Highlander III – maybe.*' While aware of the star's monetary contributions to his native land, the succession of turndowns left Wardell just a tad bitter.

It is true that Connery's contributions to his homeland, judged purely in filmmaking terms, are few and far between; in October 1981, when Fred Zinnemann's *Five Days One Summer* unit moved briefly to a Glasgow shipyard, Ferguson Brothers of Port Glasgow, this represented his first filming on Scottish soil – excluding *The Bowler and the Bunnet* and a documentary on Edinburgh – since 1963, when he worked briefly in Lochgilphead, Argyll for scenes in *From Russia With Love*. Since then only *Highlander*, with offshore financing, had managed to lure him back.

Life, of course, doesn't consist entirely of making movies and lending support to home-grown movies. Connery, very much his own man, is perfectly entitled to make his own career decisions independently. Meanwhile, time *and* money can be spent on many causes just as worthy – indeed, some would argue, even worthier . . .

At the start of the 1980s Connery backed a Scottish Office drive for kidney donors with his invitation to the public to become 'a Special Agent for Life'. The added message: 'I lived through six death-defying Bond films, threatened by rockets, lasers, guns, beautiful women and always managed to walk away unscathed. The magic of the cinema is like that. The reality of life is not.'

A £70,000 thirty-minute movie to promote tourism in Edinburgh, *Sean Connery's Edinburgh*, was shot in three weeks in June 1981. Connery not only appeared in the film driving a horse and cart as in days of yore, visiting a few old drinking haunts – and using brother Neil as a stand-in – but delivered the narration as well.

A friend for some time of Edinburgh Festival director Frank Dunlop, Connery accepted membership of the Festival Council in 1988. A year later he lent his voice to a campaign intended to prevent a blood supply crisis in Scotland, providing a backing commentary to a seven-week television advertising campaign to recruit new donors. 'I particularly welcome the chance to appeal to the young people of Scotland,' he declared. 'They represent the new generations of blood donors, the lifeblood of the Scottish Blood Transfusion Service. They're the future and I'm glad to be part of that.'

Apart from being entirely serious, the rivalry between Edinburgh and Glasgow, Scotland's two major cities, has always provided a rich vein of humour for comedians. When Glasgow was named European City of Culture in 1990, one columnist described it as 'the final kick in the teeth' for the beleaguered Edinburgh. Michael Kelly, a public relations consultant appointed by Edinburgh's Chamber of Commerce, decided that enough was enough and sprang into action. Already engaged in the production of a video about the city, both for resident and potential businessmen as well as the citizenry, he suddenly thought of Connery as 'the best person in the world' to do the voice-over. What a boost that would prove for Auld Reekie!

Phoned direct in Marbella, Connery said he would be delighted to do it, but had to be in America within a couple of days. Quick as a flash the enterprising Kelly grabbed a sound recorder, caught the first available flight to Marbella and arrived at Connery's villa that very evening. Edinburgh's most famous son duly provided a truly splendid voice-over, and recaptured for his home town at least a modicum of snook to cock at Glasgow.

A year earlier the non-partisan Connery had performed similar whistle-stop duties for Edinburgh's rival neighbour. The management of Glasgow's Film Theatre, planning a futuristic Screen 2, a 145-seater complex costing close on half a million pounds, was on the lookout for a big name to endorse the project. Hearing that Connery was resident at the Hospitality Inn, just round the corner from Rose Street and the GFT, Brenda Carson, the cinema's development officer, contacted him while he was relaxing between a round of golf at Turnberry and a planned showbusiness dinner.

Having presided over the theatre's original conversion from Cosmo cinema to GFT, the star's endorsement was readily granted, his views promptly enshrined in a brochure sent to five hundred top companies requesting financial backing.

Apart from time, there are two types of monetary contributions – the systematic type, exemplified by Connery's admirable twenty-year support for his Scottish International Educational Trust, together with the equally humanitarian, but decidedly impulsive variety . . .

While filming *Name of the Rose* at Cinecitta, and occupying Federico Fellini's marvellously old-fashioned dressing room, the bath Connery was in overflowed. He found a ten-day-old *Sunday Times* stuffed underneath, that carried an article about the imminent demise of Britain's National Youth Theatre.

It seemed that Michael Croft, the Theatre's director and founder, had just had his request for support from the Arts Council turned down. £50,000 had been the sum sought, with Croft hopeful of matching the figure from private donations. Although Connery had no connection with the theatre and had never acted in it, he was well aware of the NYT's track record, how it had produced successful graduates that included Helen Mirren, Derek Jacobi, Hywel Bennett, Michael York and Ben Kingsley. 'I had met the guy who runs it when I was first in London,' Connery recalled, 'and I always remember him as kind of tubby, a little like Dylan Thomas, with curly hair and round eyes. He was mad about the theatre (and had) started the NYT, which had been going all these years. It was always failing, but he always got by, but then suddenly he realized he was going to go under.'

Connery promptly phoned Croft and asked, 'Is it true what I read in the paper?'

'Yes,' Croft replied, 'but that was a couple of weeks ago.'

'Oh – then you've gone under?'

'No, but the bailiffs are coming on Wednesday.'

By this time Connery had made up his mind. 'I'll have to clear it,' Croft was told, 'but I'll give you your £50,000.'

'Oh, Christ, that's terrific. We must make an announcement.'

'I don't want you to make an announcement, but you've got it. I'll telex you with confirmation so that you can act on it.'

A few moments later Croft called his benefactor back: 'You know, it's terrific, but you spoil it completely if you don't let me make an announcement, because I will not be able to embarrass anybody else into giving us more money, because your £50,000 will only just save the production we're supposed to do.' Connery agreed, sticking to his first instinct that a source of the finest British acting talent should not be required to go cap in hand for cash.

Although the NYT was able to carry on, Croft himself died only days after the star's donation was received. Friends said that he had been fearful that Connery's magnanimity might be taken as proof by the Arts Council that they were right all along in withdrawing their support and insisting that funds be raised from private sources; a Catch-22 situation with which Croft had clearly grown weary.

'British actors and actresses, writers and directors,' Connery asserted, 'are among the best in the world. We come second to no one. The NYT is one source of this talent, a source everyone should be proud of.'

The experience left him shaken and led him to another attack on paltry government funding and cut-backs. He conceded that the Prime Minister had started well: 'She's got more chutzpah and balls than anyone that preceded her, but I think she's reached a crisis now. She's gone a little – not a little, but a long way too far, too extreme, too removed from what is really happening.'

Gareth Wardell, like many others, has his own axe to grind. And as a talented, home-grown filmmaker who has given a lot of untested talent their first chances – directors Michael Caton-Jones and Gillies Mackinnon being the two latest examples – he is entitled to grind it. What is incontrovertible is the tremendous boost to filmmaking in Connery's native heath that would result from his returning in a really significant movie. Who knows? It could yet happen.

Old habits die hard. A year and a half after Andy Vajna resigned from his co-chairmanship of Carolco Pictures, having sold his shares to ex-partner Mario Kassar for a cool $106 million, he had bastardized the dreaded eighties buzzword and had his own brand new 'Cinergi Productions' off and running.

First recipients of his renewed largesse were *Dead Poets Society* scriptwriter Tom Schulman, pocketing between $2.5 and $3 million, *Hunt for Red October* helmer John McTiernan with an estimated $6 million, and Sean Connery, coffers swollen by an upfront $10 million and a promised 15 per cent of the gross.

The project, at first entitled *The Stand: The Last Days of Eden*, eventually boiled down to *Medicine Man* and was filmed on location in Catemaco, Mexico, much of it a hundred feet above the rainforest floor. Schulman's scenario had Connery playing Dr Robert Campbell, an eccentric, silver-pony-tailed research scientist living among the native Indians and discovering a cancer cure. After seeing her performance in *Good-Fellas*, co-star Lorraine Bracco had been Connery's immediate choice for the role of the feisty head-office snoop: 'We needed someone who could be tough, dynamic and had a sense of humour about it.'

Ten weeks was spent in temperatures of up to 115 degrees and humidity of 98 degrees during the summer of 1991, with Connery quaffing two litres of water a day to prevent dehydration. Incredibly, the hardy sixty-one-year-old was the only member of the cast and crew who didn't fall ill at some point. ('I wasn't sick only because I drank too much vodka,' Connery claimed.)

The movie proved a troubled shoot, even with McTiernan enthusing that not only could he 'get away' with telling Connery what he thought, but that his star, whom he described as 'an encyclopedia of film actors' skills', positively *encouraged* the process. A few crew members had a different tale to tell, maintaining that Connery was 'grouchy' for much of the shoot, even clearing the set at one point to accommodate a shouting match with McTiernan. 'Sure it's ninety to a hundred degrees and there are mosquitos and he's eighty feet up in a tree doing stunts,' said one, 'but he's making a million dollars a week. It's hot for everybody.' Others praised Connery's professionalism, while McTiernan dismissed the tales of conflict, with Connery at least, as amounting to just 'a couple of mornings'. His relationship with Bracco, apparently, was a different matter entirely.

Connery's admission that Schulman's high-priced script was still being rewritten well into shooting was evidenced in the finished movie, *Variety* describing the dialogue as 'very weak', even with apparent additions by Sally Robinson and an uncredited Tom Stoppard. They also considered Bracco, with her 'screeching New York accent', 'lethal miscasting': 'Rarely has one less wanted two romantic leads to end up together than in this concoction.' In their apportionment of blame for the misfire, Connery's credit as executive producer was not overlooked: '[He] remains watchable, as always, but these are not two of his better hours.'

Even with a reasonable box-office start early in 1992, medium-term profitability for the $40 million feature looked extremely dicey. The prospects for Connery's latest venture, an adaptation of Michael Crichton's bestselling *Rising Sun*, look distinctly brighter.

Chapter 38

'He's a huge personality and he plays himself to the hilt.'

John Huston

'Looking back on it now, Sean, I think it fair to say we were disadvantaged. We grew up in an area of social deprivation. But in those days, of course, we didn't have social workers to tell us that! Consequently, we were happy as pigs in shit!!'

Craigie Veitch, Connery's Darroch contemporary,
Edinburgh 1991

The term 'movie star' at once defines and limits Connery as an actor; Connery can usually be relied upon, however magnificently, to be pure and simple Connery, loaded with grace, charm, sex appeal and charisma no matter how impaired his script. He is not Hoffman, De Niro, Pacino or Nicholson – actors who tackle an enormous spectrum of roles and are not, by definition, movie stars, more *character* actors. Connery accepts what he finds comfortable with, which often amounts to what he himself is feeling at the time, or what he is aspiring to.

Bond fantasies apart, he fits easily into the romantic, deluded jingoism of Danny Dravot in *The Man Who Would Be King*, the roguishness of Edward Pierce in *The Great Train Robbery*, the erudite Father William of *The Name of the Rose*, the free-spirited professor of *Indiana Jones and the Last Crusade*, the loud-mouthed space-age gunslinger of *Outland*, the down-to-earth Irish cop of *The Untouchables*, the patriarchal rapscallion of *Family Business*.

These are not, however superbly played, taxing roles; it is necessary to go back as far as *The Offence* (significantly, his own production), to find Connery playing, in the tormented Detective Sergeant Johnson, a character completely outside this otherwise narrow range. His most fully realized perform-ance since then, in Richard Lester's *Robin and Marian*, together with his most perfectly understated, in Fred Zinne-mann's *Five Days One Summer*, come closest to fusing the twin strands of Connery's artistry. At his very considerable best he combines the integrity of Tracy with the physicality of Cooper, the raw energy of Cagney with the sex appeal of Gable, together with the same vein of sly humour all four tapped to such devastating effect.

One additional approach to his craft Connery employs is to acknowledge his own mortality and incorporate it into his roles. After Sean had played the fathers of both Harrison Ford and Dustin Hoffman, Michael Caine cracked, 'Sean, if you hadn't given up bodybuilding, you could have played *Arnie's* father!'

Staggered as he was to be offered the Freedom of the City by his native Edinburgh, Connery did not at first realize the full significance of the honour. When he studied its history, he learned that it had previously been reserved for such illustrious figures as Sir Walter Scott, Disraeli, Garibaldi, Ben Jonson, Ben Franklin, Dickens, Asquith, Gladstone, David Livingstone and Sir Winston Churchill. The award had last been made twenty years earlier; there were only five living recipients, including the Queen, the Prince of Wales having been proposed and turned down in the 1970s. Looking through them all, Connery was less than astonished to find he was the first from Fountainbridge.

The honour had been given to celebrate his distinguished contribution to world cinema, to recognize his largely unpublicized work for the Scottish Education Trust he had founded – said to be doling out upwards of £60,000 a year to deserving Scots – and particularly as a token of the esteem and affection in which he was held in Edinburgh. The motion had been proposed by the Lord Provost of the City and seconded by Councillor Irene Kitson, daughter of Alex, the former head of the Transport and General Workers' Union, Connery's original milk round driver.

Despite the enthusiastic reception on the streets of Edinburgh when he and Micheline arrived for the ceremony in June 1991, Connery still felt it necessary to clarify, at a press conference to mark the occasion, a couple of items that had 'got up his nose a little' in the *Scotsman* that morning. The first concerned the newspaper's attempts to quantify his charity contributions, with Connery explaining that his fee for a one-day appearance, at Kevin Costner's request, in *Robin Hood: Prince of Thieves*, was $250,000, not $500,000 as reported. Furthermore, the role had been undertaken only on condition that his fee would be presented direct to charity, and he had reached an understanding with Britain's Inland Revenue that this would not be announced. 'Each of the charities asked if they could advertise (my contribution),' he added, 'because they were always looking for donations and covenants. What I give to charity is a very personal thing and I don't like the taste of that (the *Scotsman* article) ... The way it read was as if one were getting $250,000 and professing to be giving it to charity ...'

Clarification of his tax situation was next on the agenda. 'Another reference is that I don't pay taxes, which is entirely untrue ... When I moved out of Britain in 1974 I paid nothing but taxes on everything that was frozen in the country; you're not allowed to take your money. I pay full tax in Britain and

America, wherever I work, without the benefits of living in the country. It's a very important fact, that, to me, and I'd just like that matter cleared up.'

Although there was no doubt about Connery's spontaneity, he would have been hard pressed to find a less appropriate platform for his ripostes. For many they only served to pose another question: why *does* Connery feel obliged to respond to every sling and arrow? Surely he hasn't grown so far apart from Joe Public, the vast majority of whom feel nothing but the deepest affection and admiration for one of the greatest movie stars ever, a hero, an idol, *legitimately* avoiding tax, something that should be every right-thinking person's sworn aim and duty, as well as steadily and conscientiously donating to charity? Their collective attitude, 'Right *on*, Sean,' seems to be lost on him. Perhaps he should heed Elbert Hubbard's advice: '*Never explain.* Your friends don't need it – and your enemies will not believe it anyway!'

An inspiration to all concerned during the trip was Connery's visit to Scotland's only AIDS hospice, Milestone House, where he insisted on meeting every one of the twenty patients in turn.

Reduced to skin and bone, Eddie 'L', who had contracted the disease from an infected syringe, had tried desperately to hang on for Connery's visit, but died just a few days earlier. 'Sean put his arms around me,' said his widow, Olive, her two children by her side. 'He held me very tight. He kissed my cheeks and my hands, stroking them and soothing me. I could hardly speak I was so choked with emotion. He was so big, he was like a bear, yet so gentle. He lifted the kids, one under each arm, and jokingly whispered to me, "Will you be my knock-about?" I was crying, but I said, "Of course I will."'

Spotting a nurse holding a year-old baby girl, Connery grasped the pathetic bundle and rocked her in his arms, tears welling up as he was told the child was dying.

Twenty-three-year-old Sally White, weighing barely four stone, had contracted the HIV virus that led to her full-blown AIDS from her boyfriend. 'I know I'm dying,' she said, 'but

Sean gave me hope. He held me in his arms and kissed me. You can't know what that means to someone in my condition, when a man of his magnitude will do that. He's a giant.' Two months after his visit, Sally was dead.

'It seems ironic he made *The Untouchables*,' said another patient. 'To many people *we* are the untouchables – but certainly not to Sean. He made us feel like human beings.'

Connery had been a reliable source of funds for the Scottish National Party – the SNP – since the 1960s. These sympathies notwithstanding, he had seemed to question, early in 1991, whether they were ready and able to lead Scotland on the march to separatism from the rest of the United Kingdom.

He had unequivocally declared his views on separatism twenty years earlier, and not without a fair degree of prescience: 'I don't believe in the Common Market, in the US or in the Soviet Union, because there will always be national differences and skirmishes. And the world's in a highly dangerous situation when it splits up into three uncontrollable superpowers. Scotland should pull away somewhat after those hundreds of years of taking second place to England. The sad thing is the indifference of the Scottish electorate, more than 60 per cent of which didn't bother to vote when given the choice of devolution.'

His decision to participate in an SNP party political television broadcast in September 1991, still came as a surprise. So, for that matter, did the lack of cogency in the broken-backed contention he put over. After dwelling on the various deductions made from Scottish working men's pay packets and suggesting that further deductions were on some sort of secret agenda, he switched the argument to the old saw of Scots oil revenues travelling south to subsidize England. Then he promised that no less than £2 billion of these revenues would be ploughed back into Scotland by the SNP so that 'everyone in Scotland who wants a job, has a job'; instead of lashing out money on nuclear weapons, the money would be used to provide improved housing and better health service, schools and standard of living for senior citizens. The promises, as well as the populist 'Scotland's oil revenues for Scotland' argument, were effectively – if simplistically – delivered.

With membership swollen by five hundred new members as a direct result of the broadcast, and predicted to rise to a thousand, proud-as-a-puggy SNP leader Alex Salmond declared the other political parties 'shaken, stirred and panicked'. Connery, he maintained, had delivered a 'rocket boost' for his party's fortunes.

Edinburgh Central's Labour MP Alistair Darling was appalled at the 'presumption' behind Connery's participation: 'I think Scotland's future should be decided by people who live in Scotland, pay taxes in Scotland and have a personal stake in the nation's future. As far as I am aware Mr Connery has made his future in a villa in Spain. He is an excellent ambassador for the city and should stick to that.' Another Labour MP, George Galloway of Glasgow Hillhead, put it this way: 'As a tax exile living in Marbella who spends most of his time on the rolling golf courses of the Iberian peninsula, he ought perhaps to think twice about lecturing the rest of us unlucky enough to have lived through these last twelve years of Tory government.' In a rare show of unanimity Michael Hirst, president of the Scottish Conservative Party's voluntary wing, chipped in with a similar message: 'Sean Connery would be more credible if he was based in Scotland and paid money to the British exchequer instead of living in a tax haven.'

Political commentators like Allan Massie in the *Sunday Times* were no more generous, his views encapsulated in the headline: 'Absence Makes The Heart Grow Softer'. 'Sceptics,' he wrote, 'will find Connery's attachment to the cause of an independent Scotland unconvincing until he announces his intention to reside here, and to pay the taxes an independent Scotland would require.' Massie conceded that, natural as it was to see Scotland through a romantic mist while living abroad, actually living in the country would dispel the mist and reveal the intimate connections between Scotland and the rest of the United Kingdom. Stung by the reaction, Connery chose to hit back at his critics. Had anyone doubted that he would? 'I am entitled to be interested and involved,' he protested. 'I have a birthright in Scotland.' Connery for President?

Only weeks later, now firmly allied in the public consciousness as backing Scotland, the SNP and separatism through and through, he threw a curved ball that astounded everyone, his 'rocket boosted' political allies not least. Surely it couldn't be true – the archetypal Scot signing on the dotted line with Suntory of Japan to promote Suntory Crest, 'a blend of the finest aged whiskies'? It seemed that if the cheque were large enough, all other 'petty' considerations were tossed out of the window. What price 'birthright' now? All that remained was for the Scottish Whisky Association – ridiculous though it may sound – to rope in Toshiro Mifune to push their own brands. How much money, it was asked, did Connery *need*? (According to *Variety*, he came sixth in 1990's 'highest paid' movie-star league, with total earnings of $35 million.)

Many saw his promotion of Suntory whisky in Japan as at best hypocritical, at worst unpatriotic. A spokesman for the Scottish Whisky Association came straight to the point: 'It certainly shows where [Connery's] loyalties lie. Considering his strong pro-Scottish stance, he might have had second thoughts and put patriotism before greed.' Alex Salmond was left with little alternative but to rush to Connery's defence, pointing out that what he did as a 'professional performer' should be divorced from his political activities. Was he preaching separatism – or schizophrenia? He also had a suggestion for the Scottish whisky producers, who contributed $2.6 billion to British exports and employed 15,000 Scots: 'They should have got off their backsides and signed up Mr Connery themselves.'

Connery found himself bitterly attacked in the House of Commons over his decision, while one letter to the press in Scotland suggested that his Freedom of the City award should be promptly rescinded. Unabashed, Connery formally joined the SNP in February 1992.

Apart from the monetary reason for his 'defection to Japan', one Edinburgh worthy, displaying the same twinkle often employed by the star under fire, summed up the situation in typically pawky fashion. 'It's just Big Tam being lovable,' he suggested.

In an ironic twist, Jam Jar's Gareth Wardell established a further tenuous link with his elusive object of desire, from the distance of the actor's second contributed voice-over to an SNP party political broadcast he was brought in to elevate to the level of Connery's international status.

After all the brouhaha over the SNP 'surge' and Alex Salmond's confident prediction that his party was 'about to deliver a triple whammy to the Tories', the SNP gained only 7 per cent and lost a seat, while the Tories gained two.

The lost seat, causing maximum embarrassment, was that of Salmond's deputy Jim ('All our returns show a decisive shift toward the SNP') Sillars in the Govan district of Glasgow. In the *Sunday Times*'s list of Election Winners and Losers they featured Connery – 'who advertises Japanese whisky, lives in Marbella and pledged his support to the Scottish Nationalists' – prominently in the Losers section.

In addition to his Oscar for *The Untouchables* and BAFTA Best Actor award for *The Name of the Rose*, Connery found himself on the receiving end of a whole slew of other awards in the latter half of the 1980s. These included the Commandeur des Arts et les Lettres, France's highest artists' honour; the Honorary Doctorate of Letters from both St Andrew's and Heriot-Watt Universities; a Fellowship from the Royal Scottish Academy of Music and Drama; the Man of Culture Award, presented in Rome by the President of Italy, as well as 1990's BAFTA Silver Mask presentation where Jason had made his outstanding, clearly heartfelt speech.

Michael Caine saw the occasion as marking another watershed for Connery, one that affected him as profoundly as his reception at the Oscars. As one by one the testimonials were delivered – by, among others, Gina Lollobrigida, Steven Spielberg, Ursula Andress and Sir Richard Attenborough – a mixture of pride and delight, tinged with regret, was evident in Connery's reaction. Billy Connolly, tongue firmly planted in cheek, spiced the schmaltz of the glitzy occasion and turned the tables on Connery in London by delivering his message live by satellite from a poolside in Hollywood. 'It's absolutely magic that they're honouring you in this sycophantic fashion,' he said, grinning broadly. 'I'd like to embarrass you even further. I think you're the nicest man on earth. If not the *entire universe*!'

Her Royal Highness Princess Anne summed up the feelings of both the public and Connery's peers: 'We are very fortunate in the British film and television business to have such a wealth of talent. But there are some really shining examples of professionalism' – a nod to Connery, barely able to control his feelings – 'and "professionalism" is really the word to describe his work. I suspect everything he has ever done has had a really professional attitude, with a prevailing sense of humour. He is professional about everything and works very hard – and that is not only on-screen. The things he has done for young people in this country off-screen are tremendous. Maybe we are short of heroes, but he's a shining example of a hero for a whole generation.'

A clearly humbled and bemused Connery referred in his speech to the 'thirty years' filmic odyssey' he had enjoyed and the 'marvellous people' he'd met along the way. 'What's become apparent, watching this evening,' he confessed, 'was that I haven't *seen* them as much as I should have.' After the ceremony he told Michael Caine, 'I don't know why I've locked myself away like I have . . .'

His 'homecoming' was completed a year later in Edinburgh with the ceremonial handing over of the keys to the city. The feelings Connery expressed in his acceptance speech can be applied not only to his movie career, but to his entire, remarkable sixty-odd-year odyssey. 'I feel like I've gone fifteen rounds with Mike Tyson,' he declared, before gleefully adding, '*But I won*!'

FILMOGRAPHY

NO ROAD BACK (Gibraltar/RKO-Radio 1957)
DIRECTOR: Montgomery Tully
SCREENPLAY: Charles A. Leeds and Montgomery Tully, adapted from the play, *Madame Tic-Tac* by Falkland L. Cary and Philip Weathers
PRODUCER: Steve Pallos
CAMERAMAN: Lionel Banes
EDITOR: Jim Cannock
MUSIC: John Veale
RUNNING TIME: 83 minutes
CAST: Skip Homeier, Paul Carpenter, Patricia Dainton, Norman Wooland, Margaret Rawlings, Eleanor Summerfield, Alfie Bass, Sean Connery as 'Spike'.

HELL DRIVERS (Aqua/J. Arthur Rank 1957)
DIRECTOR: C. Raker Endfield (Cy Endfield)
SCREENPLAY: John Kruse and C. Raker Endfield
PRODUCER: S. Benjamin Fisz
CINEMATOGRAPHY: Geoffrey Unsworth (VistaVision)
EDITOR: John D. Guthridge
MUSIC: Hubert Clifford
RUNNING TIME: 108 minutes

CAST: Stanley Baker, Herbert Lom, Peggy Cummins, Patrick McGoohan, William Hartnell, Wilfrid Lawson, Sidney James, Jill Ireland, Alfie Bass, Gordon Jackson, Vera Day, Beatrice Varley (Sean Connery unbilled).

TIME LOCK (Romulus/Independent/British Lion 1957)
DIRECTOR: Gerald Thomas
SCREENPLAY: Peter Rogers from the play by Arthur Hailey
PRODUCER: Peter Rogers
CINEMATOGRAPHY: Peter Hennesy
EDITOR: John Trumper
MUSIC: Stanley Black
RUNNING TIME: 73 minutes
CAST: Robert Beatty, Betty McDowall, Vincent Winter, Sandra Francis, Lee Patterson (Sean Connery unbilled)

ACTION OF THE TIGER (MGM 1957)
DIRECTOR: Terence Young
SCREENPLAY: Robert Carson, based on a book by James Wellard
PRODUCER: Kenneth Harper
CINEMATOGRAPHY: Desmond Dickinson (Cinemascope/Technicolor)
EDITOR: Frank Clarke
MUSIC: Humphrey Searle
RUNNING TIME: 93 minutes
CAST: Van Johnson, Martine Carol, Herbert Lom, Gustavo Rocco, Tony Dawson, Anna Gerber, Yvonne Warren, Helen Haye, Sean Connery as 'Mike'.

ANOTHER TIME, ANOTHER PLACE (Paramount 1958)
DIRECTOR: Lewis Allen
SCREENPLAY: Stanley Mann, from the novel by Lenore Coffee
PRODUCERS: Lewis Allen, Smedley Aston
CINEMATOGRAPHY: Jack Hildyard (VistaVision)
EDITOR: Geoffrey Foot
MUSIC: Douglas Gamley
RUNNING TIME: 95 minutes

CAST: Lana Turner, Barry Sullivan, Glynis Johns, Sean Connery as 'Mark Trevor', Sidney James, Terence Longdon, Doris Hare, Martin Stephens.

DARBY O'GILL AND THE LITTLE PEOPLE (Disney/ Buena Vista 1959)
DIRECTOR: Robert Stevenson
SCREENPLAY: Lawrence Edward Watkins, suggested by H.T. Kavanagh's Darby O'Gill stories
PRODUCER: Walt Disney
CINEMATOGRAPHY: Winton C. Hoch (Technicolor)
EDITOR: Stanley Johnson
MUSIC: Oliver Wallace
RUNNING TIME: 90 minutes
CAST: Albert Sharpe, Jimmy O'Dea, Janet Munro, Sean Connery as 'Michael McBride', Kieron Moore, Estelle Winwood, Walter Fitzgerald, Dennis O'Dea, J.G. Devlin, Jack MacGowran.

TARZAN'S GREATEST ADVENTURE (Solar/Paramount 1959)
DIRECTOR: John Guillermin
SCREENPLAY: Berne Giler, John Guillermin, from a story by Les Crutchfield, based on Edgar Rice Burroughs's characters
PRODUCER: Sy Weintraub
CINEMATOGRAPHY: Skeets Kelly (Technicolor)
EDITOR: Bert Rule
MUSIC: Uncredited
RUNNING TIME: 84 minutes
CAST: Gordon Scott, Anthony Quayle, Sara Shane, Sean Connery as 'O'Bannion', Niall MacGinnis, Scilla Gabel, Al Mulock.

THE FRIGHTENED CITY (Zodiac/Anglo Amalgamated 1961)
DIRECTOR: John Lemont

SCREENPLAY: Leigh Vance from a story by Leigh Vance and John Lemont
PRODUCERS: John Lemont, Leigh Vance
CINEMATOGRAPHY: Desmond Dickinson
EDITOR: Bernard Gribble
MUSIC: Norrie Paramor
RUNNING TIME: 98 minutes
CAST: Herbert Lom, John Gregson, Sean Connery as 'Paddy Damion', Alfred Marks, Yvonne Romain, Olive McFarland, Kenneth Griffiths, David Davies.

OPERATION SNAFU (UK Title: **ON THE FIDDLE**) (Anglo Amalgamated/American International Pictures 1961)
DIRECTOR: Cyril Frankel
SCREENPLAY: Harold Buchman, from R.F. Delderfield's novel, *Stop at a Winner*
PRODUCER: S. Benjamin Fisz
CINEMATOGRAPHY: Edward Scaife
EDITOR: Peter Hunt
MUSIC: Malcolm Arnold
RUNNING TIME: 97 minutes
CAST: Sean Connery as 'Pedlar Pascoe', Alfred Lynch, Cecil Parker, Wilfrid Hyde-White, Stanley Holloway, Kathleen Harrison, Eleanor Summerfield, Eric Barker, Terence Longdon, Alan King, Ann Beach, John Le Mesurier, Victor Maddern.

THE LONGEST DAY (20th Century-Fox 1962)
DIRECTORS: Ken Annakin (British exterior episodes), Andrew Marton, Elmo Williams, Bernhard Wicki, Darryl F. Zanuck
SCREENPLAY: Cornelius Ryan, based on his book
PRODUCER: Darryl F. Zanuck
CINEMATOGRAPHY: Jean Bourgoin, Henri Persin, Walter Woffitz (CinemaScope)
EDITOR: Samuel E. Beetley
MUSIC: Maurice Jarre
RUNNING TIME: 180 minutes

CAST: Richard Burton, Kenneth More, Peter Lawford, Richard Todd, Leo Genn, Michael Medwin, Sean Connery as 'Private Flanagan', Norman Rossington, John Robinson, Patrick Barr, Donald Houston, Trevor Reid, John Wayne, Robert Mitchum, Henry Fonda, Robert Ryan, Richard Beymer, Mel Ferrer, Jeffrey Hunter, Sal Mineo, Roddy McDowall, Eddie Albert, Edmond O'Brien, Red Buttons, Henry Grace, Irina Demick, Bourvil, Jean-Louis Barrault, Christian Marquand, Arletty, Madeleine Renaud, Georges Wilson, Fernand Ledoux, Curt Jurgens, Werner Hinz, Paul Hartmann, Hans Christian Blech, Wolfgang Preiss, Peter Van Eyck.

DR NO (Eon/United Artists 1962)
DIRECTOR: Terence Young
PRODUCERS: Harry Saltzman, Albert R. Broccoli
SCREENPLAY: Richard Maibaum, Johanna Harwood, Berkely Mather from the novel by Ian Fleming
CINEMATOGRAPHY: Ted Moore (Technicolor)
EDITOR: Peter Hunt
MUSIC: Monty Norman
RUNNING TIME: 105 minutes
CAST: Sean Connery as 'James Bond', Ursula Andress, Joseph Wiseman, Jack Lord, Anthony Dawson, John Kitzmiller, Zena Marshall, Bernard Lee, Lois Maxwell, Eunice Gayson, Lester Prendergast, Margaret LeWars, Reggie Carter, Peter Burton.

FROM RUSSIA WITH LOVE (Eon/United Artists 1963)
DIRECTOR: Terence Young
SCREENPLAY: Richard Maibaum, Johanna Harwood, based on the novel by Ian Fleming
PRODUCERS: Harry Saltzman, Albert R. Broccoli
CINEMATOGRAPHY: Ted Moore (Technicolor)
EDITOR: Peter Hunt
MUSIC: John Barry
RUNNING TIME: 116 minutes

CAST: Sean Connery as 'James Bond', Daniela Bianchi, Pedro Armendariz, Lotte Lenya, Robert Shaw, Bernard Lee, Eunice Gayson, Walter Gotell, Francis de Wolff, Georges Pastell, Nadja Regin, Lois Maxwell, Martine Beswick, Vladek Sheybal, Desmond Llewelyn.

WOMAN OF STRAW (Novus, United Artists 1964)
DIRECTOR: Basil Dearden
SCREENPLAY: Robert Muller, Stanley Mann, Michael Relph, based on the novel by Catherine Arley
PRODUCER: Michael Relph
CINEMATOGRAPHY: Otto Heller (EastmanColor)
EDITOR: John D. Gutheridge
MUSIC: Muir Mathieson
RUNNING TIME: 117 minutes
CAST: Gina Lollobrigida, Sean Connery as 'Anthony Richmond', Ralph Richardson, Johnny Sekka, Laurence Hardy, Danny Daniels, A.J. Brown, Peter Madden, Alexander Knox, Edward Underdown, George Curzon, André Morell.

MARNIE (Universal-International 1964)
DIRECTOR: Alfred Hitchcock
SCREENPLAY: Jay Presson Allen, from the novel by Winston Graham
PRODUCER: Alfred Hitchcock
CINEMATOGRAPHY: Robert Burks (Technicolor)
EDITOR: George Tomasini
MUSIC: Bernard Herrmann
RUNNING TIME: 130 minutes
CAST: Sean Connery as 'Mark Rutland', 'Tippi' Hedren, Diane Baker, Martin Gabel, Louise Latham, Bob Sweeney, Alan Napier, S. John Launer, Mariette Hartley, Bruce Dern.

GOLDFINGER (Eon/United Artists 1964)
DIRECTOR: Guy Hamilton
SCREENPLAY: Richard Maibaum, Paul Dehn
PRODUCERS: Harry Saltzman, Albert R. Broccoli

CINEMATOGRAPHY: Ted Moore (Technicolor)
EDITOR: Peter Hunt
MUSIC: John Barry
RUNNING TIME: 109 minutes
CAST: Sean Connery as 'James Bond', Honor Blackman, Gert
    Frobe, Shirley Eaton, Tania Mallet, Harold Sakata, Bernard
    Lee, Martin Benson, Cec Linder, Austin Willis, Lois Max-
    well, Bill Nagy, Alf Joint, Varley Thomas, Nadja Regin,
    Raymond Young, Richard Vernon, Bert Kwouk.

THE HILL (Seven Arts/MGM 1965)
DIRECTOR: Sidney Lumet
SCREENPLAY: Ray Rigby, based on the play by Ray Rigby and
    R.S. Allen
PRODUCER: Kenneth Hyman
CINEMATOGRAPHY: Oswald Norris
EDITOR: Thelma Connell
MUSIC: None
RUNNING TIME: 123 minutes
CAST: Sean Connery as 'Joe Roberts', Harry Andrews, Ian
    Bannen, Alfred Lynch, Ossie Davis, Roy Kinnear, Jack
    Watson, Ian Hendry, Michael Redgrave, Norman Bird, Neil
    McCarthy.

THUNDERBALL (Eon/United Artists 1965)
DIRECTOR: Terence Young
SCREENPLAY: Richard Maibaum, John Hopkins, based on a
    story by Kevin McClory, Jack Whittingham, Ian Fleming,
    based on Ian Fleming's novel
PRODUCER: Kevin McClory
CINEMATOGRAPHY: Ted Moore (PanaVision/Technicolor)
EDITOR: Peter Hunt
MUSIC: John Barry
RUNNING TIME: 125 minutes, originally 130 minutes
CAST: Sean Connery as 'James Bond', Claudine Auger, Adolfo
    Celi, Luciana Paluzzi, Rik Van Nutter, Bernard Lee, Martine

Beswick, Guy Doleman, Molly Peters, Desmond Llewelyn, Lois Maxwell, Roland Culver, Earl Cameron.

A FINE MADNESS (Pan Arts/Warner Bros 1966)
DIRECTOR: Irvin Kershner
SCREENPLAY: Elliott Baker, based on his own novel
PRODUCER: Jerome Hellman
CINEMATOGRAPHY: Ted McCord (Technicolor)
EDITOR: William Ziegler
MUSIC: John Addison
RUNNING TIME: 104 minutes
CAST: Sean Connery as 'Samson Shillitoe', Joanne Woodward, Jean Seberg, Patrick O'Neal, Colleen Dewhurst, Clive Revill, Werner Peters, John Fiedler, Kay Medford, Jackie Coogan, Zohra Lampert, Sue Ann Longdon, Sorrell Brooke.

YOU ONLY LIVE TWICE (Eon-Danjaq-United Artists 1967)
DIRECTOR: Lewis Gilbert
SCREENPLAY: Roald Dahl
PRODUCERS: Harry Saltzman, Albert R. Broccoli
CINEMATOGRAPHY: Freddie Young (PanaVision/Technicolor)
EDITOR: Peter Hunt
MUSIC: John Barry
RUNNING TIME: 116 minutes
CAST: Sean Connery as 'James Bond', Akiko Wakabayashi, Tetsuro Tamba, Mie Hama, Teru Shimada, Karin Dor, Lois Maxwell, Desmond Llewelyn, Bernard Lee, Charles Gray, Tsai Chin, Donald Pleasence, Alexander Knox, Burt Kwouk, Robert Hutton.

SHALAKO (Kingston Films/Warner Bros 1968)
DIRECTOR: Edward Dmytryk
SCREENPLAY: J.J. Griffith, Hal Hopper, Scot Finch, based on a novel by Louis L'Amour (Story: Clarke Reynolds)
PRODUCER: Euan Lloyd (a Dimitri de Grunwald Production)
CINEMATOGRAPHY: Ted Moore (Franscope/Technicolor)
EDITOR: Bill Blunden

MUSIC: Robert Farnon
RUNNING TIME: 113 minutes
CAST: Sean Connery as 'Shalako', Brigitte Bardot, Stephen Boyd, Jack Hawkins, Peter Van Eyck, Honor Blackman, Woody Strode, Eric Sykes, Alexander Knox, Valerie French, Julian Mateos, Donald Barry, Rodd Redwing.

THE MOLLY MAGUIRES (Paramount 1970)
DIRECTOR: Martin Ritt
SCREENPLAY: Walter Bernstein, suggested by a book by Arthur H. Lewis
PRODUCER: Martin Ritt, Walter Bernstein
CINEMATOGRAPHY: James Wong Howe (PanaVision/Technicolor)
EDITOR: Frank Bracht
MUSIC: Henry Mancini
RUNNING TIME: 125 minutes
CAST: Richard Harris, Sean Connery as 'Jack Kehoe', Samantha Eggar, Frank Finlay, Anthony Zerbe, Bethel Leslie, Art Lund, Anthony Costello, Philip Bourneuf, Brenda Dillon, Francis Heflin, John Alderson.

THE RED TENT (Italian Title: *La Tenda Rossa*/Russian Title: *Krasnaya Palatka* (Vides Cinematografica, Rome/Mosfilm, Moscow/Paramount 1970)
DIRECTOR: Mikail K. Kalatozov
SCREENPLAY: Ennio de Concini, Richard Adams, story by Ennio De Concini
PRODUCER: Franco Cristaldi
CINEMATOGRAPHY: Leonid Kalashnikov (Technicolor)
EDITORS: John Shirley, Peter Zinner
MUSIC: Ennio Morricone
RUNNING TIME: 121 minutes (English version)
CAST: Peter Finch, Sean Connery as 'Amundsen', Claudia Cardinale, Hardy Kruger, Mario Adorf, Massimo Girotti, Luigi Vannucchi, Edward Marzevic.

THE ANDERSON TAPES (Columbia 1971)
DIRECTOR: Sidney Lumet
SCREENPLAY: Frank R. Pierson, based on the novel by Laurence Sanders
PRODUCER: Robert M. Weitman
CINEMATOGRAPHY: Arthur J. Ornitz (PanaVision/Technicolor)
EDITOR: Joanne Burke
MUSIC: Quincy Jones
RUNNING TIME: 99 minutes
CAST: Sean Connery as 'Duke Anderson', Dyan Cannon, Martin Balsam, Ralph Meeker, Alan King, Christopher Walken, Val Avery, Stan Gottlieb, Anthony Holland, Richard B. Schull, Conrad Bain, Margaret Hamilton, Judith Lowry, Scott Jacoby.

DIAMONDS ARE FOREVER (Eon/Danjaq/United Artists 1971)
DIRECTOR: Guy Hamilton
SCREENPLAY: Richard Maibaum, Tom Mankiewicz
PRODUCERS: Harry Saltzman, Albert R. Broccoli
CINEMATOGRAPHY: Ted Moore (PanaVision/Technicolor)
EDITOR: Bert Bates, John W. Holms
MUSIC: John Barry
RUNNING TIME: 120 minutes
CAST: Sean Connery as 'James Bond', Jill St John, Charles Gray, Lana Wood, Jimmy Dean, Bruce Cabot, Putter Smith, Bruce Glover, Norman Burton, Joseph Furst, Bernard Lee, Desmond Llewelyn, Leonard Barr, Lois Maxwell, Margaret Lacey, Joe Robinson, Donna Garratt.

THE OFFENCE (Tantallon/United Artists 1973)
DIRECTOR: Sidney Lumet
SCREENPLAY: John Hopkins, based on his play *This Story of Yours*
PRODUCER: Denis O'Dell
CINEMATOGRAPHY: Gerry Fisher (DeLuxe Color)
EDITOR: John Victor Smith

MUSIC: Harrison Birtwhistle
RUNNING TIME: 113 minutes
CAST: Sean Connery as 'Johnson', Trevor Howard, Vivien Merchant, Ian Bannen, Derek Newark, John Hallam, Peter Bowles, Ronald Radd, Anthony Sagar, Howard Goorney, Richard Moore, Maxine Gordon.

ZARDOZ (20th Century-Fox 1974)
DIRECTOR: John Boorman
SCREENPLAY: John Boorman, Story Associate Bill Stair
PRODUCER: John Boorman
CINEMATOGRAPHY: Geoffrey Unsworth (DeLuxe Color)
EDITOR: John Merritt
MUSIC: David Munrow
RUNNING TIME: 105 minutes
CAST: Sean Connery as 'Zed', Charlotte Rampling, Sara Kestleman, Sally Anne Newton, John Alderton, Niall Buggy, Bosco Hogan, Jessica Swift, Bairbre Dowling, Christopher Casson, Reginald Jarman.

MURDER ON THE ORIENT EXPRESS (EMI/Paramount 1974)
DIRECTOR: Sidney Lumet
SCREENPLAY: Paul Dehn, based on the novel by Agatha Christie
PRODUCERS: John Brabourne, Richard Goodwin
CINEMATOGRAPHY: Geoffrey Unsworth (Technicolor)
EDITOR: Anne V. Coates
MUSIC: Richard Rodney Bennett
RUNNING TIME: 131 minutes
CAST: Albert Finney, Lauren Bacall, Martin Balsam, Ingrid Bergman, Jaqueline Bisset, Jean-Pierre Cassel, Sean Connery as 'Col. Arbuthnot', John Gielgud, Wendy Hiller, Anthony Perkins, Vanessa Redgrave, Rachel Roberts, Richard Widmark, Michael York, Colin Blakely, George Coulouris, Denis Quilley, Vernon Dobtcheff, Jeremy Lloyd, John Moffatt, George Silver.

THE TERRORISTS (UK Title: **RANSOM**) (Lion International/British Lion 1975)
DIRECTOR: Caspar Wrede
SCREENPLAY: Paul Wheeler
PRODUCER: Peter Rawley
CINEMATOGRAPHY: Sven Nykvist (Eastman Color)
EDITOR: Thelma Connell
MUSIC: Jerry Goldsmith
RUNNING TIME: 98 minutes
CAST: Sean Connery as 'Nils Tahlvik', Ian McShane, Norman Bristow, John Cording, Isabel Dean, William Fox, Richard Hampton, Robert Harris, Harry Landis, Preston Lockwood, James Maxwell, John Quentin.

THE WIND AND THE LION (MGM/Columbia 1975)
DIRECTOR: John Milius
SCREENPLAY: John Milius
PRODUCER: Herbert Jaffe
CINEMATOGRAPHY: Billy Williams (PanaVision/Metrocolor)
EDITOR: Robert L. Wolfe
MUSIC: Jerry Goldsmith
RUNNING TIME: 119 minutes
CAST: Sean Connery as 'Mulay El Raisuli', Candice Bergen, Brian Keith, John Huston, Geoffrey Lewis, Steven Kanaly, Roy Jenson, Vladek Sheybal, Darrell Fetty, Nadim Sawalha, Mark Zuber, Antoine St John, Simon Harrison, Polly Gottesman, Deborah Baxter.

THE MAN WHO WOULD BE KING (Persky-Bright/Devon/Allied Artists/Columbia 1975)
DIRECTOR: John Huston
SCREENPLAY: John Huston, Gladys Hill, based on a story by Rudyard Kipling
PRODUCER: John Foreman
CINEMATOGRAPHY: Oswald Morris (PanaVision/Color)
EDITOR: Russell Lloyd
MUSIC: Maurice Jarre

RUNNING TIME: 129 minutes

CAST: Sean Connery as 'Danny Dravot', Michael Caine, Christopher Plummer, Saeed Jaffrey, Karroum Ben Bouih, Jack May, Doghmi Larbi, Shakira Caine, Mohammed Shamsi, Paul Atrim.

ROBIN AND MARIAN (Rastar/Columbia 1976)

DIRECTOR: Richard Lester

SCREENPLAY: James Goldman

PRODUCER: Denis O'Dell

CINEMATOGRAPHY: David Watkin (Technicolor)

EDITOR: John Victor Smith

MUSIC: John Barry

RUNNING TIME: 107 minutes

CAST: Sean Connery as 'Robin Hood', Audrey Hepburn, Robert Shaw, Richard Harris, Nicol Williamson, Denholm Elliott, Kenneth Haigh, Ronnie Barker, Ian Holm, Bill Maynard, Esmond Knight, Veronica Quilligan, Peter Butterworth, John Barrett, Kenneth Cranham.

THE NEXT MAN (Artists Entertainment Complex/Allied Artists 1976)

DIRECTOR: Richard C. Sarafian

SCREENPLAY: Mort Fine, Alan R. Trustman, David M. Wolf, Richard C. Sarafian

PRODUCER: Martin Bregman

CINEMATOGRAPHY: Michael Chapman (Technicolor)

EDITOR: Aram Avakian, Robert Q. Lovett

MUSIC: Michael Kamen

RUNNING TIME: 108 minutes

CAST: Sean Connery as 'Khalil Abdul-Muhsen', Cornelia Sharpe, Albert Paulsen, Adolpho Celi, Marco St John, Ted Beniades, Charles Cioffi, Jaime Sanchez, James Bullett, Salem Ludwig.

A BRIDGE TOO FAR (Joseph Levine/United Artists, 1977)

DIRECTOR: Richard Attenborough

SCREENPLAY: William Goldman, based on the book by Cornelius Ryan
PRODUCERS: Joseph E. Levine, Richard P. Levine
CINEMATOGRAPHY: Geoffrey Unsworth (PanaVision/Technicolor)
EDITOR: Antony Gibbs
RUNNING TIME: 175 minutes
CAST: Dirk Bogarde, James Caan, Michael Caine, Sean Connery as 'Maj. Gen. Robert Urquhart', Edward Fox, Elliott Gould, Gene Hackman, Anthony Hopkins, Hardy Kruger, Laurence Olivier, Ryan O'Neal, Robert Redford, Maximilian Schell, Liv Ullman, Arthur Hill, Wolfgang Preiss and 'cast of thousands'.

THE GREAT TRAIN ROBBERY (UK Title: **THE FIRST GREAT TRAIN ROBBERY**) (Starling/United Artists, 1978)
DIRECTOR: Michael Crichton
SCREENPLAY: Michael Crichton, based on his novel
PRODUCER: John Foreman
CINEMATOGRAPHY: Geoffrey Unsworth (PanaVision/Technicolor)
EDITOR: David Bretherton
MUSIC: Jerry Goldsmith
RUNNING TIME: 108 minutes
CAST: Sean Connery as 'Edward Pierce', Donald Sutherland, Lesley-Anne Down, Alan Webb, Malcolm Terris, Robert Lang, Michael Elphick, Wayne Sleep, Pamela Salem, Gabrielle Lloyd, George Downing, James Cossins, John Bett, Peter Benson, André Morell.

METEOR (Paladium/Allied Artists/Warner Bros, 1979)
DIRECTOR: Ronald Neame
SCREENPLAY: Stanley Mann, Edmund H. North (story: Edmond H. North)
PRODUCER: Arnold Orgolini, Theodore Parvi
CINEMATOGRAPHY: Paul Lohmann (PanaVision/Movielab)

MUSIC: Laurence Rosenthal
RUNNING TIME: 107 minutes
CAST: Sean Connery as 'Dr Paul Bradley', Natalie Wood, Karl Malden, Brian Keith, Martin Landau, Trevor Howard, Richard Dysart, Henry Fonda, Joseph Campanella, Bo Brundin.

CUBA (Holmby/United Artists, 1979)
DIRECTOR: Richard Lester
SCREENPLAY: Charles Wood
PRODUCERS: Alex Winitsky, Arlene Sellars
CINEMATOGRAPHY: David Watkin (Technicolor)
EDITOR: John Victor Smith
MUSIC: Patrick Williams
RUNNING TIME: 122 minutes
CAST: Sean Connery as 'Major Robert Dapes', Brooke Adams, Jack Weston, Hector Elizondo, Denholm Elliott, Martin Balsam, Christ Sarandon, Danny De La Paz, Lonette McKee, Alejandro Rey, Louisa Moritz, Dave King, Walter Gotell, David Rappaport.

OUTLAND (Ladd Co., Warner Bros, 1981)
DIRECTOR: Peter Hyams
SCREENPLAY: Peter Hyams
PRODUCER: Richard A. Roth
CINEMATOGRAPHY: Stephen Goldblatt (PanaVision/Technicolor)
EDITOR: Stuart Baird
MUSIC: Jerry Goldsmith
RUNNING TIME: 109 minutes
CAST: Sean Connery as 'Marshal O'Neill', Peter Boyle, Francis Sternhagen, James B. Sikking, Kika Markham, Clarke Peters, Steven Berkoff, John Ratzenberger, Nicholas Barnes, Manning Redwood, Pat Starr, Hal Galili.

TIME BANDITS (HandMade/Avco Embassy, 1981)
DIRECTOR: Terry Gilliam

SCREENPLAY: Michael Palin, Terry Gilliam
PRODUCER: Terry Gilliam
CINEMATOGRAPHY: Peter Biziou (Technicolor)
EDITOR: Julian Doyle
MUSIC: Mike Moran (percussion sequences Ray Cooper, Greek dance music, Trevor Jones)
RUNNING TIME: 113 minutes
CAST: John Cleese, Sean Connery as 'King Agamemnon', Shelley Duvall, Katherine Helmond, Ian Holm, Michael Palin, Ralph Richardson, Peter Vaughan, David Warner, David Rappaport, Kenny Baker, Jack Purvis, Mike Edmonds, Malcolm Dixon, Tiny Ross, Craig Warnock, David Baker, Charles McKeown, Winston Dennis.

WRONG IS RIGHT (UK Title: **THE MAN WITH THE DEADLY LENS** (Rastar/Columbia, 1982)
DIRECTOR: Richard Brooks
SCREENPLAY: Richard Brooks, based on the novel *The Better Angels* by Charles McCarry
PRODUCER: Richard Brooks
CINEMATOGRAPHY: Fred J. Koenekamp (PanaVision/Metrocolor)
EDITOR: Geroge Glenville
MUSIC: Artie Kane
RUNNING TIME: 118 minutes
CAST: Sean Connery as 'Patrick Hale', George Grizzard, Robert Conrad, Katharine Ross, G.D. Spradlin, John Saxon, Henry Silva, Leslie Nielsen, Robert Webber, Rosalind Cash, Hardy Kruger, Dean Stockwell, Ron Moody, Cherie Michan.

FIVE DAYS ONE SUMMER (Ladd Co/Warner Bros, 1982
DIRECTOR: Fred Zinnemann
SCREENPLAY: Michael Austin, based in part on the short story 'Maiden, Maiden', by Kay Boyle.
PRODUCER: Fred Zinnemann
CINEMATOGRAPHY: Guiseppe Rotunno (Technicolor)

EDITOR: Stuart Baird
MUSIC: Elmer Bernstein
RUNNING TIME: 108 minutes
CAST: Sean Connery as 'Dr Douglas Meredith', Betsy Brant-
ley, Lambert Wilson, Jennifer Hilary, Isabel Dean, Gerard
Buhr, Anna Massey, Sheila Reid, Georges Claisse, Kathy
Marothy.

NEVER SAY NEVER AGAIN (Taliafilm/PSO/Warners,
1983)
DIRECTOR: Irvin Kershner
SCREENPLAY: Lorenzo Semple Jr., story by Kevin McClory,
Jack Whittingham, Ian Fleming
PRODUCER: Jack Schwartzman
CINEMATOGRAPHY: Douglas Slocombe (PanaVision/Techni-
color)
EDITOR: Ian Crafford
MUSIC: Michel Legrand
RUNNING TIME: 134 minutes
CAST: Sean Connery as 'James Bond', Klaus Maria Brandauer,
Max Von Sydow, Barbara Carrera, Kim Basinger, Bernie
Casey, Alec McCowen, Edward Fox, Pamela Salem, Rowan
Atkinson, Valerie Leon, Milow Kirek, Pat Roach. Anthony
Sharp, Prunella Gee, Gavon O'Jerlihy, Ronald Pickup.

SWORD OF THE VALIANT (*The Legend of Gawain and
The Green Knight*) (Cannon/MGM, 1984)
DIRECTOR: Stephen Weeks
SCREENPLAY: Stephen Weeks, Howard C. Pen, Philip M.
Breen. Story consultant Roger Towne. Additional dialogue
Rosemary Sutcliff, Therese Burdon
PRODUCERS: Menahem Golan, Yoram Globus
CINEMATOGRAPHY: Freddie Young, Peter Hurst (Scope/Fuji-
color)
EDITORS: Richard Marden, Barney Peters
MUSIC: Ron Geesin
RUNNING TIME: 102 minutes

CAST: Miles O'Keefe, Trevor Howard, Sean Connery as 'The Green Knight', Peter Cushing, Ronald Lacey, Cynrielle Claire, Emma Sutton, Douglas Wilmer, Lila Kedrova, Leigh Lawson, John Rhys-Davies, David Rappaport, Wilfred Brambell.

THE NAME OF THE ROSE (Neue Constantin, West Berlin/ Cristaldi, Rome/Film Ariane, Paris/20th Century-Fox, 1986)
DIRECTOR: Jean-Jacques Annaud
SCREENPLAY: Andrew Birkin, Gerard Brach, Howard Franklin, based on the novel *Il Noma della Rosa* by Umberto Eco
PRODUCER: Bernt Eichinger, co-producers Franco Cristaldi/ Alexandre Mnouchkine
CINEMATOGRAPHY: Tonino Delli Colli (Eastmancolor)
EDITOR: Jane Seitz
MUSIC: James Horner
RUNNING TIME: 129 minutes (originally 131 minutes)
CAST: Sean Connery as 'William of Baskerville', Christian Slater, Helmut Qualtinger, Elya Baskin, Michael Lonsdale, Volker Prechtel, Feodor Chaliapin Jr., William Hickey, Michael Habech, Urs Althaus, Valentin Vargas, Ron Perlman.

HIGHLANDER (20th Century-Fox, 1986)
DIRECTOR: Russell Mulcahy
SCREENPLAY: Gregory Widen, Peter Bellwood, Larry Ferguson
PRODUCERS: Peter S. Davis, William N. Panzer
CAMERAMEN: Gerry Fisher, Tony Mitchell (NY) (Technicolor)
EDITOR: Peter Honess
MUSIC: Michael Kamen, Queen
RUNNING TIME: 111 minutes
CAST: Christopher Lambert, Roxanne Hart, Clancy Brown, Sean Connery as 'Ramirez', Beatie Edney, Alan North, Sheila Gish, Joe Polito, Hugh Quarshie, Christopher Malcolm, Peter Diamond, Billy Hartman, James Cosmo.

THE UNTOUCHABLES (Paramount, 1987)

DIRECTOR: Brian de Palma
SCREENPLAY: David Mamet, suggested by the television series and based on the works of Oscar Fraley with Eliot Ness and Paul Robsky
PRODUCER: Art Linson
CINEMATOGRAPHY: Stephen H. Burum (Panavision/Technicolor)
EDITOR: Jerry Greenberg, Bill Pankow
MUSIC: Ennio Morricone
RUNNING TIME: 120 minutes
CAST: Kevin Costner, Sean Connery as 'Jim Malone', Charles Martin Smith, Andy Garcia, Robert de Niro, Michael Bradford, Jack Kehoe, Brad Sullivan, Billy Drago, Patricia Clarkson, Vito D'Ambrosio, Steven Goldstein.

THE PRESIDIO (Paramount, 1988)

DIRECTOR: Peter Hyams
SCREENPLAY: Larry Ferguson
PRODUCER: D. Constantine Conte
CINEMATOGRAPHY: Peter Hyams (Panavision/Technicolor)
EDITORS: James Mitchell, Diane Adler, Beau Barthel-Blair
MUSIC: Bruce Broughton
RUNNING TIME: 98 minutes
CAST: Sean Connery as 'Lt-Col. Alan Caldwell', Mark Harmon, Meg Ryan, Jack Warden, Mark Blum, Dana Gladstone, Jenette Goldstein, Marvin J. McIntyre, Dan Calfa, Rich Zumwalt.

MEMORIES OF ME (MGM/UA 1988)

DIRECTOR: Henry Winkler
SCREENPLAY: Eric Roth, Billy Crystal
PRODUCERS: Alan King, Billy Crystal, Michael Hertzberg
CINEMATOGRAPHY: Andrew Dintenfass (Color)
EDITOR: Peter E. Berger
MUSIC: Georges Delerue
RUNNING TIME: 105 minutes

CAST: Billy Crystal, Alan King, JoBeth Williams, Sean Connery as himself, Janet Carroll, David Ackroyd.

INDIANA JONES AND THE LAST CRUSADE (Lucas-film/Paramount, 1989)
DIRECTOR: Steven Spielberg
SCREENPLAY: Jeffrey Boam, story George Lucas, Menno Meyjes, based on characters createdby George Lucas, Philip Kaufman
PRODUCER: Robert Watts
CINEMATOGRAPHY: Douglas Slocombe (Eastman Color, prints De Luxe)
EDITORS: Michael Kahn, Colin Wilson
MUSIC: John Williams
RUNNING TIME: 127 minutes
CAST: Harrison Ford, Sean Connery as 'Dr Henry Jones', Denholm Elliott, Alison Doody, John Rhys-Davies, Julian Glover, River Phoenix, Michael Byrne, Kevork Malikya, Robert Eddison, Richard Young, Alexei Sayle, Alex Hyde-White, Paul Maxwell.

FAMILY BUSINESS (TriStar Pictures, 1989)
DIRECTOR: Sidney Lumet
SCREENPLAY: Vincent Patrick (based on his novel)
PRODUCER: Lawrence Gordon
CAMERAMAN: Andrzej Bartkowiak (Technicolor)
EDITOR: Andrew Monshein
MUSIC: Cy Coleman, arrangements Sonny Kompanek (orchestrations)
RUNNING TIME: 113 minutes
CAST: Sean Connery as 'Jessie McMullen', Dustin Hoffman, Matthew Broderick, Rosana DeSoto, Janet Carroll, Victoria Jackson, Bill McCutcheon, Deborah Rush, Marylyn Cooper, Salem Ludwig, Rex Everhart, James S. Tolkan.

THE HUNT FOR RED OCTOBER (Paramount, 1990)
DIRECTOR: John McTiernan

SCREENPLAY: Larry Ferguson, Donald Stewart
PRODUCER: Mace Neufeld
CINEMATOGRAPHY: Jan de Bont (PanaVision/Technicolor)
EDITORS: Dennis Virkler, John Wright
MUSIC: Basil Poledouris
RUNNING TIME: 135 minutes
CAST: Sean Connery as 'Marko Ramius', Alec Baldwin, Scott
    Glenn, Sam Neill, James Earl Jones, Joss Ackland, Richard
    Jordan, Peter Firth, Tim Curry, Courtney B. Vance, Stellan
    Skarsgard, Jeffrey Jones, Timothy Carhart, Larry Ferguson.

THE RUSSIA HOUSE (MGM/PATHE, 1990)
DIRECTOR: Fred Schepisi
SCREENPLAY: Tom Stoppard, based on the novel by John le Carré
PRODUCER: Paul Maslansky
CINEMATOGRAPHY: Ian Baker (Technicolor: Technovision)
EDITOR: Peter Honess
MUSIC: Jerry Goldsmith (trumpet, Branford Marsalis)
RUNNING TIME: 123 minutes
CAST: Sean Connery as 'Barley Blair', Michelle Pfeiffer,
    Roy Scheider, James Fox, John Mahoney, Michael Kitchen,
    J.T. Walsh, Ken Russell, David Threlfall, Klaus Maria
    Brandauer.

HIGHLANDER II: THE QUICKENING (InterStar 1991)
DIRECTOR: Russell Mulcahy
SCREENPLAY: Peter Bellwood (Story Brian Clemens, William
    Panner, based on characters created by Gregory Widen)
PRODUCERS: Peter S. Davis, William N. Panzer
CINEMATOGRAPHER: Phil Meheux (Eastern color)
EDITORS: Hubert C. de la Bouillerie, Anthony Redman
MUSIC: Stewart Copeland
RUNNING TIME: 100 minutes
CAST: Christopher Lambert, Sean Connery as 'Ramirez',
    Virginia Madsen, Michael Ironside, Allan Rich, John C.
    McGinley, Phil Brock, Rusty Schwimner, Ed Trucco,
    Stephen Grives, Jimmy Murray, Pete Antico.

ROBIN HOOD: PRINCE OF THIEVES (Morgan Creek, Warner Bros, 1991)
DIRECTOR: Kevin Reynolds
SCREENPLAY: John Watson from a story by Pen Densham, Richard B. Lewis
PRODUCERS: John Watson, Pen Densham, Richard B. Lewis
CINEMATOGRAPHY: Doug Milsome (Technicolor)
EDITOR: Peter Boyle
MUSIC: Michael Kamen
RUNNING TIME: 138 minutes
CAST: Kevin Costner, Morgan Freeman, Mary Elizabeth Mastrantonio, Christian Slater, Alan Rickman, Geraldine McEwan, Michael McShane, Brian Blessed, Michael Wincott, Nick Brimble, Soo Druet, Daniel Newman, Daniel Peacock, Walter Sparrow, Harold Innocent, Jack Wild, Sean Connery as 'King Richard'.

MEDICINE MAN (Cinergi/Hollywood Pictures/Buena Vista 1992)
DIRECTOR: John McTiernan
SCREENPLAY: Tom Schulman, Sally Robinson (Story by Tom Schulman)
PRODUCERS: Andrew G. Vajna, Donna Dubrow
EXECUTIVE PRODUCER: Sean Connery
CINEMATOGRAPHY: Donald McAlpine
EDITOR: Michael R. Miller
MUSIC: Jerry Goldsmith
RUNNING TIME: 105 minutes
CAST: Sean Connery as 'Dr Robert Campbell', Lorraine Bracco, Jose Wilker, Rodolfo de Alexandre, Francisco Tsirene Tsere Rereme, Elias Monteiro da Silva, Edinei Maria Serrio Dos Santos, Bec-Kana-Re Dos Santos Kaiapo, Angelo Barra Moreira, Jose Lavat.

RISING SUN (20th Century-Fox, 1993)
DIRECTOR: Philip Kaufman
SCREENPLAY: Philip Kaufman, based on the novel by Michael Crichton

PRODUCER: Peter Kaufman
CINEMATOGRAPHY: Michael Chapman
CAST: Sean Connery, Wesley Snipes, Harvey Keitel, Kevin Anderson, Tia Carrere, Stan Egi, Mako, Cary-Hiroyuki, Tagawa, Ray Wise.

FINANCIAL HISTORY OF SEAN CONNERY MOVIES, BASED ON US/CANADIAN RENTAL FIGURES*

JAMES BONDS

DR NO (1962)	$6.4 million
FROM RUSSIA WITH LOVE (1963)	$10.0 m
GOLDFINGER (1964)	$23.0 m
THUNDERBALL (1965)	$28.0 m
YOU ONLY LIVE TWICE (1967)	$19.0 m
DIAMONDS ARE FOREVER (1971)	$19.7 m
NEVER SAY NEVER AGAIN (1987)	$28.0 m

(NON-CONNERY) BONDS:

ON HER MAJESTY'S SECRET SERVICE (1969)	$9.1 million (1)
LIVE AND LET DIE (1973)	$15.9 m (2)
THE MAN WITH THE GOLDEN GUN (1974)	$9.4 m (2)
THE SPY WHO LOVED ME (1977)	$24.3 m (2)
MOONRAKER (1979)	$33.9 m (2)
FOR YOUR EYES ONLY (1981)	$26.5 m (2)
OCTOPUSSY (1983)	$34.0 m (2)
A VIEW TO KILL (1985)	$25.3 m (2)
THE LIVING DAYLIGHTS (1987)	$27.8 m (3)
LICENCE TO KILL (1989)	$16.6 m (3)

   (1) Starring George Lazenby
   (2) Starring Roger Moore
   (3) Starring Timothy Dalton

CAMEO/SUPPORTING ROLES

MURDER ON THE ORIENT EXPRESS (1974)	$19.0 million
A BRIDGE TOO FAR (1977)	$20.4 m
TIME BANDITS (1981)	$20.5 m
SWORD OF THE VALIANT (1984)	Virtually unreleased
HIGHLANDER (1986)	$2.8 m
THE UNTOUCHABLES (1987)	$38.0 m
INDIANA JONES AND THE LAST CRUSADE (1989)	$116.0 m
HIGHLANDER II (1991)	$8.0 m (approx.)
ROBIN HOOD: PRINCE OF THIEVES (1991)	$86.0 m

STARRING ROLES (NON-BOND)

WOMAN OF STRAW (1964)	under $1.0 million
MARNIE (1964)	$3.3 m
THE HILL (1965)	under $1.0 m
A FINE MADNESS (1966)	under $1.0 m
SHALAKO (1968)	under $1.0 m
THE MOLLY MAGUIRES (1970)	$1.1 m
THE RED TENT (1970)	under $1.0 m
THE ANDERSON TAPES (1971)	$5.0 m
THE OFFENCE (1973)	under $1.0 m
ZARDOZ (1974)	under $1.0 m
THE TERRORISTS (1975)	under $1.0 m
THE WIND AND THE LION (1975)	$4.9 m
THE MAN WHO WOULD BE KING (1975)	$11.0 m
ROBIN AND MARIAN (1976)	$4.0 m
THE NEXT MAN (1976)	under $1.0 m
THE GREAT TRAIN ROBBERY (1978)	$5.0 m
METEOR (1979)	$6.0 m
CUBA (1979)	under $1.0 m
OUTLAND (1981)	$10.0 m
WRONG IS RIGHT (1982)	under $1.0 m

FIVE DAYS ONE SUMMER (1982)	under $1.0 m
THE NAME OF THE ROSE (1986)	under $4.0 m
THE PRESIDIO (1988)	$9.6 m
FAMILY BUSINESS (1989)	$5.5 m
THE HUNT FOR RED OCTOBER (1990)	$58.5 m
THE RUSSIA HOUSE (1990)	$10.0 m
MEDICINE MAN (1992)	approx. $20 m.

*A note on film 'rentals': this is the figure actually returned to the film's distributor as his share of the box-office gross. Rentals vary, between 45–55 per cent of the box-office, and give a better idea of a movie's profitability than quoting box-office figures. Only US/Canadian rentals are quoted in most cases, and exclude worldwide figures (mostly unavailable) as well as subsequent television sales, video release, etc. In this way, like is being compared with like. The only significant 'breakout' worldwide, at odds with the US results, was with *The Name of the Rose*, which broke records across Europe (excluding the UK).

Index

Woman of Straw, 90–91, 92, 98, 202, 357, 374
Wood, Charles, 223–4, 227
Wood, Natalie, 215–16
Woodfall Films, 67, 82
Woodward, Joanne, 57, 117
Woolf, Jimmy, 82–3
Woolf, John, 68, 82
'World's Sexiest Man' accolade, 288
Wrede, Caspar, 172
Wright, Ian, 99
Wrong Is Right, 234, 241, 243–5, 367, 375

York, Michael, 174, 266, 339

Young, Terence, 12, 48, 69, 72–3, 74, 85, 88–90, 100, 102–3, 106, 109, 114, 115, 116, 127
Young Cassidy, 96, 102
You Only Live Twice, 119, 123–4, 148, 359, 374

Zardoz, 164–8, 172–4, 202, 362, 375
Zerbe, Anthony, 133
Zinnemann, Fred, 236, 242, 246–7, 248–50, 337
Zulu, 163, 182, 336
Zumwalt, Rick, 288